Variation and change in the lexicon

LANGUAGE AND COMPUTERS: STUDIES IN PRACTICAL LINGUISTICS

No 63

edited by
Christian Mair
Charles F. Meyer
Nelleke Oostdijk

Variation and change in the lexicon

A corpus-based analysis of adjectives in English ending in *-ic* and *-ical*

Mark Kaunisto

Amsterdam - New York, NY 2007

Cover photo:
Jane M. Sawyer, www.morguefile.com

Cover design: Pier Post

Online access is included in print subscriptions:
see www.rodopi.nl

The paper on which this book is printed meets the requirements of
"ISO 9706:1994, Information and documentation - Paper for documents -
Requirements for permanence".

ISBN-13: 978-90-420-2233-1
©Editions Rodopi B.V., Amsterdam - New York, NY 2007
Printed in The Netherlands

Table of contents

viii

Preface

This book presents a corpus linguistic study into one of the peculiar features of the English lexicon, that of the variation and change in the occurrence of adjectives ending in -ic/-ical. It is a revised version of my doctoral dissertation examined in June 2004. Some of the revisions include references to recently published works on the subject, and the comments I have received on the manuscript.

I would like to thank a number of people for their kind help, assistance, and encouragement throughout my work on this book. I am very grateful to my supervisor Dr Juhani Norri for his warm support, insightful comments, and good humour during my research. I also wish to acknowledge and thank all the members of staff of the Department of English at the University of Tampere who were instrumental in helping to bring it to fruition. I am indebted to Professors Juhani Rudanko, Anna Mauranen, and Juhani Klemola for valuable advice and inspiration. David Robertson, Ian Gurney, and Robert Cooper also deserve special thanks for their tireless assistance in answering my never-ending questions on the semantic intricacies of the English lexicon.

In addition to colleagues in Tampere, several other people have given me useful comments and assistance. I would especially like to thank Professor Laurie Bauer, the official examiner of my thesis, for his highly valuable and helpful comments and suggestions. Thanks are also due to Christian Kay, one of the pre-examiners of this thesis, as well as Emeritus Professor Matti Rissanen, Professor Irma Taavitsainen, and Professor Terttu Nevalainen for their comments when I was doing my research in the Langnet Graduate School in Language Studies. In the same vein, I would like to express my gratitude to all the other scholars and non-scholars in Finland, the UK, the USA and elsewhere who have kindly shared their views on the -ic/-ical issue.

I am grateful to Emil Aaltonen Foundation, Oskar Öflund Foundation, Leo and Regina Weinstein Foundation, the Langnet Graduate School in Language Studies, the University of Tampere Support Foundation, and Tampere City Science Fund for financial support, without which this study could not have been completed. I would also like to thank Taylor & Francis Group for giving me permission to include short extracts of my 1999 article "*Electric/Electrical* and *Classic/Classical*: Variation Between the Suffixes -*ic* and -*ical*" (published in *English Studies*) in this book. I would also like to give warm thanks to the editors of the Language and Computers series, and Eric van Broekhuizen at Rodopi for their comments during the editing process.

I would finally like to thank my dear wife Sari for her love, understanding, and patience, and all my relatives and friends for their support and much-needed distraction from academic life.

Chapter 1

Introduction

Corpus linguistics has opened up whole new avenues into language research. The introduction and availability of large electronic corpora have enabled a more focussed and detailed investigation into a number of linguistic phenomena. Ever since the very first corpora came to be used by linguists, the development of these "microscopes" into language use has been rapid. Corpora and the relevant computer software have become more refined and efficient, providing linguists with research tools which enable more accurate and valid descriptions of language. The accuracy and validity of the results, of course, depends heavily on how representative the corpus is, and also on its suitability for the examination of the phenomena in question.

    The challenges and difficulties related to corpus linguistics have not gone unnoticed by linguists examining and/or compiling corpora. The key problems have to do with the size of the corpus used, and the kind of material it contains. Bauer (1994: 50–51), for instance, has discussed the common problems with the adaptability of corpora for different kinds of lexical and grammatical research. He correctly observes that the requirements as regards corpus size depend to a great extent on the linguistic items that are being examined. The occurrence of some elements in language can be investigated with relatively small corpora, while other issues may demand research material consisting of millions of words in order to provide enough examples of the elements in question. Another obvious factor influencing the representativeness of one's research material – thus also influencing the generalisability of the results – is the actual content and structure of the corpus. For example, an examination of the leading articles in five years' issues of the *Wall Street Journal* might be representative of the language used in the world of finance, but such a corpus alone might not be sufficient for making observations on, say, American English as a whole. Moreover, it is important that the texts in a corpus should be written by a relatively large number of people; even a massive corpus loses a great deal of its value if the number of the authors represented is small.

    Discussing the difficulties involved in historical corpus linguistics, Rissanen (1989) distinguishes three basic problems. Firstly, he emphasises the importance of the scholar becoming familiar with the research material, i.e. learning about earlier forms of the language through actually reading the texts. Secondly, there is the danger that the use of corpora without a deeper knowledge of their contents may give a researcher a distorted idea of the generalisability of the results that they yield. The third problem relates to the large number of variables used in coding the background information for the texts in a corpus; the greater the number of variables, the more difficult it is to have every variable represented fully in the corpus (which is solved by the compilation of larger corpora). Although Rissanen considers these dilemmas and dangers to be relevant mainly in diachronic corpus work, they are, in fact, very important in the analysis of present-day materials as well.

1.   Corpus-based research on word-formation and lexicology

The study of word-formation and lexicology will undoubtedly benefit from the availability of large electronic corpora. Before the age of computerised language research, work in these fields was very much based on the examination of dictionaries, as well as texts in printed form. There are, in fact, plenty of things to investigate in greater detail: for example, one ultimate common goal for linguists in this field could be a comprehensive revision of Hans Marchand's *The Categories and Types of Present-Day English Word-Formation* (1969), which is still one of the standard works on the subject.

In recent years, many corpus-based studies on word-formation have concentrated on derivational morphology, especially on the question of the productivity of different affixes. Quantitative methods for measuring productivity have been developed and/or employed by e.g. Baayen and Lieber (1991), Baayen (1993), Baayen and Renouf (1996), Plag (1999; 2000), Bolozky (1999), Bauer (2001), and Cowie and Dalton-Puffer (2002). The examination of productivity sheds new light on the question of competing processes, as the notion of productivity is to a great extent also a relative issue. In addition to a word-formational process being productive or non-productive, two productive processes may differ noticeably as to how productive they actually are. The very words *competition* and/or *rivalry* have been used in studies by e.g. Plag (2000), Kjellmer (2001), and Bauer (2001).

Given that the main focus has recently been on the issue of productivity, studies on competing affixes have so far been mostly concerned with the extent of the application of the affixes, i.e. the numbers of types and tokens of words containing the affixes under investigation. Less attention has been given to the competing lexemes resulting from morphological rivalry. For example, Plag (2000) examines the occurrence of the verb-producing suffixes *-ify*, *-ate*, and *-ize* in present-day English, and notes the phonological and semantic conditions in which the endings are used. There are some areas of overlap, and Plag finds in his research material synonymous doublets such as *sinicize/sinify*, *plasticize/plastify*, and *technicize/technify*. Examining competing processes of nominalisation, Bauer (2001: 179–181) likewise observes competition between pairs such as *implantation/implant* (the latter through conversion) and *insurgency/insurgence*. From a historical point of view, the existence and use of such cases of rival formations could be of great interest. One could expect there to have been a greater number of competing derivatives sharing the same base or root in earlier centuries, particularly the sixteenth and seventeenth centuries, which were a period characterised by "an atmosphere favouring linguistic experiments" (Görlach 1991: 138).

Recent years have also seen a growing interest in studies on historical derivational morphology in English, discussed in e.g. Dalton-Puffer (1996), Aronoff and Anshen (1998), Bauer (1998; 2001), and Cowie and Dalton-Puffer (2002). These studies again make observations on the competition between word-formational processes. However, the discussion of individual lexemes does not go much further than the moment of their coinage. That moment could arguably be regarded as the point where the study of word-formation ends, and that of lexicology, that is, analysing the actual use of the words, begins. But there are grounds for arguing that the investigation of morphological rivalry would benefit from a close study of the corresponding (or resulting) lexical rivalry. In fact, although the title of Marchand's (1969) book refers first and foremost to word-formational questions, he does touch on some lexicological issues as well.[1]

In all likelihood, the reason why most of the studies so far have concentrated on the level of coinage is practical. Instead of consciously limiting their scope of investigation so as to exclude lexical study, linguists had to face the simple fact that lexical corpus studies set particularly high requirements for corpus size, at least when compared to the study of derivational affixes. This causes difficulties especially when studying the uses of words in earlier centuries, as historical corpora have not been comparable in size to corpora consisting of present-day materials. The 1990s, however, has witnessed the introduction of electronic collections of historical texts, either commercially available or accessible on the Internet. Together with more carefully structured historical corpora compiled by linguists, the total number of words in electronically analysable historical materials has begun to reach such levels as to enable more detailed diachronic studies of competing lexical items, as noted by Nevalainen (1999), among others. Although the situation is still far from perfect – we do not have equally large or representative collections of texts representing all types of texts – it has now become possible to take initial steps in studying the use of competing derivatives from both a diachronic and synchronic point of view. Some diachronic studies employing large corpora on lexical variation have been conducted, e.g. by Kwon (1997), who examined the variation between words beginning with *un-* and *in-* in Chadwyck-Healey's English Poetry Full-Text Database (which contains more than 45 million words).

This book aims to illustrate how corpora can today be used to carry out a diachronic study on lexical competition, addressing questions such as

---

1   Despite the reference to "present-day English word-formation" in the title of the book, historical details play an important role in the work as a whole: Marchand's assertions are heavily based on research into the first edition of the *Oxford English Dictionary* (*OED*), and the etymological aspects of the word-formational processes are discussed in some detail.

- what kinds of sources can be examined?
- how should we analyse their contents?
- to what extent are corpus-linguistic tools sufficient in the study of lexicon?

As a base and a platform for the discussion of these issues, I will concentrate on examining one particular set of words in the English lexicon involving competition between word-formational patterns, namely, adjectives ending in -ic and -ical. Although the subject may at first seem rather narrow, the close analyses of different competing pairs of words ending in -ic/-ical reveal a large number of different kind of factors which have had an effect on the developments in this part of the lexicon.

Although the book aims to illustrate the possibilities of the corpus-based approach into lexical studies, it is by no means to be assumed that I will only highlight the favourable sides of using corpora in this fashion. Instead, I feel that it is of vital importance to be duly critical of the approach, and even to observe its potential pitfalls: in addition to pointing out instances where I think the study of corpora alone is not sufficient, I will also observe cases where results gleaned from the corpora may perhaps be misleading. When one examines the lexicon from a diachronic or a synchonic point of view, I would very strongly recommend a method that includes a number of different sources of information. Alongside corpora, I will also take a close look into other sources, such as historical dictionaries, grammars, and language usage manuals.

2.   The topic for our closer study: words ending in *-ic* and *-ical*

If we consider lexical competition in English, the words ending in -ic and -ical stand out in a number of ways, perhaps most prominently because of the large number of competing adjectives which contain these endings. From a present-day point of view, the array of -ic/-ical words appears rather puzzling. There are a great many adjectives with which only the form in -ic is attested (e.g. *atomic, basic, electronic, melodic,* and *patriotic*), alongside those where only the -ical ending is to be found (e.g. *biblical, medical, nonsensical, oratorical,* and *theatrical*). In addition, there are pairs of adjectives ending in -ic and -ical, some of them being more or less synonymous (e.g. *ironic/ironical, pedagogic/ pedagogical,* and *satiric/satirical*), some manifesting a noticeable semantic differentiation between the two forms (e.g. *classic/classical, economic/ economical,* and *historic/historical*). In many cases, the words in -ic/-ical have nominal functions as well, usually developed through elliptical or absolute uses of the adjectives (alternatively, the adjectives in -ic/-ical may stem from a noun ending in -ic). As a result of conversion, some words in -ic, such as *magic* and *panic*, even have a verbal use. Considering the various uses of the words as regards different word-classes, the behaviour of words ending in -ic and -ical is quite heterogeneous. This can be seen from Table 1, which represents different kinds of functional combinations of *-ic/-ical* words in present-day English (based on the definitions of the words in the *Longman Dictionary of the English Language* (1991; henceforth abbreviated to *LDEL*) and *The New Oxford Dictionary of English* (1998; *NODE*).

Table 1. Different combinations of word-class functions of words ending in *-ic* and *-ical*.

-ic			-ical	
Adj	N	V	Adj	N
magic	magic	magic	magical	-
panic	panic	panic	-	-
comic	comic	-	comical	-
public	public	-	-	-
periodic	-	-	periodical	periodical
pedagogic	-	-	pedagogical	-
majestic	-	-	-	-
-	music	-	musical	musical
-	logic	-	logical	-
-	-	-	radical	radical
-	-	-	theatrical	-

The table above includes *-ic/-ical* words sharing the same root and also cases where only one variant exists. Considering the slots horizontally, we detect eleven different kinds of combinations of nominal, adjectival, and verbal uses. The list is not exhaustive; there are possibly other kinds of combinations as well. Moreover, if historical dictionaries such as the *Middle English Dictionary* (*MED*) or the *OED* were looked into from this perspective, the number of the various sets of combinations might be considerably different.

    Considering only the adjectives ending in *-ic* and *-ical*, the number of such formations is high: as regards words beginning with ten letters alone (*a, c, f, i, k, l, n, r, t*, and *u*; chosen at random), the *OED* contains 2554 instances of adjectives ending in *-ic* and 770 instances of those in *-ical*. The very fact that adjectives of this type are so numerous has perhaps discouraged scholars somewhat from examining them in greater detail. Burchfield (1996) s.v. *-ic(al)*, who makes some interesting observations on the application and use of the suffixes, notes that "the mathematical unattractiveness of analysing the relevant evidence in large computerized corpora is self-evident" (cf. Marsden 1985: 26). The unpleasantness connected with the issue is also reflected in the title of Hawkes' (1976) article "'*-ic*' and '*-ical*': the terrible twins".

    The number of academic articles concentrating on the question of the use of *-ic/-ical* adjectives is small. The list includes studies by Hawkes (1976), Marsden (1985), Ross (1998), Kaunisto (1999; 2001), and Gries (2001; 2003). However, the subject has certainly not escaped language scholars. As regards works on word-formation, Marchand's (1969) observations are the most detailed. Comments on the use of the adjectives can also be found in several grammars and usage manuals. The discussion in such sources varies a great deal in its extensiveness, the most notable or original treatments being those made by Elphinston (1765), Earle (1871), Sweet (1891), Fowler (1926) – as well as the subsequent editors of Fowler's work, Gowers (1965) and Burchfield (1996) – and Jespersen (1942). Moreover, recently published dictionaries, having adopted the practice of including additional usage notes alongside traditional entries in potentially problematic instances, often have a word or two to say on certain pairs ending in -ic/-ical.

In all honesty, another likely reason for the relative shortage of research into -ic/-ical adjectives is that the question can easily be regarded as being of minor importance. The difference between the adjective pairs as regards their external appearance is very small – only the additional -al separates them. The issue may therefore be easily shunned, and rather than providing impetus for purely descriptive lexicological curiosity, it may be regarded as belonging to those mental minefields trodden only by characters afflicted with incurable pedantry and ultra-prescriptive notions on language. Considering the everyday use of adjectives in -ic/-ical, some might think that a haphazard use of the forms does not constitute a thing to be overly concerned about. Where the two forms have developed separate meanings, the use of the "wrong" or unusual form does not present any serious threat to the overall meaning to be conveyed, as the intended sense in most cases becomes evident from the context.

It is true that "errors" or "slips from the norm" in the use of -ic/-ical adjectives can be and are made very easily. Instances of this type are to be found in e.g. quotations. To take one example, at the Florida Supreme Court Hearing on November 21, 2000, concerning the controversy over the Florida vote count in the presidential election, Chief Justice Charles Wells opened the hearing with these words:[2]

> Good afternoon, ladies and gentlemen, and welcome to the Florida Supreme Court. The court is certainly aware of the historic nature of this session and is aware that this is a matter of utmost and vital importance to our nation, our state and our world.

2   Chief Justice Wells' opening words were transcribed from an audio-tape recording of the court hearing, broadcast through the *BBC World* television channel. The transcribed version here is identical with the corresponding section in the transcription of the whole hearing on *The Washington Post* Internet site, http://washingtonpost.com/wp-srv/onpolitics/elections/courttext112000.htm, retrieved November 21, 2000.

In an article in the *Washington Post* on the day following the hearing, the Chief Justice was quoted as saying "The court is certainly aware of the histori*cal* nature of this session" [emphasis mine].[3]

Apart from errors, one can also encounter instances of synonymous use of the two forms, or instances of free variation (or inconsistent use of the forms) in the reportage of individual authors. For example, the following extract includes both *geometric* and *geometrical* used in the same meaning, with an identical head word.

(1)   Victor Vasarely, who has died aged 88, was considered the master of Op Art, known for his combinations of hard-edged geometrical forms which produce dazzling optical effects. [...] Vasarely established himself as the father of the movement with a number of manifestos describing his theories on form and colour, and his 'planetary folklore', an alphabet of geometric forms, which, combined with certain colours, could create varying calculable effects.   (*The Daily Telegraph*, Mar. 18, 1997, "Obituary of Victor Vasarely: Father of Op Art who sought to make visual images that anyone could appreciate")

On the other hand, as mentioned earlier, there are some adjective pairs in *-ic/-ical* with which the forms have developed different meanings, including *classic/classical*, *economic/economical*, and *historic/historical*. In some cases, the two non-synonymous forms can be used in connection with the same head word:

(2)   a. Which of us who loves music does not treasure the memory of the first time we heard the voice of the soprano Elisabeth Schumann as Sophie on those classic records of extracts from Strauss's Rosenkavalier? (*The Sunday Telegraph*, Mar. 14, 1993, "Books: Sex lives of the great composers")

        b. Sales of classical records now account for less than 10 per cent of the market. (*The Daily Telegraph*, Oct. 16, 1993, "The Arts: Music-makers crank up the sales pitch")

In examples (2a) and (2b), *classic* and *classical* modify the same noun, but the meanings are different. In (2a), the adjective means 'of recognized excellence' or 'of the first rank', while *classical* in (2b) refers to a particular type of music.

As has been noted, normative aspects in the use of adjectives ending in *-ic* and *-ical* have indeed aroused a good deal of attention, but there are more important linguistic considerations involved as well, and a closer analysis reveals processes and tendencies that might otherwise remain undetected. By examining

3   "Fla. High Court Considers Recounts" by Peter Slevin and Dan Balz, November 21, 2000, page A01; http://washingtonpost.com/wp-dyn/articles/A46540-2000Nov20.html, retrieved November 21, 2000.

both the overall occurrence of the adjectives and the developments in the uses of individual -*ic*/-*ical* pairs, it is possible to find some explanations for the complexity of the current situation.

3.   The origin of the suffixes -*ic* and -*ical*

The earliest words with the ending -*ic* in English date from the Middle English period: according to the *OED*, among the earliest words were the nouns *arithmetic* 1250, *physic* 1297, and *phthisic* 1340, and the adjectives *authentic*, *choleric*, and *phlegmatic* (first citations for each in the *OED* dating from 1340). These words were adoptions of French, Latin, or Greek words ending in -*ique*, -*icus*, and -*ικος*, respectively; later on -*ic* became a "proper" English suffix (*OED* s.v. -*ic*; Marchand 1969: 294).[4] In many cases, the immediate source of the foreign loan word remains uncertain (see e.g. Earle 1892: 395, 399; Jespersen 1935: 106; Görlach 1999: 107).

The first citations of adjectives ending in -*ical* date from the late fourteenth century, i.e. later than the earliest occurrences of those in -*ic*. The earliest words in -*ical* in the *OED* include *philosophical* 1374, and *poetical* 1384. These adjectives had the same kind of foreign models as those in -*ic*. In other words, *philosophical* and *poetical* were based on the words *philosophique* (or *philosophicus*) and *poétique* (or *poeticus*), with the suffix -*al* added. The suffix -*ical* is often referred to as a compound suffix (Maetzner 1874: 462; Ramsey 1892: 290; *OED* s.v. -*ical*).[5] Interestingly enough, the shorter forms of these adjectives, *philosophic* and *poetic*, came into use as well, and they seem to have entered the lexicon after the forms in -*ical* (first recorded citations dating from ca. 1454 (*MED*) and 1530 (*OED*), respectively). Other -*ic*/-*ical* pairs with the -*ical* form being attested earlier – which are quite numerous – include e.g. *chirurgic* 1660/*chirurgical* 1541, *emphatic* 1708/*emphatical* 1555, *geometric* 1630/*geometrical* 1392, *heroic* 1549/*heroical* 1514, *monastic* 1449/*monastical* 1401, *sophistic* 1549/*sophistical* 1483, *tactic* 1604/*tactical* 1570, and *theoretic* 1656/*theoretical* 1616, (the year of the first citation recorded in either the *MED* or

---

4   According to Jespersen (1942: 386), the very first loan word in -*ic* in English was *clerk*, which in Old English had the forms *cleric, clerec*, and *clerc*. The word was adopted from the Latin *clericus*, which in the Early Modern English period was adopted again, producing *cleric* and *clerical*. There are, of course, a number of words ending in -*ic* in English which are irrelevant to the present study, such as the nouns *bishopric, abbotric* (which include the Old English suffix -*ric*, derived from *riche* or *rike* 'kingdom' or 'realm'), and *garlic* (an OE compound of *gár* 'gare' + *léac* 'leek'; *OED* s.v. *garlic*).

5   It is not uncommon to find comments to the effect that (all) adjectives in -*ical* have been formed by adding -*al* to already existing adjectives in -*ic*. This is particularly the case in nineteenth century grammars, e.g. Morris (1872: 234, 237), Bain (1879: 247, 249), Richardson (1885: 56), and Meiklejohn (1890: 125) (but see also Sinclair 1991, s.v. -*al*).

the *OED*; see also Danielsson 1948: 222; Barber 1976: 187; Marchand 1969: 241; Urdang 1982: 194; Nevalainen 1999: 403).

Earle (1892: 404) explains the entrance of -ic/-ical pairs into English as resulting from the (increased) nominal use of words in -ic in general:

> The adjectives in French -ique, English -ic ran with unusual celerity into substantival significations, as domestique, *domestic*; physique, *physic*; logique, *logic*. Hence there rose a further demand for an adjectival form which should be unequivocal. This may well be the account of that strain of adjectives in -ical which is one of the notes of the literature of the sixteenth and seventeenth centuries, and which has been largely discarded in recent times.

Marchand (1969: 240–241; see also Krapp 1927 s.v. -ic, -ical) traces the origin of -ic/-ical doublets to the influence of Latin adjectives ending in -icus and -icalis. The Latin adjectival suffix -icus occurred both in words of Latin origin (e.g. *civicus, classicus, domesticus*) and in adoptions of Greek adjectives in -ικος (e.g. κωμικός *cōmicus*, οἰκονομικός *œconomicus*). As observed in *The Oxford Dictionary of English Etymology* s.v. -ic, the Greek adjectives were also used absolutely as nouns, and the feminine forms (denoting "names of arts, or systems of thought, knowledge, or action") of these nouns ended in -ικέ (in the singular) or -ικά (in the plural). Nouns of this type were also adopted into Latin, where the ending came to be -ica, as in *grammatica, musica,* and *physica*. In Medieval and Late Latin, nouns in -ica served as bases for adjectives formed with the suffix -alis, producing adjectives such as *grammaticalis, musicalis,* and *physicalis*, although corresponding adjectives in -icus, i.e. *grammaticus, musicus,* and *physicus* (loans from Greek) had been in use long before (some of which had developed nominal uses as well, whereas words in -alis were only adjectival). Marchand (1969: 241) notes that the forms in -alis were then erroneously perceived to be derivations from the words ending in -icus. The Latin adjective pairs ending in -icus/-icalis include *canonicus/canonicalis, chīrurgĭcus/chīrurgĭcalis, hæreticus/hæreticalis, inimicus/īnĭmīcālis, rusticus/rusticalis,* and *sacrificus/sacrificalis* (all of these words have had their corresponding -ic/-ical borrowings in English).

Marchand (1969: 241) observes two main currents as regards the pouring of words in -ic and -ical into English. Firstly, he claims that the Latin -icus/-icalis pairs were at some stage understood as representing a noun/adjective pattern (cf. Earle's comment quoted above), resulting in pairs such as *music/musical* and *physic/physical*. Supporting the idea of the influence of this pattern, and thus also the idea that the words in -ic should be "reserved" for nominal uses only, is the fact that several English coinages in -ical never had a corresponding Latin adjective in -icalis (or French adjective in -ical), such as *historical* (L *historicalis) and *pathetical* (L *patheticalis). But apparently the influence of the pattern was not strong enough, as Latin adjectives ending in -icus came to be adapted (or adopted) with the -ic ending as well, producing e.g. the forms *historic* and *pathetic* (both entering the lexicon after the longer forms). Marchand points to this tendency as "a second current in the language". The influence of French may have facilitated this current, as French did not produce many words ending in *-ical* (two examples are *clérical* and *médical*), preferring *-ique* instead (*OED* s.v. *-ical*).

Thus the foreign models discussed here were at first made use of by means of adoption (or adaptation), on the one hand, and by affixation with *-al*, on the other. According to Marchand (1969: 294), *-ic* began to be used as a proper English suffix in forming new words around the year 1600. Interestingly enough, loan words ending in *-ic* from French, Latin, and Greek kept entering the language as well. The production of competing pairs in *-ic/-ical* continued, as the suffixes were in some cases added to the same base. For example, *majestic/majestical* and *symmetric/symmetrical* are presented in the *OED* as English formations from *majesty* and *symmetry*. As in the case of many other *-ic/-ical* pairs, the form in *-ical* was the earlier one (for further details, see Chapter 4).

As noted earlier, the Early Modern English period witnessed the application of several ways of supplying the need for new words, resulting in a great number of competing lexemes (see e.g. Baugh 1959: 272; Adams 1973: 199; Nevalainen 1999: 400). Some adjectives in *-ic/-ical* pairs did not only compete with each other, but had other comparable formations as their rivals, often ending in *-(i)al* or *-(i)ous*. For example, the *OED* gives *symmetral, symmetrial*, and *symmetrous* competing with *symmetric/ symmetrical*. Other sets of synonyms include e.g. *tyrannial/tyrannic/tyrannical/tyrannious/tyrannish/ tyrannous* and *symphoniac/symphoniacal/symphonial/symphonic/symphonical/ symphonious/symphonous*.

In reference to the almost feverish application of various word-formational processes during the Early Modern English period, Görlach (1991: 138) notes that "this proliferation was not cut back until the late seventeenth/eighteenth centuries, as a consequence of natural selection or as a result of grammarians' or lexicographers' prescriptivism". As for the process of deletion or attrition of one of the forms in the case of competing *-ic/-ical* adjectives, these changes are for the most part the result of natural selection rather than any deliberate attempt at systematizing the lexicon (see also Fowler 1926 s.v. *-ic(al)*, Krapp 1927 s.v. *-ic, -ical*). This conclusion is a fairly safe one to make. Between the years 1600 and 1800, Elphinston (1765; 1790) was the only grammarian to have commented on the adjectives (Sundby 1995 s.v. *-ic: -ical*). His observations were not notably prescriptive (see Chapter 3), and the influence he had on the subsequent developments in the use of the adjectives in *-ic/-ical* was probably marginal at best, the author having gained notoriety amongst his profession for his unfashionable and unsuccessful attempts at a spelling reform (Walker 1791: iii).[6]

---

6   A good example of Elphinston's proposed spelling conventions is his grammar *Inglish Orthoggraphy Epittomized* (1790), printed entirely in his radical system of phonetic spelling.

Neither are lexicographers likely to have been responsible for changes in the uses of the adjectives in question, at least to any great extent. In eighteenth century dictionaries, such as Johnson's *The Dictionary of the English Language* (1755), adjective pairs in -ic and -ical were often grouped together with a brace, without indicating any clear difference between the two forms. Even when one of them was rare, the practice of including both variants was followed in dictionaries well into the nineteenth and twentieth centuries. A third group of people who might be suspected of being the "culprits" in the changes during the Early Modern English period is printers. For example, Osselton (1984: 132–133) attributes the historical change in the spelling of the word-final suffix -al – from the former -all to -al – to printers, based on a survey of seventeenth and eighteenth century printed texts compared with letters from the same period. The shift in the spelling was observed to have occurred considerably earlier (approximately fifty years) in printed texts. It is doubtful, however, that printers' practices would have affected the choice between the adjectives in -ic/-ical. It is likely that the possible influence of the printers was limited to spelling only, rather than extending to the morphemic level, although a more in-depth investigation on the issue awaits the compilation of sufficiently large electronic corpora of letter-writing from the period.[7]

Considering the phenomenon of lexical competition, Fowler (1926) s.v. -ic(al) discusses two processes functioning in language in cases where two or more words can be perceived as being alternative forms. As referred to above, one of the "self-purifying" tendencies of language for ridding itself of superfluous items is to assign different meanings to the forms. Fowler considers these developments in language highly laudable, saying that "every well established differentiation adds to the precision & power of the language" (see also Earle 1892: 405). The second tendency, which, in the same way as semantic differentiation, in Fowler's opinion should be "assisted", is the deletion or "clearing away" of one of the forms, especially if lines for division into different senses are not particularly forthcoming. Examples of -ic/-ical adjectives that have eventually given way to their rivals include forms both in -ic and -ical, such as *ethic, hypothetic, theoretic, typic*, and *tyrannic,* on the one hand, and *dramatical, enigmatical, scientifical, symbolical,* and *tragical*, on the other. Both Earle and Fowler, as well as Krapp (1927) s.v. -ic, -ical point out that the processes affecting the use of -ic/-ical adjectives have not resulted in patterns which would at first glance (or a second or a third) appear overwhelmingly systematic or logical (as well illustrated by Table 1 in the previous section).

As the adjectives in -ic/-ical constitute a large group of lexical items competing with one another, it is most fascinating to examine the intricacies of the tendencies functioning to "purify" the language of superfluous elements. One may ask why the rivalry led to semantic differentiation in the case of some

---

7   The largest historical collection of letters in electronic form at the moment is *The Collection of Early English Correspondence*, compiled at the University of Helsinki, the 1998 version containing some 2.7 million words from early fifteenth century to 1681.

adjective pairs, and to deletion of one of the forms in others. What kind of set of meanings must an *-ic/-ical* pair have so that it promotes semantic differentiation between the two forms? Conversely, is there something "lacking" in some other adjective pairs, resulting in the survival of only one member of the pair? Similarly of interest is the rate or rapidness of the changes, as well as the influence that preference for one of the forms in existing pairs may have had on the coinage or adoption of new lexemes.

4.   Outline of the study

This book examines the appearance, whether through adoption or coinage, and subsequent use of English adjectives ending in *-ic* and *-ical*, investigating the regularities and irregularities therein. It is therefore important to point out that this is not a study of derivational morphology in the strictest sense, because the status of the elements *-ic* and *-ical* as suffixes is not clear-cut in a large number of the adjectives. The morphological complexity of the issue is discussed by Bauer (1983: 115), who observes that the problem of determining whether an element is a suffix or not "arises particularly frequently when the base is a root from a foreign – usually classical – lexeme". The words ending in *-ic/-ical* are here examined rather from a lexicological perspective, with due attention given to recently formulated methods used in the study of derivational morphology. The decision to examine loan words and domestic derivatives together can be justified with the similarities in the historical behaviour of some of the *-ic/-ical* pairs. For example, *authentic* was adopted, according to the *OED*, from Old French (*autentique*) in the fourteenth century. *Authentical* was coined some two hundred years later, at a time when several adjectives ending in *-ical* entered the language. *Majestic/majestical*, on the other hand, are both English coinages, with the *-ical* form occurring earlier (and thus *-ical* in *majestical* may be regarded a proper English suffix).[8] What the two adjective pairs have in common, however, is that in the case of both pairs, the form ending in *-ical* was dropped from use, at roughly the same time. Therefore, even though the adjectives are etymologically different, they probably have been perceived – and eventually treated – as if they were morphologically and lexicologically comparable. In the present study, however, I consciously speak of adjectives ending in *-ic* and *-ical* rather than the suffixes *-ic* and *-ical*.

As observed above, the number of such adjectives is vast, and some limitations in the scope of the research are necessary. As regards different varieties of English, main attention has been given to the use of the adjectives in British English. Some arguments have been made about regional differences in

---

8   Given the earlier existence of pairs such as *authentic/authentical*, one could argue that the occurrence of *majestic* after *majestical* is actually a result of back-formation instead of coinage from *majesty* by adding the suffix *-ic*.

the use of certain adjective pairs as concerns the two forms. Comments of this type mainly relate to the differences between American and British usage. In a few individual cases, the validity of these claims is looked into or checked by examining corpora of American texts. On the whole, however, the occurrence of *-ic/-ical* adjectives in American English will be discussed only cursorily.

Chapter 2 describes the materials used in the study, both the corpora of British English texts and the main reference works consulted. Chapter 3 introduces previous studies on the subject, discussing the main observations or theories put forward regarding the application of the endings, on the one hand, and the uses of the words ending in *-ic/-ical*, on the other. Ideas relating to morphological productivity are examined in Chapter 4, with the aim of studying their applicability to the adjectives in *-ic* and *-ical*.

The results of the analysis of the use of different adjective pairs in corpora of historical and present-day English texts are discussed in Chapters 5–12. The first adjective pairs to be discussed are ones which manifest semantic differentiation between the two forms. This is because compared to instances where one of the forms has become rare or obsolete, semantically differentiated pairs have a more prominent role in grammar books, usage manuals, dictionaries, and popular discussion. In addition, semantic differentiation may in some cases have played a role in the eventual disappearance of one of the forms.

The uses of six semantically differentiated adjective pairs will be examined in greater detail. These pairs are *classic/classical*, *comic/comical*, *economic/economical*, *electric/electrical*, *historic/historical*, and *magic/magical*.[9] Of all the *-ic/-ical* pairs, these have attracted by far the greatest attention among linguists. Each pair is investigated in a separate chapter (5–10). The chapters include descriptions on the etymological background of the individual adjectives, followed by analyses of their uses "yesterday and today". As the differences between the meanings of the two forms are in some cases no more than minor nuances, the discussion of the semantic features is fairly detailed. A close semantic scrutiny is highly important considering the tabular presentations, where the occurrences of the adjectives in the corpora are listed according to their meanings. Therefore a careful description of the decisions made when analysing the meanings is necessary in the interests of repeatability of the survey. One must, of course, acknowledge the fact that perhaps no linguistic study involving a semantic analysis is entirely repeatable, as different people might always analyse some items differently. For that reason, it is of utmost importance to explain in detail the principles adhered to in the semantic categorisations, so that following the same principles in analysing the same material, other scholars are likely to

---

9   In Kaunisto (1999), the present-day uses of *classic/classical* and *electric/electrical* were examined in the 1993 issues of *The Daily Telegraph/The Sunday Telegraph* (on CD-ROM). The corresponding chapters in the present study are more extensive, including investigation on the etymological background and the uses of the adjectives in earlier centuries as well.

arrive at results which give rise to conclusions similar to mine.[10] The close analysis of the meanings of the adjectives also involves examining their definitions in dictionaries.

Chapter 11 concentrates on the tendency to oust one of the variants from the language. The most prominent pairs of this type, or pairs manifesting the greatest degree of competition between the two forms in the corpora, are looked into. The frequencies of occurrence of the rival forms in different periods are presented in tabular form. Although the pairs discussed in this chapter may have had multiple meanings, they did not show any major signs of semantic differentiation between the competing forms. In other words, the result of the competition was the deletion of one of the forms, even if some minor semantic differences in the use of the two forms may be observed at some point in history. This chapter expands an earlier investigation (Kaunisto 2001), which concentrated on the use of *-ic/-ical* adjective pairs in the prose fiction works in the Chadwyck-Healey *Literature Online* text collection.

Some of the "minor" semantically differentiated pairs are investigated in Chapter 12. Most of the pairs discussed in this chapter are ones that are not often commented on in usage manuals, either because they represent reasonably clear or fully established differentiation (*politic/political*) or are somehow less prominent among semantically differentiated *-ic/-ical* pairs, largely because one of the pairs is considerably rarer than the other (*diabolic/diabolical, fantastic/fantastical,* and *optic/optical*). However, only those pairs will be discussed for which a reasonable number of occurrences was found in both the historical and present-day corpora, so that observations could be made on the developments in the use of the adjectives through history. The results of the research are summarised and discussed in Chapter 13.

---

10   As regards the analyses of the occurrences of the six adjective pairs, several native English speakers were consulted on a number of occasions. This was very helpful especially in cases where the meanings of the two forms were very similar, but minor differences could nevertheless be perceived.

Chapter 2

Materials used in the study

As established in the Introduction, for conducting a close analysis on the use of individual lexemes, a large corpus is usually required, obviously depending very much on the relative frequency of the words to be examined. This is true for both synchronic and diachronic studies. As regards the study of present-day English, the advent of the 100-million-word *British National Corpus* (*BNC*; for further details on the corpus, see Aston and Burnard 1998), containing extracts of many different types of written and spoken British English, has undoubtedly expanded the scope of corpus linguistic studies a great deal. However, the *BNC* plays only a secondary role in the present study, for several reasons. The first very simple and practical reason is that I did not have access to the *BNC* at the time I started this project. There are also some features in the *Sara* search programme of *BNC World* which make its use unattractive, especially when it comes to the semantic analysis of words. In many instances, the assessment of particular shades of meaning carried by e.g. *classic* or *classical* requires the examination of the word in a wider context than just the sentence the word appears in, but unfortunately that is all that the search programme provides. Thus instances of the type "It is ~" or "I thought it was ~" would have to be excluded from the survey, as the analysis of the meaning of the adjective would be virtually based on guessing. Another potential danger in the use of the corpus lies in the fact that some of the extracts are rather long, increasing the possibility of idiosyncratic uses having an effect on the assessment of typicality of expressions. For example, the significance of a word in the lexicon can be easily misinterpreted if it has relatively numerous occurrences in the corpus but a large number of them are actually from only a few individual texts. This does not need to constitute any problem for the linguist at all, as long as one pays careful attention to the numbers of texts as well as to the numbers of occurrences of a given word.

While the *BNC* is used in the study as an important supplementary source, the analysis of the present-day British English usage of the adjectives in *-ic* and *-ical* is mainly based on the examination of the CD-ROM containing the 1995 issues of *The Daily Telegraph/The Sunday Telegraph*. The newspaper CD-ROM is useful in many ways. First of all, the material is relatively large in size, approximately 35 million words, and the search programme allows one to browse the searched items in larger contexts, even to view the articles in their entirety.[1] As the articles in newspapers are relatively short, the danger of idiosyncratic

---

1   I would like to thank Ian Gurney for making the estimate on the word count in the 1995 issues of the newspaper, based on a number of different calculations, e.g. the number of words in the articles from two days, and the file sizes on the CD-ROM, all pointing toward a word count of 35 million.

usage affecting the results is rather small when compared to the *BNC*.[2] Although it is obvious that newspaper material represents one register (as opposed to e.g. academic writing, fiction), it is nevertheless fairly representative of general English usage, as it includes articles from a wide spectrum of human activities, covering all kinds of subjects from international politics to gardening tips. As supplementary material, the CD-ROM versions of other yearly issues (from the 1990's) of the newspaper were also consulted, as well as *Collins WordbanksOnline* corpus (including 56 million words of the *Bank of English* collection).

A decade or so ago, examining the semantic developments and the competition between *-ic/-ical* adjectives in historical corpora would have been very difficult, if not altogether impossible, because of the size of the corpora available (although they obviously were and still are very useful in examining some other kinds of linguistic elements). For example, one could not draw any far-reaching conclusions on the changes of meanings of *classic/classical* in a corpus of eighteenth century texts including, say, five instances of *classic* and seven instances of *classical*, and comparing them with a handful of nineteenth century examples. One of the largest collections of historical texts in electronic form nowadays is the commercially available Chadwyck-Healey *Literature Online* collection (*LION*). The "online library" (see http://lion.chadwyck.co.uk) contains at present over 300,000 texts, including works of English and American poetry, drama, and prose fiction. The ever-growing collection first became available in 1996, and new databases have been continually added. For the present study, the British prose fiction works in *LION* were examined. Influencing this decision was the fact that some of the earlier published databases in the collection were prose texts, e.g. the Early English Prose Fiction database (containing texts from 1514 to 1700), and the Eighteenth Century Fiction database (1700–1780). In the end, the material investigated included prose fiction works from 1514 to 1903.[3]

The word counts (approximated to the nearest 1,000 words) and the numbers of books and authors in the *Literature Online* material, viewed in blocks of fifty years, are presented in Table 2 below:

---

2   It is of course possible that some reporters use a particular expression repeatedly in a number of articles. The search programme on the CD-ROM also gives the names of the authors of the articles, thus enabling one to keep tabs on the possible effect of idiosyncratic uses on the results.

3   In addition to the search engine on the *Literature Online* web site, the texts were examined by using the *MonoConc Pro 2.0* programme, which allows the temporary loading of texts from the Internet. With the *MonoConc* programme, it was possible to create word frequency lists of the texts, and the study of these electronic lists made it considerably easier and quicker to find instances of various spellings of the adjectives. The spelling of the endings alone varies greatly, the variants including e.g. *-ique, -icque, -yque, -yk, -yke, -yck, -ycke, -icke, -ick, -ik, -icalle*, and *-ycall*.

Table 2. Authors/books/word count in the prose fiction texts in the *Literature Online* corpus.

	authors	texts	word count
1514–1550		4 (all by anonymous authors)	68,000
1550–1599	33	52 (+ 7 anon.)	3,130,000
1600–1649	32	48 (+ 16 anon.)	2,566,000
1650–1699	36	59 (+ 24 anon.)	4,214,000
1700–1749	13	56	5,526,000
1750–1799	36	66	9,828,000
1800–1849	37	89	13,698,000
1850–1903	60	135	22,127,000

As can be observed from the table above, the material is fairly voluminous as regards word counts, enabling studies on the uses of competing words in blocks of fifty years.[4] An exception is the first half of the sixteenth century, which is only represented by four books by anonymous authors. This material was therefore excluded from the study, which does not, however, constitute a significant problem, because many of the adjective pairs examined entered the lexicon after this period.

A thing worth noting is that the fifty-year blocks include varying numbers of authors and books. As regards the number of authors, one peculiar period that stands out is the first half of the eighteenth century, including texts by only thirteen authors, i.e. fewer than in the other periods. This is simply a fact that must be born in mind when evaluating the results. The word counts also differ considerably – the material from 1850–1903 is almost ten times as large as that from the first half of the seventeenth century. The structural differences between the subperiods are not problematic at all, because what is being examined is the

---

4   The texts were grouped in the fifty-year periods according to the year in which they were printed. Therefore some authors' texts are included in two different periods, e.g. the works of Emanuel Forde, Henry Roberts, and Richard Johnson are found both among the late sixteenth century and early seventeenth century texts. One possibility, often used in sociolinguistic research, would have been to organize the texts into fifty year blocks according to the authors' birthyear. Unfortunately the birthyears of some of the authors (particularly those who flourished in the sixteenth century) is unknown, which is why this option was not applied. There are two exceptions, however, in the grouping of the texts: the *LION* corpus includes Parts 1 and 2 of Richard Johnson's *The Seuen Champions of Christendome*, the first part transcribed from a print from 1608, the second from a 1597 print. As the first part was unquestionably written before the second, the occurrences of the -ic/-ical adjectives examined found in this text were included in the figures of the 1550–1599 period. Similarly, the non-fiction texts examined include *Christian Morals* by Thomas Browne, which was published posthumously in 1716, but which was written in the latter half of the seventeenth century.

relation between the uses of the -*ic* and -*ical* variants in different periods. Thus normalisation of the figures in the tabular presentations is not necessary. As an example, we could observe Table 3, which presents the absolute numbers of occurrences of the rival adjective forms *majestic* and *majestical* in the *Literature Online* material. The numbers in parentheses denote the numbers of authors using the words, and the figures in the column on the far right denote the number of authors who used both forms in their texts. Observing the numbers of authors is, as mentioned earlier, important, as it is in theory possible that a large number of occurrences of any given word in -*ic* or -*ical* derives from the texts of just one author.

Table 3. The numbers of occurrences of *majestic/majestical* in the prose section of *Literature Online*.

	majestic	*majestical*	number of authors using both forms
1550–1599	1 (1)	14 (10)	-
1600–1649	15 (7)	19 (8)	2
1650–1699	67 (15)	10 (3)	1
1700–1749	33 (7)	-	-
1750–1799	79 (21)	1 (1)	1
1800–1849	224 (29)	4 (4)	4
1850–1903	190 (30)	2 (2)	2

The figures in Table 3 can be analysed rather easily without any normalisation. The way to read the table is to look at the relation between the numbers of occurrences (or numbers of authors using the forms) of *majestic* and *majestical*, and then compare it with the corresponding relations in other periods.[5]

It would appear from Table 3 that the first period of fifty years, 1550–1599, witnessed a preference for the use of *majestical* over *majestic*. The following period, however, shows an increase in the use of the shorter form. This tendency seems to have strengthened, with the form in -*ical* becoming less and less common. Although it is already known that *majestical* is nowadays an archaic form, the table provides us with more detailed information about the timing of the shift from the use of the form in -*ical* to the use of the variant in -*ic*. Also worth pointing out is that the clarity of the shift that can be observed speaks for the usefulness of the material in the examination of historical tendencies in the usage of the competing forms.

---

5   One option would be to present the figures in percentages, i.e. the percentage of the absolute occurrences of the forms in -*ic* and -*ical*, or the numbers of authors using these forms in different periods. It was nevertheless thought that the figures as presented in Table 3 speak well for themselves without any further adjustment.

Although the *Literature Online* material examined, including over 60 million words, is a massive corpus, it would obviously be desirable to be able to study other types of historical texts than just fiction. As the corpora designed especially for linguistic research are relatively small, non-fiction texts in electronic form were sought from various collections of texts on the Internet.

Historical texts on the Internet are plentiful, but there are some practical difficulties in using them in linguistic research. From the viewpoint of corpus linguists working with electronic corpora, a recent, rather worrying tendency is the practice of making texts available in page images which are in unsearchable formats. This is perhaps considerably easier and simpler for those wanting to make the texts widely accessible, but unfortunately electronic searches cannot be made from such files (and manual searching is not a very attractive option). Another problematic feature often encountered in electronic versions of historical texts is modernisation of spelling. Although it is possible, or even likely, that the modernised spelling would not have either deleted or added an extra *-al* as far as adjectives in *-ic/-ical* are concerned, modernised editions of historical texts were not selected among the research material for the present study. It is also regrettably typical of historical texts on the Internet not to be accompanied by detailed bibliographical information on the edition on which the electronic version was based. Such texts were likewise not included in the material examined.[6]

Altogether 318 non-fiction texts by British authors (written or published between 1550 and 1950) met the rather strict criteria for inclusion in the study. As regards the Early Modern English period, one of the major sources was the Brown University *Renaissance Women Online* collection, which includes many different kinds of writings, e.g. parliamentary pamphlets, prophesies, and cook books. There are also a number of web sites devoted to a particular subject (e.g. chemistry, psychology, economics) or the life and works of a particular person (e.g. John Milton, Sir Thomas Browne). These sites also provided useful material

---

6   One of the web sites from which electronic texts were retrieved was *Renascence Editions* ("An Online Repository of Works Printed in England Between the Years 1477 and 1799", http://www.uoregon.edu/~rbear/ ren.htm). Most of the electronic versions of the historical texts on the site are accompanied by detailed bibliographic information about the editions that the transcripts are based on. The web site nevertheless has a disclaimer, which states that the "texts published by *Renascence Editions* are not peer reviewed in the strict sense" and that "[g]raduate students and scholars who base their *research* on any of these texts may find their work questioned in the academic community, and rightly so". However, nine of the non-fiction texts from the sixteenth and seventeenth centuries were included in the collection of non-fiction texts examined for the present study. The occurrences of the relevant *-ic* and *-ical* adjectives in this material were checked against the page images of the original works in the *Early English Books Online* (*EEBO*) collection. In this respect, no discrepancies were found between the electronic versions and the page images included in *EEBO*.

for the study. The numbers of non-fiction texts, authors, and word counts are given in Table 4 below (a full list of texts is given in the Bibliography).[7]

Table 4. Authors/books/word count in the Internet non-fiction texts studied.

	authors	texts	word count
1550–1599	17	20	564,000
1600–1649	38	49 (+ 4 anon.)	1,265,000
1650–1699	48	80 (+ 6 anon.)	2,016,000
1700–1749	19	21	488,000
1750–1799	25	30	1,640,000
1800–1849	28	40	1,222,000
1850–1899	28	49	1,060,000
1900–1950	17	25	385,000

To supplement these texts, four corpora of historical English writing were made use of, namely the *Helsinki Corpus of English Texts* (the sections covering the period 1420–1710), the *Corpus of Early English Medical Writing* (1375–1750), the *Century of Prose Corpus* (1680–1780), and the *Corpus of Nineteenth-Century English* (1800–1899). Some of these corpora also include extracts from works of fiction; these parts of the corpora were excluded from the study.

Considering the non-fiction material examined, it has to be noted that the different periods are not entirely comparable as they contain different kinds of texts at varying volumes, i.e. the representation of texts on economics or chemistry may be more prominent in one period than in another. In the present study, the different types of texts or scientific fields represented are not examined individually, but as a whole.[8] This is because the different subcorpora would not be large enough to enable diachronic investigation. Corpus-based research on texts on evolving scientific disciplines presents many difficulties in general: for example, early writings on chemistry are bound to be drastically different from twentieth century academic articles in style as well as in content. The vocabulary attested in writings on natural sciences through history may show great variation, since in the Early Modern English period, theological aspects – and thus also

---

7   Additionally, some American non-fiction texts were gleaned from the Internet, and these were examined for the sake of comparison. The American texts from 1850–1899 include 43 texts by 31 individual authors, and 1900–1961 are represented by 116 texts by 74 authors.

8   In the case of some *-ic/-ical* adjective pairs, occurrences were considerably more frequent in certain kinds of texts. For example, *economic/economical* were understandably attested more often in texts on economics than on, say, chemistry. The close analyses of the *-ic/-ical* adjectives will include comments on instances where a given discipline or text type contributed to a significant degree to the occurrences of the adjectives examined.

religious terminology – were very often incorporated into the descriptions of natural phenomena. Given the smaller number of words in the non-fiction corpus studied, it is obvious that attention must be paid to the results from this material in relation to those from the *Literature Online* prose texts.

In the case of those adjective pairs where one of the forms has been ousted or has become notably rarer than the other form, the occurrences of *-ic/-ical* adjectives were also examined in the *OED* citations to gain additional data; in general, the token frequencies of such pairs was smaller than those of semantically differentiated pairs (although there are some exceptions). As the quotes in the *OED* include short passages of both fiction and non-fiction texts, this third source thus serves as an additional database, the results of which are then compared to the ones from the *Literature Online* prose works and the non-fiction material. Interestingly enough, the timing of the shifts observed was remarkably similar in the three corpora (see Chapter 11).

The first citations of *-ic/-ical* adjectives in the *OED* are also looked into in order to study the popularity of the endings in neologisms in different periods. While it has been observed that the *OED* often is not absolutely reliable as regards first citations, it has nevertheless been acknowledged that examining the dictionary provides an indication or a good estimate on the actual tendencies of usage in the language (Bauer 1998; 2001). As the subject of studying *-ic/-ical* adjectives is obviously of lexicographical interest, a survey is made on the occurrence of such forms in other dictionaries as well. A very useful source in this respect is the *Early Modern English Dictionaries Database* (*EMEDD*; http://www.chass.utoronto.ca/english/emed/emedd.html), which contains altogether sixteen lexicographical works from 1530–1657). Full texts of three dictionaries from this period (Mulcaster 1582, Coote 1596, and Cawdrey 1604) are also available on the Internet. Other dictionaries from the seventeenth, eighteenth, and nineteenth centuries were furthermore examined at the British Library. More recent dictionaries likewise play an important role in the study. The main goal in their investigation is not to compare the dictionaries in detail. Instead, the intention is to make observations on the general problematic aspects encountered in the definitions of the adjectives. A full list of the dictionaries consulted is given separately in the References section.

Chapter 3

Earlier observations and empirical studies

This chapter presents and discusses the most notable observations, theories, and empirical research on the occurrence of adjectives in *-ic* and *-ical* so far. The first section deals with ideas and generalisations proposed to account for cases where only the form in *-ic* or *-ical* is nowadays in use. As regards semantic differentiation between the two forms, linguists have likewise attempted to find some unifying patterns in their use. These suggestions are examined in section 2, while section 3 discusses other factors, e.g. regional differences and language rhythm, which have the potential of governing the choice of one form over the other. In section 4, attention is given to the empirical studies on the subject by Marsden (1985) and Gries (2001; 2003).

1. The preference for one of the forms over the other

Through the years, linguists have made observations on certain types of adjectives which seem to manifest a preference for one of the endings, either at the stage of their coinage, or as a result of the gradual disappearance of the rival form. The most interesting set of arguments in this respect are found in Marchand (1969: 241–243). Marchand's presentation of the overall use of adjectives in *-ic* and *-ical* is rather problematic, with some of the ideas suggested appearing contradictory. This is largely perhaps because the author attempts to describe processes of change which are temporally quite diverse, and no clear timeline of the various changes is evident. Marchand (1969: 242–243) himself humbly noted that his portrayal of the use of the adjectives in question does not manage to account for all of the cumbersome issues involved. Moreover, he observed that his statements were "tendencies rather than rules", and that "it will be possible to find words used contrary to the general trend".

One peculiar (and perhaps mistaken) point in Marchand's presentation is his emphasis on the general prevalence of the forms in *-ical* in cases where forms in *-ic* and *-ical* have competed with one another. For example, he says that "the language has shown a tendency to throw out one member (usually the form in *-ic*) from common usage". This statement does not correlate with that of Earle (1892: 404) quoted on page 9, who noted the obsolescence of a number of adjectives in *-ical*, e.g. *Germanical*, *magnifical*, and *domestical*. There are, however, a number of *-ic/-ical* pairs where the rivalry has ended in favour of the longer form, including *mathematical, tactical,* and *theoretical*. Marchand's main attention appears to have been drawn to instances of this type: he points out the dominance of the forms in -*ical* particularly in adjectives derived from names of sciences (or in adaptations from Latin adjectives in -*icus* relating to a science), saying that the "by-forms in -*ic* are, as a rule, weaker and newer than the extended forms" (1969: 241).[1]

From a present-day point of view, this pattern has not always been adhered to with absolute strictness in the use of the adjectives, as we now have names of sciences such as *phonetics, linguistics, semantics,* and *genetics,* which all have corresponding adjectives in -*ic* rather than in -*ical*. In some cases, the form in -*ical* preceded the shorter form in the same way as with *mathematic* 1549/*mathematical* 1522. For example, *linguistical* (1823) preceded *linguistic* (1856). However, according to the *OED*, the adjectives *linguistic/linguistical* were not derived from the name of the science, but instead from the word *linguist*. Additionally, the corresponding nouns in -*ics* for these nineteenth century adjectives usually came into use after at least one of the adjectives had already been coined, as with e.g. *phonetic* 1826, *phonetical* 1845, and *phonetics* 1841.

In his commentary on -*ic*/-*ical* adjectives, Marchand (1969: 242) makes some other rather awkward statements concerning the strength of the forms in -*ical*. The following is particularly confusing:

> There is another tendency [. . .] to use adjectives in -*ical* when the word is in wider, common use: *analytical, biblical, chemical, clinical, critical, geometrical, periodical, surgical, theatrical, theoretical, typical* are more frequent than their unextended counterparts; but such words as *aesthetic, angelic, apologetic, artistic, dramatic, dynamic, pathetic, static* are the ones commonly used.

It is not immediately evident what Marchand actually means by "wider, common" usage here, especially as the list of words in -*ical* in the extract includes adjectives with scientific (e.g. *chemical, geometrical*) as well as non-scientific (e.g. *theatrical, typical*) referents. The purpose of the list of adjectives in -*ic* that follows is puzzling. The adjectives listed do not seem strikingly different from the -*ical* adjectives given in the previous sentence, and this in fact undermines the main argument concerning the prevalence of the forms in -*ical*. On the other hand, if the intention was indeed to present some prominent counterexamples, the fact that there are so many counterexamples to the general tendency similarly weakens the proposed argument (see also Gries 2001: 79). In fact, is not difficult to present further examples of commonplace, everyday adjectives in -*ic*, including e.g. *basic, characteristic, domestic, drastic,* and *patriotic*; these are adjectives

---

1   In some cases, there existed no underlying noun denoting a field of science in English predating the corresponding adjective adapted from a Latin word in -*icus*. For example, *botany* was coined after *botanic/botanical* (adapted from the Latin word *botanicus*) to match the pattern of names of sciences ending in -*y* and the corresponding adjectives in -*ic* or -*ical*, as in *astronomy* and *astronomic/astronomical* (*OED* s.v. *botany*).

presented by Marchand himself (1969: 243) as cases where the rivalling forms in *-ical* are rarely encountered.

Marchand also proposes that except in names of sciences, scientists are more prone to use the shorter forms, which reflects the notion that forms in *-ic* are, almost as a rule, semantically closer to the idea denoted by the root of the adjective. In contrast, adjectives in *-ical* in Marchand's view have a comparatively more remote connection with the sense of the root (see also p. 31). This idea, which Marchand presents in particular as "characteriz[ing] the general tendency of differentiation", thus applies to the process of choosing only one of the two forms as well. Marchand (1969: 242) explains the logic behind this distinction in the following way:

> [. . .] as derivatives in *-ic* are, morphologically speaking, derivatives from the basic substantive, they have notionally also a direct connection with the idea expressed by the root. On the other hand, formations in *-ical* are secondary derivatives, i.e. they are derived from adjectives in *-ic* by means of *-al*. This will partly explain why they usually have a remoter and looser relation to the basic substantive.

The explanation clashes with some of the earlier statements made by Marchand himself on the entrance of *-ic/-ical* adjectives, according to which many adjectives in *-ical*, in fact, preceded their rivals in *-ic*. Moreover, in several cases it is uncertain whether the adjectives were modelled after Latin adjectives in *-icus* or whether they were pure English formations. An interesting and actually rather plausible idea, however, is to regard Marchand's observation as representing how the adjectives in *-ic* and *-ical* came to be perceived (which is something that perhaps should have been explicitly stated), which then was reflected in more or less clear preferences in the use of the forms.

As regards the question of the scientists' general preference over the forms in *-ic*, Marchand (1969: 242) claims that "the scholar uses the unextended forms much more, as for him the quality expressed by the adjective is more directly and intimately connected with the thing to which it is applied than it is for a non-scientist" (see also *OED* s.v. *-ical*). Regardless of the morphological aspects relating to the "primary" or "secondary" adjectival status, and whether scientists are/were aware of them or not, the argument seems to suggest that the additional *-al* would have had some kind of symbolic value, distinguishing it from the variants in *-ic*. As support for his argument, Marchand (1969: 242) presents the following observations:

> Scientific terms have therefore mostly *-ic*: *electrolytic, eolithic, geodesic, geostatic, linguistic, magnetic, phonemic, phonetic, plutonic, semantic, sematic, tannic, tectonic, toxic, volcanic,* etc. The directness of relation and their corresponding designation is clearly seen in medical terms, which all have the suffix *-ic*, as they are

generally applied to phenomena of the body and therefore 'primary attributes': *allergic, anemic, antiseptic, apathetic, asthmatic, entric, gastric, gastrocolic, hyperemic, metabolic, metagastric, nephritic, neurasthenic, neuritic, pneumogastric, pneumonic, rachitic,* etc. Though dictionaries often quote forms in *-ical* also, they are hardly ever used.

In addition to the unspecific reference to "primary attributes", one problem in Marchand's argument is that it does not take into account the possibility that the scientists' use of the adjectives might have changed through history. Instead, the passage quoted implies that scientists have always preferred to use the shorter forms.[2] In fact, looking up the abovementioned adjectives in *-ic* in the *OED*, it can be observed that most of them were coined in the eighteenth and nineteenth centuries. In contrast, most of the *-ic/-ical* adjectives in "wider, common use" presented by Marchand as examples are older, their first citations dating back to the sixteenth and seventeenth centuries. As will be observed in the following chapter, the coinage of all adjectives in either *-ic* or *-ical* according to the first citations in the *OED* shows the competition between the two endings being closer in the sixteenth and seventeenth centuries, after which new words ending in *-ic* exceeded those in *-ical* (particularly in the nineteenth century). Based on Marchand's evidence alone, one remains doubtful whether the preference for the use of the shorter forms in scientific terminology truly reflects scientists' uses of the adjectives, or whether these words have been affected by larger, more general trends at the time of their coinage.

Marchand was not the first linguist to suggest that the semantic differences between the endings *-ic* and *-ical* themselves (explained by their different origins) are reflected in the use of the corresponding adjectives in clearly definable ways. As early as in the eighteenth century, James Elphinston (1765: 323–324) presented the following argument:[3]

> *ic* is a foreign, and *ical* a domestic termination. The former therefore is used upon solemn, the latter on familiar occasions; as *seraph seraphic* or *seraphical, microscope microscopic* or *microscopical.* Where the subject then is naturally solemn, the solemn ending prevails; and where familiar, the familiar. So we say almost only

---

2   One could also ask why the preference of scientists to use the shorter forms was not more strongly applied on *-ic/-ical* adjectives relating to whole branches of sciences, as in *mathematic(al)* and *geographic(al)*, with which the shorter forms are nowadays rare. In his reference to the scientists' use of *-ic/-ical* adjectives, Marchand (1969: 242) does not point out this discrepancy.

3   Marchand (1969) does not refer to Elphinston's (1765; 1790) observations, which actually seem to have escaped most scholars writing on the *-ic/-ical* adjectives. Of the reference material consulted for the present study, only Jespersen (1942) and Evans and Evans (1957) mention them.

majestic, miltonic, from *majesty, Milton,* &c. and *whimsical, finical,*
from *whimsy, fine,* &c.

The dichotomy 'solemn versus familiar' is, in fact, not far away from Marchand's
ideas on the basic characteristics of words in *-ic/-ical.* Elphinston's ideas (1765:
323–324; 326–328) of adjectives inherently describing "a solemn subject", and
thus mostly taking the *-ic* form, as in *angelic, heroic,* and *majestic,* will be
discussed further in Chapter 4 (see also Kaunisto 2001).

In the same way as Marchand, Jespersen (1942: 388–390) appears to
emphasise the relative "strength" and "popularity" of adjectives in *-ical* when
compared with those in *-ic.* For example, he points out that the use of the *-ical*
form as the adjective is "virtually obligatory whenever there is a subst. in *-ic* or
-ics in use" (p. 390), but even Marchand (1969: 243) dismisses Jespersen's idea
as an exaggeration. Like other linguists, Jespersen and Marchand note the fact
that adjectives in both *-ic* and *-ical* form adverbs in *-ically.* In fact, they present
this as a major factor explaining the prominence of adjectives in *-ical.* According
to Jespersen (1942: 389), the dominance of *-ically* over *-icly* is "the chief reason"
why the *-ical* ending in English came to be employed to a greater extent than its
equivalents in Latin (*-icalis*) and French (*-ical*). Marchand (1969: 243) in turn
regards the dominance of *-ically* over *-icly* (which is today only seen in *publicly*)
as a reason behind "the dominance of *-ical* in commonly used words".

Many scholars, however, tend to suggest an overall tendency in the use of
-ic/-ical adjectives that is opposite to the ideas of Jespersen and Marchand. As
observed in the Introduction, Earle (1892: 404) referred to a backlash after the
"strain of adjectives in *-ical*", with many *-ical* adjectives disappearing from the
language while their shorter rivals prevailed (see also Partridge 1957 s.v. *-ic,
-ical*; Barber 1964: 114; Swan 1980 s.v. *-ic* and *-ical*; Todd and Hancock 1986
s.v. *-ic, -ical words*; Ross 1998: 41).[4] Instead of considering the deletion of one of
the forms to have been systematic – so that as a result particular kinds of
adjectives more frequently have the *-ic* ending, while some others feature the
-ical ending – Earle sees no prominent regularities in the process. He points out
the obsolescence of e.g. *domestical* and *magnifical*, but adds that "it almost
excites a surprise to find that after all we have been rather arbitrary in our
discontinuance of some, while we have continued to use others whose case is
nowise different", presenting e.g. *archaeological, categorical, cynical,
ecclesiastical, ecumenical, methodical,* and *symmetrical* as examples (Earle 1892:
404–405). Krapp (1927) s.vv. *-ic, -ical* and Kennedy (1935) s.vv. *-al, -ical* share

---

4   Bain (1879: 249), however, observes that in cases where *-al* has been added to *-ic*
(see also Chapter 1, fn. 5), "[o]ften the form in *-ic* does not now exist". The examples Bain
provides are *angelical, canonical, comical, historical,* and *whimsical*, which hardly
support his argument very well: *whimsical* never had a rival form in *-ic, angelical* itself
has become obsolete, and the remaining ones do nowadays have a corresponding form in
-ic (with *comic* and *historic* having a firm stand in the lexicon, *canonic* being admittedly
rare).

this view, both as regards the tendency to oust forms in -*ical*, and the conceptual irregularity with the remaining adjectives in -*ic*/-*ical*. Presenting adjectives such as *athletic, barbaric, chaotic, idiotic, magnetic*, and *scientific*, on the one hand, and *allegorical, astronomical, clerical, critical, dropsical, farcical, genealogical, identical, piratical, surgical*, and *typical*, on the other, Krapp concludes that "[t]he groupings in present use appear to rest upon accidental conventions", since "*athletical* would seem to be as natural a form as *identical*, and *identic* as *athletic*" (see also Fowler 1926 s.v. -*ic(al)*).

The main difference in the presentations by Jespersen and Marchand, on the one hand, and e.g. Earle, on the other, is that the former seem to base their arguments mainly on the origins of -*ic* and -*ical* in English (resulting in basic semantic differences between -*ic* and -*ical*), and the present-day use of the adjectives, but they pay almost no attention at all to the chronologically intermediate changes in the use of the adjectives, i.e. between the moment of their entrance into the lexicon and the present day. As noted earlier, Marchand comments briefly on the tendency of clearing away one of the forms, but he portrays it as generally favouring the longer forms. In contrast, the historical changes in the use of the words, especially the processes of deletion have a greater role in the argumentation of Earle, Fowler, and Krapp. In their view, the forms in -*ic* are seen as being usually the victors of the rivalry. In slightly exaggerated terms, one could argue that the approach of Jespersen and Marchand puts more weight on the endings -*ic* and -*ical* themselves, whereas Earle focusses on the entire words or word pairs.

The claims about the overall strength and popularity of -*ical* are also in opposition to the observations according to which -*ic* is more likely to be used in more recent coinages, i.e. -*ic* being relatively more productive than -*ical*. This idea has been suggested by e.g. Swan (1980) s.v. -*ic* and -*ical*, Marsden (1985: 29), Todd and Hancock (1986) s.v. -*ic, -ical words*, and Ross (1998: 41), with words such as *allergic, bionic, electronic, moronic*, and *synthetic* given as examples. The examination of first citations of -*ic*/-*ical* adjectives in the *OED* corroborates this argument (see Chapter 4).

As to certain specific groups of words singled out as manifesting a preference for either -*ic* or -*ical*, linguists show greater agreement over adjectives derived from proper names denoting persons, places, or races (see e.g. Elphinston 1765: 328; Sweet 1891: 490; Jespersen 1942: 389; Marchand 1969: 243, 294). These adjectives, which refer to ethnic features, languages (e.g. *Celtic, Gaelic, Germanic, Gothic, Slavic*) or an influence/adherence to certain styles or lines of thought (e.g. *Aristotelic, Byronic, Platonic, Miltonic*), show in present-day English a clear preference for the use of the forms in -*ic* rather than -*ical*.[5]

---

5   Chapman (1939: 71) notes that some of the earliest English words ending in -*ic* denote seas (e.g. *Atlantic, Adriatic, Baltic*), following the respective Greek and Latin models in -ικος and -*icus*. He also believes that the model of the classical languages explains the present-day prevalence of the shorter forms over the obsolete alternatives in -*ical* (i.e. adjectives of this type in Latin did not have the cumulate -*icalis* ending).

Marchand (1969: 243) claims that the extensions into -*ical* are not possible, as -*al* is not used to produce adjectives from "proper names of persons, places, nations, or races". However, what he does not mention is that in the sixteenth and seventeenth centuries, adjectives of this type ending in -*ical* did exist (some of them actually predating the corresponding forms in -*ic*), e.g. *Galenical, Germanical, Homerical, Junonical, Platonical,* and *Socratical* (Earle 1892: 396, 404; Chapman 1939: 68–70). The corpora studied also included instances of e.g. *Adamical, Aesopical, Babylonical, Hippocratical, Mosaical, Pythagorical, Satanical,* and *Skeltonical,* most of them indeed from the late sixteenth century and seventeenth century. Jespersen (1942: 389) argues that as adjectives of this type do not usually form adverbs (in the same way as adjectives in "chemical and other technical nomenclature"), the adverbial ending -*ically* did not promote the usage of -*ical*. The corpus evidence would rather suggest that the application of -*ical* with proper names increased along with other -*ical* adjectives in the late sixteenth century.[6] The process of discarding the longer forms later on seems to have taken place in a rather uniform manner, and as a result we have a clearly definable group of words where -*ic* is the preferred ending.

It has also been suggested that formations in -*ical* are seen more often than those in -*ic* in adjectives derived from native bases with a basic meaning paraphrased by Marchand (1969: 243) as "queer, odd, spleeny". As examples Marchand has *coxcombical, farcical, frenzical, lackadaisical, nonsensical, quizzical, twistical,* and *whimsical,* some of which also have connotations of 'ludicrous' or 'haphazard, lazy'. Marchand further observes instances of native-based nonce-formations with the -*ical* ending, including *good-sensical, hobbyhorsical, pillarboxical,* and *spleenical.* Jespersen presents some nonce-words ending in -*ic* as well, such as *dryasdustic(al), gigmanic,* and *mushroomic.* These words often have quite negative shades of meaning.

In some cases, it is possible that a part of the base of the adjective together with the -*ic(al)* element has been perceived as an ending in its own right, which could account for the historical changes in the uses of certain groups of adjectives. For example, adjectives ending in -*cratic/-cratical,* as in *aristocratic(al), democratic(al),* and *theocratic(al),* corresponding to nouns ending in -*crat,* may have, by analogy, developed so that only the -*ic* forms are nowadays usually encountered. Marchand (1969: 242–243) observes that whenever -*ic/-ical* adjectives have an ending which can also stand as an independent word, the corresponding form is normally selected. Marchand presents adjectives in -*logical* as the most prominent example (cf. Swan 1980 s.v.

---

6   As regards the significance of the adverbs in -*ically* on the use of adjectives in -*ic/-ical,* it is difficult to accept the argument that they would have had a crucial effect in favour of the corresponding adjectives in -*ical,* i.e. adjectives which most naturally form adverbs would have the -*ical* ending. Instances speaking against the idea include the nowadays obsolete or rare forms *domestical, heroical, majestical, pathetical, poetical,* and *tragical,* which undoubtedly have received plenty of "lexical support" over the years from their corresponding adverbs in -*ically.*

-ic and *-ical*; see, however, pp. 36, 49). More variation, however, can be seen between adjectives ending in *-graphic/-graphical* and *-metric/-metrical*.

Finally, there is one semantically distinct type of adjective where the *-ical* form has probably never been encountered. While both the *-ic* and *-ical* endings have the basic meanings 'of or pertaining to', 'relating to', 'resembling', 'having the quality of' or 'characterised by', in chemistry, only *-ic* has been used in a more specified meaning denoting a relation on the level of valence in chemical compounds, or that of a charge in ions. In this case, *-ic* contrasts not with *-ical* but with *-ous*, so that the level of oxidation or charge in adjectives with *-ic* is higher than in those with the suffix *-ous*, as in *nitric/nitrous* and *phosphoric/phosphorous* (*OED* s.v. *-ic*; Urdang 1982 s.v. *-ic*[1]; Metcalfe & Astle 1995: 202). *The Oxford Dictionary of English Etymology* (1966) s.v. *-ic* attributes this use to the practice adopted in French, citing *Nomenclature Chimique* (1787) as the work establishing this distinction in chemical terminology.

It has been observed that the presentations of different scholars on the *-ic/-ical* issue differ from each other, even as regards which of the forms is the "preferred" or "stronger" form on the whole. In fact, it appears that the synchronic point of view is notably visible in many descriptions of the use of the adjectives, and linguists have not always been able to distinguish between different tendencies. For example, some groups of words have shown a preference for the use of one of the endings from the very moment of their coinage, while in the case of others, the preference seen today is a result of lexical competition, which was "settled" with the deletion or attrition of one of the forms.

2.   Semantic differentiation

As noted earlier, in the case of some adjective pairs in *-ic/-ical*, the two forms have developed different meanings, among them *classic/classical*, *economic/economical*, *historic/historical*, and *politic/political* (see e.g. Fowler 1926 s.v. *-ic*, *-ical*, Marchand 1969: 241–242, and Adams 2001: 36). Some scholars have set out to observe common features or patterns in the ways in which semantic differentiation manifests itself in such adjective pairs. The present section will discuss some of the ideas that have been put forward.

Many accounts on the matter base their arguments on the (perceived) semantic differences between the endings. As already observed in the previous section, Elphinston (1765; 1790) emphasised the "foreign versus domestic" aspect in the origins of the endings *-ic* and *-ical*, respectively, and claimed that where pairs in *-ic/-ical* exist, the shorter form tends to be preferred on "solemn" occasions, while the *-ical* forms are used in "familiar" contexts. The examples he provided (1765: 323), e.g. *seraphic/seraphical* and *microscopic/microscopical*, with no surrounding context, are not very illustrating. A related theory can be found in the *OED* s.v. *-ical* and *The Concise Oxford Dictionary of Current*

English s.v. *-al*. According to the latter, the shorter forms are in general semantically closer to the base word, whereas the *-ical* form "indicates vaguer connexion".[7] The *OED* s.v. *-ical* describes the distinction by stating that the shorter forms are "often restricted to the sense 'of' or 'of the nature of' the subject in question", while the longer forms tend to have the sense 'dealing or practically connected with'.

This is also the view held by Marchand (1969: 242). However, the question of the semantic distance of the adjectives from "the idea expressed by the root" is rather problematic. It appears that "measuring" this feature is disturbingly vague, and depends too heavily on the paraphrases given for the adjectives. In fact, some of the example phrases presented in the *OED* s.v. *-ical* to illustrate the semantic differentiation between the two forms appear to not only simplify, but also to distort the issue with sometimes questionable paraphrases, as also observed by Gries (2001: 74, 79). For example, the distinction between *historic/historical* is described by saying that "[a] *historic* book is one mentioned or famous in history, a *historical* treatise contains or deals with history" (see also Marchand 1969: 242), an example presented in support of the idea that forms in *-ic* have the sense 'of' or 'of the nature of', while *-ical* forms mean 'dealing or practically connected with'. What complicates the issue is the fact that semantically differentiated forms commonly have a number of different meanings instead of only one sense per form (which is often disregarded when making generalisations on the uses of *-ic/-ical* pairs; see e.g. Quirk et al. 1985: 1554). For example, *historical* is also used in the sense of 'belonging to or having existed in history', as in "it was a genuine historical event" (as opposed to being merely a legendary or rumoured one). Considering this meaning of *historical* together with the sense 'making history or important in history' of *historic*, the issue of measuring semantic distance seems questionable, since it is difficult to say which one of the adjectives is then closer to the notion of history.[8]

---

7   This comment is found in the 4th edition (1951) of the dictionary. However, no such comment appears in the 8th edition (1990).

8   The pair *economic/economical* is exemplified in the *OED* s.v. *-ical* with the phrases *economic science* and *economical wife*. It seems that *economic science* is chosen as the example phrase because it is phraseologically more common to refer to "the science *of* economics" than to "the science dealing with economics", while the paraphrase 'practically connected with' conveniently covers the meaning 'thrifty' in *an economical wife*. However, *an economic treatise* is one that 'deals with' economics in the same way as *a historical treatise* would relate to history. As in the case of *historic/historical*, *economic/economical* have other uses as well, e.g. the sense 'profitable' (*economic* being the more frequently occurring form, as in *an economic rent*). Taking this sense into account in the overall "measurements" of semantic distance from the core meaning again causes obvious difficulties. What exactly is the difference between the senses 'profitable' and 'thrifty' as regards their distance from the core idea of managing one's resources (for more on *economic/economical*, see Chapter 7)? Hawkes (1976: 98), who basically reiterates Marchand's arguments, contributes to the treatment of the issue by providing some awkward comments. For example, the observation that "a 'problematic question' is

As regards the suggested glosses of the meanings distinguishing between adjectives in *-ic/-ical* in the *OED*, pondering on the relational difference between senses such as 'of the nature of' and 'dealing with' is perhaps not very practicable[9]. The same can be said of descriptions such as 'of', 'pertaining to', or 'having to do with'. In considerably clearer terms, it has been suggested that competing forms in *-ic/-ical* are often differentiated as regards their adjectival function. According to e.g. Schibsbye (1970: 140), the forms in *-ic* typically have 'a limiting value', whereas those in *-ical* are usually 'descriptive' (see also Hansen and Nielsen 1986: 70, and Bache and Davidsen-Nielsen 1997: 451). This has usually been linked with the positioning of the adjectives in the sentence, limiting (or classifying) adjectives being more often found in the attributive position, whereas descriptive adjectives (sometimes referred to as qualitative adjectives or epithets) can be used more freely, i.e. either attributively or predicatively (cf. Warren 1984; Halliday 1985; Downing and Locke 1992; Bache and Davidsen-Nielsen 1997).

One adjective pair used by Schibsbye (1970: 140) and Todd and Hancock (1986) s.v. *-ic, -ical words* is *lyric/lyrical*. Todd and Hancock illustrate the difference in the usage of the two forms with the sentences "Keats has often been praised for his lyric gifts" and "John was lyrical in his praise of the meal". It is suggested that *lyric* is used more often as a classifier, i.e. denoting a type, while *lyrical* has a descriptive meaning. Leaning on the example of this pair, Todd and Hancock say that "*-ical* adjectives are more widely used than *-ic* adjectives and are also more likely to be used metaphorically".[10] The argument thus builds up into a view (echoing that of Marchand) on the semantic differentiation between the forms in *-ic/-ical*, according to which one of the forms relates to a specific genre or activity in some field of science, whereas the other form would be reserved for metaphorical uses or other senses derived from the (perceived) root of the word.

Interestingly enough, all adjective pairs in *-ic/-ical* do not behave similarly as to the differentiation between the forms along these lines. In the case of *politic/political* and *historic/historical*, the uses denoting a genre or scientific field are assigned to the *-ical* forms, while with e.g. *comic/comical*, *economic/economical*, and *lyric/lyrical*, these senses are carried by the forms in

---

one to which the answer is difficult; whilst a 'problemat*ical* question' can be one to which there is no possible answer at all, but which is posed simply for the intellectual discussion to be derived from it" is perhaps unlikely to meet with widespread agreement.

9   It must be noted that the distinction proposed in the *OED* s.v. *-ical* is by no means presented as applying to all *-ic/-ical* adjectives. The entry also adds that "in many cases this distinction is, from the nature of the subject, difficult to maintain, or entirely inappreciable".

10   This observation on the use of *lyric/lyrical* is also given by Fowler (1926) s.v. *lyric(al)*, who notes that "[*l*]*yrical* is in some sort a parasite upon *lyric*, meaning suggestive of lyric verse. *Lyric* classifies definitely, while *lyrical* describes vaguely".

-ic. Schibsbye (1970: 140) himself also notes that the use of many adjectives in *-ic/-ical* does not conform with the idea he proposed. Moreover, *theoretic*, which he cites as one of the examples illustrating the distinction, is nowadays rare, with *theoretical* actually being more common in all senses where the shorter form is still found.

Marsden (1985) examines the uses of eight *-ic/-ical* adjective pairs, namely *classic/classical*, *comic/comical*, *economic/economical*, *electric/ electrical*, *historic/historical*, *lyric/lyrical*, *magic/magical*, and *poetic/poetical*. He bases his assessment of the use of the words on a handful of monolingual English dictionaries, English-German dictionaries, and a few English usage manuals. Drawing from the definitions in these works, Marsden points out three features which he observes as reoccurring in the uses of the adjectives, and thus showing that there is 'some underlying system' in how the *-ic/-ical* adjectives are used (even though the features are not systematically assigned). The "marked" features in question are value judgement, imitation, and the ability to occur in predicative position. The forms he presents as manifesting a notion of value judgement are e.g. *classic* ('of the highest quality'), *comic* ('funny'), *economical* ('thrifty, saving'), *historic* ('important in history'), and *magical* ('wonderful, enchanting'). By the component of "imitation" – based on the frequent occurrence of the word *resemblance* in dictionary definitions – Marsden points to the metaphorical uses of the adjectives, uses outside "the genuine article". One adjective presented as having an imitative use is *lyrical*, which is used to describe emotions and atmospheres, as opposed to *lyric*, which denotes a genre. Marsden then gives a tabular presentation of the uses of the eight adjective pairs, showing how the different forms stand as regards the three features described. Based on this componential analysis, he considers *historic/historical* and *economic/economical* to be "mirror images" of each other as regards the criteria examined: in the former pair, the denotative and neutral senses are assigned to the longer form, and in the latter to the shorter form. Correspondingly, the "chiasmus" is completed with the senses of *historic* and *economical* involving the notion of value judgement (see also Bache and Davidsen-Nielsen 1997: 451). Rather elegantly, Marsden (1985: 30) concludes that "the morphology is at variance with the semantics".[11]

However, Marsden's observations and conclusions appear to be very similar to those of Schibsbye, that is, not at all far from the dichotomy of "classifying versus descriptive use". Value judgement and imitation are typical features of descriptive adjectives, which in turn can usually occur both attributively and predicatively. In contrast, the lack of these features is characteristic of adjectives used in a classifying function. One can therefore ask

---

11   The third feature examined by Marsden (1985), the ability to occur in a predicative position, is not discussed in any greater detail. In the tabular presentation, Marsden merely states whether the forms have this ability or not. Its connection with meaning (i.e. descriptive versus classifying function) is not explored in connection with the eight adjective pairs, either.

whether the breakdown into different components actually brought anything genuinely new to the semantic characterisations of -ic/-ical adjectives, particularly when the conclusion appears to be the same, i.e. the pairs seem to vary as to what kinds of senses are assigned to the two forms. Although Marsden's (1985) attempt to explore the -ic/-ical issue in itself should be recognised, his overall treatment of the uses of the eight -ic/-ical adjective pairs is regrettably superficial. For example, the figurative use of *electric* (as in *the atmosphere was electric*) as well as the sense 'profitable' of *economic* are not mentioned at all. Furthermore, *comic* is presented as having only classifying uses (e.g. *comic actor/opera/strip*) and thus not being used predicatively. In stark contrast, the corpora examined for the present study shows that *comic* is used descriptively as well, and in that function can be used in a predicative position in a sentence (see Chapter 6). One possible reason for the deficiencies in Marsden (1985) may be the relatively limited reference material, in which Fowler (1926) appears to be represented perhaps too prominently at the expense of others.[12] Considering the fact that Fowler did not hesitate to put forward his views on ideal usage instead of describing the (then) current linguistic behaviour, the almost authoritative role of his comments in Marsden's argumentation gives some reason for concern.

Ross (1998) suggests that forms in -ic and -ical in many differentiated pairs follow the pattern of 'specific versus general', so that the shorter form usually has a more specific reference, while -ical is more general. The idea harks back in many ways to that of semantic distance, both as regards the perceived difference as well as the method of formulating the argument. Again, one finds several senses neglected when making the generalisations (e.g. 'having existed in history' for *historical*, 'amusing' for *comic*, 'profitable' for *economic*), and the uses are paraphrased as reflecting a "wider" use when appropriate. For example, Ross (1998: 42) notes that "*economic* is strictly related to the world of economics (*an economic cycle, economic recovery*), while *economical* is used in the wider sense of not wasting money (*an economical floor-covering, an economical little car*)" (cf. Crystal 1991 s.v. *economic*). As also pointed out by Gries (2001: 79), it could be argued that the paraphrase would be equally convincing if one were to

---

12   It is interesting to note that although Fowler (1926) comments on the "classifying versus descriptive" distinction between the two forms in the case of a number of different -ic/-ical pairs, he does not make any generalisation to this effect under the entry for -ic(al). One reason for this could be the very lack of regularity as to the functions assigned to the two forms. The idea does appear in Jespersen (1942: 391), who cites a letter written to him by Ian Maxwell, including the comment "[m]y impression is that the forms in ic may indicate either the quality or the category of a thing, but that those in ical always, or almost always, indicate the quality only". However, Jespersen appears to have been content to merely include the observation instead of developing the argument any further (or even commenting on it in any way). In fact, he continues by illustrating the differences in use between the -ic/-ical forms in a number of pairs (e.g. *comic/comical*, *electric/electrical*, *politic/political, theatric/theatrical*), which on the whole do not provide ample support for the suggestion of Mr. Maxwell.

change the places of the words *strictly* and *wider* in the paraphrases, so that "*economic* is related to the world of economics in a wider sense, whereas *economical* is strictly used in the sense of not wasting money". However, while many accounts on the semantic differentiation between *-ic/-ical* adjectives oversimplify the issue, implying that there is no overlap in their uses, Ross (1998: 42) points out that "there are nevertheless some indications that [...] *-ical* may in some cases eventually lose out to the shorter *-ic*", referring e.g. to the corpus-based *Collins COBUILD English Dictionary* (1995).

Although the ideas proposed on the overall trends in semantic differentiation between adjectives in *-ic/-ical* are most interesting, they should be considered with a certain measure of caution because of the scantiness of hard evidence provided by the scholars behind them. It appears that many linguists have, in fact, made generalisations based on the generalisations of others.[13] Similarly troubling is the fact that the various accounts provide no clear diachronic picture of the trends in the application of the endings in new words, or the changes in their subsequent use. The problems perceived in the theories proposed therefore speak for the necessity of investigating the use of the adjectives more closely, preferably in a corpus as large and comprehensive as possible.

3.   Other factors affecting the choice of the form

In addition to the comments relating to the two processes discussed in the two previous sections, other remarks have been made on the factors that may affect the choice between the forms in *-ic* and *-ical*. One interesting suggestion is that the rhythm of the sentence could in some cases determine the choice of the form. This idea has been put forward by e.g. Burchfield 1996 s.v. *-ic(al)*, who does not, however, present any practical example of how rhythm would have an effect on the choice (see also Marchand 1969: 244). The effect would presumably be more likely with those pairs in *-ic/-ical* where a clear semantic difference has not been established. The problem with this idea is that its validity is very difficult to examine empirically. Furthermore, it is possible that rhythmic(al) factors are more likely to come into play in spoken language than in writing; Todd and Hancock (1986) s.v. *-ic, -ical words* even suggest that when the two adjective

---

13   Crystal (1991) s.v. *classic* withheld from making hasty generalisations, pointing out that the "distinction between *-ic* and *-ical* is found in dozens of cases in English, but it is not easy to generalize about usage preferences, as different factors are involved".

forms are used synonymously, it is possible that "the *-ic* ending is more likely to occur in the written medium and the *-ical* variant in the spoken".

Relating to the question of rhythm, the placing of the word-stress in *-ic/-ical* adjectives has also been commented on, e.g. by Jespersen (1942: 387), Danielsson (1948: 162–187), Chomsky and Halle (1968: 88), Hill (1974), and Bauer (1983: 113–122). Basically adjectives in *-ic/-ical* are similar as to the placing of the stress, which usually falls on the syllable preceding *-ic* (see also Fudge 1984: 40–43). The earliest words in *-ic*, however, used to have the stress on the first syllable, which is still seen in adjectives such as *Arabic*, *politic*, and *catholic*. Some words in *-ic* also have an antepenultimate stress, such as the noun *arithmetic*. Bauer (1983: 114) regards these kinds of instances as "phonologically lexicalized" forms (see also Hill 1974: 11). By the time the first words in *-ical* were coined, *-ic* and *-ical* conditioned the stress of the word; the pronunciation of some of the previously existing words in *-ic* also changed (e.g. from *a'postolic* to *apos'tolic*).[14] However, the exceptionally stressed adjectives in English nowadays do not appear to have played a very significant role as regards the choice of the form in *-ic* or *-ical*, since the number of the early adjectives before the "flood" of the forms in *-ical* is relatively small. An interesting case is *politic/political*, which today have different meanings: in all likelihood, the stress patterns of the two forms have always been different.

Some scholars suggest that the choice of either the *-ic* or the *-ical* form occasionally shows regional variation. For example, Burchfield (1996) s.v. *-ic(al)* suggests that "for those pairs where there appears to be no difference of sense, I have formed a broad impression that the *-ic* forms are favoured in AmE and *-ical* ones in BrE; but the distribution is erratic, and is much influenced by the practice of particular publishing houses". The same general observation is made by Evans and Evans (1957) s.v. *-ic; -ical*, who note that "the short form in *-ic* is preferred, and the long form in *-ical* leaves many people wondering why the speaker went to the trouble of pronouncing that unnecessary syllable". Ross (1998) and Barbeau and Barbeau (2000) argue that British usage shows a greater preference for the use of the *-logical* ending than for *-logic*, while in American English, the shorter forms are relatively more visible (e.g. *gynecologic, pathologic*), though the forms in *-logical* are still dominant.[15]

---

14   Hill (1974: 12) proposes an interesting theory on why some words in *-ic* resisted the shift of the word-stress to the penultimate syllable, and thus still have the antepenultimate stress. In the three-syllable words where this stress-pattern is attested, the pre- or post-vocalic consonant (or both) in the middle syllable is liquid or nasal. Words with this feature are thus "subject to variation in the number of syllables, since a weakly stressed vowel in such a middle syllable can be replaced by a syllabic consonant, and the syllabicity may be unstable". The words which Hill sees as having the potential to be recognised as either a two- or a three-syllable word are *Arabic, arsenic, catholic, choleric, climacteric, dominic, heretic, lunatic, politic,* and *rhetoric*.

15   A quick survey of a number of adjectives ending in *-logic/-logical* in the 1994 issues of *The Washington Post* and the 1995 issues of *The Daily Telegraph* shows that

Another factor suggested by Kaunisto (1999: 347) as possibly having an effect on the use of *-ic/-ical* adjectives is prefixation. One could assume that as languages favour economy, the shorter forms of the adjectives tend to be the ones that are prefixed.[16] An interesting example in this respect is the prevalence of *prehistoric* over *prehistorical*: as regards the meaning of *prehistoric*, the semantic differentiation between *historic* and *historical* would, in fact, promote the use of *prehistorical* as the prefixed form (for further details on *historic/historical*, see Chapter 9). Thus it would be tempting to consider that the desire for economy in this case overrides (the need for) semantic differentiation.[17] Gries (2001: 98–100) examined the prefixed forms of fifteen *-ic/-ical* adjective pairs in the *BNC* (the domains of written language), and compared their numbers of types and tokens with those of the unextended forms. Gries observed that the prefixed forms in general ending in *-ic* appeared to be considerably more frequent than one might have expected compared with the numbers of types and tokens of their base forms, thus supporting the idea of economy. Two exceptions to these results were *economic/economical* and *classic/classical*. Gries concludes that in these cases, the semantic differentiation is probably so well established that the distinction is reflected in the prefixed forms as well. However, instead of reducing or simplifying the issue into mere frequencies of types and tokens, one would wish for a more detailed account of the meanings of the prefixed forms and the corresponding bases. Some adjectives may carry senses which do not readily

---

-logical is indeed the dominant form in British English: one instance of *immunologic* was the sole occurrence in the *Telegraph* texts of any adjective ending in *-logic*. The *Washington Post* material contained 16 articles including the adjective *geologic*, and 38 articles including *geological* (excluding the instances in which the adjectives were a part of a proper name). *Pharmacologic* was found on five, and the corresponding *-ical* form on eight occasions. The other pairs examined – *archaeologic(al), biologic(al), ecologic(al), gynecologic(al), meteorologic(al), neurologic(al), pathologic(al), physiologic(al), psychologic(al),* and *theologic(al)* – showed generally a greater preference for the use of the longer forms, with only a couple of occurrences (or none at all) of the *-ic* forms.

16   Gries (2001: 75) points out that the idea of the effect of prefixation on the choice between *-ic* and *-ical* was suggested already by Marsden (1985: 29). Under the section on *electric/electrical*, Marsden does mention the fact that the shorter form is "favoured in derivatives such as *photoelectric*", but his observation appears to underline the claim on 'the growing ascendancy of the shorter form'. In other words, Marsden presents the prefixed form as an example of recent coinages, instead of observing prefixation and the choice between *-ic* and *-ical* as having to do with language economy in general.

17   As regards lexical competition, the tendency towards economy has by no means governed the outcome of the rivalry. For example, in her discussion on multiple borrowing, Nevalainen (1999: 361) observes the occurrence of rivalling verbs borrowed from Latin, e.g. *captive/captivate, exone/ exonerate,* and *reverb/reverberate* (see Reuter 1936). The former variants in these pairs were based on the present stems of the Latin verbs, the latter ones on the past participle forms. Economy obviously was not the crucial factor in the choice between the two forms, as time has shown the longer verb forms as having eventually prevailed.

promote further derivation, e.g. the notion of being unintentionally amusing in the uses of *comic/comical*.

In some cases, it may also be possible that the choice of the *-ic/-ical* form is influenced by the proximity of another *-ic/-ical* adjective (cf. Marsden 1985: 29). An interesting passage is found in Sterne's *Tristram Shandy*:

> Thus,---thus my fellow labourers and associates in this great harvest
> of our learning, now ripening before our eyes; thus it is, by slow steps
> of casual increase, that our knowledge physical, metaphysical,
> physiological, polemical, nautical, mathematical, ænigmatical,
> technical, biographical, romantical, chemical, and obstetrical, with
> fifty other branches of it, (most of 'em ending, as these do, in ical)
> have, for these two last centuries and more, gradually been creeping
> upwards towards that Akme of their perfections, from which, if we
> may form a conjecture from the advances of these last seven years, we
> cannot possibly be far off. (Laurence Sterne, *Tristram Shandy* (1760),
> 143–144)

In the extract above, a generalisation is made on adjectives relating to the knowledge or learning of various subjects as often having the *-ical* ending. However, as we know today, the forms *enigmatical, obstetrical*, and *romantical* have given way to their rivals in *-ic*, even if used in a similar fashion to the occurrences in the quote from Sterne. The corpora examined also reveal these three adjectives as showing more variation between the two forms in the eighteenth and nineteenth centuries than the others in the list in the above passage. It is possible that the choice of the *-ical* forms here was partly influenced by a certain desire towards harmony (which was emphasised explicitly inside the parentheses). In present-day English, however, such a passage would perhaps be even less likely, because *enigmatic, obstetric*, and *romantic* have taken over the longer variants (the last one in particular). Again, the significance of this factor remains a mere theoretical possibility, as its effect is difficult to verify with absolute certainty.

4.   Empirical studies

As mentioned in Chapter 1, only a few academic articles have been published studying the use of *-ic/-ical* adjectives. As is the case with any scientific work, the measure of their successfulness in adding to the overall knowledge of the issue depends to a great extent on the aims and the level of ambition at the outset of the study. The article by Hawkes (1976) does very little apart from introducing the subject, and in substance and observation owes a good deal to Marchand (1969). Ross (1998) presents an overview into some of the problems in the use of *-ic/-ical* adjectives, and summarises the generalisations made in a handful of usage manuals and dictionaries. Empirical research is involved in Marsden (1985), Kaunisto (1999; 2001), and Gries (2001; 2003). The work in Kaunisto (1999; 2001) is generally expanded on in the present study, and will not be discussed in detail here.

4.1   Marsden (1985)

Marsden (1985), whose theoretical observations were discussed in the previous section, includes in his article the results of a small-scale elicitation test on the use of eight adjective pairs in *-ic/-ical*. In the test, Marsden presented some native English-speaking informants with a set of noun phrases containing an empty slot to be filled with one of the suggested adjectives in *-ic* and *-ical*. For example, the phrases *an ~ light* and *an ~ fault*, were to be filled with *electric* or *electrical*, and *an ~ miracle* and *the car is ~ to run* with *economic* or *economical*. The informants showed greatest uniformity in their choices of the *-ic/-ical* forms with *electric/electrical*, *economic/economical*, *magic/magical*, *comic/comical*, and *classic/classical*, which suggests that a clear division has become established between the two forms. The responses for *lyric/lyrical* and *poetic/poetical* showed greater variation. Although the results also corrclate fairly well with the picture emerging from usage manuals, the setup of the test itself can be criticised for many reasons. Firstly, the adjectives are in reality used in a large number of different collocations, and also in many different senses – the elicitation test only measured the possible use of the adjectives in two phrases, representing only two senses. In the case of some *-ic/-ical* pairs, dictionaries and some usage manuals give senses in which the use of the two forms overlap, but the use of the adjectives in such instances was unfortunately not elicited[18]. Gries (2001: 77) also demands further information on the number of informants, and criticizes the fact that the informants were, by Marsden's description, probably teachers, and therefore more likely to have based their responses on previous knowledge of the issue.

4.2   Gries (2001; 2003)

Whereas Marsden's examination of the *-ic/-ical* issue can be seen as having relatively modest goals, the articles by Gries (2001; 2003) are considerably more ambitious, aiming at a more thorough, corpus-based quantitative analysis on the use of a large number of adjective pairs in *-ic/-ical*. The first article analyses 15

---

18   It would appear that setting up an in-depth elicitation test on the use of adjective pairs in *-ic/-ical* is quite difficult, especially considering the number of different uses that even one adjective pair may have, and the number of factors potentially influencing the choice.

adjective pairs, and the latter altogether 57 pairs, based on their occurrences in the written language section of the *BNC*. However, although the ultimate goal of developing a corpus-linguistic method of lexical analysis as objective as possible is in itself most important, the quantitative approach Gries promotes in connection with the analysis of adjectives in *-ic/-ical* and the practical handling of the corpus material are open to serious criticism, which I will elaborate on below.

Instead of inspecting every occurrence of the adjectives in their surrounding contexts individually, the analysis proposed by Gries is based on the examination of the first right-hand collocates of the adjectives – more specifically, the subset of significant first right-hand collocates.[19] By using statistical calculations (the log-likelihood ratio -2logλ, and the Chi-square test), Gries (2001) obtained a set of significant collocates for the two forms, which were compared with each other. To examine the degree to which the forms can be used in place of each other, he looked at the percentages of the significant collocates shared by both forms from the total numbers of significant collocates of the individual forms. For example, Gries found 36 significant first right-hand collocates for *symmetric*, and 18 for *symmetrical*. Of these collocates, five were shared by both forms. Thus the percentage of the shared significant collocates from all the significant collocates of the two adjective forms is 13.89 (5/36) for *symmetric*, and 27.78 (5/18) for *symmetrical*.

The assessment of the degree of differentiation between the forms in *-ic/-ical*, then, was based on these percentages. In practice, the closer the percentages for both forms are to zero (in which case the sets of significant collocates for the two forms are entirely different), the more differentiated the use of the pair is. In fact, Gries further suggests that the percentages in question can be used as coordinates in a two-dimensional diagram, with "each axis represent[ing] the percentage of significant collocates of one word that are also shared by the other" (2001: 86). Each adjective pair then is represented in the diagram by a dot, and by examining the placing of the adjective pairs in the diagram, one can compare the degree of differentiation between them.

The percentages themselves, however, do not say anything about the semantic aspects of the differentiation, which Gries (2001: 84) himself observes. While Gries suggests that observations on the semantic aspects can be made by examining the sets of significant collocates, he regards some instances as problematic, especially those *-ic/-ical* pairs which have a "number of [significant] collocates that do not lend themselves to manual analysis easily" (2001: 92). For example, *magic/magical* is presented as such a pair, having "92 and 89 significant collocates respectively". In order to further reduce the number of items to be analysed, Gries applies a variant of the *t*-test proposed by Church et al (1991),

---

19   Concentrating on R1 collocates alone does not provide an accurate view into the use of the adjectives in a predicative position. Gries (2001) makes rough assessments on this factor based on the number of function words among the significant collocates (i.e. the adjective is followed by words like *the* or *that*). All sentence-final predicative occurrences were excluded from the analysis.

producing sets of "discriminating collocates" for the adjective forms, i.e. collocates which occur significantly more often with one of the forms rather than the other.[20]

There are many arguments that can be made against the method of research proposed by Gries. The basic problem with the comparison of sets of significant collocates is that it plays down the significance of semantic aspects, of both the adjectives as well as the collocates. First of all, what may potentially result in distortions in the conclusions following the "estimation of significant collocate overlap" is the fact that some adjective pairs may modify the same collocate, but have different meanings, as in *a historic event* 'an important event in history', and *a historical event* 'an event that occurred in history, as opposed to being mythical or legendary'. Gries (2001: 83–84), however, argues against the possible weight of this factor:

> I would like to anticipate an objection that might be raised by sceptical readers. The objection is: while it is possible to use significant collocates for the differentiation of the meanings of polysemous individual words such as *right* or *certain*, it is not possible to use the same technique for comparing two (or more) words. This is so because the fact that both *blue* and *expensive* might have *car* as a significant R1 collocate does not render their meaning similar at all: *blue* and *expensive* mean something completely different, and, therefore, the whole approach is bound to fail.
>
> Admittedly, this objection has some intuitive appeal – at a second glance, however, it does not pose too much of a problem for two reasons. Firstly, note that the present approach (just like Biber's [(1993)] technique, on which it is based) does not attempt to formulate a definition of the meaning of a word on the basis of its significant collocates; it uses significant collocate overlap as a measure of similarity of linguistic usage. Secondly, and much more importantly, the objection misses an important point of the technique, namely the inclusion of significant collocates *not* shared by the two words to be compared. Even if *blue* and *expensive* share a significant collocate such as *car* (or even a few more), the number of collocates they do not share is even larger. Thus, given the inclusion of the non-shared significant collocates [...], it is impossible that two words so different

---

20   The *t*-test may perhaps be a useful tool in producing rough generalisations on the distinction between forms in *-ic* and *-ical*, which conceivably could be applied, as Biber (1993: 537) observes, as a "*complementary* perspective to traditional lexicographic methods" [emphasis mine]. It cannot be used, however, for studies requiring more accurate analysis, because it does not distinguish between cases where there is slight overlap between the forms and those where there is no overlap at all (information which may be most interesting, or even critical, in e.g. describing diachronic changes in the use of the adjectives).

in meaning as *blue* and *expensive* accidentally result in being synonymous just because they happen to share a few collocates.

In this connection, one might raise the question of whether meaning/semantics and collocational behaviour are in fact two different aspects of a word's behaviour, a question also brought up by Kaunisto (1999:349). Given his way of analysis, however, he implicitly seems to assume that there is a close enough relation between the two to investigate the former in terms of the latter.

The defence presented by Gries is not fully satisfactory. Firstly, although the examples *blue* and *expensive* as words with clearly different meanings illustrate the fact that the analysis probably would not provide results to the effect that they are synonymous, one remains concerned about its useability or accuracy with words which are not semantically so far apart. Secondly, it should be pointed out that instead of merely "comparing two (or more) words" with each other as regards their collocational behaviour, Gries extends the comparison one step further, to different pairs of words. The semantic relevance in this 'comparison between the results of the comparisons' is then on an even shakier ground. In other words, what Gries' approach misses is that different adjectives in *-ic/-ical* may differ as to the extent to which the two forms can share collocates but still have different meanings. Let us take a hypothetical example: consider that two pairs ending in *-ic/-ical*, say, *Xic/Xical* and *Yic/Yical*, were completely differentiated semantically, with each of the forms carrying only one sense and never being used in the sense of the other. However, the different senses of *Xic* and *Xical* could be such that the two forms never have the same collocates, whereas with *Yic/Yical* this could happen to a significantly greater extent. In this hypothetical instance, Gries' analysis would then provide different results for the two pairs, with the difference reflecting only collocational behaviour, and not semantic differentiation at all. While scholars such as Biber (1993) have indeed drawn attention to the relation between meaning and collocational behaviour, and the applicability of examining it for various purposes, Gries assumes, rather dangerously, that the relation between semantic differentiation and collocational behaviour is exactly the same from one *-ic/-ical* pair to another.[21]

---

21   As regards the reference to Kaunisto (1999: 349), the page in question discusses the use of the adjectives *electric/electrical*, in which case the role of collocation indeed appears to be important. However, there is no suggestion that the behaviour of all *-ic/-ical* pairs could be likewise assessed by examining the immediately following collocates. In the section on *classic/classical* in Kaunisto (1999: 356), it is emphasized that the analysis of the pair must involve an examination of the adjectives in larger contexts, since the two forms can collocate with the same noun but still have clearly different meanings (e.g. *classic records* 'excellent, outstanding' versus *classical records* 'records of classical music').

In addition to the hesitations one might have on Gries' approach, the practical analysis of the material is also somewhat questionable. An examination of the *BNC* as regards the lists of significant collocates and discriminating collocates identified reveals that the data should perhaps have been examined more closely. For example, in the identification of significant collocates, Gries seems to have relied on the absolute frequencies of the collocates, without sufficiently taking into account the possible effects of idiosyncratic uses. The attention paid to the numbers of different texts in which the adjectives were found is hardly sufficient. As a result, most of the significant collocates identified for *symmetric* (e.g. *matrix, matrices, modes, section, vibrations,* and *combination*) are actually collocates occurring in just one text. For some of the other collocates considered significant, the number of different texts appears to be greater: for example, the collocate *multi-processing* occurs with *symmetric* 41 times in 21 texts. However, the 21 texts in question are all extracts from two magazines or publications, namely, *Unigram X* and *Computergram international*, which again raises doubts as to the generalisability of the data. A similarly questionable practice is that instances where the adjective is a part of a proper name were not excluded from the analysis, as such cases may be regarded as fixed and not allowing any variation. For example, when examining the discriminating collocates Gries lists for *magic*, one finds in the *BNC* numerous instances of *Magic Kingdom* (a Disney theme park), *The Magic Flute* (the opera), *Magic Bus* (the song), *Magic Roundabout* (children's TV show in the UK), *Magic Night* and *Magic Ring* (racehorses), and *The Magic Music Man* ('a video for young learners in their first year of English'). Considering the extent of the distortions that these types of inaccuracies in the analyses must have had on the overall results in both Gries (2001) and (2003), (lists of significant collocates for all the adjectives examined for the articles are not provided), I will not comment on the results in any greater detail here[22].

---

22   The method of analysis of the 57 *-ic/-ical* pairs in Gries (2003) is slightly different from the one applied in Gries (2001), although it retains the basic principle of characterising the extent of differentiation of *-ic/-ical* pairs by comparing the extent of overlap between their significant collocates. In the 2003 article, Gries included in the assessment of significant collocates only those R1 collocates which occurred in the corpus more than twice. However, the occurrences of several of the collocates deemed by Gries as significant (or even distinctive) for some adjectives – e.g. *burner* and *implant* for *optic*; *axis, bistability,* and *encoder* for *optical* – are found in only one article represented in the corpus (even though they may have occurred many times in the article).

5.   General remarks

The overall treatment of the *-ic/-ical* question by linguists appears somewhat heterogeneous and erratic. Among the main reasons for the deficiencies in general is that many of the analyses have been based on intuition, emphasizing the present-day situation in the use of the adjectives. Because of the lack of a diachronic perspective, it is possible that much of the previous work has not been able to identify the different historical tendencies at work. This in part has led to contradictory statements as regards the generalizations on the present-day stance of *-ic/-ical* adjectives in the lexicon today. The surveys involving empirical research, on the other hand, have regrettably been unsatisfactory, being problematic or questionable in their overall approach into the issue and/or the methodology applied. However, the array of claims proposed have left the linguistic world many questions to look into, for which an examination of corpora and dictionaries may provide the most accurate answers.

Chapter 4

The history of new adjectives ending in *-ic* and *-ical*

The present chapter examines the relation between the numbers of new coinages of adjectives ending in *-ic* and *-ical* in different periods. One could also talk of the productivity of *-ic* and *-ical* as derivational suffixes – but as has been noted earlier, all adjectives ending in *-ic/-ical* have actually not resulted from a simple word-formational process such as N + *-ic/-ical*. In fact, many adjectives ending in *-ic* were adopted (or adapted) from Greek, Latin or French. As regards adjectives in *-ical*, some were adoptions of French or Latin adjectives in *-ical* or *-icalis*, respectively. In addition, several words in *-ical* were based on the foreign models in *-ique*, *-icus*, and *-ικος*, with the *-al* suffix added in English, even though there may not have been forms corresponding with the *-ical* ending in the source languages.

In many instances it may be difficult to determine whether or not the *-ic/-ical* elements are genuine English affixes (see e.g. Bauer 1983: 114–115).[1] The *OED* is not very helpful in this respect, as it is sometimes undecided on the etymologies of *-ic/-ical* words: for example, *cadaveric* s.v. is regarded as either a direct adoption of the French *cadavérique* or an English formation with *-ic* based

---

1   The question of distinguishing between loan words and words coined in English using affixes of foreign origin may actually be regarded as a classic one. The problem has been observed in general terms e.g. by Görlach (1991), Dalton-Puffer (1996), Nevalainen (1999), and Bauer (2001). One aspect into the issue that has received attention relates to the analysability of the words (see e.g. Görlach 1991: 171). In her study of the French influence on the derivational morphology of Middle English, Dalton-Puffer (1996: 29–31; 209–211) analyses stem-based derivatives in different ways according to how remote they are from genuinely word-based derivatives. Stem-based derivatives regarded as closest to word-based ones are exemplified by *conspiracy* and *declaration*, the stems of which (*conspir-* and *declar-*) are analysed as verbal "stems which are somehow historically close to becoming words in their own right". More clearly stem-based derivatives include e.g. *desolation*, in which the base of the word (*desol-*) is not an existing word in English, but occurs in more than just one word (e.g. *desolation* and *desolate*). Yet another separate group includes simplex items, i.e. instances where a recurring stem cannot be found (as in *confederacy*, which is not an English formation of **confeder-* + *-acy*). Dalton-Puffer proposes that the greater the number of derivatives of the type *conspiracy* and *declaration*, the more rapidly the ending can be borrowed (or identified) as a derivational affix to be used independently.

on the Latin loan word *cadaver*.[2] As mentioned in the Introduction, given the fact that many adjectives in *-ical* occurred before the corresponding variants in *-ic*, one could even regard the shorter forms in such cases to have been formed via back-formation through the deletion of *-al* (instead of being adopted from French, Latin, or Greek). The question of productivity of *-ic* and *-ical* as derivational affixes is therefore a complex one, as there is often no clarity as to the origin of the adjective. Even if one were able to separate loan words from genuine English derivatives, the adjectives in *-ical* would present some problems. One can argue that the coinage of adjectives ending in *-ical* is to some extent a result of the productivity of the suffix *-al*. In fact, it would be difficult to distinguish whether the word was derived from a foreign adjective ending in *-ique*, *-icus*, or *-ικος* with the addition of *-al*, or formed from an underlying stem by adding *-ical*. In some instances, forms in *-ic* existed before the longer variants, in which case the *-al* ending is more likely to have been a derivational element. However, the first citations of some of the competing formations are not at all far apart, and it may be questionable which form actually occurred first.[3]

As the emphasis in the present study is on the competition between words ending in *-ic* and *-ical*, the complex issue of the extent of the use of these elements as genuine English affixes can be bypassed, since the origin of the word is largely irrelevant from the perspective of competition. In other words, a loan word in *-ic* may have had an English derivative in *-(ic)al* as its rival, or competition may have existed between a word in *-ical* and its variant in *-ic* produced via back-formation or shortening. To study the competition of the two patterns – resulting from a variety of processes of adding to the lexicon – one must investigate the relative popularity of all of the words having these endings in different times. Whilst doing so, it is nevertheless most interesting and useful to consider the theories and methods used in the examination of the productivity of individual derivational processes. In his review of the recent methods used in the study of morphological productivity, Bolozky (1999: 3–7) observes three ways of

---

2   As regards the origins of individual *-ic/-ical* adjectives, the different alternatives have not always been given in the *OED*. The influence of Latin is emphasized in the etymology given for *amuletic*, which is presented as a formation on the Latin word *amulētum* with the suffix *-ic*, "as if ad. L. *amulēticus*". Another possibility would be to regard the adjective as being formed from the noun *amulet*, which had become established in the English lexicon well before the time that the adjective was coined.

3   Danielsson (1948: 218) also makes the following most important point: "[...] it should be borne in mind that a learned or scientific word may have been adopted or adapted or coined on Latin or Greek analogies by different writers who were not acquainted with the adoption, adaption, or coinage of the same word by earlier authors. One author may have adopted or adapted the word from a French source that he made use of; another, who was well versed in Latin, may have adopted or adapted the same word – perhaps a hundred years later – from Latin (or Greek) or may have coined it from a Latin, Greek, or Romance primitive. In such cases a word may have two (or more) etymologies, cf. for instance *arithmetic, authentic, pentastich, phrenetic, prenostic, spasmodic*, etc."

examining the issue, namely elicitation tests, study of dictionaries, and the investigation of word-frequencies in corpora. Bolozky (1999: 7) also promotes the idea of applying different kinds of methods and comparing the results when investigating productivity, as "none of the methods is totally reliable in itself" (see also Plag 1999: 117 and Bauer 2001: 161). Of the three methods mentioned, the latter two will be addressed in the present study, as elicitation tests cannot be applied to studies with a diachronic perspective.[4]

As far as examining dictionaries is concerned, many scholars have raised doubts about the reliability of the results gleaned by this method. For example, Baayen and Renouf (1996) have noted that present-day dictionaries cannot possibly include entries for every conceivable derivative which might be a perfectly normal and acceptable formation. This is true for highly productive derivational affixes, such as the suffixes -*ness* and -*ly* (see also Bolozky 1999, and Cowie and Dalton-Puffer 2002). Bauer (2001: 144–145) also points out that when examining a dictionary or a corpus, the differences in productivity between two or more word-formation rules cannot be determined simply on the basis of type frequencies of the words produced by these processes. This is because mere lists of words only provide information on the rate of application of a given process in the past; they do not indicate the potential of the process to produce new words. For diachronic studies on the rate of production of words in given periods of time, however, the numbers of first citations of the words in the *Middle English Dictionary* and the *Oxford English Dictionary* provide opportunities for comparing different means of word-formation. Although several scholars have also been duly wary of the accuracy of the record of first instances of words, as well as the weaknesses of the *OED* as regards its compilation (see e.g. Görlach 1991; Bauer 1998, 2001; Nevalainen 1999; Cowie and Dalton-Puffer 2002; McDermott 2002), the *OED*'s usefulness as a tool for investigating word-formational processes through history has nevertheless been acknowledged. The results gained from the study of the *MED* and *OED* have been thought of by linguists as showing at least an indication of the actual historical application of the processes examined. Studies based on the *OED*, in particular the numbers of

---

4   As regards the frequencies of words in corpora, I will pay closer attention to the methods based on the investigation of the so-called hapax legomena, that is, items occurring only once in the corpus. Some notable studies have also examined the frequencies of types and tokens of words with particular affixes. For example, Dalton-Puffer (1996) examined the type and token frequencies of words with a number of affixes in different sections of the *Helsinki Corpus of English Texts*. Cowie and Dalton-Puffer (2002) also introduce an interesting new method of studying morphological productivity from a diachronic point of view: they used the Early Modern section of the *Helsinki Corpus* (until 1640) as "a starting lexicon", and examined the occurrence of "new" types of words with a set of affixes in subsequent periods of fifty years in the *ARCHER* corpus (beginning from 1650). As Cowie and Dalton-Puffer (2002: 431) point out, the new words encountered in this fashion may not be neologisms in reality, but the results were nevertheless considered indicative of historical trends in the application of the affixes studied.

first citations of words created via different processes in different periods, have been conducted, for example, by Anshen and Aronoff (1989), Aronoff and Anshen (1998), and Bauer (2001). The results of a similar survey on the first citations of adjectives ending in -ic and -ical in the second edition of the OED (covering the adjectives beginning with the randomly chosen letters a, c, f, i, k, l, n, t, r, and u) is presented in Table 5 below.[5]

Table 5. The numbers of first citations of adjectives ending in -ic and -ical in the OED.

	-ic	%	-ical	%
1250–1299	1	100.0	-	0.0
1300–1349	2	100.0	-	0.0
1350–1399	15	93.8	1	6.2
1400–1449	2	66.7	1	33.3
1450–1499	10	66.7	5	33.3
1500–1549	12	30.8	27	69.2
1550–1599	38	29.7	90	70.3
1600–1649	111	44.2	140	55.8
1650–1699	176	56.8	134	43.2
1700–1749	81	65.3	43	34.7
1750–1799	113	74.8	38	25.2
1800–1849	392	78.2	109	21.8
1850–1899	1043	89.2	126	10.8
1900–1949	396	91.7	36	8.3
1950–1989	162	89.0	20	11.0
total	**2554**		**770**	

Although the absolute figures of first citations of -ic/-ical words are of some interest, what is even more illuminating is the relation between the numbers of new words in -ic and -ical attested in different fifty-year periods.[6] As can be

---

5   In some instances, the dates of the first recorded instances in the OED are only approximations (e.g. ca. 1390), or span several years (e.g. 1432–1470). Here, the approximations have been accepted as such; in cases spanning several years, the last year has been selected to represent the year of the first attested occurrence.

6   The drop in the type frequencies in the eighteenth century figures may be a reflection of the overall decrease in neologisms in this period, but it may also result from the uneven volumes of source material from different periods used by the dictionary-makers (see e.g. Nevalainen 1999: 338). One way of normalizing the figures would be to calculate the numbers of first citations of -ic/-ical adjectives in relation to the total numbers of neologisms from each fifty-year period. However, such normalized figures would not alter the picture of the relation between the numbers of new words in -ic and -ical in different periods (cf. Bauer 2001: 185–186).

seen from the table, the first adjectives in -*ic* (including *authentic, fantastic, lunatic, rhetoric,* and *rustic*), occurred before those in -*ical* (e.g. *canonical, radical, rhetorical, rustical,* and *tragical*). A clear increase in the numbers of words in -*ical* can be seen in the sixteenth century, when the adoptions or coinages of words in -*ical* seem to have dominated over those in -*ic*. In the seventeenth century, however, the number of new adjectives ending in -*ic* appears to have increased in relation to those in -*ical*. In the latter half of the seventeenth century, the shorter forms were more numerous among the neologisms, and the relation in favour of new words ending in -*ic* only seems to have increased ever since. Adjectives ending in -*ical* seem to have become less and less popular in new coinages. As regards the lexical fields represented by the adjectives, both endings seem to have been used in fairly similar kinds of words well into the seventeenth century. In the eighteenth and nineteenth centuries (especially in the latter), however, the -*ic* ending was clearly favoured in new scientific words, relating to e.g. chemistry and mineralogy (for example, *aconitic, aluminic, amylic, isatoic, ferritic,* and *tantalic*), and in many cases rival forms in -*ical* were not coined. As mentioned in Chapter 3, adjectives derived from proper names (either loan words or corresponding formations in English, e.g. *Aristotelic(al), Franklinic, Miltonic, Noachic(al), Robinson Crusoic*) showed more variation between the -*ic*/-*ical* endings in new words in the sixteenth and seventeenth centuries, after which the -*ical* ending did not occur anymore.

The figures in Table 5 do not include instances of prefixed -*ic*/-*ical* words. Although prefixed items themselves are in theory of great interest, and variation between -*ic*/-*ical* is possible, these cases were excluded from the examination of the *OED* entries as they are perhaps not represented as comprehensively as their base forms in the dictionary. However, the figures do include cases where the -*ic(al)* ending could be regarded as a part of a final combining form. The greatest type frequencies in the *OED* material studied were found with the endings -*graphic(al)*, -*logic(al)*, and -*metric(al)* (corresponding to nouns ending in -*graph(y)*, -*logy*, and -*metre*/-*metry*, respectively). In the case of -*graphic(al)* and -*metric(al)*, the numbers of first citations for the -*ic*/-*ical* forms are to a great extent parallel to the overall figures in Table 5, i.e. in 1550–1599, more new words were attested for -*ical* than for -*ic*, followed by a surge in new words ending in -*ic*. With words ending in -*logic(al)*, however, the longer forms have almost always been more frequent among the neologisms, most clearly in the nineteenth century. Since the nineteenth century, many new words were created ending in -*blastic*, -*genic*, -*genetic*, -*lithic*, -*lytic*, -*morphic*, -*philic*, -*phobic*, -*trop(h)ic*, -*uric*, and -*zoic*, which all could be regarded as final combining forms (cf. Görlach 1999: 111–113). Instances of these elements with the additional -*al* are quite rare in the dictionary.

Some other groups of words ending in -*ic*/-*ical* are worth mentioning: for example, the numbers of first citations of words ending in -*istic(al)* – usually derived from words ending in -*ist* or -*ism* by adding -*ic(al)* – again seem to follow the overall pattern seen in Table 5, with the coinages of shorter forms being considerably more frequent than the longer ones from the nineteenth century onwards. The same goes for adjectives ending in -itic(al), from words ending in either -ite or -itis.[7] The derivation from names of minerals, e.g. albinite, aphanite, and chlorite, shows a clearer preference for the use of -ic at all times, whereas slight variation between -ic/-ical is seen with adjectives based on nouns referring to followers of a sect or ethnic groups (e.g. Ishmaelite, Islamite, Israelite) or illnesses (e.g. arthritis, cellulitis, fibrocitis). On the other hand, -ical appears to have been the preferred form in words where the -ic- element is ultimately not an affix, but a part of the stem of a Latin word ending in -ix or -ex, such as cervix, cortex, mātrix, rādix, and vertex. In Latin, adjectives were derived from these nouns with the affix -ālis, producing e.g. cervicālis, corticālis, mātricālis, rādicālis, and verticālis. Most of these words were adopted or adapted directly from either Latin or French, in which the Latin final -is had been deleted.[8] However, the OED also includes entries for adjectives such as matric and vertic, which are most likely the results of shortening or back-formation of the earlier matrical and vertical.[9] Instances of this type show that in practice, almost any adjective in -ic or -ical could conceivably have had a rival form at some stage. It is therefore justified to include the Latin-based adjectives where the -ic element was originally a part of the stem in the overall analysis, although they differ from the majority of adjectives in -ic/-ical having foreign models.

While Table 5 shows the numbers of first citations of all adjectives ending in -ic/-ical (with the exception of prefixed forms) in the OED, one could also take a closer look at the first citations of those adjectives in particular which have a rival form in -ic or -ical. These figures – again based on the examination of -ic/-ical adjectives beginning with the letters a, c, f, i, k, l, n, t, r, and u – are presented in Table 6. The table, divided into two main sections, gives the numbers of first citations of the adjectives, indicating whether the form in

---

7   Marchand (1969: 296) presents a series of correlating patterns between nouns (often loan words from Greek) and adjectives ending in -ic (see also Nevalainen 1999: 403–404), such as words ending in -y (e.g. astronomy, geography, geometry, philology), -ia (e.g. amnesia, anaemia, hydrophobia), -sis (e.g. electrolysis, genesis, mimesis), -itis (e.g. bronchitis, encephalitis, enteritis), -ite (e.g. dynamite, parasite), -cracy (e.g. aristocracy, democracy, plutocracy), and -m(a) (e.g. aroma, drama, problem). As Marchand presents the patterns under the section on the suffix -ic, what remains unmentioned is the fact that many of the corresponding adjectives did in fact have rival forms in -ical.

8   According to the OED, some adjectives in -ical were derived in English from Latin loan words in -ix/-ex in accordance with the Latin model. For example, apical and vortical s.vv. are said to be not loan words, but English formations (with -al) based on the Latin stems of apex and vortex.

9   While the OED describes vertic as 'an irregular shortening' of vertical, 'after tropic etc.', matric is surprisingly considered a formation from the stem mātric- of Latin mātrix, which is perhaps inaccurate, as a formation from mātric- with -ic would have produced matricic (cp. filicic from filic-, the stem of L filix).

question was adopted or coined before or after its rival.[10] From this kind of presentation, it is possible to look into the temporal aspects of the competition itself.

Table 6. The numbers of first citations of competing adjectives ending in -ic/-ical in the *OED*.

	-ic occurring before -ical	-ic occurring after -ical	-ical occurring before -ic	-ical occurring after -ic
1250–1299	1	-	-	-
1300–1349	2	-	-	-
1350–1399	11	-	-	-
1400–1449	1	-	-	-
1450–1499	8	-	2	2
1500–1549	7	1	13	9
1550–1599	16	12	55	15
1600–1649	20	42	74	21
1650–1699	24	56	56	20
1700–1749	5	17	14	9
1750–1799	10	28	12	4
1800–1849	19	50	24	24
1850–1899	17	53	18	36
1900–1949	4	9	3	3
1950–1989	-	4	1	2
total	**145**	**272**	**272**	**145**

There are many things to observe in Table 6, and it is furthermore revealing to investigate the figures in Tables 5 and 6 together. One immediately prominent detail in Table 6 is the total figures of adjectives where either the -ic or -ical form occurred in the language first; of all the -ic/-ical pairs, in approximately two out of three cases the form in -ical is of earlier origin. Of these adjectives in -ical (i.e. where the rival form in -ic was coined or adopted later), the majority entered the language between 1550 and 1699, further demonstrating that the period in question was the "golden age" of new adjectives in -ical, which also contributed significantly to the overall variation and competition between forms in -ic/-ical. Subsequent fifty-year periods show a somewhat more balanced situation as regards which of the forms occurred first. In addition, the numbers of coinages or adoptions in either -ic or -ical for which a competing form was to appear later are considerably lower than in 1550–1699. Conversely, when

---

10   In addition to the first citations presented in the four columns in Table 6, there were altogether 25 pairs of -ic/-ical adjectives sharing the year of their first recorded citation. Most of such instances (seven pairs) were first cited in texts from the period 1650–1699.

examining the numbers of those adjectives which constituted a rival form for an earlier existing adjective in -*ic*/-*ical* in relation to all new adjectives in -*ic* and -*ical* in different fifty-year periods, it turns out that from 1500 until the late eighteenth century, the percentages range between 23.8 and 29.0, whereas in the first half of the nineteenth century, the percentage of new words contributing to the lexical competition drops to 16.0. For 1850–1899 and the twentieth century, the corresponding percentages are even lower (1850–1899: 8.3 %; 1900–1949: 4.2 %; 1950–1989: 3.3 %). In other words, although the absolute figures of new adjectives in -*ic* forming a competing word for their -*ical* variants e.g. in the nineteenth century appear relatively high, their relation to all new adjectives in -*ic* in the period is lower than in earlier times. These results are thus in perfect agreement with Görlach's (1991: 138) characterization of the Early Modern English period as the era of linguistic experimentation.

There are, however, some points as regards the figures in Table 6 that merit further discussion. One important issue concerns the significance of the difference in time between the first recorded instances of adjectives in -*ic* and -*ical*. The figures in the fifty-year blocks include cases where the difference in time between the first recorded instances may have been not more than one or two years, whereas with some other pairs the difference may be considerably greater. It can be questioned how well a relatively small difference actually illustrates larger tendencies in the occurrence of new adjectives in -*ic* and -*ical*, especially in the light of possible inaccuracies as regards the reliability of the first recorded instances in the *OED* in general. In other words, what kind of temporal difference between the appearance of competing items can be regarded as reflecting any wider trends? One possibility to examine this issue further would be to produce a number of tables of the same type as Table 6. In these different tables, one could leave out those cases where the difference between the dates of the first attestations is 10, 20, 30, or 40 years, for example. A comparison of the results presented in such tables would provide more information on the matter.

Tables 5 and 6, including all of the adjectives ending in -*ic* and -*ical*, on the one hand, and only the competing pairs, on the other, nevertheless give rise to similar conclusions as regards the most notable changes in the overall numbers of the first recorded instances of adjectives in -*ic* and -*ical* in different periods. The same kind of observations can also be made on the numbers of those adjectives which are included in Table 5, but not in Table 6, i.e. uncontested adjectives in -*ic* and -*ical*. The numbers of the first citations of these adjectives are presented in Table 7.

Table 7. The numbers of first citations of uncontested adjectives ending in -*ic* and
-*ical* in the *OED*.

	-*ic*	%	-*ical*	%
1250–1299	-	-	-	-
1300–1349	-	-	-	-
1350–1399	4	80.0	1	20.0
1400–1449	1	50.0	1	50.0
1450–1499	2	66.7	1	33.3
1500–1549	4	44.4	5	55.6
1550–1599	10	33.3	20	66.6
1600–1649	49	52.1	45	47.9
1650–1699	96	62.3	58	37.7
1700–1749	59	74.7	20	25.3
1750–1799	75	77.3	22	22.7
1800–1849	323	84.1	61	15.9
1850–1899	973	93.1	72	6.9
1900–1949	383	92.7	30	7.3
1950–1989	158	90.3	17	9.7
total	**2137**		**353**	

As can be observed from Table 7, the new adjectives in -*ical* are again more
numerous than those in -*ic* in the latter half of the sixteenth century. As in Table
5, the period 1600–1649 shows a more balanced situation; in Table 7, however, it
is the number of adjectives in -*ic* that slightly outnumbers the figure for -*ical*. The
subsequent periods in both tables show a very similar development in the
relations between new adjectives.

The relatively greater popularity of adjectives ending in -*ical* in the late
sixteenth and early seventeenth century can also be observed from the numbers of
entries of adjectives in -*ic*/-*ical* in dictionaries from this period. Three full-text
electronic versions of Mulcaster (1582), Coote (1596), and Cawdrey (1604),
downloaded from the Internet, were examined, and as shown in Table 8, the
adjectives in -*ical* outnumber those in -*ic*.

Table 8. The numbers of entries of adjectives ending in -*ic*/-*ical* in Early Modern
English dictionaries.

	# of entries ending in -*ic*	# of entries ending in -*ical*
Mulcaster (1582)	8	16
Coote (1596)	6	9
Cawdrey (1604)	17	29

As regards other methods of investigating the productivity of derivational affixes, the statistical corpus-based measures of productivity proposed in Baayen and Lieber (1991), Baayen (1993), and Baayen and Renouf (1996) are perhaps the most notable, having given rise to plenty of discussion and further research on the issue (see e.g. Bolozky 1999, Plag 2000, and Bauer 2001). An important role in these measurements is played by the so-called *hapax legomena* (often referred to as hapaxes), i.e. words occurring in a corpus just once. The basic premise in the approaches examining the number of hapaxes is that when comparing word-formational processes as regards their productivity, a more productive process is also more likely to have produced words which are rare. In the words of Baayen and Renouf (1996: 74), "unproductive morphological categories will be characterized by a preponderance of high-frequency types, by low numbers of low-frequency types, and by very few, if any, hapax legomena, especially as the size of the sample (corpus or text) increases". As one measure of productivity, Baayen and Lieber (1991) put forward the relation of the number of hapaxes with a given affix in a corpus to the token frequency of words with that same affix. This measure has also been presented as the formula

$$\mathcal{P} = n_1 / N$$

where $\mathcal{P}$ is the measure for productivity, n_1 the number of hapaxes in the corpus examined, and N the token frequency of the words containing the affix in question. It is important to note that the hapaxes themselves are not necessarily neologisms themselves; instead, the idea is that the number of hapaxes is indicative of the number of new words.[11] Baayen and Lieber (1991: 809) note that the productivity measure $\mathcal{P}$ "expresses the rate at which new words are to be expected to appear when N tokens have been sampled".

Bauer (2001: 151), however, expresses some doubts about this measure. One of the problems is that it is uncertain when exactly a corpus is large enough for the productivity measures achieved to be regarded as reliable. Furthermore, the relation between the number of hapaxes and productivity has not been precisely defined, and thus conclusions on the productivity of any affix must be based on the comparison of a number of affixes. While it has been assumed that unproductive processes have a higher average token frequency, the formula for the productivity measure has nevertheless been criticized for having token frequency as the denominator. One of the concerns in this regard is that single

---

11   Baayen and Renouf (1996) examined the words with five affixes (*in-*, *un-*, *-ity*, *-ness*, and *-ly*) in an 80-million-word corpus consisting of issues of *The Times* newspaper from September 1989 to December 1992. Comparing the words in the corpus against *Webster's Third New International Dictionary of the English Language* (1961/1993), it was observed that many of the words in the *Times* corpus that did not appear in the dictionary were lexemes of very low frequency. In fact, the proportion of such words among the hapax legomena was considerably greater than among the words occurring in the corpus twice or three times.

lexemes with a high token frequency can affect the productivity measure $\mathcal{P}$ quite drastically (Bauer 2001: 152–153; see also Cowie and Dalton-Puffer 2002: 426). In fact, Baayen (1993: 192) has proposed another formula to measure productivity, $\mathcal{P}^*$, in which the number of hapaxes containing a given suffix is divided with the number of all hapaxes in a corpus. This measure, which emphasizes the significance of hapaxes even more than $\mathcal{P}$, is in Baayen's (1993: 205) words "particularly suited to ranking productive processes according to their degree of productivity". As the denominator in this measurement (i.e. the number of all hapaxes in a corpus) is the same for the calculations of all of the different affixes, what Baayen suggests in effect is that comparisons between the productivity of different derivational processes can be made by comparing directly the numbers of hapaxes containing the affixes.

Considering the adjectives ending in -*ic* and -*ical*, some objections might be raised against applying the above formulae on these words, since many of them are not actually the results of derivational affixation with -*ic* or -*ical*, as already stated in the present chapter.[12] However, an examination of the numbers of hapax legomena in the historical corpora presents interesting results:

Table 9.   The numbers of hapax legomena of adjectives in -*ic* and -*ical* in the prose section of *Literature Online*.

	-*ic*	%	-*ical*	%
1550–1599	16	29.6	38	70.4
1600–1649	36	38.3	58	61.7
1650–1699	52	49.5	53	50.5
1700–1749	35	52.2	32	47.8
1750–1799	67	52.3	61	47.7
1800–1849	86	62.8	51	37.2
1850–1903	122	70.9	50	29.1

---

12   The reservations are particularly serious in the case of the measure $\mathcal{P}$: the adjectives with the highest token frequencies in both the historical and present-day corpora are clearly loans (e.g. *catholic*, *characteristic*, *domestic*, *public*, and *physical*). The inclusion of the token frequencies of such items in the calculations of the productivity measure $\mathcal{P}$ might cause distortions in the results. For example, an examination of the $\mathcal{P}$ values of the "endings" -*ic* and -*ical* in the *Literature Online* material from 1800–1849 would indicate that one was actually less likely to encounter new words ending in -*ic* than those in -*ical*. Compared with the relation between the numbers of first citations of adjectives ending in -*ic* and -*ical* in the corresponding period in the *OED* (see Table 5), this result seems rather surprising.

Table 10.   The numbers of hapax legomena of adjectives in -*ic* and -*ical* in the
        non-fiction material examined.

	-*ic*	%	-*ical*	%
1550–1599	17	40.5	25	59.5
1600–1649	39	45.3	47	54.7
1650–1699	32	34.8	60	65.2
1700–1749	35	57.4	26	42.6
1750–1799	40	54.1	34	45.9
1800–1849	64	70.3	27	29.7
1850–1899	83	67.5	40	32.5
1900–1951	52	57.8	38	42.2

Tables 9 and 10 represent the numbers of hapaxes within fifty-year periods in the
Literature Online material, and the non-fiction texts examined, respectively. It is
interesting to observe that the relations between the hapaxes ending in -*ic* and
-*ical* in different periods are notably similar in the two tables, although the
smaller size of the non-fiction corpus might justifiably raise some doubts about
the reliability of the results. The tables do differ somewhat as to the relations
between the hapaxes: for example, in the non-fiction material, the difference in
the relation of hapaxes in 1650-99 shows a greater number of words in -*ical*,
whereas in the *LION* collection, the figures of -*ic* and -*ical* hapaxes are roughly
equal in the same period. However, the major "changes" in the relations of the
hapaxes through the times are similar – in the latter half of the sixteenth century,
hapaxes ending in -*ical* were more numerous than those in -*ic*. In the eighteenth
century, however, the numbers of hapaxes are closer to one another, with those
ending in -*ic* slightly exceeding the hapaxes in -*ical*. A clear increase in favour of
the -*ic* forms is seen in the nineteenth century figures. The results in Tables 9 and
10 are thus remarkably close to the numbers of first citations of adjectives in -*ic*
and -*ical* in the *OED*, presented in Table 5, the only major difference being that
the rise of the new words in -*ic* (after the "dominance" of the -*ical* ending in the
late sixteenth and early seventeenth centuries) is seen earlier in Table 5.

It must be emphasized, however, that the numbers of hapaxes can only be
regarded as indicative of the actual numbers of neologisms ending in -*ic* and -*ical*.
Many hapaxes in the corpora examined for the present study, in fact, are not new
words at all (especially in the smaller corpus of non-fiction texts). Interestingly
enough, some of the hapaxes encountered were adjectives which were becoming
obsolete, e.g. *domestical*, *majestical*, *organical*, *rustical*, *scientifical*, and
Socratical in 1750–99, and *democratical* and *prophetical* in 1850–99 (see
Chapter 11). As a result of the existence of (often redundant) competing forms in
-*ic*/-*ical*, a number of adjectives (especially the forms in -*ical*) were dropped from
use. It must be noted that the use of hapaxes in the study of productivity of
derivational processes has so far concentrated on synchronic rather than
diachronic studies, and the studies by Baayen et al have been based to a great

extent on corpora of present-day English. One could argue that the possible role of obsolete items has perhaps not been sufficiently taken into account, especially as regards the diachronic perspective, but also in general. While Bolozky (1999: 6) – who examined Modern Hebrew – briefly mentions that hapaxes in a corpus may include obsolete as well as otherwise rare words, he says that "it is only argued that they are less likely to occur only once than single neologisms are". One could ask then whether this likelihood holds equally well for all affixes in every period in history. As observed by e.g. Görlach (1991: 139; 1999: 134), the overall obsolescence of words in a language may have changed through times. These changes may, in fact, be quite significant when assessing the illustrativeness of the hapax legomena as indicators of lexical innovation. Considering Tables 9 and 10, one might actually entertain the possibility that the process of obsolescence is reflected in the relation between hapaxes in -*ic* and -*ical* being more "balanced" in the figures for the eighteenth century, rather than indicating a clearer preference for new adjectives ending in -*ic* (as one might conclude from Table 5).

In summary, it can be said that the results of different analyses based on dictionaries and corpora are in agreement with each other to a great extent. While the first adjectives ending in -*ic* occurred before those in -*ical*, it appears that new adjectives in -*ical* were more frequent than those in -*ic* in the sixteenth century. The following centuries, on the other hand, show a relative increase in new words in -*ic*, with the shorter forms being considerably more common among new words in the nineteenth century, with the exception of adjectives ending in -*logic(al)*. These changes through history were visible in, or supported by, the first citations of adjectives in -*ic* and -*ical* in the *OED* (both as regards all the adjectives in -*ic* and -*ical* beginning with *a, c, f, i, k, l, n, r, t*, and *u*, as well as only those adjectives constituting a competing -*ic/-ical* pair), the lists of entries in three dictionaries from the Early Modern English period, and the hapax legomena in the historical corpora examined. As noted earlier, the tendencies observed should not be regarded as reflecting the productivity of the suffixes -*ic* and -*ical*, because the words examined here have entered the lexicon as a result of different kinds of processes. However, given the fact that the endings -*ic* and -*ical* were most likely perceived as word-formational elements in almost all words that they appear in, one can justifiably consider the results here to reflect the overall popularity of the endings among new words in different periods, regardless of their etymological status.

The following chapters will present the analyses of individual -*ic/-ical* adjective pairs in the corpora examined. As regards the two main processes involved in lexical competition, semantic differentiation will be looked into first, as it is potentially – as well as in practice – more complex than the tendency of merely abandoning one of the variants from use. Six adjective pairs will be discussed in greater detail, with a chapter devoted to each pair. These are: *classic/classical*, *comic/comical*, *economic/economical*, *electric/electrical*, *historic/historical*, and *magic/magical*. The pairs in question will be presented in alphabetical order in Chapters 5–10. What makes these pairs stand out from all semantically differentiated *-ic*/*-ical* pairs is that they are the ones most frequently commented on in usage manuals and in the brief usage notes given in recently published dictionaries (roughly from the early 1990s onwards). To illustrate the various semantic nuances in the use of the adjectives, concrete examples from the corpora will be presented. The relative frequencies of pairs will also be looked into. As will be observed, the differences in frequencies of use may depend on the kind of texts the corpora contain. In this respect, brief comments will be made based on examinations of different written and spoken domains represented in the *BNC*.

Chapter 11 turns to those adjective pairs where one of the forms has been dropped from use. As will be seen, although signs of semantic differentiation were detected in connection with some of these *-ic*/*-ical* pairs at some point in history, only one member of the pair ultimately survived. Authentic instances of the use of the adjectives will be presented in this chapter as well (although not to the same extent as in connection with semantically differentiated pairs). The analyses will not cover all *-ic*/*-ical* pairs; the adjectives discussed include only those pairs for which a sufficient number of occurrences (as regards the historical material, at least twenty occurrences of the rarer form in both the fiction and non-fiction texts) were found in the historical and present-day corpus material. The discussion will therefore not include those pairs where one of the forms has at all times dominated strongly over the less frequently occurring form, e.g. *mathematic/mathematical*. In other words, the pairs examined in Chapter 11 will be ones which manifest a higher degree of lexical competition between the two forms than for example mathematic/mathematical.

Among the semantically differentiated pairs, the six pairs examined in detail in Chapters 5–10, partly through their relatively high frequency in most corpora of English, may be considered to be of greater significance especially as regards the vocabulary of everyday speech and writing. This does not, of course, mean that other pairs showing semantic differentiation are less important in general. For example, the pair *politic/political* is remarkable in being perhaps the first *-ic*/*-ical* pair for which different meanings ultimately came to be assigned to the two forms. Chapter 12 takes a brief look into the use of four pairs, *diabolic/diabolical*, *fantastic/fantastical*, *optic/optical*, and *politic/political*. One feature that these pairs share is that one of the forms is nowadays considerably rarer than the other. In some cases, one can argue that the uses of the forms manifest both semantic differentiation and signs of one of the forms becoming rare, if not totally obsolete.

Chapter 5

Excellence, tradition, and ancient Greeks: *classic/classical*

The adjectives *classic* and *classical*, once practically identical as regards their use, have in the course of time diverged from each other so far semantically that in present-day English one can find instances such as (1), in which the two adjectives are used in one and the same sentence, making use of the observed contrast in their meanings:

(1)   To ensure again that TV viewers will be exposed to more opera on this one show than in the rest of the year, five of the women [entering the Miss America beauty contest] promise a 'classical vocal.' Classical, perhaps; classic, perhaps not. (*Time*, 18 Sept., 1995, "Dream Girls", p. 54)

In the example above, the idea conveyed by means of *classic* and *classical* is that the performances, pertaining to a certain musical genre (*classical*), may not be of any particular excellence (*classic*). The great extent of the semantic differentiation between the forms in -*ic* and -*ical*, in other words, becomes evident from the fact that they can, with different meanings, be used to modify the same head word, as was also seen in examples (2a) and (2b) in Chapter 1.

Classic/classical is a pair frequently commented on in usage manuals, which most often tend to emphasize the preference for *classic* when relating to things considered to be of high quality, while *classical* is the usual form in expressions referring to the arts, authors, and other things of ancient Greece or Rome, as well as in the phrase *classical music*, denoting a more or less specific type of orchestral music. There are, however, some uses of the two forms where an overlap can be perceived, or the difference between the meanings is perhaps merely a question of slight nuances. For example, Crystal (1991) s.v. *classic, classical* draws attention, on the one hand, to the differences between *a classic treatise*, which is of the highest rank, and *a classical treatise*, one concerning ancient times. On the other hand, he also notes the occasional interchangeability of the two forms, pointing out that "there is little to choose between them in such phrases as *classic design* and *classical design*".

The polysemous nature of the adjectives also presents some problems of interpretation, as it is not always a straightforward task to separate a particular sense from one which has been derived from it, e.g. 'pertaining to (the culture) of ancient Greece or Rome' and 'adhering to the idealized styles and forms of the ancient Greek or Roman culture'. The number of different uses of the adjectives, as well as the closeness of some of them, can be observed, for instance, in the various definitions they have been given in dictionaries, as in the following ones from *LDEL* (1991):

classic

1a of recognized or historical value or merit; serving as a standard of excellence <*these are ~ recordings whose loss would be disasterous*>
1b characterized by simply tailored and elegant lines that remain in fashion year after year <*a ~ suit*>
2 CLASSICAL 2a
3 CLASSICAL 3a
4 noted because of special literary or historical associations <*in Bath we are on ~ ground*>
5a authoritative, definitive
5b being an example that shows clearly the characteristics of some group of things or occurrences; archetypal <*the ~ case of this motif is the Cinderella story*>
6 CLASSICAL 4b(1)

classical

1 standard, classic
2a of the ancient Greek and Roman world, esp its literature, art, architecture, or ideals
2b expert in the classics <*a ~ scholar*>
3a *of a work of art, style, etc* adhering to traditional standards, derived ultimately from the work of ancient Greece and Rome, and characterized by such qualities as balance, restraint, and simplicity in form – compare ROMANTIC 4a, b
3b(1) of or being music of the late 18th and early 19th centuries characterized by an emphasis on simplicity, objectivity, and proportion; also of or being a composer of this music
3b(2) of or being music in the educated European tradition that includes such forms as chamber music, opera, and symphony as distinguished from folk or popular music or jazz
4a being both authoritative and traditional
4b(1) of or being systems or methods that formerly constituted the accepted approach to a subject < ~ *Mendelian genetics versus modern molecular genetics*>
4b(2) based on long-standing theories of physics, esp those of Newton rather than more recent ones (e g quantum theory) < ~ *mechanics*>
4c conforming to a pattern of usage sanctioned by a body of literature rather than by everyday speech < ~ *Arabic*>
5 concerned with or giving information in the humanities, the fine arts, and only the broadest aspects of science <*a ~ education*>

The definitions of the adjectives above seem to confirm the observations made as regards the general semantic differentiation between the forms, and also the notable degree of overlap (observe the number of cross-references under the entry for *classic* to various senses of *classical*). Interestingly enough, some of the definitions assigned to *classic* and *classical* seem quite similar[1], without the lexicographer, however, resorting to cross-references, as, for example, *classic* 5a 'authoritative, definitive' and *classical* 4a 'being both authoritative and traditional', which unfortunately have not been furnished with example phrases so as to illustrate differences between these uses. Any possible differences, as well as the question of the degree of interchangeability – whether there is a clear preference for using one of the forms or free variation – demand careful investigation. The number of different uses itself undoubtedly has brought along a danger of confusion, which has been noticed by lexicographers; Beckson and Ganz (1990: 41) observe that *classical* "has carried so many different meanings at different times that no single meaning can any longer be said to appertain to it" and that therefore "this term should be used with discretion."

As one of the core meanings of the adjectives relates to the categorization of things by their quality, it is no great surprise that the "proper" application of the words has also become a question of debate. For example, the authors of some (mostly American) usage manuals have complained about the overuse – or misuse – of *classic*, as in the following extracts (see also Partridge 1957; Bernstein 1965; and Bremner 1980 s.v. *classic, classical*):

> Sports writers label any game between two schools or teams that have played before a *classic* and in this sense the word is sadly overworked. (Evans and Evans 1957 s.v. *classic* and *classical*)

> Contemporary speakers and writers overuse *classic* in describing sports events, books, television shows, and the like; the term should be applied only to works and performances of the first rank that adhere to established standards. (Shaw 1975 s.v. *classic, classical*)

As will be seen in this chapter, these cases are not the only ones that have occasioned sometimes heated arguments on what should be designated *classic* or *classical*.

This problem is by no means a modern one: considering the basic meaning of the Latin model word *classicus*, 'of the first class', it is obvious that what was originally regarded as fulfilling this measure depended on what was held in high esteem at the time. Since the opinions of individuals – let alone generations – as to what can be considered 'of the first class' vary, the use of the word is not entirely objective (even if the use was based on a general consensus), at least not

---

1   The first definition under *classical*, 'standard, classic', appears rather infelicitous, as it is not entirely obvious how 'classic' is to be interpreted here; presumably it is related in meaning to *classic* 1a and 1b.

in the same manner as the application of adjectives such as *electric* and *electrical*. This inherent vagueness of the idea denoted by the base word can also be seen in the possibility of the evaluation being applied to different levels of the same thing: rather than applying the word *classicus* (or the English *classic/classical*) to literature of ancient Greece and Rome in general, the words have also been used to refer only to the "best" and "choicest" writers and works of these cultures. For example, according to *The Royal Dictionary-Cyclopædia* (1862–1867), "Aristotle, Plato, Demosthenes, Thucidides, and others, among the Greeks; and Cicero, Virgil, Horace, Juvenal, Livy, Sallust, Caesar, and Tacitus, among the Latins, are *classical* authors" (s.v. *classic, classical*). Similarly, the words can be applied either to the whole period of Greek and/or Roman antiquity or, more specifically, as pointed out in *The Oxford Companion to the English Language* (1992) s.v. *classical*, to the fifth century B.C. in Greece, or to the period between second century B.C. and second century A.D. in Rome, considered by historians to represent the most productive and vital periods of these ancient cultures.

The tendency of human beings to classify and categorize different kinds of works of art by the evaluation of their artistic merit was, according to Ernst Langlotz's long and extensive article on *classic art* in *Encyclopedia of World Art* (1960), already visible in the attitudes of the ancient Greek thinkers. Thus the idea of a "canon", based on the nostalgic notion that works of the past "are unsurpassable and that current times are decadent", had already been in existence for a long time before this sense was assigned to the word *classicus* and its descendants in the sixteenth and seventeenth centuries. In the same way as in ancient Greece, theories were formulated on the correctness and perfection of the forms and styles employed in the admired works of ancient times, with a desire for "fixed norms and unchanging values" (*Encyclopedia of World Art* s.v. *classic art*). Some of the attributes often used to describe the classic(al) style are symmetry, balance, restraint, and proportion; the aims of this style can also be seen in Haggar's (1984: 80) description of classical art as "an art which directs its appeal to the mind of the beholder, is entirely rational, and intellectually satisfying." Although the general idea of this style can be thus described, the fact that people have had differing ideas as to which works of art and which periods of the Greek and Roman antiquity represent the apex of these cultures has meant that there is no single exact definition of classic(al) style. Finding such a definition became in theory even more difficult as the usage of *classicus* referring to canonical works of art was extended to not only the works of ancient Greece and Rome, but also the masterpieces of the Western culture (more or less modelled after the ancient ideals). Ancient culture influenced different Western cultures in different ways; Langlotz points out that "a classic style per se does not exist, and that every age important to intellectual history has had the task of formulating an attitude toward the past and of defining as classic whatever could be considered productive [...] for its particular time."

1.   Etymology and early history of the pair

The foreign model words for the adjectives *classic* and *classical* are, then, the Latin *classicus* and the French *classique* (the French word was itself obviously an adoption of the Latin word). The Latin adjective *classicus* was first used in reference to the highest class of Roman citizens (the Romans being divided into five classes according to their property by Servius Tullius; see Lewis and Short (1879) s.v. *classicus*; *OLD* s.v. *classis*; *OED* s.v. *classic*). Assigned to entities other than people, the later Latin sense 'of the highest rank, superior, standard' has been regarded as a figurative use of the original notion of *classicus*. According to the *Encyclopedia of World Art* (1960) s.v. *classic art*, the Romans did not, however, use the word in relation with art; Langlotz points out that "in antiquity the word *classicus* was never commonly used to denote intellectual facts and values".[2]

During the Renaissance, *classicus* was used to refer to writers whose works were taught in schools and considered "worthy of preservation and study" (*Encyclopedia of World Art* s.v. *classic art*; Beckson and Ganz 1990: 42). In fact, the influence of the word *class* in the sense of 'classroom' has also been suggested as influencing the assignment of this meaning to *classicus*, as well as to *classique/classic/classical* (see *The Oxford Dictionary of English Etymology* s.v. *classic*). As writers taught in schools were usually those of ancient Greece and Rome, and because of the growing interest in these ancient cultures, the words were later applied generally to the arts and the period of these cultures, as well as the Greek and Latin languages themselves (*OED* s.v. *classic*).

The second edition of *Le Grand Robert* dates the first recorded instance of *classique* in French 1548. In English, *classic* and *classical* made their entrances into the lexicon in the latter half of the sixteenth century, at roughly the same time, judging from the first citations in the *OED*. The first recorded instance of *classical* in the dictionary is from 1586, in the sense of 'pertaining to (a classis in) a Presbyterian system of church-government' ("To take new callings from classical ministers, renouncing their calling from bishops", from the 1621 edition of T. Rogers, *Thirty-Nine Articles of Religion*, 334).[3] Under the entry for *classic* in the *OED*, the first citation is from 1613, but an earlier instance of the word is found under *bandon*: "Forgo thy solenne walks, bandon Classic wood" (from

---

2   Langlotz further writes that "During the entire Middle Ages the word [*classicus*] disappeared, and it was revived in the Renaissance with a different meaning, describing an author whose works were taught in the schools (implying only the Humanistic schools), and remained thus in all the lexicons until 1900" (*Encyclopedia of World Art*, s.v. *classic art*).

3   In the Presbyterian Church, *classis* referred to an 'inferior judicatory consisting of the elders or pastors of the parishes or churches of a district' (*OED* s.v. *classis*, sense 3.a). Interestingly enough, the first citation of *classis* in this sense in the *OED* is from the 1590's – i.e. after that of *classical* with similar reference, although it must be noted that first citations do not necessarily follow the actual chronological sequence.

George Turberville, *Tragical Tales and Other Poems* (1837, originally written in 1587), 53). In this instance, *classic* can either relate to the historical connection of the "wood" with Roman antiquity, or it may also mean, in a derived sense, 'famous in history'.

Classic/classical is a pair where the shorter form can also function as a noun, e.g. "Orwell's *1984* is now regarded as a classic", in the sense of 'a work of art belonging to a canon'. The nominal use of *classic* was derived from its adjectival use, and began to increase in the eighteenth century. As in the case of other *-ic/-ical* adjective pairs, the nominal function of the shorter form did not result in the form in *-ical* ultimately taking over all the adjectival uses. Considering merely the frequencies of the adjectives' uses in the corpora studied, the adjective *classic* appears to have been the less frequent member of the pair at all periods. This can be seen from Tables 11 and 12, presenting the numbers of occurrences of the adjectives in fictional and non-fictional texts, respectively (the figures in parentheses denoting the numbers of authors using the adjectives).

Table 11. *Classic/classical* in the prose section of *Literature Online*, 1700–1903.

	1700–1799	1800–1849	1850–1903
classic	9 (6)	60 (18)	68 (22)
classical	45 (17)	133 (22)	142 (27)
authors using both forms	5	13	15

Table 12. *Classic/classical* in the non-fiction texts studied (British and American authors), 1700–1961.

	1700–1799	1800–1849	1850–1899	1900–1961
classic	4 (3)	1 (1)	7 (5)	22 (14)
classical	10 (8)	10 (6)	29 (12)	200 (23)
authors using both forms	1	1	3	6

Opdycke (1935: 556) likewise lists *classical* among those words which are "preferably spelled with *ical*" as opposed to *-ic*. In contrast, in the July–December 1995 issues of *The Daily Telegraph*, the occurrences of *classic* outnumbered those of *classical* (673 vs. 497).[4] However, the relative frequencies of the

---

4   These figures include only those occurrences which were analysed for the study; cases in which the adjectives were part of a proper name or fixed subheading of a particular section of a newspaper (e.g. "The Arts: Spades trumped – Classical Records") were left out from the analysis, because in these cases one would not expect any variation as to the choice of the adjective form.

adjectives themselves are not very illuminating, and they can vary considerably across genres. In fact, the semantic multiplicity as regards purely descriptive senses, on the one hand, and, quite significantly, specialised uses in various walks of life (e.g. *classical music*), on the other, ultimately increases the influence of the subject matter on the numbers of occurrences of the adjectives. For example, a higher relative frequency of *classical* over *classic* in texts relating to arts could simply be a reflection of the greater number of references to things such as classical ballet or classical music rather than an overall preference to use *classical* in all senses of both *classic* and *classical*. The significance of the subject matter is perhaps also reflected in Tables 11 and 12, the latter showing a relatively greater number of occurrences of *classical*.

2.   *Classic/classical* in dictionaries and usage manuals

The first English monolingual dictionary to list either member of the pair *classic/classical* was Robert Cawdrey's *A Table Alphabeticall* (1604), including an entry for *classic* with the paraphrase "chiefe, and approued". *Classical* is the listed form of the adjective in Blount (1656), described as having the sense 'pertaining to a ship' as well.[5] Entries of only the longer form of the pair are also found in Bullokar (1680) and Kersey (1702). Both *classic* and *classical* are included under the same entry in dictionaries by Coles (1676), Bailey (1721), Johnson (1755), Sheridan (1780), Walker (1791), as well as in nineteenth century works such as those by Barclay (1819), Todd's second edition of Johnson (1827), Webster (1828), and Richardson (1836). The usual senses assigned to the adjectives in the early dictionaries are 'authors of the first class' or 'authors read in the classes at schools'.[6] The general idea of 'approved' without reference to authors is given in the definition in Cawdrey (1604) and Coles (1676). The latter also includes the sense 'belonging thereto', i.e. relating to a class or the idea of classification.

Annandale's edition of *The Imperial Dictionary of the English Language* (1882) still gives *classic* and *classical* under the same entry, but one additional comment is made on the preference for *classical* when referring to "Greek and

---

5   In Classical Latin, the noun *classis* was also used of 'a naval force, fleet', and the adjective *classicus*, correspondingly, was used in the sense 'of or connected with fleets' (Lewis and Short 1879; *Oxford Latin Dictionary* s.vv. *classicus; classis*). The *OED* also notes this sense as nowadays obsolete for *classical* (sense 9), but merely with a reference to Blount's dictionary – no actual quotation is given. This use of *classic/classical* was not encountered in the historical corpora studied, either.

6   Among the dictionaries studied, Johnson (1755) is the first one to include a specific reference to ancient Greek or Latin literature in the definitions of *classic/classical*. It is surprising that this aspect in the use of the adjectives did not appear in dictionaries earlier, considering that the first citation of *classical* in the sense 'of the standard Greek and Latin writers' in the *OED* dates from as early as 1607.

Roman authors of the first rank or estimation". The dictionary separates between this sense and the more general 'pertaining to ancient Greece or Rome'. Furthermore, the descriptive sense 'pure; chaste; correct; refined' – derived from the classifying application 'pertaining to ancient Greek and Latin literature' – is included, with the examples *a classical taste/style/work of art*.

The definitions of the adjectives in the second edition of the *OED* are cited in full (except for the quotations) below:

> *classic*
> 1. Of the first class, or the highest rank or importance; approved as a model; standard, leading.
> 2. Of or belonging to the standard authors and literature of Greek and Latin antiquity; also, of the art and culture of the same age.
> 3. More widely: Belonging to Greek and Latin antiquity.
> 4. In the style of the literature and art of Greek and Latin antiquity; = CLASSICAL 6. (Opposed to *romantic*.)
> 5. *transf.* Of literary note, historically famous.
> 6.a. In a burlesque or humorous sense: Approved, recognized 'standard'.
>   b. *classic races*: a name given to the five chief annual horse-races (the Two Thousand, One Thousand, Derby, Oaks and St. Leger).
>   c. Of clothes: made in simple, conventional styles that are almost unaffected by changes in fashions.
> 7. = CLASSICAL 7. *Obs*.
> 8. With capital initial. Of or pertaining to a period of advanced Meso-American civilization (c 300-900), esp. to that of the mayas. Cf. POST-CLASSIC a. b, PRE-CLASSIC a.
>
> *classical*
> 1. Of the first rank or authority; constituting a standard or model; especially in literature.
> 2.a. Of the standard Greek and Latin writers; belonging to the literature or art of Greek and Roman antiquity.
>   b. Designating the form of a language (esp. Greek and Latin) used by its ancient authors.
>   c. Designating the language, art, or culture of a period deemed to represent the most perfect flowering of the civilization that produced it.
> 3. Of persons: Learned in the classics, i.e. in ancient Greek and Latin literature.
> 4. Of or pertaining to Greek and Latin literature and antiquities; relating to the classics.
> 5. = CLASSIC a. 5.

6.a. Of literature: Conforming in style or composition to the rules or models of Greek and Latin antiquity; hence *transf.* to art having similar qualities of style (see quot. 1885); opposed to *romantic*.

b. Of painting, landscape, etc.

c. Of music: (see quot. 1885); spec. opp. JAZZ.

d. Of a style of ballet: (see quots.).

e. Of physics, mechanics, etc., used esp. of conclusions based on concepts and theories established before the discovery of quantum theory, the theory of relativity, etc.

7. *Hist.* Of or pertaining to a classis in a Presbyterian Church (see CLASSIS 3); belonging to this system of church-government.

8. Of or belonging to a class; class-. *Obs.*

9. [= L. *classicus* belonging to a fleet.] 'Pertaining to a ship' (Blount *Glossogr.* 1656).

10. Short for *classical style, art*, etc.

11. *Comb.*, as *classical-minded* adj.

The definitions were not altered significantly from the first edition of the dictionary; new senses added in the second edition were 6.c and 8 for *classic*, and 2.b, 2.c, 6.d, and 6.e for *classical*. While cross-references to the *-ic/-ical* counterparts are employed in some cases, in some others nearly identical paraphrases are given, and differences between the uses in such cases are not at all evident. For example, the first senses of both *classic* and *classical* appear very similar to one another, as well as *classic* 2 and *classical* 2.a. One could also suggest that *classic* 8, relating specifically to the "peak period" in the Maya civilization, is semantically comparable to *classical* 2.c.

As regards the overall division of the senses in the *OED*, the remark "a burlesque or humorous sense" under *classic* 6.a raises one's eyebrows (see also Marsden 1985: 28). From a historical point of view, references to "articles of female want" as *classic*, as in a quotation under *classic* 6.a, may originally have been characterized by something of a "tongue-in-cheek" notion, but today it would be very difficult to separate such cases from the more "serious" uses, as in *classic* 1. As observed earlier, the issue of subjectivity may easily cause problems in the application of the adjectives in this sense. Another potentially confusing point in the definitions is found in the wordings of *classical* 2.a 'belonging to the literature or art of Greek and Roman antiquity' and *classical* 4 'of or pertaining to Greek and Latin literature and antiquities; relating to the classics', as they do not suggest any difference whatsoever. However, the quotations provided under the two senses show that while sense 2.a is exemplified by cases such as *classical art*, sense 4 appears to pertain to the education and knowledge of Greek and Latin literature and art (e.g. *classical education/learning/instruction*). In other words, the division into two sense groups itself is justifiable, but the paraphrases unfortunately do not convey the idea behind it.

What appears slightly surprising in the *OED* definitions of *classic(al)* is the absence of the sense 'typical; archetypal; suitable for standing as a representative of a type', as in *The patient showed all the classic symptoms of tuberculosis*. This sense is usually noted in the dictionaries published in the 1990's, for example in the *LDEL* (s.v. *classic*, sense 5b), as was observed earlier (see p. 60). Although this use of the adjectives is perhaps among the more recent ones considering all the senses they have carried (noted e.g. by Crystal 1991 s.v. *classic, classical*), instances of this type can be found in the *OED* citations – not under the entries for *classic* or *classical*, however – dating from the early twentieth century.

As regards more recent dictionaries, the overall presentations of the uses of *classic/classical* resemble for the most part that of *LDEL*, with only minor differences in the division into different senses. Some of these differences will be noted in the following sections which discuss the individual senses in greater detail.

Turning now to usage manuals, it is most interesting to examine the observations made by Fowler in his *Modern English Usage* (1926), particularly when compared with Gowers' (1965) edition of the same book:

Fowler (1926):
classic(al).
The adjectives are distinguished rather by suitability to different contexts than by difference of meaning. *Classical* is the usual word, & it would perhaps never be noticeably the wrong one, even where *classic* is more idiomatic (e.g. we can say, if we choose, *This is classical ground*); on the other hand, there are many combinations in which *classic* would sound ridiculous; *classic education, classic allusions*, are impossible. *Classic*, however, is often preferred (1) where the language is of an ornate kind (compare *steeped in classic lore* with *learned in classical mythology*); (2) where the speaker's emotion of admiration or respect is to be conveyed (compare *Do you prefer the classical or the romantic style?* with *A style classic in its perfect self-restraint; I did not ask for classical regularity of features* with *The classic regularity of his features; St Andrews, the classic home of golf* with *R.v.Hobbes was cited as the classical case*).

Gowers (1965):
classic(al).
These adjectives, in their senses of relating to the classics and conforming to the rules of Greek and Latin antiquity, are distinguished rather by suitability to different contexts than by difference of meaning. *Classical* is the usual word, and it would perhaps never be noticeably the wrong one, even where *classic* is more idiomatic (e.g. we can say, if we choose, *This is classical ground*). On the other hand, there are many combinations in which *classic* would sound ridiculous; *classic education, classic allusions*,

are impossible. *Classic*, however, apart from being used in the plural
as a noun meaning the general body of Greek and Latin literature, has
its own separate meaning of outstandingly important or authoritative.
*St. Andrews is the classic home of golf. / Rylands v. Fletcher was cited
as the classic case. / The Derby is one of the five classic flat races.*

As can be seen from the entries above, one of the most notable changes made by
Gowers is the specification of the comment on the adjectives being distinguished
rather by "suitability to different contexts than by difference of meaning" to
pertain only to the sense relating to Greek and Latin antiquity, instead of
suggesting that *classical* is "the usual word" by and large. In fact, whereas Fowler
seems to argue that the difference between *classic* and *classical* is mostly
pragmatic (or governed by collocational selection) rather than semantic, Gowers
significantly tones down this sentiment, and clearly promotes the idea of semantic
differentiation instead; for example, 'outstandingly important or authoritative' is
considered a genuine "separate meaning". As for Fowler's observation of *classic*
being preferred "when language is of an ornate kind", no conclusive evidence is
found in the historical corpora studied to support the argument, and it is perhaps
no wonder that Gowers excluded it from his edition of Fowler's book. From the
viewpoint of present-day use of the adjectives, the changes made by Gowers may
be considered necessary improvements, although it should be noted that the
pragmatic aspects in the adjectives' use are perhaps not altogether irrelevant, as
will be seen in the following sections.

Considering the issue of interchangeability, Copperud (1964: 81) echoes
Fowler in saying that "*classical* may often be substituted for *classic* (*a classical
example*) but the reverse is not true". Crystal (1991) s.v. *classic, classical* also
argues that because of the recent developments in the use of *classic*, e.g. the
senses 'typical', 'appropriate', and the "widespread ironic use in informal
speech", *classic* is "less likely these days to be a substitute for *classical*".

3. Different uses of *classic/classical*

Reflecting on the significance of the various notions, concepts, and views that
have affected the use of *classic* and *classical* during their history, Howard (1993)
s.v. *classic or classical* argues that "understanding the different ways in which
classic and *classical* are used is one indicator of cultural awareness". The
following sections will discuss the different uses of the adjectives, concentrating
especially on the complex aspects in the analysis of actual uses of the words. As
will be seen, teasing out the exact meanings of *classic* and *classical*, on the one
hand, and setting up semantic categories of the uses in a plausible way, on the
other, is not an altogether straightforward task.

3.1   Positive value judgement

As the fundamental, original meaning of *classic* and *classical* has to do with ranking, and things considered to be of the first rank, one of the most central semantic components perceivable in the usage of these adjectives is, naturally, positive value judgement, which is conveyed in their usage in different ways. Senses such as 'belonging to a canon', 'of the first class', 'authoritative', and 'famous' are discussed in the following sections.

3.1.1   'Belonging to a canon', 'of the first class', 'authoritative'

One of the senses entailing positive value judgement can be paraphrased as 'belonging to a canon' or 'of acknowledged excellence'. Although this sense is usually assigned to *classic* in dictionaries and usage manuals, both forms of the adjectives are found in this sense today, as can be seen from examples (2a–d):

(2)   a.   There she sits at the desk at which her mother wrote Rebecca, on a chair from the old house, with her mother's volumes of classic writers in front of her and the illustrations from Peter Pan that once hung on the nursery walls. (*The Daily Telegraph*, 17 Mar., 1993, "Wednesday Matters: Why Daphne's daughter is not shocked")

   b.   Central to the dispute is the question of the canon. Are there certain recognised great works of literature, or great writers, which all pupils should spend some time studying? [...] True, the classic texts may seem more remote from children's experience than much inferior, more modern writing. (*The Sunday Telegraph*, 31 Jan., 1993, "Education: Are children canon fodder?")

   c.   Last week the National Curriculum Council made proposals for a revised English syllabus, which stressed the use of standard English, knowledge of grammar and acquaintance with a broad range of classical English texts. (*The Sunday Telegraph*, 18 Apr., 1993, "Sunday Comment: Save our schools – stand up to the teachers")

   d.   The images here come not so much from the Bible as from idyllic portrayals of rustic life in classical poetry: Milton works on the age-old feeling that a vegetable diet is somehow more harmonious, more simple, more natural. (*The Sunday Telegraph*, 18 Apr., 1993, "Books: Eating up your greens")

One may question the nature of the value judgement in cases such as these. In fact, it can be argued that the greatness of canonical works is self-explanatory, regardless of the speaker's own opinion, and that the adjectives are merely used to denote the status of the referent as an objectively observable fact. The possibility of these two differing viewpoints of evaluation becomes evident in (2b), in which it is observed that what is classic is not necessarily always liked or appreciated, although belonging to a canon.

What exactly can be regarded as belonging to a canon, however, is an issue where subjective viewpoints again enter the scene, and disputes on the matter are highly likely in the absence of an absolute authority. To some extent, postulations even on what is commonly acknowledged to be great may be based on personal assumptions. Aiming at some kind of objective criteria, one could argue that the idea of a canon, by definition, should not be extended to recent works of art. It has been suggested, for example, that "it takes a generation or two for classic status to become established" (*The Daily Telegraph*, 14 Jan., 1993, "Education: Classic case of confusion"). The phrase *modern classic(al) writers* is thus not impossible, but in order to restrict the use of *classic(al)*, some argue that there cannot be any living classic(al) writers.

In some cases, the positive value judgement is more clearly subjective, as in "Had Graham Taylor been at Highbury to watch another classic performance from Ian Wright he would have banished any thoughts of dropping the striker from the English team to play Holland next month" (*The Daily Telegraph*, 13 Sept., 1993, "Soccer: Campbell grabs the goals but Wright gets the glory"). Instances of this type can be easily paraphrased as 'first-class' or 'excellent'; the idea of 'belonging to a canon' is less evident, though certainly not entirely impossible. Interestingly enough, some dictionaries assign the label "slang" to this use of *classic* (e.g. *The Chambers Dictionary* (1993) s.v. *classic*, in which the slang sense 'excellent, definitive' is distinguished from 'of the highest class or rank').

It is often practically impossible to distinguish conclusively between the senses 'canonical' (classifying) and 'excellent' (descriptive)[7]: for example, in "Billy Wilder's classic film *Some Like It Hot*", determining between the two possible senses simply cannot be done. Such ambiguous cases are, of course, more frequent when the adjective is used in reference to relatively recent works. Although there are easily analysable instances as well, e.g. *classic status*, all cases paraphrasable as 'of high quality', 'excellent', or 'belonging to a canon' are in the present analysis placed in the same semantic category.

In the context of scientific studies, the use of *classic* and *classical* also suggest notions of being groundbreaking or authoritative:

---

7   As classifiers are considered e.g. by Warren (1984) to be somewhat awkward in a predicative position, one might postulate that in the phrase *the book is classic*, the adjective is to be interpreted as meaning 'excellent' rather than referring to the book's canonical status. In *OALD* (1995), however, both adjectives, regardless of their meaning, are said to be used mainly in the attributive position, which was also observed in the July–December 1995 issues of *The Daily Telegraph* (see Table 17).

(3)   a. But where did these amino acids come from? For years, the answer was thought to have been found by a classic experiment performed in 1952 by Stanley Miller at Chicago University. (*The Sunday Telegraph*, 10 Dec., 1995, "Scope: We came from Outer Space...")

     b. After taking a first in botany at Bangor, he embarked on a PhD at Cambridge, for a year of which he worked in the USA with Harlan and Martini, then engaged on their classical investigations into the selection of barley in different environments. (*The Daily Telegraph*, 2 July, 1993, "Obituary of George Bell")

When referring to scientific publications, 'groundbreaking', 'of high quality', and 'belonging to a canon' are all possible paraphrases of *classic(al)*, as in "Why did this "phenomenal explosion of creative energy", as Dr Heinz Kiosk calls it in his classic study *Aspects of Football Hooliganism in a West Midland City* (1978) falter and die?" (*The Daily Telegraph*, 16 Jan., 1998, "Peter Simple"). In the present analysis, all instances suggesting these notions, i.e. denoting achievements of the human mind, are therefore classified under the same semantic category.

3.1.2 'Famous', 'outstanding'

In present-day English, *classic* is also used of other kinds of things considered for various reasons special or outstanding, 'excellent' or 'of high quality' not being suitable paraphrases, as in examples (4a) and (4b):

(4)   a. At the time of writing, however, my optimism is not being supported by reports of any notable catches from some of the classic Scottish rivers. (*The Daily Telegraph*, 15 Mar., 1993 "Angling: Spring's arrival whets the angler's appetite")

     b. Walker was the first to the century and, indeed, the big New Zealander was the outstanding favourite to crack the classic time barrier [of running a mile in under four minutes] at 40. (*The Daily Telegraph*, 1 Feb., 1993, "Athletics: Chairman back on the boards aiming to break barrier")

The "classic Scottish rivers" are, in (4a), rivers in Scotland that are probably well-known among angling enthusiasts, and 'well-known', 'outstanding', or, more likely, 'famous' perhaps best describes the usage of *classic* in (4b) as well. These instances can be likened to those paraphrased in the *OED* s.v. *classic*, sense 5, as 'of literary note, historically famous', originally used of most often in connection with places of historical interest:

(5)   a. They crossed from the Angel into St. John's road, struck down the
small street which terminates at Sadler's Wells theatre, through
Exmouth-street and Coppice-row, down the little court by the side of
the workhouse, across the classic ground which once bore the name of
Hockley-in-the-hole, thence into Little Saffron-hill, and so into
Saffron-hill the Great, along which the Dodger scudded at a rapid pace,
directing Oliver to follow close at his heels. (Charles Dickens, *Oliver
Twist* (1838), 128)[8]

b. [...] he had not only built himself a fine palace, but had finished putting
the black and white marble façade to the church of Santa Maria
Novella; he had planted a garden with rare trees, and had made it
classic ground by receiving within it the meetings of the Platonic
Academy, orphaned by the death of Lorenzo; [...]   (George Eliot,
Romola (1863), 211)

Another group of things with which this shade of meaning of *classic* can
be associated today is cars. According to *The Chambers Dictionary*, a classic car
is "a motor car of classic design, esp. manufactured between 1925 and 1942" (see
also Green 1991 s.v. *classic*). There are, however, varying opinions about what
constitutes a classic car:

(6)   a. 'My only classic car now is a 1961 Riley,' says Steel, who is practising
on winding roads near his Borders home.   (*The Daily Telegraph*, 1
Jan., 1993, "Peterborough: Big wheel")

b. Before contemplating a classic car which may be anything from 30 to
60 years old, it is essential to take advice on such matters as spare parts
availability and insurance which can often be fairly cheap on a
restricted mileage basis.   (*The Daily Telegraph*, 24 Aug., 1993,
"Special Report on Second Cars: A classy chassis for high days and
holidays")

It is possible that the term *classic car* is understood in different ways among
collectors and other car enthusiasts, nevertheless sharing the semantic component
of 'famous' or 'outstanding'. Resembling debates on which books, paintings,
buildings or films belong to a canon of works of acknowledged excellence, the
application of the label "classic" has been criticized. For example, in his article in
The Daily Telegraph (24 Aug., 1993, "Special Report on Second Cars: A classy
chassis for high days and holidays"), Colin Dryden writes that "to become a
classic, a car does not even need to have been good in its day – merely to have
acquired a patina over the years and become cocooned in nostalgia."

---

8   Hockley-in-the-hole was a famous meeting-place of the lower classes in 18th
century London.

A somewhat similar use of the adjective *classic*, that is, 'famous' and 'outstanding', occurs in connection with wines, perhaps also involving a notion of 'having a long tradition', as in "Hermitage La Greal from Sorrel (£9.98) is actually a classic wine – all smoky raspberry and brambles and a whiff of violets – but classic in the Rhone is never very mainstream" (*The Daily Telegraph*, 13 Mar., 1993, "Drinking: Wacky wines at winter's end"). Providing a slightly more detailed description in *Wine Lover's Companion* (1995), Herbst and Herbst define *classic* as "a broad wine term used to suggest that a wine is consistent with the established characteristics of that particular wine's type and style". They add that "even though the term is sometimes used on wine labels (for example, 'Classic Cabernet'), it has no official definition." Along the same lines, *classic* is also used of beers and other beverages. Partly because of the semantic ambiguity of the uses of the adjective with these types of referents, the instances of *classic(al)* when relating to wines and beers will be categorized as a separate group.

Classic races, according to the *OED* and *The Chambers Dictionary*, denote "the chief five annual horse-races (the Two Thousand, One Thousand, Derby, Oaks and St. Leger)". It is possible that in the world of horse racing, *classic* only applies to these particular races. However, this sense of the adjective, 'famous through having a long history', has been applied to other kinds of races as well, as in "Thirty three cars roared around the Indianapolis circuit three weeks ago in the classic Indy 500 race, the high point of the American motor racing season" (*The Daily Telegraph*, 19 June, 1993, "CITY: British winners hand laurels to America").

The different uses of the adjectives implying positive value judgement can all be applied to the nominal use of *classic*, that is, classic books, films, cars, wines, races and other things can also be referred to as *classics*.

Owing to the vagueness in the use of the adjectives, coupled with the fact that their meanings can be described with many different paraphrases, there is some degree of ambiguity as regards the senses defined in the last two sections. This is an important fact considering the setup of semantic categories in the analysis of the corpora. In fact, the senses 'famous' and 'outstanding' could naturally be applied to cases analysed as meaning 'canonical', 'excellent' or 'groundbreaking', because such things are very likely to be famous as well. Correspondingly, some of the instances described in the current section may suggest the notion of 'belonging to a canon'. Their arrangement into separate subgroups was nevertheless considered appropriate; the various dictionaries consulted follow a similar policy in separating cases such as *classic cars/races* from other instances.

3.2   Representing a type: 'exemplary', 'typical', 'archetypal'

In present-day English, one of the central applications of *classic* concerns the suitability of the referent to stand as a representative of its type. The most usual nouns collocating with *classic* when used in this sense are *example* and *case*, as in (7a) and (7b):

(7)   a.   Trevor Francis, their manager, has made light of his injury problems, and the success of defender Paul Warhurst as emergency striker is a classic example of his belief that every setback can bring an unexpected bonus. (*The Daily Telegraph*, 1 Mar., 1993, "Soccer: Francis puts his theory on trial")

        b.   Director Chris Tame said: 'This is a classic case of medical scaremongering which has become such a feature of the smoking debate.' (*The Daily Telegraph*, 18 Aug., 1995, "Heart attack risk 6 times bigger for young smokers")

As noted earlier, the *OED* does not mention this usage of *classic(al)*. One possible explanation for the omission is that this application resembles those discussed in the previous section, the things denoted being regarded as models. There is a difference between the two usages, however. In cases such as (7a) and (7b), the positive value judgement is not directly pointed at the thing itself with regard to its qualities but at its very potential to stand as a model or a representative of its type. In the sense of 'of high quality' or 'canonical', what is described as *classic(al)* is a worthy model because of its greatness, and its qualities are thus considered to be worth striving for, whereas in the sense of 'representing a type', *classic(al)* can also be used of things viewed in a negative light, as in "The classic error for any business in trouble is to appoint a chief executive before a chairman" (*The Daily Telegraph*, 16 Nov., 1995, "CITY COMMENT: Middleton rides away from sluggish Lloyd's").

The positive value judgement is, in a way, more prominent when the head word is *example*, as in such cases the word *classic* could be replaced by the phrase *very good* or *excellent* without change of meaning. In the case of *a classic error/mistake*, however, this is not possible. If this replacement is made, in order to retain the original meaning one must add the phrase *example of*, which also underlines the difference between the shades of meaning of *classic(al)* discussed in the present section and the previous one.

The most frequent word used in recent dictionaries and usage manuals as a synonym or paraphrase for *classic* in this sense is *typical* (see e.g. *Cambridge International Dictionary of English* 1995, *Random House Compact Unabridged Dictionary* 1996, *Collins COBUILD English Dictionary for Advanced Learners* 2001 s.v. *classic*). As opposed to *classic*, however, *typical* is neutral as to its value judgement, other similar words being *usual*, *regular*, and *common*. Some dictionaries, in fact, include a modifier of *typical* in their paraphrases for this use, e.g. 'quintessentially typical' (*The Chambers Dictionary* 1993), 'remarkably typical' (*The Concise Oxford Dictionary of Current English* 1990), and 'very typical' (*Oxford Advanced Learners' Dictionary* 1995). It would seem that the use of *classic(al)* instead of the more neutral substitutes involves an element of evaluation of the suitability of the referent to represent its type; e.g. Urdang (1988) s.v. *classic/classical* phrases this sense as denoting a "perfect example that epitomizes exactly what is being exemplified".

Classical is nowadays occasionally also found in this sense, although it is considerably rarer than the shorter form. In the nineteenth century, as well as in the early twentieth century, however, it may have been more common in this sense than *classic*.[9]

(8) a. We won't go with pitiful faces to the stern father, and ask for food and shelter, only to be refused in long Johnsonian sentences, and made a classical example of for the benefit of the neighbourhood. (M. E. Braddon, *Lady Audley's Secret* (1862), 61)

     b. That four Tests should have been won largely through the efforts of two bowlers, Shane Warne and Merv Hughes, is a classical example of the way in which diligent practice, the confidence which comes from success and a real esprit de corps can make up for setbacks and fallible areas. (*The Daily Telegraph*, 25 Aug., 1993, "Cricket: Batting and Warne made Australia almost great")

As in the case of *classic(al)* used with a positive value judgement, there are many different aspects as regards the useability of the referent as a representative of a type, which results in a number of different possible paraphrases for the adjectives in question. In some instances, *classic* might be interpreted as 'archetypal':

(9) a. It's a classic saloon: wood, wood and more wood – benches, tables, chairs, bar, floor. (*The Daily Telegraph*, 20 Nov., 1993, "Travel: After Nelson's Blood and Norfolk Nog")

     b. She would be the classic capable British nanny, familiar in literature from When We Were Very Young to Mary Poppins. (*The Daily Telegraph*, 25 Aug., 1993, "Wednesday Matters: The hand that rocks the cradle")

In some cases, *classic* has the additional flavour of 'basic', 'central' or 'quintessential', as in "The central bank's classic role as lender of last resort is to put back the cash that has leaked out of the damaged bank or out of the system"

---

9   Some indications of *classical* being at first more common in this sense can be found in the *OED* citations. As regards the most typical phrases in which the adjectives occur having this particular meaning, i.e. *classic(al) case/example/instance*, the citations dating from the first half of the twentieth century include two occurrences of *classic* as opposed to fifteen occurrences of *classical*. The post-1950 quotations, on the other hand, include twenty occurrences of the phrases with *classic*, but only three with *classical*.

(*The Daily Telegraph*, 25 Mar., 1993, "CITY COMMENT: The real world is a mean place"). Some instances of *classic* might be interpreted either as 'typical' or 'traditional', as, for instance, in the case of "At the heart of the unique sound that is in demand round the world is the boy soprano voice, but unlike the classic English cathedral choir, it comes unadulterated by male tenor and bass" (*The Daily Telegraph*, 11 Nov., 1995, "The Arts: High voices, higher spirits"). The borderline between the traditional and the typical can be problematic. In the *Random House Compact Unabridged Dictionary* (1996) s.v. *classic*, one of the different definitions of *classic* is simply 'traditional or typical', accompanied with the example phrase *a classic comedy routine*.

In this sense, *classic(al)* is usually found in the attributive position, but predicative instances are also possible:

(10)   Yes, the advanced aluminium overhead cam 875cc lump mounted in the rear was prone to meltdown, but only if neglected. My symptoms were classic: the engine consumed water rapidly, and performance became increasingly gammy until the final hillside Chernobyl ensued. (*The Daily Telegraph*, 10 July, 1993, "Classic cars: Angelic side of the Imp")

3.3   Relating to ancient cultures

Both *classic* and *classical* have been and still are used in relation to ancient Greece and Rome, or their language, literature, and arts:

(11)   a.   Sir Peter Hall took a classic Greek play to Athens. It has much to say about our times but what, he wondered, would the locals think? (*The Daily Telegraph*, 17 Aug., 1993, "The Arts: On manoeuvres with the sex war")

       b.   [Calasso] mixes together primitive myths bound up with obscure local cults and rituals, folk-wisdom mythology of the 'how the leopard got his spots' variety, the earliest classic stories of the Olympian gods in Homer and Hesiod, the mystical-theoretical cosmology of much later 'Orphic' cults [...] (*The Sunday Telegraph*, 13 June, 1993, "Books: Can we still believe in mythology?")

       c.   The Middle Ages, instead of being a dull, confused interval between classical antiquity and the modern world became thrillingly sinister – the era of gothic horror. (*The Sunday Telegraph*, 20 June, 1993, "Books: Can we trust our picture of the past?")

       d.   Western civilisation, with its classical and Judaeo-Christian roots, is the greatest collective achievement of humanity. (*The Sunday Telegraph*, 2 May, 1993, "Leading Article: The shock of the old")

As noted earlier, what is understood to be the classic(al) period varies. The phrase may denote a period within the cultures of ancient Greece or Rome or, as in (11c) and (11d), the whole period of both ancient Greek and Roman antiquity.

Considering the analysis of historical corpora for the present study, phrases such as *classic(al) books/writers* are potentially ambiguous, as they can either mean 'of the first rank' or 'relating to ancient Greece or Rome'. Therefore it is necessary to examine a larger context around the occurrences of the adjectives; only those instances where it becomes evident from the context that reference is being made to a thing connected with ancient Greece or Rome, or the culture in question, are classified in the present category.

Although dictionaries include this usage among the definitions of both *classic* and *classical*, the latter is usually said to be the more common form in this sense. Similarly, *classical* is considered the normal form when referring to studies of ancient Greece and Rome, as in the phrases *classical scholar/learning*. Thus commenting on the different senses of *classic* and *classical*, Greenbaum and Whitcut (1988) s.v. *classic, classical* observe that "Shakespeare's *Julius Caesar* is *classic* as to its literary status and *classical* as to its subject matter." Reference to the (works of) ancient Greek or Roman artists is also possible in the nominal use of *classic* (usually in the plural), as in "At Louvain he afterwards devoted himself to the study of the classics, giving special, and sometimes almost undivided, attention to the acquisition of Ciceronian Latin" (G. Benson Clough, *A Short History of Education* (1904)). This usage has become established even though *classical* is the preferred adjectival form. In fact, it might even be regarded as one reason why the shorter form of the adjectives is still occasionally seen with this kind of reference. It has also been suggested that the noun and the adjectives should be written with a capital letter when used in this sense (e.g. Phythian 1979: 28).

The adjectives *classic* and *classical* are also used to denote historically outstanding periods of other cultures. According to *The Oxford Companion to the English Language* (1992) s.v. *classical*, "the cultures of Sanskrit in India, Arabic at the time of Muhammad, and Confucian China are classical". The shorter form appears in *The New Encyclopedia Britannica* (1974) s.v. *Classic period* for the most productive period (from AD 100 to 900) in Meso-American civilization; i.e. the Maya culture.

As the adjectives in these cases refer to a specific culture or a period within its history, they are clearly classifiers, and thus not very common in a predicative position.

3.4   'Adhering to the ancient Greek/Roman ideals'; 'simple, restrained, elegant'

As opposed to the Renaissance, history has also witnessed times when the works of the classic(al) period have been regarded with less enthusiasm. Romanticism, arising sometime in the middle of the eighteenth century, was a countermovement to classicism (or neoclassicism, as it is also sometimes called). The principles and ideals of romanticism, as described by the philosophers and poets of the era, were consciously opposite to those of classicism. Rather than emphasizing the importance of adhering to fixed norms and rules of composition, romanticists called for originality, individuality, and invention (Barnet, Berman and Burto (1964: 28); for a more detailed discussion of the derivation and usage of the word *romantic* and its relation to classicism, see Smith 1943). The vehement attitude against the notion of the inherently authoritative status of ancient Greek and Roman art naturally had an effect on how the classic(al) style was later defined; classicism and romanticism were regarded as antonyms, and more objective definitions for classic(al) style, free of value judgement, were sought. For instance, according to the generalisations illustrated by Barnet, Berman and Burto (1964: 28), "the classical mind delights in the probable or typical, the unified, the static, the finite" and "the romantic mind delights in the improbable, the varied, the dynamic, the infinite."[10] A lack of positive value judgement for classic(al) art can also be seen in the definition "marked by conservatism" by Urdang (1988) s.v. *classic/classical* (see also Hudson 1977 s.v. *classic*).

In some cases it may be difficult to decide whether *classic/classical* should be interpreted as pertaining directly to ancient Greece and/or Rome or to the different movements reviving the ideals of these periods, thus having the sense 'marked by classicism', as described in the *Random House Compact Unabridged Dictionary* (1996) s.v. *classical*. The corresponding definition in *The Chambers Dictionary* (1993) s.v. *classic or classical* is "chaste, refined, restrained, in keeping with classical art". In order to avoid this ambiguity, it has been suggested that the word *classicistic* be used in the derived, "revivalist" sense. As regards the analysis of *classic/classical* in the corpora studied, it was decided that those instances the context of which contained references to ancient Greece and/or Rome (or other ancient cultures) would be included in a group(s) of their own, while the others relating to artistic style and design were to be placed in the 'classicism' group.

Classical seems to be the preferred form when used in this sense or denoting the period of classicism in the context of architecture, with few exceptions of the shorter form (e.g. "Even the '70s decor in the sumptuous drawing room cannot diminish its classic proportions"; *The Daily Telegraph*, 4 Sept., 1993, "Travel: A few words about that place with the funny name"). The interpretation of *classical* may again depend on the focus. For example, the *Random House Compact Unabridged Dictionary* (1996) ascribes four different

---

10   Smith (1943: 117–118) considers these kinds of explanations "over-emphasized", saying that "the variety of meanings attributed to [the words *romanticism* and *classicism*] shows that they are employed without any precise and accepted understanding of what their signification really is", and adding that "there are both romantic and classical elements in almost every work of art."

definitions to *classical* in the context of architecture.[11] The sense 'marked by classicism' of the adjectives is also applied to the fine arts and other things, among them furniture and landscape gardening, as in examples (12a–c):

(12)   a.   *In House of Edinburgh and Glasgow* has some good-value, classic, upholstered furniture with a contemporary twist.   (*The Daily Telegraph*, 24 Sept., 1993, "Furnishings: Dress up tired rooms in style")

        b.   Bolingbroke makes and sells classical garden furniture and specialist joinery such as trellis-work, dovecotes, garden seats and summerhouses [...] (*The Daily Telegraph*, 19 Mar., 1993, "Consumer News: Shopping")

        c.   Stowe gardens, which comprise the finest and most important 18th century classical landscape in Europe, are to be given the most ambitious restoration ever undertaken by the National Trust [...] (*The Daily Telegraph*, 26 June, 1993, "£15m revival for birthplace of landscape gardening")

In this sense, *classic(al)* is often also contrasted with Romanticism; referring to the various different usages of *classic* and *classical*, *The Oxford Dictionary of Art* (1988) s.v. *classicism* observes that "it would be legitimate, if wilfully confusing, to refer to Delacroix as the classic Romantic artist."

Observed as adhering to ancient Greek and Roman ideals, *classic* and *classical* have been used of people's physical appearance as well:

(13)   a.   And he directed the attention of Lord St. Patrick to a young lady, rather tall, a brilliant complexion, classic features, a profusion of light brown hair; a face of intelligence and a figure rich and yet graceful. (Benjamin Disraeli, *Tancred* (1847), 176)

        b.   His cousin was pretty, his uncle's wife was lovely, but Clara Talboys was beautiful. Niobe's face, sublimated by sorrow, could scarcely have been more purely classical than hers. Even her dress, puritan in its grey simplicity, became her beauty better than a more beautiful dress would

---

11   The four senses relating to architecture listed in the dictionary are: (a) 'noting or pertaining to the architecture of ancient Greece and Rome, esp. the religious and public architecture, characterized by the employment of orders', (b) 'noting or pertaining to any or several styles of architecture closely imitating the architecture of ancient Greece or Rome; neoclassic', (c) noting or pertaining to architectural details or motifs adapted from ancient Greek or Roman models', and (d) '(of an architectural design) simple, reposeful, well-proportioned, or symmetrical in a manner suggesting the architecture of ancient Greece and Rome'.

have become a less beautiful woman. (M. E. Braddon, *Lady Audley's Secret* (1862), 94)

Relating to style on the whole, without necessarily having a pronounced connection with the classicist movement, *classic* and *classical* thus signify 'characterised by simplicity, restraint, order, harmony and symmetry', as in "She dressed almost exclusively at Dior for many years with classic elegance, and the fashion house bought back three creations for its museum in Paris" (*The Daily Telegraph*, 30 June, 1993, "Film star's costumes fetch £29,000"). According to *Bloomsbury Good Word Guide* (1988) s.v. *classic, classical*, the former adjective is used in this sense, and "*classical*, too, can suggest elegance, but there is a definite link with the standards and forms of ancient Greece and Rome". The use of *classic* for clothes, as in "I don't deliberately go to sales, but if I happen to see something classic like a cashmere sweater, shoes from Ferragamo or beautiful silk lingerie I will be tempted" (*The Daily Telegraph*, 21 June, 1993, "Fashion: Everybody loves a bargain"), has also been noted in dictionaries and usage manuals, usually with the additional attributes "following traditional lines", "ever-popular" and "never going out of fashion". Because of the notion of 'ever-popular', *classic(al)* here involves an element of positive value judgement as well. As in the case of classic cars, the usage of *classic(al)* in relation to fashion has been questioned and criticized, and sometimes the adjective has even been regarded as "a euphemism for 'boring'" (*The Daily Telegraph*, 3 Jan., 1993, "Fashion: A classical tale").

3.5   Traditional systems and methods

The sense of 'traditional' is one of the central elements in many of the applications of the adjectives *classic* and *classical*, and its presence has already been observed in the previous sections. This element is clearly perceivable when the adjectives are used of methods, systems and schools of thought. In present-day English, *classical* is the usual form given in this sense by dictionaries and usage manuals, e.g. *classical economics/physics*. The particular methods and ideologies may have been later challenged by other theories; for example, *classical* in relation to physics is according to *Chambers Science and Technology Dictionary* (1988) "said of theories based on concepts established before relativity and quantum mechanics, i.e. largely in conformity with Newton's mechanics and Maxwell's electromagnetic theory". Some instances may include a obvious suggestion of the outdated nature of the practices adhered to by tradition, as in "This method is infinitely more economical of tubes than the classical method and seems to produce effective remedies" (*BNC*, C9V 481).

    In relation to ballet, *classical* seems to refer to a traditional style of ballet, which can be regarded as a school, and which, according to *The New Encyclopedia Britannica*, emphasises a technique consisting of a "formalized set of movements and positions of the arms, feet, and body". The technique seems to be the most important factor in the question of what is called *classical* here. In the case of famous works such as *Swan Lake* or *The Nutcracker*, however, there can be some confusion over whether the adjective refers to the style or the school or is used in the sense 'of high quality' or 'belonging to a canon' (see also e.g. Wilson 1974 s.v. *classical ballet*).

The traditional, accepted methods and techniques, as opposed to modern or improvised ones, are referred to as *classic* or *classical* in other fields as well, including sports in examples (14a) and (14b):

(14) a. Later on I saw him batting, sometimes improvising like a jazz musician and every so often leaning into a cover drive of classic style just to remind us that, as with all great players, the foundation of his genius was a marvellous technique. (*The Daily Telegraph*, 26 Apr., 1993, "Cricket: The Brylcreem boy even Yorkshire fans took a shine to")

       b. Lewis, having more than likely grown used to the round-arm, kidney-slapping stuff that senior American heavyweights routinely dish out, seemed disconcerted by the literal straightforwardness of this direct and almost classical lead, so he was frequently off balance when Bruno's less textbook follow-up, the over-arm right, came crashing round his ears. (*The Sunday Telegraph*, 3 Oct., 1993, "Boxing: Fight fans are getting raw deal")

In both (14a) and (14b) the adjectives *classic* and *classical* suggest an adherence to traditional methods. The context shows, however, that *classic* has a stronger positive loading, whereas the longer form suggests the notion of 'textbook'.

A similar usage of the adjectives is seen in texts about cooking. In some instances, the context suggests that *classic* or *classical* denotes a particular style or even a school of cooking:

(15) a. I have always felt that this lack of formal training can free the cook from the rigid constraints of classic cuisine, and so makes for some of the most exciting and interesting dishes. (*The Daily Telegraph*, 2 Oct., 1993, "Cooking: Glossy chefs write glossier books")

       b. The kitchen hasn't gone berserk and jettisoned the trappings of classical French cooking; indeed it helpfully translates some of the more basic technical terms at the front of the menu just to prove it, from coulis and terrine to the dreaded supreme. (*The Daily Telegraph*, 21 Aug., 1993, "Eating Out: Too good to be sent up in flames")

According to native English informants, while both forms have the meanings 'traditional' and 'conforming to an approved pattern', the shorter form usually also implies a stronger positive value judgement, whereas the longer form again suggests the notion of 'textbook' or 'orthodox'.

3.6   Classical music

Rather than the form of the adjective, the problems confronted in the interpretation of the phrase *classical music* concern the definition and application of the phrase in the first place (see e.g. Urdang 1994: 21). In present-day English, the longer form of the adjective has become the norm in this expression.

In a more specific sense, *classical* is applied to the style of music of the late eighteenth century and early nineteenth century, preceded by the Baroque period and followed by the Romantic period. The adjective was originally applied in this sense by the Romanticists, and contrasts with *Romantic*.[12] The attributes that are ascribed to the classical style in music as opposed to Romantic are similar to those assigned to ancient Greek and Roman ideals. In the *Harvard Dictionary of Music* (1944) s.v. *classicism*, the classical style and form is said to emphasize "greater stability, repose, clarity, balance, self-reliance, objectiveness, traditionalism", whereas Romanticism is described with words such as "unrest, exaggeration, experimentation, ostentation, diffusion, subjectivism". The so-called "Viennese classics", i.e. Haydn, Mozart, Beethoven and Schubert, have been generally regarded as the most notable representatives of the classical style. The attributes used to describe the style have, however, been criticized. For example, according to Room (1988) s.v. *classical/romantic*, some of Beethoven's works have features usually assigned to Romanticism.

Although the use of *classical* in its specific sense is in *The Oxford Companion to Music* (1970) s.v. *classical* said to be "the sense in which today nine musicians out of ten use the word" – obviously referring to *classical* musicians – this is probably not the sense in which the word is most commonly used in connection with music. Finding a suitable definition for the more extensive meaning of *classical*, i.e. classical music as distinct from other types of music, such as jazz, folk, and pop music, has resulted in rather strange statements in dictionaries and encyclopedias. In such recent dictionaries as *Cambridge International Dictionary of English* (1995; henceforth *CIDE*) and *Collins COBUILD English Dictionary for Advanced Learners* (2001; henceforth *COBUILD*), *classical music* is defined as 'music that is considered to be serious and of lasting value', which seems to reflect the dictionary-makers' own opinions rather than objective characteristics of the type of music in question. Definitions of this kind are also found in some earlier works of reference, where this sense is considered to be based on the similar use of *classic(al)* 'canonical' in relation to literature and other art forms, the classical works having "stood the test of time" (*Collins Encyclopedia of Music* s.v. *classical music*).[13] This argument, as well as

---

12   Thus what is understood by *classical* could also be thought to include the Baroque period, as pointed out in *The Oxford Companion to Music* (1970).

13   Even more awkward are the comments openly reflecting the hostility between the enthusiasts and non-enthusiasts of classical music; *The Oxford Companion to Music* (1970) rather bluntly states that "amongst less educated people 'Classical' is used in antithesis to 'Popular'", accompanying the claim with the dreadful example "'Do you like

the use of the phrase 'of lasting value' in definitions of classical music, are unsuccessful, because one can talk about *modern* classical music, which would then involve a contradiction in terms. A more objective approach to the question can be seen e.g. in *LDEL*, in which classical music in the wider sense is defined as 'of or being music in the educated European tradition that includes such forms as chamber music, opera, and symphony as distinguished from folk or popular music or jazz.'

3.7   Other uses

Classic and *classical* are also used in relation to the productions of plays of the Shakespearean period, as witness examples (16a) and (16b):

(16)   a.   Saturday night's Performance: *The Changeling* (BBC2) was a wretched disappointment; indeed the opening 10 minutes must rank as some of the worst classic drama ever staged on television. (*The Daily Telegraph*, 13 Dec., 1993, "The Arts: Devil-may-care immortality tale – Television")

   b.   Nonetheless, [*The Good Life*] bracketed him somewhat in suburban sitcom until Kenneth Branagh convinced a wide audience of Briers's classical ability [...] it was his portrayal of Malvolio in Branagh's 1989 stage production of Twelfth Night that opened audiences' eyes. (*The Daily Telegraph*, 30 Oct., 1993, "Telegraph Magazine: Beyond the pullover")

This use of the adjectives has not been separately mentioned in dictionaries and usage manuals. It seems that what is referred to by the classic(al) stage is in some ways a school, bearing a certain resemblance to classical ballet. In this case, however, it is the programme or the repertoire (i.e. the adjectives refer to the production of "canonical" works) that is emphasized rather than the techniques or methods. When used in relation to theatre, the adjectives *classic* and *classical*, then, can refer to the production of Shakespearean plays, or to ancient Greek or Roman theatre, or, according to *The New Encyclopedia Britannica*, French drama of the latter half of the seventeenth century (e.g. the works of Racine and Corneille).

---

classical music?' 'No, I like something with a tune to it!'" Commenting on the unfortunate vagueness of the definitions of classical music, and also on the needlessly inflammable nature of the question, *The New Oxford Companion to Music* (1983) s.v. *classical* includes the humorous remark that "perhaps the nearest to an accurate definition is that it is music considered respectable by respectable people".

4.   *Classic/classical* in the material studied

The seventeenth century texts in the corpora studied – both fiction and non-fiction – contain only a few instances of *classic* and *classical*, mainly in relation to authors considered to be of the first rank. The eighteenth century material in the *Literature Online* collection include a greater number of instances of the adjectives, the different uses being presented below in Table 13. The earliest instances date from 1742, so the figures on the whole perhaps reflect more accurately the usage of the adjectives in the second rather than the first half of the century. The figures indicate the numbers of uses of *classic/classical* in different senses; the figures given in parentheses denote those instances where the adjectives occurred in a predicative position. For example, of the total 45 instances of *classical* in the *Literature Online* texts from 1740–1799, four were used predicatively. With the exception of references to historically famous locations, *classical* is in all senses more common than *classic*. The adjectives are most frequently used to refer to things relating to Greek or Roman antiquity. This is also the case in the eighteenth century non-fiction texts examined, although the overall number of occurrences of *classic/classical* in this material was fairly low.

Table 13. *Classic/classical* in the prose section of *Literature Online*, 1740–1799.

	classic	classical
1. positive value judgement		
a. 'of the first rank', 'of high quality', 'authoritative'	-	3
b. 'famous' (locations)	5	-
2. pertaining to a historical period in a particular culture:		
a. ancient Greece or Rome		
1. arts, literature	1	15 (2)
2. others	-	4
a'. pertaining to the study and knowledge of ancient Greek/Latin cultures	1	11
a''. pertaining to people learned in ancient Greek/Latin cultures	1	3
3. 'pertaining to classicism', 'characterised by simplicity, harmony, symmetry, etc.'	1	8 (1)
4. pertaining to old, "pure" literary form of languages	-	1 (1)
total	**9**	**45 (4)**
# of authors using the forms:	6	15
# of authors using both forms: 5		

Table 14 presents the different uses of the adjectives in the *Literature Online* material from the first half of the nineteenth century. The first notable feature in the figures is the relative increase in the use of *classic*, although the longer form is still more frequently used. As in the eighteenth century texts, *classic* is the more common form when referring to famous places. It is also interesting to observe the use of the two forms relating to Greek and Roman antiquity: *classic* is still the less frequent form, but there are, relatively speaking, fairly numerous occurrences of it in reference to ancient Greek/Roman art or the antiquity in general, while the shorter form is distinctly rarer than *classical* when relating to the study and knowledge of the languages and cultures, as well as people learned in the classics.

Table 14. *Classic/classical* in the prose section of *Literature Online,* 1800–1849.

	classic	*classical*
1. positive value judgement		
a. 'of the first rank', 'of high quality', 'authoritative'	1	2 (1)
b. 'famous', 'outstanding'		
1. locations	12	4 (1)
2. others	2	3
2. pertaining to a historical period in a particular culture:		
a. ancient Greece or Rome		
1. arts, literature	14	18 (1)
2. others	12 (1)	27 (2)
a'. pertaining to the study and knowledge of ancient Greek/Latin cultures	2	29
a''. pertaining to people learned in ancient Greek/Latin cultures	2	19 (1)
3. 'pertaining to classicism', 'characterised by simplicity, harmony, symmetry, etc.'		
a. architecture	2	4
b. clothing	-	5 (2)
c. physical appearance	6	2
d. others	6 (1)	18 (3)
4. 'ancient' = 'old'	1	2
total	**60 (2)**	**133 (11)**
# of authors using the forms:	18	22
# of authors using both forms: 13		

It is noteworthy, furthermore, that the use of *classic/classical* in the sense of 'of
the first class' or 'canonical' is – somewhat surprisingly – quite rare among the
nearly two hundred instances in this period. In some cases, the adjectives were
used with a touch or irony or jocularity (group 4), relating to the sense of
'ancient', as in "He surveyed me from head to foot with an air of benign and
fatherly complacency, and ragging forth from its sullen rest a large arm chair, on
whose cushions of rusty horse-hair sat an eternal cloud of classic dust, too sacred
to be disturbed, he plumped me down upon it, before I was aware of the cruel
hospitality" (Edward Bulwer Lytton, *Eugene Pelham* (1828), 272).

No great change in the use of the adjectives is seen in fictional texts of the
latter half of the nineteenth century (Table 15); *classical* is still the "dominant"
form of the two in most senses, the clearest instances being collocations such as
classical learning/knowledge/studies/scholar.

Table 15. *Classic/classical* in the prose section of *Literature Online,* 1850–1899.

	classic	*classical*
1. positive value judgement		
a. 'of the first rank', 'of high quality', 'authoritative'	6	4
b. 'famous', 'outstanding'		
1. locations	4	1
2. others	-	3
2. being representative of a type: 'typical', 'archetypal', 'regular', 'traditional'	-	1
3. pertaining to a historical period in a particular culture:		
a. ancient Greece or Rome		
1. arts, literature	10	18
2. others	15 (1)	22 (1)
a'. pertaining to the study and knowledge of ancient Greek/Latin cultures	5 (1)	34 (1)
a''. pertaining to people learned in ancient Greek/ Latin cultures	3	16 (1)
b. other cultures	4	2
4. 'pertaining to classicism', 'characterised by simplicity, harmony, symmetry, etc.'		
a. architecture	4	4 (1)
b. clothing ('ever-popular')	2	1
c. physical appearance	6	13 (3)
d. others	9 (1)	17 (4)

	classic	*classical*
5. denoting orchestral music (symphonies, chamber music)	-	2
6. pertaining to old, "pure" literary forms of languages	-	3 (1)
7. 'ancient' = 'old'	-	1
total	**68 (3)**	**142 (12)**
# of authors using the forms:	22	27
# of authors using both forms: 15		

The dominance of *classical* in the nineteenth century can also be perceived in the non-fiction material studied, the results being presented in Table 16 below. The table indicates the uses of *classic/classical* by British authors; the texts by American authors contained only a handful of instances of the two adjectives, the meanings being among those given in Tables 14, 15, and 16.

Table 16. *Classic/classical* in the non-fiction texts studied, 1800–1899 (British authors).

	classic	*classical*
1. positive value judgement		
a. 'of the first rank', 'of high quality', 'belonging to a canon', 'authoritative'	1	9 (1)
b. 'famous' (locations)	2	-
2. pertaining to a historical period in a particular culture:		
a. ancient Greece or Rome		
1. arts, literature	-	4
2. others	-	10
a'. pertaining to the study and knowledge of ancient Greek/Latin cultures	-	9
3. 'pertaining to classicism', 'characterised by simplicity, harmony, symmetry, etc.'	-	1 (1)
4. pertaining to traditional and (formerly) accepted methods, systems or ideas	1	1
5. pertaining to old, "pure" literary forms of languages	-	1
total	**4**	**35 (2)**
# of authors using the forms:	4	19
# of authors using both forms: 3		

The numbers of occurrences of *classic/classical* in the British non-fiction texts dating from the first half of the twentieth century were also fairly low. As the figures from this period are thus perhaps not very illustrative of the actual use of the adjectives at the time, they are presented in an appendix (Appendix A, Table 1). However, in the same way as in the corresponding material by American authors (see Appendix A, Table 2), a notable detail is the preference for *classical* in connection with traditional or (formerly) accepted scientific methods or ideas. This preference was prominent in texts on economics, chemistry, psychology, and literary theory alike; this use was the most frequently occurring one in the material.

Turning now to the present-day situation, the 1993 issues of *The Daily Telegraph* were analysed for Kaunisto (1999). While the setup of semantic categories is slightly different in the present analysis, the same overall observations on the adjectives' use can be made based on the results of six months' issues of the newspaper ranging from July to December 1995, which included 673 analyzed instances of *classic* and 497 instances of *classical*. The results are summarized in Table 17. The different applications of the adjectives are arranged into groups similar to those discussed above.

Table 17. *Classic/classical* in the July–December 1995 issues of *The Daily Telegraph*.

	classic	*classical*
1. positive value judgement		
a. 'of the first rank', 'of high quality', 'belonging to a canon', 'authoritative'	212 (2)	9
b. 'famous', 'outstanding'		
1. cars/motorcycles/bikes	79	-
2. wines/beers	8	-
3. races	11	-
4. others	39	2
2. being representative of a type: 'typical', 'archetypal', 'quintessential', 'regular', 'traditional'	238	10
3. pertaining to a historical period in a particular culture:		
a. ancient Greece or Rome		
1. arts, literature	-	10
2. others	2	58 (1)
a'. pertaining to the study and knowledge of ancient Greek/Latin cultures	-	12

	classic	*classical*
a''. pertaining to people learned in ancient Greek/ Latin cultures	-	6
b. pertaining to the period of ca. 4th c. BC in ancient Greece (as opposed to the Archaic and Hellenistic periods)	-	3
c. pertaining to the tradition or the productive periods of non-Western cultures	-	6
4. 'pertaining to classicism', 'characterised by simplicity, harmony, symmetry, etc.'		
a. architecture	6	41 (1)
b. clothing ('ever-popular')	33 (4)	-
c. physical appearance	2	3
d. others	21	27 (4)
5. pertaining to traditional and (formerly) accepted methods, systems or ideas:		
a. cooking	4	6
b. sport	8	7
c. others	3	5
d. of or pertaining to established schools		
1. ballet	-	63 (2)
2. ideologies and scientific theories	1	3
6. pertaining to distinguishable styles of music:		
a. orchestral music (symphonies and chamber music, general sense)	1	197 (7)
b. pertaining to the style and period of Viennese classicism, contrasted with Baroque, Romanticism, etc.	1	7
7. pertaining to the productions of plays of the Shakespearean period	4	17
8. pertaining to old literary forms of languages	-	5
total	**673 (6)**	**497 (15)**

The results as a whole seem to confirm the generalizations found in dictionaries and usage manuals concerning the usage of the adjectives: *classic* is clearly the preferred form for conveying a positive value judgement, whether the viewpoint is subjective or objective, and also in the sense of 'typical'. It is likewise the normal form when used of clothes that are considered ever-popular, regarded as simple and traditional in style (and which can, in fact, also be famous!). *Classical* is preferred when used in relation to ancient Greece and Rome and the subsequent artistic movements in Western culture based on the principles of ancient Greek and Roman art (i.e. classicism). It is also used when referring to the orchestral music of the period from about 1780 to 1830, as opposed to that of the Romantic period, as well as to these types of music in a wider sense. When used of traditional methods or scientific theories, it seems that *classical* is preferred in cases where there is clearly an established school. The 1993 issues of the newspaper contained three instances of *classic*, and seventeen instances of *classical* referring to ideologies or scientific theories regarded as traditional or constituting the formerly accepted way of thinking (e.g. the classical school of economics). This tendency is strikingly evident when referring to ballet. When it comes to cooking and sports, however, there seems to be some variation as to the choice of the adjective, although, as pointed out by native English informants, the shorter form suggests a stronger sense of positive value judgement. Another notable fact is that the predicative occurrences were only a handful in the case of both adjective forms.

The present-day material also contained instances where a prefix or initial combining form was tagged on to the adjectives, e.g. *neo-classic(al)*, *post-classic(al)*, and *pseudo-classic(al)*. In most cases, these formations tend to relate to senses in which *classical* is today the prevalent form, and the forms ending in *-ical* outnumber those ending in *-ic*. In the July–December 1995 material studied, three formations of this type had the *-ic*, 24 the *-ical* ending (in the 1993 issues the corresponding figures were three and 45). In other words, the added elements did not result in a preference for the shorter form of the adjectives. Instead, the semantic differentiation between *classic* and *classical* was the overriding factor. The historical material did not contain enough instances of these kinds of formations so as to warrant drawing any definite conclusions on the matter.

5.   General remarks

Based on the corpora studied, the most prominent change in the use of the adjectives has been the rise in the use of *classic*. In the nineteenth century texts, the increase in the use of this form was seen in the senses relating to historically notable places, and generally to ancient Greece and/or Rome. More crucial developments have been since taking place as regards the senses 'of the first rank', 'excellent', 'canonical' or 'authoritative' plus 'typical' or 'archetypal', in which *classical* has obviously given way to the shorter form. Some variation between the forms, as well as an overall vagueness in the use of the adjectives are nevertheless still seen. This can be perceived as reflecting the fact that the different uses of *classic* and *classical* are different kinds mixtures of the same basic semantic ingredients, including high status, high quality, tradition, with some additional elements such as purity, simplicity and correctness.

Classic/classical today is, in fact, one of the most "mosaicked" of all *-ic/-ical* adjective pairs, resulting in some difficulties in interpretation. It was observed that the examination of the usage of *classic/classical* could not be based solely on the study of their immediate right-hand collocates, as the two forms could be used in different senses with the same head word.

On the basis of the results presented in Table 17, one can agree with Marsden's (1985: 28) observation on the overall differentiation between *classic* and *classical*, according to which "a broad distinction may be drawn between a generalized, universally applicable sense of *classic* as opposed to the more restricted, historically or culturally specific sense of *classical*". The shorter form seems to be more directly connected with one of the original ideas of the Latin word *classicus*, 'of the first class'. As to the semantic components differentiating between the adjective forms, considering value judgement as a component in the case of this adjective pair may at first seem somewhat strange here, because the etymon inherently had a close connection with evaluation itself. The present-day use of the adjectives shows, however, that this component can safely be assigned to *classic*, in contradistinction to *classical*.

Considering the comments by Fowler and Gowers discussed earlier, none of the figures in Table 17 suggest that *classical* could today more readily replace *classic* than vice versa. The uses of *classic/classical* in the historical corpora, however, show that Fowler's idea on *classical* being "the usual word" in most uses of the pair was perhaps not altogether unjustified considering the time when Fowler wrote his comment. In fact, it could be argued that most of the drastic developments in the semantic differentiation between the two forms, and the increase in the relative frequency of *classic* occurred in the twentieth century, after the publication of Fowler's book.

Although adjectives in *-ic/-ical* in proper names are in the present study not included in the tabular presentations, nor are they otherwise examined in greater detail, some general comments are perhaps worth mentioning. In the English-speaking world today, *classic* is a very popular adjective, used in the names of a great number of products. Its high marketing value is due to its readiness to be used in many different senses while still always being associated to the sense of 'excellent' or 'of highest quality'. For instance, the idea of 'original' of the word *classic*, together with its nostalgic flavour, has been successfully made use of in *Classic Coke*. The notions of 'basic' and 'simple, restrained' sometimes suggest themselves in the names of car models, as in "The C-class is offered as four 'lines': Classic (basic specification), Esprit (bright colours, young image), Sport and Elegance" (*The Sunday Telegraph*, 30 May, 1993, "Motoring: Star turn from Benz") and "The Classic is the 'understated' – that is, basic – model, which continues where the 190 left off [...]" (*The Daily*

Telegraph, 9 Oct., 1993, "Motoring: Hey, doc, you're getting it in the groove"). In contrast to the shorter form, *classical* is not usually favoured in names of products. A "classic" example of the attractiveness of *classic* is its usage in the name of the classical music radio station *Classic FM*.

Chapter 6

Perspectives on amusement: the use of *comic/comical*

One of the most striking and intriguing comments on the present-day use of *comic/comical* is to be found e.g. in Swan (1995: 256):

> *Comic* is the normal adjective for artistic comedy.
> > **comic** verse   Shakespeare's **comic** technique
> > **comic** opera
> *Comical* is a rather old-fashioned word meaning 'funny'.
> > a **comical** expression

Attention is immediately caught by the word "old-fashioned", an inescapably subjective observation on the use of *comical*, which is almost impossible to directly corroborate by corpus linguistic means. However, it could be argued that there is some *in*direct evidence supporting the view, namely the fact that *comic* is today used more frequently than *comical* (noted, for example, by Partridge 1957, and more recently by Burchfield 1996). In the *British National Corpus*, *comic* as an adjective appears 719 times, whereas *comical* appears 122 times (excluding instances where the adjectives appear as part of a proper name). In the 1995 issues of *The Daily Telegraph*, the relation is even greater in favour of the shorter form, the corresponding figures being 706 against a mere 68. The problem in assessing the vitality of a word on the basis of the numbers of occurrences, however, is that a relatively lower frequency of one of the forms does not necessarily correlate with old-fashionedness, especially in cases where the forms in *-ic* and *-ical* have been observed to have different uses. No parallel argument on old-fashionedness has been made, for example, on *economical*, although in both the *BNC* and *The Daily Telegraph* material, instances of *economic* are far more numerous than those of *economical*. In addition, the issue of the frequencies of use is not at all straightforward, depending to some extent also on the type of the texts examined, as will be seen in later sections.

Considering all the semantically differentiated adjective pairs, the relative infrequency of one of the forms is nevertheless a prominent feature in the present-day use of the pair *comic/comical*. The situation resembles the pair *politic/political* somewhat (see Chapter 12), of which the shorter form has shown a steady decline in use. Moreover, looking at the definitions of *comical* in the *OED*, and examining the historical text material, it appears that the adjective has had a number of uses which have later disappeared, and this in turn may have played some part in the overall impression that some people may have of the word being nowadays "dated". Aiming at a general distinction on the use of *comic* and *comical*, Swan does not mention the fact that *comic* is also used in the sense 'amusing' or 'funny', as in *I found it comic to watch his drunken behaviour.*[1] As in the case of other semantically differentiated *-ic/-ical* pairs, the use of *comic/comical* shows a certain degree of overlap. It will also be seen that the possibility of having different viewpoints when approaching the central themes denoted by the words – comedy, amusement, and the act of amusing people – to a great deal explains the choice of the adjective form in different contexts, something worth keeping in mind when one speculates on the semantic differentiation of the two forms.

1.   Etymology and early history of the pair

As in the case of most *-ic/-ical* pairs, the models for the English *comic* and *comical* are to be found in French (*comique*), Latin (*comicus*), and, ultimately, Greek (κωμικός). The words had both a nominal and an adjectival function, the adjective originally having the meaning 'of or pertaining to comedy', and the noun denoting a person involved in the production of comedy, e.g. a writer or an actor. The adjectival use is in all four languages the dominant one. First citations of *comice* and *comicalle* in the *MED* are both from translations of Higden's *Polychronicon*, *comice* appearing in a manuscript translated before 1387, while the manuscript with *comicalle* is in the *MED* dated ?a1475 (?a1425). However, in the *OED* these uses of the words are regarded as non-anglicized occurrences, and the citations are given inside square brackets.[2] The "proper" first citation of *comic* in the *OED* dates from 1576[3], that of *comical* from 1557. The first attested substantival use of *comic* in the dictionary dates from 1581.

It is interesting to note that the history of *comic* and *comical* differs in some respects from that of *magic/magical* (discussed in Chapter 10), another pair of which the shorter form is also used as a noun, since the adjectives *comic* and *comical* seem to have entered the English language at approximately the same time. The nominal uses of *comic* and *magic* themselves are also significantly different: *magic* as a noun refers to the whole phenomenon and practice of

---

1   At the other end of the spectrum of comments on the use of *comic/comical* in usage manuals, one finds claims that the two forms do not show any significant difference in meaning (Barber 1964: 114; Roberts 1967: 233; Sinclair 1991 s.v. *-al*).

2   It is possible that presenting these instances of *comice* and *comicalle* as non-anglicized items has to do with the fact that they appeared in a translated work instead of being in an originally English text. Such a decision would, however, seem somewhat unjustified, considering that *comicalle* certainly is an anglicized form.

3   The *Literature Online* material includes an instance of *Comike Poet* in William Painter's *The Palace of Pleasure, Tome 1* (1566), antedating the first citation of *comic* in the *OED*.

supernatural powers, whereas the noun *comic* was originally used only of *people* involved in the production of humorous plays, poems, etc., the noun *comedy* designating the more extensive concept. As will be observed in Chapter 10, the adjective form *magic* was used more frequently than *magical* in the late sixteenth century (reflecting the fact that the adjectival use of *magic* had become established before the longer form entered the scene), whereas other *-ic/-ical* pairs have manifested a strong preference for the longer forms during this period in most cases. The use of *comic* and *comical* in earlier centuries seems to adhere to the general pattern, as seen from the numbers of their occurrences in the *Literature Online* material, presented in Table 18 (the numbers in parentheses denote the numbers of authors using the adjectives, the number of books by anonymous authors being separated with a slash).[4]

Table 18. *Comic/comical* in the prose section of the *Literature Online* corpus, 1550–1903.

	1550–1599	1600–1699	1700–1799	1800–1849	1850–1903
comic	4 (4)	8 (5)	49 (13)	106 (12)	156 (28)
comical	18 (10/1)	33 (14/4)	75 (18)	67 (16)	97 (26)
authors using both forms	2	3	11	7	17

Table 18 shows a degree of preference for the use of *comical* in the sixteenth and seventeenth centuries (with due reservations regarding the relatively low numbers of authors). It is difficult to argue anything conclusive about the effect of the use of *comic* as a noun; one could postulate that the preference for *comical* reflects its "unequivocally adjectival" nature. However, in the *Literature Online* material studied, the Early English Prose Fiction database (1513–1699) and the Eighteenth Century Fiction database (1700–1780) each contained only one instance of *comic* as a noun, while in the considerably larger Nineteenth Century Fiction database (1781–1903) no nominal uses of the word were found. Therefore the nominal use of *comic*, keeping in mind its relative frequency, does not seem to have presented a major hindrance for its adjectival use.[5] Instead, the

---

4   In the non-fiction texts, as well as in the citations in the *OED*, the occurrences of *comic/comical* were unfortunately too low to merit closer analysis and discussion here.

5   In the twentieth century, *comic* has developed new nominal uses, which is perhaps reflected in the relative increase in the overall number of nominal occurrences of the word: e.g. in the *BNC*, *comic* appears as a noun 568 times, and compared to the number of adjectival uses, nominal cases are relatively speaking considerably more frequent than they were in earlier centuries. This fact, however, does not appear to have had any direct effect on the choice between the two adjectives, least of all in the way of presenting a hindrance

increasing popularity in the use of the adjectival *-ic* forms from the seventeenth century onwards seems to have had an effect on *comic/comical* as well, as can be seen from the figures for the eighteenth century, where the relation between the numbers of uses and authors for the two forms shows a clear increase in the use of *comic*. As will be seen in subsequent sections, the eighteenth century also marks the period during which the semantic differentiation of the two forms begins, or at least becomes clearly visible in the material studied. Therefore the relation between the occurrences of uses of *comic* and *comical* from this period onwards is of less significance, although it may have some relevance as regards the "old-fashionedness" of *comical*. One interesting observation considering these relations is that compared to the shorter form, *comical* was still used quite frequently in prose fiction in the latter half of nineteenth century, suggesting that the "obsolescence" of this form would be to a great extent a process occurring in the twentieth century.[6]

2.   *Comic/comical* in dictionaries and usage manuals

The earliest appearances of *comical* in dictionaries, be they monolingual or bilingual, usually precede those of *comic*, corresponding with the general trend in the case of *-ic/-ical* adjectives in early dictionaries observed in Chapter 4. In early bilingual dictionaries, *comical* (but not the shorter form) is given as the English equivalent of foreign words, for example, in Thomas's (1587) Latin-English dictionary s.v. *comicus*, and Florio's (1598) Italian-English dictionary s.v. *comico*. *Comical* is also the sole adjective form of the pair appearing in such monolingual dictionaries as Cawdrey (1604), Bullokar (1616), Cockeram (1616), Blount (1656), Phillips (1658), Kersey (1702), and Bailey (1721). Both forms are given in Minsheu's (1617) multilingual dictionary, and among the works consulted, the earliest instance of both forms given as synonyms in a monolingual dictionary is the sixth revised version of Bullokar's dictionary (1680). The practice of including both *comic* and *comical* is seen also in Johnson's dictionary

---

for the adjectival use of *comic*, as in the twentieth century, it is *comical* that has been withering away.

6   The numbers of occurrences of *comic/comical* per one million words in the *Literature Online* material are as follows: 1.2 and 5.6 in 1513–1599, 1.2 and 4.9 in 1600–1699, 3.2 and 4.9 in 1700–1799, 7.7 and 4.9 in 1800–1849, and finally 7.1 and 4.4 in 1850–1903.

(1755), after which it became the norm (see e.g. Sheridan (1780), Walker (1791), Barclay (1819), and Richardson (1836)).

It is interesting that in Johnson's dictionary, *comic* and *comical* are given in separate entries, which are, however, almost identical (cf. Johnson's definitions of *magic/magical*, discussed in Chapter 10): *comic* is paraphrased as 'relating to comedy' and 'raising mirth', while *comical* is ascribed the senses 'raising mirth; merry' and 'relating to comedy'. One wonders whether Johnson could have been hinting that there was at least a slight degree of semantic differentiation between the two forms through his ordering of the senses (i.e. with *comic*, the sense 'relating to comedy' is given first, whereas with *comical*, that sense is the second one), adding the word "merry" for *comical*, as well as through drafting two separate entries. The same ordering of the senses also appears e.g. in Walker (1791), probably much due to the influence of Johnson.[7]

In the *OED*, the original sense 'of or having to do with comedy', is assigned to both forms (s.vv. *comic*, sense 1; *comical*, sense 1), the quotations for both forms including the phrase *comic(al) poet*. This use of *comical* is marked as obsolete. While sense 1 of *comic* and *comical* covers instances which have to do with comedy "in the dramatic sense", sense 2 of *comic* relates to products which are not necessarily connected with theatrical productions. The paraphrase in question reads '[a]iming at a humorous or ridiculous effect: applied to literary compositions, songs, journals, etc., which have it as their express aim to excite mirth; burlesque, funny'. The sense as given in the *OED* apparently relates to performers as well, as the citations provided include the example *comic vocalist*. This use of *comic* is considered in the dictionary "a modern downward extension of the notion", i.e. distinguishing it from the notion of 'having to do with comedy' in the narrow, restricted sense. The *OED* does not include any instances of *comical* in connection with literary compositions aiming to cause amusement. However, the distinction between senses 1 and 2 may be difficult to apply to an analysis of the adjectives' use in a corpus, particularly in present-day English, in which comedy as a genre encompasses a wider spectrum in fiction than drama. For example, problems may arise in distinguishing whether *a comic performance/poet/song/vocalist* actually relates to theatrical comedy or to other kinds of performances. Additionally, the adjective phrases such as *a comic genius/talent* could be regarded as having two distinct meanings according to whether the person is a playwright or a novelist. It is therefore not all that

---

7   In Todd's second edition of Johnson's dictionary (1827), the two adjectives are still remarkably similar as regards the ordering of the senses, but with more "differentiating" additional words (such as 'diverting') given in the definitions. Also notable is the astonishing use of *tragick* and *tragical* in connection with parallel *-ic/-ical* forms (the entries in the original work were in a different order from that below, due to the *-ick* spelling of the shorter form):

        comick   1. relating to comedy; not tragick 2. raising mirth
        comical   1. raising mirth; merry; diverting 2. relating to
            comedy; befitting comedy; not tragical

surprising to find that more recent dictionaries do not make a similar distinction along these lines. Instead, senses 1 and 2 are more likely to be presented as representing basically one classifying sense, 'of or characterised by comedy'.

Unfortunately, the *OED* definitions for *comic* and *comical* are – again – not totally free from oddities and inconsistencies as regards the choices in paraphrasing the different senses. *Comic*, sense 3, relating to "actions, incidents, etc.", is broken into two parts, i.e. 3.a '[c]alculated to excite mirth; intentionally funny' (exemplified by "Moody interjected, in an Irish tone, and with a comic look, 'Ah! poor George the Second'", from James Boswell, *The Life of Samuel Johnson LL.D.* (1791) 6 Apr. an. 1775) and 3.b '[u]nintentionally provocative of mirth; laughable, ludicrous' (as in "His attempt in such deep affliction to be musical is comic in the extreme", from Sir Francis B. Head, *Bubbles from the Brunnens of Nassau* (1833), iii). A cross-reference is also given to *comical*, sense 4, which reads '[r]esembling comedy, mirth-provoking; humorous, jocose, funny; ludicrous, laughable'. Surprisingly, sense 4 for *comical* is not similarly divided into two subgroups according to whether the thing causing amusement has been intentionally produced or not. Instead, the quotations provided include examples of both kinds: for example, *comical* in the sentence "A man [...] may break jests upon pain, and entertain his company with comical Representations of the Groans and Agonies of dying" (from John Scott, *The Christian Life* (1685), II. 135) clearly involves a deliberate aim on the man's part to amuse others. Other citations include e.g. "There was something extremely comical in the sight of the archbishop lying flat on his back" (from J. Athelstan Riley, *Athos* (1887), xiii), representing in turn a case where amusement has been caused unintentionally. There does not seem to be any reason why a more detailed subdivision should be used for *comic* but not for *comical*. The different treatment of the adjectives in this part of the semantic spectrum makes one wonder to what extent the definitions in the *OED* have influenced subsequent dictionary-makers and writers of grammars and usage manuals. The issue can, in fact, be considered rather important, as the presence or absence of intention is a major factor used to explain the difference between these two forms.

Apart from the sense 'of or having to do with comedy', the *OED* lists some other senses of *comical* which are marked obsolete, such as '[b]efitting comedy; trivial, mean, low; the opposite of tragical, elevated or dignified' (sense 2, used of 'style, subject, etc.'), 'low, mean, base, ignoble; or ? clownish' (sense 2.b, used of persons), as in "This Comical mention of the power and goodness of God [...] in a place so improper and unnatural for those reflexions" (from Edward Clarendon, *A Brief View and Survey of the Errors to Church and State in Hobbes' Leviathan* (1676), 18). Likewise obsolete is sense 3 of *comical*, which reads '[l]ike the conclusion of a comedy; happy or fortunate', with the example "That all might appear to be knit up in a comical conclusion, the duke's daughter was afterwards joined in marriage to the lord Lisle" (from Sir John Hayward, *Annals of the first four years of the reign of Queen Elizabeth* (a1627)). This sense has not been assigned to *comic*, but instances of both forms are found in the *Literature Online* material, as in the following excerpts by Richard Brathwait:

(1)   a. Forestall our History we must not; the issue of this Plot shall disclose it
            selfe in this our ensuing and closing discourse: which, as Comick
            conclusions suit best with love, where vertue drawes the line, makes it
            the least of our meaning to set in a Cloud, but to cleare all preceding
            stormes with a cheerefull calme. (Richard Brathwait, *The Two
            Lancashire Lovers* (1640), 275)

        b. Ismenia and Himself: but ever temper'd and allay'd with that Candor,
            as they ended ever with a Comical Conclusion: [...]   (Richard
            Brathwait, *Panthalia* (1659), 63)

Sense 5 of *comical* in the *OED* reads '[q]ueer, strange, odd', and is
labelled as 'colloquial'. One of the examples given here is "I think it likely he
may grant thy request, though, by my honour, it is a comical one!" (from Walter
Scott, *Quentin Durward* (1823), xxxi). This particular sense, appearing mostly in
nineteenth century English (but not labelled as either obsolete or archaic),
presents some problems as regards the analysis of corpus material. Although
some isolated examples of *comical* can be clearly said to represent this sense,
there can also be cases where even the context does not provide enough
information for distinguishing the sense 'strange' without any doubt or hesitation
from the sense 'amusing, ludicrous', especially when the amusement is
unintentional or unprovoked. The two senses are, in fact, "dangerously" close to
each other in that things considered ludicrous can often be ones that seem strange
or odd in one way or another: for example, in *LDEL, comical* is defined as 'of a
kind to excite laughter, esp because of a startlingly or unexpectedly humorous
impact'. In other words, the problem often seen in connection with the word
funny (i.e. "funny ha-ha or funny peculiar?") also applies to the interpretation of
comic and *comical* (cf. Marsden 1985: 28).
        Sense 5 of *comical* is further divided into subgroups, 5.b reading '"Queer"
in the sense of 'peculiar or disagreeable in temper or nature, difficult to deal with,
awkward, troublesome, dangerous'', a usage labelled as "dialectal".[8] This sense is
interesting in that *comical* can be said to involve a negative value judgement (as
noted by Copperud (1964) s.v. *comic, comical,* although he probably refers to
uses of *comical* in general instead of this sense specifically), while in most of the
other semantically differentiated *-ic/-ical* pairs, if one of the forms carries a
notion of value judgement, it tends to be regarded as positive (cf. Marsden's
(1985) analyses of e.g. *classic, economical,* and *historic*). Sense 5.c, 'strangely
out of sorts, unwell, ill', again a dialectal use, relates to physical conditions

---

8   A similar division of the senses of *comical*, along the lines of sense 5.a and 5.b of
the word in the *OED*, can be found in the *English Dialect Dictionary* s.v., which separates
between the more "general" sense 'odd, peculiar, singular, unusual; queer, cracky' (which
the *OED* labels "colloquial"), and the use describing a person's behaviour, i.e.
'disagreeable, queer in temper, captious, bad-tempered; pert, impertinent'.

considered untoward. These senses are still, according to native informants, currently used in some parts of Britain.

In more recent dictionaries, definitions of the two forms show a definite semantic distinction between *comic* and *comical*, in most cases along the lines of *comic* meaning both 'of comedy' and 'amusing', *comical* having the senses 'amusing', 'ludicrous', and 'strange or queer'. In usage manuals, a common generalization is that *comic* denotes the specific *aim* and *intention* to cause laughter, whereas *comical* describes the *effect*. This idea was probably first put forward by Fowler (1926; s.v. *comic, comical*), and later "reiterated" by e.g. Wood (1962), Tennant (1964), Clark (1987), and Greenbaum and Whitcut (1988). Other sources of the same type have different descriptions for basically the same thing, emphasizing more specifically that what is *comic* is usually intentional, whereas *comical* denotes unintentionally amusing things (see e.g. Clark 1990; Hardie 1991; Todd 1997), often neglecting cases of overlap, as in the sentence "It was a very comic/comical situation" given in Crystal (1991; s.v. *comic/comical*).

Comparing the usually rather generalizing treatments of *comic* and *comical* in usage manuals to the comments on other *-ic/-ical* pairs, one interesting observation can be made. No remark is made on the syntactic functions that the two adjective forms are likely to carry, as in the case of *magic* and *magical*, although one could point out the fact that only *comic* is now used in a sense which is predominantly classifying, i.e. 'of comedy' (e.g. *comic novelist*, where the adjective denotes a literary genre). In this sense, one could therefore expect that the adjective is rarely seen in a predicative position. As will be seen later with the pair *magic/magical*, the metaphorical use of the shorter form has become more frequent only relatively recently, whereas similarly "derived" or "extended" uses (i.e. 'amusing') of both *comic* and *comical* are older. It is possible that instances of both *comic* and *comical* in a predicative position when used in such senses may have had an effect on the overall perception of the adjectives' use, resulting in no comments regarding the syntactic functions of the words. One can also assume that the example of influential sources is an important factor: had the *OED*, for example, added the comment 'not in predicative use' to sense 1 of *comic*, a note arguably just as fitting and justifiable as it is in connection with *magic*, sense 1, we would probably have a great number of usage manuals emphasizing this very point distinguishing between *comic* and *comical* as well.

3.   Different uses of *comic/comical*

The following sections will discuss some of the senses of *comic/comical* in more detail, with special attention to problematic cases as regards the analysis of the corpus material, and the question of which factors can be seen as distinguishing between the two forms.

3.1   'Of or pertaining to comedy' – the comedy "establishment"

The sense 'of or pertaining to comedy', denoting a (literary) genre, is nowadays assigned only to *comic*, earlier centuries yielding instances of both forms with no difference in meaning:

(2)   a.   [...] accompanied with speach the common behauiours and maner of life of priuate persons, and such as were the meaner sort of men, and they were called Comicall Poets, of whom among the Greekes Menander and Aristophanes were most excellent, with the Latines Terence and Plautus. Besides those Poets Comick there wer other who serued also the stage, but medled not with so base matters: [...] (George Puttenham, *The Arte of English Poesie* (1589))

       b.   Yet many most worthy monuments of heauenly wits wanted the honor and safetie of this seate, for they were drowned in the abysse of Lethes silence, especially of the most ancient Graecian Authors, as Orpheus, Linus, the first Musaeus, Aratus, Nicander, Theogonis, Phocilides, and most of all the nine Lyriques, and Elegiacke and Comicke Poets, [...] (John Dickenson, *Arisbas* (1594), 54)

       c.   [...] or as Philistione a poet comicall, and Denis the tyraunt of Siracusa, with surpassing ioy made sodayne chaunge of life: [...]   (Brian Melbancke, *Philotimus* (1583), 199)

In the *OED*, the last citation of *comical* in this sense is from 1725. As in examples (2a–c), most instances of *comic/comical* of this type in the historical material studied related to people (usually poets), but other kinds of head words were also found, as in "Let me descend and stoope my verse a while, To make the Comicke cheeke of Poesie smile" (Thomas Dekker, *The Wonderfulle Yeare* (1603), 13).

Instances of the adjectives modifying nouns relating to the performance of comedy in other ways were also placed into this category, as e.g. *comic* in "The partnership of Fred and Ginger, which captivated millions, owed everything to her extraordinary comic fluency, her irrepressible glee and her carefree, exhilarating brashness" (*The Daily Telegraph*, Apr. 26, 1995, "Ginger Rogers, dancing queen of Hollywood, dies aged 83"), as well as in phrases like *comic timing/technique/instinct*, where the adjective functions first and foremost as a classifier, referring to the realm of comedy rather than describing the humorous quality of the referent. Supporting this view, it can be observed that in such phrases, *comic* is more typically preceded by an adjective modifying the whole noun phrase than an adverb modifying *comic* alone; note, for instance, in the previous *DTL* quote the phrase *extraordinary comic fluency* (instead of *extraordinarily comic fluency* or *extraordinary, comic fluency*; other similar examples attested include *natural comic instinct, marvellous comic techniques*, and relating to people, *a fine/very average comic novelist/talent*).

The same comments also apply to those cases where the head word denotes compositions and performances, e.g. novels, plays, shows, and duets.[9] In some cases, the context helps in determining whether the adjective – usually *comic* – denotes a type of composition or performance or whether it describes a mere humorous quality, as in examples (3a–d):

(3)   a.   Here is a social history of modern Britain cleverly disguised as an eccentric but thoroughly delightful comic novel.   (*The Sunday Telegraph*, Dec. 31, 1995, "Books: Paperbacks")

       b.   Littell's breezy, comic novel of ideas has a rather soft head, and a very gooey centre.   (*The Daily Telegraph*, Feb. 4, 1995, "Books: Paperbacks")

       c.   Orton combines the manic action with Wildean epigrams and John Alderton reveals himself to be an inspired farceur, with many moments of deliriously funny comic business.   (*The Daily Telegraph*, Mar. 11, 1995, "Theatre: Critic's Choice")

       d.   (headline + subheader:)   "The Arts: How to write life's wrongs – It's no joke having multiple sclerosis. Or is it?" With the help of Jimmy McGovern, author of Cracker, a sufferer has written an unflinchingly comic film, shown next week, says Stephen Pile (*The Daily Telegraph*, Aug. 17, 1995)

In example (3a), the adjective *delightful* seems to modify the phrase *comic novel* instead of just the noun *novel*, and *comic* in this case apparently denotes a kind or type of novel. The phrase is indeed generally used in such a sense, illustrated explicitly in the sentence "The 'comic novel' is one of the most embarrassing strands in English fiction, with scarcely a competent practitioner since Evelyn Waugh" (*The Daily Telegraph*, Sept. 16, 1995, "Books: Stick to cornflake

---

9   In the analysis of the corpora, the category involving the classifying sense 'of or having to do with comedy' is divided into different groups. One category includes instances denoting people involved in the production of comedy, such as writers and performers. Another category is devoted to cases designating the products, i.e. plays, performances, and novels. A separate and rather large category, labelled "others" in the tabular presentations, includes classifying instances having other kinds of connections with comedy, such as *comic(al) genius/instinct/talent*. One question related to categorizing different instances is what exactly is regarded as a composition, or a comedy performance. Only those instances were placed into the larger group 'of comedy' which involved a pre-planned intention for a work, book, play, song, etc. to be read or performed, leaving out cases such as *a comic look/glance* or other types of more immediate acts provoking laughter.

boxes").[10] In (3b), however, *comic* more clearly has the sense 'amusing'. A comparable pair of examples of the adjectives are (3c) and (3d), the former being analysed as relating to comedy, and the latter meaning 'amusing'. In explanations of the different uses of *comic* and *comical* in usage manuals, the use of *comic* as a label of genre has been noted, and illustrated even with striking observations such as "Something can be *comic*, in that it is intended to be funny, even if it fails to arouse mirth: *His comic songs did not raise a smile*" in *Bloomsbury Good Word Guide*, s.v. *comic or comical*.[11] It is again the context in the example sentence, negating the idea of the referent being amusing, which assists in identifying the sense of the adjective.[12]

   But what about cases where even the context leaves the matter of interpretation unsettled? For example, in the sentence "Vladimir Voinovich's comic novel of Soviet incompetence has been turned into a flavourless Europudding" (*The Sunday Telegraph*, Oct. 29, 1995, "The Arts: Warm front conceals heart of ice"), one cannot be absolutely certain whether the use of *comic* should be regarded as being like that in (3a) or (3b). In the present study, when *comic* modified head words denoting authors, actors, or compositions, only those cases where the context clearly gave reason to analyse the adjective as having the sense 'amusing' were categorised as such. Other instances, such as the abovementioned description of Vladimir Voinovich's novel, were in the tabular presentations placed into the class 'of or having to do with comedy' and its subclasses.

---

10   An earlier example illustrating the classifying use can be seen in "But to let my Reader into a Secret, this Knowledge of upper Life, though very necessary for the preventing Mistakes, is no very great Resource to a Writer whose Province is Comedy, or that Kind of Novels, which, like this I am writing, is of the comic Class" (Henry Fielding, *The History of Tom Jones* (1749), Vol. 5, 112).

11   In a similar vein, Bailie and Kitchin (1988) s.v. *comic, comical* observe that "[c]omic describes the aim, or intention, of causing laughter; *comical* describes the effect. A *comic actor* is one who sets out to perform humorous roles; a *comical actor* is a man whose every word and gesture causes mirth, whether intended or not." This comment could be criticized for drawing too sharp a contrast between the use of the two forms, as it – like many other similar generalizations – implies that *comic* is not used in the sense 'causing amusement'.

12   One could take a prescriptive point of view and argue that the adjective *comedic* might actually be quite useful in clarifying the semantic situation of *comic/comical* as regards classifying and descriptive uses. As the form of *comedic* itself suggests a closer relation to comedy, it would seem logical to reserve this word for the classifying, and *comic(al)* for the descriptive uses. The use of *comedic* (*comedical* being nowadays obsolete) has, however, never become so frequent as to replace *comic* in the sense of 'relating to comedy'; the *British National Corpus* contains only seven occurrences of *comedic*. Moreover, *comedic* has not completely escaped the sense of 'amusing' (or resembling rather than being comedy) either, as can be seen from the *OED* quotation "The wedding, which took place at Caxton Hall, was comedic" (from *Parade* (1962), 10, 24 June).

The cases categorized as relating to comedy – one could say instances having to do with "establishmentalized" or professional comedy – be it authors, compositions, or other types of words denoting a genre, involve a definite intention and aim to amuse, which, as seen earlier, is a central element of *comic* in present-day English, used by linguists to highlight the semantic differences between *comic* and *comical*. The uses of *comic* in cases such as *hilariously comic novel*, however, show that there is also a difference between a genre-type characterization and the idea that something is *genuinely* amusing, while having the intention to do so as well. The *OED* groups together those instances of *comic* relating to compositions (sense 2), and in its definition combines the notions 'aiming at a humorous or ridiculous effect' and 'funny'. The example quoted earlier of the possibility of comic songs not being funny also helps in illustrating the value of distinguishing between 'intended to be funny' and '(genuinely) funny': while it could be said that a comic novel was not amusing, the same cannot be said of a hilariously comic novel.

Similar observations can be made in regard to references to humorous productions such as plays, typical head words being *characters*, *parts*, *roles*, and *scenes*. It is possible to contrast between the aim to amuse on a professional level and the actual effect achieved, as in "Funny in principle, that is to say, since Richard Eyre's production is much stronger on fantasy than on humour: one big comic scene in particular, featuring a policeman, is terribly strained" (*The Sunday Telegraph*, July 16, 1995, "The Arts: Flint behind the smile").

3.2   'Amusing'

Considering the quotations given in the *OED*, *comical* was used in the sense 'amusing; causing mirth' (whether intentional or not) before *comic*, the first instance of *comical* dating from 1685, and that of *comic* from 1751. On the basis of the findings in the *Literature Online* material, however, one can assume that the "derived", descriptive sense (Warren (1984) uses the term "shifted") developed considerably earlier (see e.g. Tables 19 and 20).

In cases which do not involve the production of humour on a professional level, amusing things referred to as *comic* or *comical* may still be intentional, as in examples (4a) and (4b):

(4)   a. She took it very calmly. She glanced up at him with a comic glance in her eyes, and a twitch at the corners of her mouth. (Margaret Oliphant, *Salem Chapel* (1863), 182–183)

        b. The lad made a comical face at Job, which met with no responsive look from the old man, whose sympathies were naturally in favour of the parent; [...] (Elizabeth Gaskell, *Mary Barton* (1849), 166–167)

In *The Daily Telegraph* material, occurrences of this type in connection with glances, looks, expressions, etc. are fewer; instead, the sense 'amusing' with intention involved often have to do with humorous actions in theatrical productions, appearing in numerous reviews in the newspaper. While such cases may thus be also considered to have a connection with professional comedy, the adjectives included in this group have a descriptive rather than a classifying sense. In present-day English, *comical* is only rarely found when it is understood that the amusement caused has been intentional:

(5) But the rare occasions on which Mosley lowers his guard are richly rewarding. One is his graphic, marvellously comical account of a Freudian analysis conducted by a practitioner who mewed like a cat, hooted like a ship's whistle, or sat silent like a mermaid on a rock, and whose verdict was much the same as Mosley's father's: 'You're a greedy baby.' (*The Daily Telegraph*, Jan. 21, 1995, "Books: What me, with my sort of novels?")

As reported by several dictionaries and usage manuals, *comical* is nowadays found more often in cases where the thing considered amusing is unintentionally funny, the words 'ludicrous' and 'ridiculous' describing the referent equally well. However, instances of both forms can be found in such contexts:

(6) a. Instead, West Ham's defence began to wobble, with goalkeeper Ludek Miklosko's authority apparently diminished in a comic misunderstanding with Kenny Brown. (*The Daily Telegraph*, Jan. 16, 1995, "Soccer: Francis fires up Spurs to keep ambition burning")

     b. In a Disneyesque resort where the lakes are coloured blue, boulders are painted beige and even some of the grass is artificial, Faldo and Price were disqualified after comical mistakes during their third rounds. (*The Daily Telegraph*, Dec. 2, 1993, "Golf: Faldo and Price out to make amends")

It can be argued that the idea of intention or the lack of it behind whatever is considered amusing is not all that strongly immersed in the meanings of the adjectives *comic* and *comical* themselves, because it is not uncommon to find words such as *intentionally* or *unintentionally* modifying them:[13]

---

13 It appears that both *comic* and *comical* are used when modifying words which in themselves suggest unintentionality of the amusing element, e.g. *misunderstanding*, *mishap*, *mistake*, *error*, etc., and where the use of *comical* would be to some extent tautological (although avoiding tautology is not a strong element in the choice of the *-ic/-ical* forms, as seen in the phrase *historical past*).

(7)   a. Syntax certainly does not matter to Levi. He has many awkward and some incomprehensible sentences, besides a few unintentionally comic ones, such as this on Milton's second marital union, to Katherine Woodcock: 'The marriage must have been arranged, so he can never have seen her.' What, never? (*The Sunday Telegraph*, June 16, 1996, "Books: A magpie's Milton")

       b. In her work the oppressed and the marginalised won small victories over their circumstances through extreme and bizarre acts of resistance. The effect is intentionally comic, but also amounts to a serious plea for a more insane, but more tolerant, world. (*The Sunday Telegraph*, Mar. 21, 1993, "Books: Suburban dreams")

       c. Because the Left do not dare to criticise Tony Blair in public, their understandable frustration is expressed in unintentionally comical obituary notices for the modern Conservative intellectual ascendancy. (*The Sunday Telegraph*, Mar. 9, 1997, "Notebook: Heroes of the Thatcherite gulag")

Both forms also appear in contexts where the question of intention is irrelevant, as in the following examples, where there can be no intention involved:

(8)   a. Penguins have an enduring fascination that goes far beyond their comic appearance. (*The Sunday Telegraph*, July 18, 1993, "Travel: To boldly go with the ice floe")

       b. We could almost lean out and touch (but you mustn't, of course) the faintly comical and totally trusting little Fiordland Crested penguins. (*The Daily Telegraph*, Nov. 20, 1993, "Travel: Nothing too wild in this wilderness")

       c. There is something faintly comic about bananas, but there are few jokes in banana politics, as the behaviour of Geest has demostrated this week. (*The Daily Telegraph*, Sept. 22, 1995, "CITY COMMENT: Making a monkey out of banana talks")

One might therefore say that the use of the adjectives does not point to there being two separate meanings, that is, 'intentionally amusing' and 'unintentionally amusing'. Instead, the adjectives simply mean 'amusing'. Instances of both forms can be found in contexts suggesting either presence or absence of intention, and the potential difference between the two forms lies in whether one of the forms is used more often in one kind of context or the other.[14]

---

14   As regards the issue of the presence or absence of the intention to amuse in the use of *comic/comical* in the sense of 'amusing', an important note must be made on the

Complicating the larger picture somewhat, there are cases where notions of intentionality and unintentionality working on different levels become mixed, especially in films, plays, etc., where a person or thing has been deliberately, and with the aim of amusing, written as being unintentionally amusing. One example of such a case would be "High hopes of British success at the Oscars were dashed on Monday night when Forrest Gump – a schmaltzy Hollywood movie about a comic simpleton – took the principal awards" (*The Daily Telegraph*, Mar. 29, 1995, "British Oscar hopes sunk by Tinseltown schmaltz"). This particular instance of *comic* is perhaps best analysed as being unintentional as regards the amusement, viewed from the perspective of the storyline (what it is about), as suggested in the sentence itself.

3.3   'Strange'

As mentioned earlier, it may not always be easy to distinguish between the senses 'amusing' without intention and 'strange', as the strangeness may sometimes be the very cause of laughter. There are some cases, however, where the context implies a sense of negative value judgement as well as the notion of the thing in question being somehow out of place (the uses in the examples below are possibly dialectal as well):

(9)   a. 'No, your honour, I hope I'm not a person as bears malice; only I could not but speak of it, because he behaves more comical every day. I thought he'd ha' beat me over and over. And as to the stories he tells about them little bits of paper, mortal patience can't bear it no longer.' (Fanny Burney, *Camilla* (1796), 127)

       b. 'O, that's another thing; if the young lady's sorry, I sha'n't think of holding out. Besides, I can't say but what I thought her agreeable enough, if it had not been for her behaving so comical just at the last. Not that I mean in the least to make any complaint, by way of getting of the young lady scolded.' (Fanny Burney, *Camilla* (1796), 290)

---

categorizations in the tabular presentations. It is argued here that the use of *comic/comical* does not involve two separate meanings 'intentionally amusing' and 'unintentionally amusing', but that the use of the forms has been differentiated according to the contexts in which the humour is either intentional or not. However, to examine the latter question, the occurrences of the adjectives have been divided into cases in which the amusement can be regarded (on the basis of the context) as being caused intentionally and those where amusement appears to have been either unintentional, or the question of intention is irrelevant, as in examples (8a–c).

There are further instances where the thing referred to as being *comic(al)* is also considered strange, but with an overall notion of amiableness rather than derision, as in example (10):

(10)   'I conjecture', says Jones, 'that thou art a very comical Fellow.' [...] 'Upon my Word,' cries Jones, 'thou art a very odd Fellow, and I like thy Humour extremely [...]' (Henry Fielding, *The History of Tom Jones* (1749), Vol. 3, 169-70)

Evans and Evans (1957) s.v. *comic and comical* note that while both forms mean 'amusing', '*comical* has a slightly different application sometimes, meaning quaint, in a tender way: *such a comical little face*'. In the present study, those instances which involve a definite sense of abnormality and a negative value judgement were categorized as having the sense 'strange', while instances of *comic/comical*, referring to people having no evident intention to amuse as in (10), but viewed in a positive light, are in the tabular presentations given as a separate subgroup under the sense 'amusing'.

4.   *Comic/comical* in the material studied

The *Literature Online* material from 1513–1599 contains a fairly low number of occurrences of *comic* and *comical*, all of them from the latter half of the sixteenth century. The figures presented in Table 19 do not show any remarkable differences between the two forms, except that only *comical* was used in the sense 'happy' or 'fortunate', as in "they were all glad to see such a comical fortune of Rowland" (in Anonymous, *The Cobler of Caunterburie* (1590), 53).

Table 19. *Comic/comical* in the prose section of *Literature Online,* 1513–1599.

	comic	*comical*
1. 'of (the production of) comedy or humorous works'		
a. authors or performers	3	3
b. products or performances	1	2
c. others	-	3 (1)
2. 'happy', 'fortunate'	-	7 (1)
3. 'amusing' (intentional)	-	3
total	**4**	**18 (2)**
# of authors (+ anonymous):	4	10 (1)
# of authors using both forms: 2		

The predicative instance of *comical* in the category 'of comedy: others' could also be paraphrased as 'befitting comedy'. It is, however, not in complete agreement with the negative sense in the *OED* s.v. *comical*, sense 2 having the same paraphrase, because the additional notion of 'undignified' is absent. Instead, the predicative occurrence involves comedy in the more classifying or labelling sense of a stage performance intended to amuse the audience:

(11)   I had heard that the Kings Players were learning a play of Esops Crowe, wherin the moste part of the actors were birds, the deuice wherof I discommended, saying it was not Comicall to make either speechlesse things to speeke: or brutish things to commen resonably. And although in a tale it be sufferable to immagin and tel of some thing by them spoken or reasonably doon (which kinde Esope lawdably vsed) yet it was vncomely (said I) and with out example of any authour to bring them in liuely parsonages to speake, doo, reason, and allege authorites out of authours. (William Baldwin, *Beware the Cat* (1584), 5)

Comic/comical in the seventeenth century prose works in the *Literature Online* material show a situation to a great extent similar to that of the previous century, with only a greater number of occurrences. In both Tables 19 and 20, a notable feature is that only the longer form appears in a predicative position. In addition, *comical* appears in both tables to have been the favoured form in the sense of 'amusing', but the figures and the numbers of authors using the adjectives in this sense are fairly low.

Table 20. *Comic/comical* in the prose section of *Literature Online,* 1600–1699.

	comic	*comical*
1. 'of (the production of) comedy or humorous works'		
a. authors or performers	-	1 (1)
b. products or performances	4	4
c. others	1	1
2. 'happy', 'fortunate'	2	8 (1)
3. 'low', 'undignified'	-	1
4. 'amusing'		
a. intentional	1	13 (3)
b. others (not intentional)	-	5 (2)
total	**8**	**33 (7)**
# of authors (+ anonymous):	5	14 (4)
# of authors using both forms: 3		

Table 21, representing the uses of *comic/comical* in the eighteenth century, shows clearer signs of semantic differentiation between the two forms. In this period, *comic* was the favoured form when referring to writers producing comedy, or their works themselves, i.e. denoting the type or genre of writing or performance. The significance of this change is remarkable, as it is probably also a major factor behind the overall increase in the use of the shorter form. The use of the words in the sense 'happy' or 'fortunate', which may be considered a somewhat secondary meaning, having to do with mere resemblance to comedy rather than actually being comedy, has by now become obsolete, or at least occurrences of the type were not found in the eighteenth century material studied. Both forms are used, however, in the other sense resembling the actual thing, i.e. 'amusing', for which *comical* is still found more often, whether the amusement has been intentional or unintentional.

Table 21. *Comic/comical* in the prose section of *Literature Online*, 1700–1799.

	comic	comical
1. 'of (the production of) comedy or humorous works'		
a. authors or performers	10	-
b. products or performances	11 (1)	4 (1)
c. relating to parts of plays, novels, etc. (*characters, roles, scenes,* etc.)	7	-
d. others	2	1
2. 'amusing'		
a. intentional	9 (1)	16 (2)
b. others (not intentional)	9 (2)	33 (12)
b'. people: 'amusing, pleasant'	1	12 (1)
3. 'strange'	-	9 (6)
total	**49 (4)**	**75 (22)**
# of authors:	13	18
# of authors using both forms: 11		

It is also interesting to note that in the sense 'amusing', *comical* appears in the eighteenth century material somewhat more often in contexts where the amusement was not intentional. Moreover, while the longer form had become less frequent relating to professional comedy or the general concept as a whole, it was gaining new ground in a semantically extended use, i.e. when relating to things considered strange or somehow out-of-place, with a pointedly negative loading.

The semantic differentiation between the forms also becomes evident when examining their use as regards individual authors. Out of the 13 authors using the form *comic*, 11 used *comical* as well. But to a great extent, the authors having both forms in their repertoire used the words in different senses: for example, in the works of Charles Richardson and Henry Fielding, *comic* is clearly the favoured form when relating to comedy on a professional level, whereas the longer form occurs in the more descriptive sense 'amusing'. This observation also underlines the diminishing significance of the absolute numbers of occurrences of *comic* and *comical* in relation to each other, although the total figures are nevertheless important in reflecting the extent to which the forms are used in general.

In the material from the nineteenth century (Tables 22 and 23), one can see a differentiation of the two forms along the same lines as in the eighteenth century works, with *comical* becoming obsolete with reference to professional comedy.[15] A thing worth noting is the relative increase in the use of *comic* in the sense 'amusing', whether the amusing element had been deliberately brought forth or not (although *comical* is somewhat more frequent than *comic* when no intention is involved). Along with this increase of *comic*, the number of its occurrences in a predicative position has risen. *Comical* is still found in the negative sense 'strange', although the figures for this use of the word are relatively low.

Table 22. *Comic/comical* in the prose section of *Literature Online*, 1800–1849.

	comic	comical
1. 'of (the production of) comedy or humorous works'		
a. authors or performers	6	-
b. products or performances	27	1
c. relating to parts of plays, novels, etc. (*characters, roles, scenes*, etc.)	5	-
d. others	22	-
2. 'amusing'		
a. intentional	27 (6)	31 (3)
b. others (not intentional)	19 (3)	27 (8)
b'. people: 'amusing, pleasant'	-	7
3. 'strange'	-	1
total	**106 (9)**	**67 (11)**
# of authors:	12	16
# of authors using both forms: 7		

15   In Table 22, the figure denoting the occurrences of *comic* in the sense 'of comedy' relating to products is affected to some extent by the numerous instances of the use of the phrase *comic song* in the works by Charles Dickens (10 occurrences). This does not, however, have a significant effect on the overall analysis of the figures of *comic/comical* in such cases, as *comic* is clearly the favoured form. Similarly, the group "others" under the sense group 'of comedy' includes 13 instances of the phrase *comic muse* – a phrase which has become fixed relatively early – in Maria Edgeworth's books, which does not drastically alter the overall conclusions either.

Table 23. *Comic/comical* in the prose section of *Literature Online,* 1850–1903.

	comic	comical
1. 'of (the production of) comedy or humorous works'		
a. authors or performers	9	-
b. products or performances	38	-
c. relating to parts of plays, novels, etc. (*characters, roles, scenes,* etc.)	3	-
d. others	19	-
2. 'amusing'		
a. intentional	51 (1)	32 (8)
b. others (not intentional)	36 (15)	55 (20)
b'. people: 'amusing, pleasant'	-	5
3. 'strange'	-	5 (4)
total	**156 (16)**	**97 (32)**
# of authors:	28	26
# of authors using both forms: 17		

As regards the semantic differentiation between the adjectives appearing in the works of individual authors, some writers, while using only the shorter form in connection with theatrical productions and other "professional" contexts., did not necessarily make a strict distinction between other types of things causing amusement (as distinct from the theatre), i.e. intentionally versus unintentionally amusing things. For example, in the following extracts by William Thackeray, both *comic* and *comical* are used in the same way in comparable contexts:

(12)   a. 'Lead on, Laura,' Pen said, with a half fierce, half comic air – 'Lead on, and say I wait upon my uncle.' (William Thackeray, *The History of Pendennis* (1849), 66)

b. As for Mr. Tummas, he, as we have seen, was quite as unfriendly to the proposition as she could be; and the corporal, with a good deal of comical gravity, vowed that, as he could not be satisfied in his dearest wisher, he would take to drinking for a consolation, which he straightway did. (William Thackeray, *Catherine* (1839), 697)

Turning to the present-day situation, and the uses of the adjectives in the 1995 issues of *The Daily Telegraph,* presented in Table 24, the distinction between the two forms is remarkably similar to the one seen in the *Literature Online* material in the latter half of the nineteenth century, a development which, as has been observed above, was first visible in the eighteenth century works.

Comparing Tables 23 and 24, one difference in the present-day material is that no instances of *comical* were found which suggested a clear negative value judgement.

As seen in Table 24, only *comic* is nowadays used when referring to comedy as a genre or things relating to professional comedy. Some new phrases with *comic* have emerged, such as *comic strip*, used of a strip cartoon in a newspaper, magazine, etc.[16] Considering the subsections of the sense 'of comedy' more closely, when referring to people involved in the production of comedy, the most frequent head words modified by *comic* in the material were *actor/actress* (23 occurrences), *genius* (14), *writer* (10), and *novelist* (9).

Table 24. *Comic/comical* in the 1995 issues of *The Daily Telegraph*.

	comic	*comical*
1. 'of (the production of) comedy or humorous works'		
a. authors or performers	81	-
b. products or performances	124	-
~ *strip*	62	-
c. relating to parts of plays, novels, etc. (*characters, roles, scenes*, etc.)	67	-
d. others	131	-
2. 'amusing'		
a. intentional	114 (19)	16 (3)
b. others (not intentional)	127 (26)	52 (23)
total	**706 (45)**	**68 (26)**

The most frequently encountered head words designating products include *masterpiece* (15 occurrences), *novel* (14), and *opera* (14), while the cases categorized in the group 'others' exhibit a large variety of head words, often referring to technical aspects in performing comedy, as in e.g. *comic timing* (13 occurrences), or abilities and talents as regards comedy in a wider sense, e.g. *comic genius* (4 occurrences). The genre-labelling or classifying function can also be seen in the fact that *comic* in such instances is rarely found in a predicative position (thus validating to some extent the choices made in setting up the different semantic categories, and the principles used in the analysis).

The figures denoting the occurrences of *comic* and *comical* in the sense 'amusing' show that when coming across an instance of *comical* in present-day English, one is more likely to see the word appearing in a context which suggests that the amusement caused was unintentional rather than intentional. This finding

---

16   The phrase *comic book* was excluded from the analysis, as *comic* could here also be considered to be a noun (a book of comics).

may be considered to be in line with the comments often seen in usage manuals. However, the corresponding figures for *comic* show that in similar contexts one is actually likely to find *comic* rather than *comical*, and that *comic* – at least in the newspaper material – is not at all rare in those contexts when compared to situations which do suggest intentionality. This gives reason for criticism towards the comments made in some usage manuals: whether the thing raising mirth was intentional or not does not itself seem to be a thing which clearly and conclusively distinguishes the uses of *comic* and *comical* from one another. The same argument can be made based on the results from earlier corpus materials, such as the nineteenth century material in *Literature Online*.

It is possible that the comments emphasizing the unintentional origin of laughter connoted by the use of *comical* stem from a notion that the situations which the word describes are somehow more ridiculous or embarrassing than those where one would use *comic*. In line with this argument, one could then hypothesize that potentially more "neutral" cases such as *she was good at seeing the comic(al) side of things* would allow variation more easily than instances involving a stronger sense of ludicrousness or even embarrassment, as in *she was wearing an incredibly comic(al) hat*. As it would be very difficult indeed to attempt to measure in some way the level of ridicule or embarrassment involved in unintentionally funny things, one has to settle for the basic division of intentional versus unintentional, especially as upon analysing the material, the instances themselves did not suggest that such a difference between the forms would exist.

Considering the total numbers of uses of *comic* and *comical* in *The Daily Telegraph* material, the figures suggest that *comical* is indeed nowadays considerably less frequent than *comic*. When comparing these results to the corresponding figures in Table 23, representing the use of the adjectives between 1850 and 1903, one might conclude that the longer form is disappearing from use. The same ratio of roughly 10:1 in favour of *comic* was also observed in all the yearly issues of the newspaper on CD-ROM between the years 1993 and 1999. In order to further examine the question whether *comical* is, in fact, dying out, it is useful to take a closer look into the use of *comic/comical* in the *British National Corpus*. In the *BNC*, the overall ratio between the occurrences of the adjectives – including all spoken and written domains – is approximately 6:1, i.e. slightly different from that in the *DTL* material. It is obvious that the figures observed in the three corpora are not totally comparable, as the kinds of texts included in them are remarkably different. Examining the numbers of uses of the adjectives in different domains of written material shows the variation in the relation between the frequencies of *comic* and *comical*. Table 25 presents the absolute numbers of occurrences and the numbers of occurrences per one million words of *comic* and *comical* in the *BNC*. The figures given in parentheses denote the numbers of texts in which the adjectives appeared.

Table 25. *Comic/comical* in different domains of written language in the *British National Corpus*.

A = # of occurrences
B = # of occurrences per 1 million words

	comic		comical	
	A	B	A	B
1. Imaginative	82 (64)	5.0	53 (44)	3.2
2. Natural and pure sciences	3 (3)	0.8	-	-
3. Applied sciences	8 (6)	1.1	4 (2)	0.6
4. Social sciences	53 (30)	3.8	4 (4)	0.3
5. World affairs	91 (55)	5.3	8 (8)	0.5
6. Commerce and finance	5 (4)	0.7	4 (3)	0.6
7. Arts	382 (115)	58.6	24 (19)	3.7
8. Belief and thought	15 (8)	5.0	3 (3)	1.0
9. Leisure	66 (49)	5.4	20 (15)	1.6
total	**705 (334)**	**8.1**	**120 (98)**	**1.4**

In the light of the figures in Table 25, the relations between the frequencies of *comic* and *comical* in different written domains can be said to vary to a significant degree. In some written domains, e.g. "Social sciences", "World affairs", and "Arts", the ratio is approximately the same as in *The Daily Telegraph* material. Considering the types of texts in these three domains, the correlation between them and the *DTL* material seems rather logical, as the newspaper contains a great many articles on social sciences, world affairs, and the arts, and, on the other hand, the three domains in the *BNC* contain articles from newspapers (e.g. *The Daily Telegraph* and *The Independent*) and magazines (e.g. *The Face*). In these types of texts, one is perhaps more likely to come across references to comedy as a genre compared to other text domains, which explains the considerably higher frequency of *comic*.

With the domains "Imaginative" and "Leisure", however, the difference between the frequencies of the two forms is much narrower. The domain "Imaginative" is particularly interesting, as it consists mainly of fictional writings, thus being somewhat more comparable to the *Literature Online* material. Considering the numbers of authors using *comic/comical* in the latter half of the nineteenth century (28 using *comic*, and 26 using *comical*), and the numbers of texts including the adjectives in the "Imaginative" domain in the *BNC*, the use of *comical* does seem to have become less frequent (64 texts including *comic*, 44 *comical*). To examine the viability of *comical*, it is therefore useful, as well as feasible, to look more closely into the uses of *comic/comical* in greater detail in the written domain "Imaginative". An analysis of the texts in this domain, presented in Table 26, shows indeed a situation reminiscent of that in

Table 23, especially when we consider the relation between the numbers of occurrences of the two adjectives in the different senses:

Table 26.   *Comic/comical* in the written language domain "Imaginative" in the *British National Corpus*.

	comic	*comical*
1. 'of (the production of) comedy or humorous works'		
a. authors or performers	2	-
b. products or performances	12	-
~ *strip*	2	-
c. relating to parts of plays, novels, etc. (*characters, roles, scenes*, etc.)	2	-
d. others	7	-
2. 'amusing'		
a. intentional	27 (3)	5
b. others (not intentional)	25 (18)	47 (35)
b'. people: 'amusing, pleasant'	2	1
3. 'strange'	-	9 (6)
total	**79 (21)**	**53 (35)**
# of texts:	64	44
# of texts containing both forms: 11		

As regards the major differences between the uses of *comic* and *comical*, the figures in Table 26 are also very similar to those for *The Daily Telegraph* material in that *comic* is clearly the preferred form when relating to professional comedy, while there is some variation between the two forms in the descriptive sense 'amusing'.

The difference between the frequencies of *comic* and *comical* (or between the numbers of texts they occur in) in the 'Imaginative" domain does not seem drastic enough to suggest that *comical* is steadily heading towards extinction. However, it would appear that the relation between the frequencies of the adjective forms depends on the type of text. It is possible that in present-day English, the use of *comical* in the sense 'amusing', when relating to unintentionally amusing things, is preserved in fictional writings, while in other types of texts, *comic* is used more often in all kinds of contexts. The changes in the use of *comic/comical* in the historical text material, consisting also of fictional writing, suggest that *comical* was originally the "stronger", more frequently used form, but gradually lost its ground in almost all meanings. One can assume that similar changes to the ones noted have in the course of time occurred in other types of texts as well – and judging from the analysis of *The Daily Telegraph* material, the results of the changes are certainly visible in present-day English – although the lack of sufficiently large corpora of non-fiction texts from earlier centuries makes it difficult to say anything conclusive about the overall rate of fading away of *comical*.

5.   General remarks

The use of *comic* and *comical* from the sixteenth century to the present day, as seen from the corpus material examined, shows a number of changes which are most interesting as regards their sharpness and drasticness. The uniformity in using *comic* for professional aspects of comedy in a classifying manner in the eighteenth century material, as opposed to the texts from the earlier centuries, is remarkable, even when taking into account the smaller size of the corpora from 1513–1699. It is difficult to find obvious reasons for this preference for *comic* developing particularly during this period, or towards the end of the seventeenth century, or at least becoming visible in fictional prose works of the period. It might be somewhat adventurous, although fascinating, to attempt to explain this development by looking into the history of the theatre, and the attitudes towards comedy as a dramatic or literary genre. As such, however, it is no great surprise that the differentiation between the two forms should have developed along those lines, as the professional aspect of comedy is conceptually an area quite easy to perceive as constituting a separate unity. The choice of *comic* rather than *comical* can perhaps be at least partially explained by the overall increase in the use of the forms in *-ic* in the seventeenth and eighteenth centuries, the effect of which may thus have led to major shifts in preference in already existing senses.

Considering the descriptive sense 'amusing', the generalizing comments in some usage manuals, as well as the implications in the *OED* definitions, may be regarded as overstating the difference between the two forms, because the corpora examined give evidence of both *comic* and *comical* being used whether the referent was intended to be funny or not. In other words, a characteristic rather describing the more typical context of use of the longer form has to some extent been misleadingly emphasized as presenting a clear and definite difference between the two forms. On the other hand, the fact that there can be different perspectives from which to view the source of amusement itself, and the reasons behind it, may to a degree explain why neither of the forms became so clearly established or fixed when used in this sense as *comic* did in the genre-marking sense.

One interesting question is the "old-fashionedness" of *comical*, of which only the lower relative frequency compared to *comic* in present-day English serves as partial or secondary evidence. Considering that the ratio of the frequency of the two forms differs according to the type of text, it could be asked whether the notion of "old-fashionedness" is, in fact, genre-related or genre-dependent, which as an idea admittedly seems rather awkward. The issue is undoubtedly related to subject matter, as in some types of texts, for example, one would not necessarily expect to see descriptions of unintentionally amusing situations. On the other hand, it does not seem very likely that factors such as low frequency in some types of texts *alone* would lead one to consider a word old-fashioned in general. There are, in fact, other changes in the overall use of *comic/comical* which may have contributed to the notion. As noted in the previous sections, *comical* has in the course of its history had more uses than *comic* which have become obsolete, both classifying and descriptive. It is also possible that *comical* having dialectal uses, and consequently observed as being partly dialectal, has become a "marked" form, the mark or label then perhaps being so weighty as to result in a gradual disappearance of the word in all of its senses. While the effect of such factors is very difficult to determine with the aid of the corpora presently available, they may at least be regarded as some of the possible reasons behind the notion of the old-fashionedness of *comical*. There seem to be no other obvious reasons or indications for *comical* all of a sudden losing its vitality or useability as far as the semantic field of comedy or amusement is concerned.

In the analysis of this particular adjective pair, it was also seen that the number of occurrences in the historical non-fiction texts was too low to enable observations on the uses of the words in previous centuries in written genres other than fiction. It is therefore possible that an examination of larger corpora of historical non-fiction texts might reveal other kinds of features in the use of *comic/comical*.

Chapter 7

Arranging the motions of resources: *economic/ economical*

The adjectives *economic/economical* constitute a word pair which has been considered by some linguists to be among the most clearly differentiated *-ic/-ical* pairs as regards the semantics of the two forms, second only to *politic/political* (Fowler 1926 s.v. *-ic, -ical*). In present-day English, a distinction between the forms is made in that the shorter form is generally considered to relate to economics or the economy, while the *-ical* form means 'not wasting money, careful, frugal'. It is notable that the development in the use of the adjectives has resulted in the pair carrying only two central meanings (if one does not make a closer distinction between different aspects relating to economics in connection with *economic*, or single out the use of the adjectives in the sense 'profitable'); as will be shown, the pair has also had other uses, most of which have more or less disappeared.

Some usage manuals include comments on the use of *economic/ economical* which would seem to suggest a rather toned-down view compared to the one above, namely that both forms are frequently confused, and used in contexts where one would usually expect the other form (e.g. Barber 1964: 114; Room 1985 s.v. *economic/economical*; *Bloomsbury Good Word Guide* s.v. *economic/economical*). Crystal (1991; s.v. *economic/economical*) in turn claims that one is more likely to see *economic* used in the sense 'thrifty, frugal' than the *-ical* form in the classifying sense. From the perspective of present-day English, the overall differentiation between the two forms would not at the outset seem to be a question of any great controversy or complexity, but examining the corpus data nevertheless sheds some light on the issue of the extent of overlap or "slips of the tongue". Some instances were found in the material where both forms were used synonymously in the same text:

(1)   Friday, August 21   9st 4, cigarettes 4 (vg), minutes worrying the Russian economic crisis also 4, minutes obsessing the Corfu villa brochures 400. [...] Jude could not get out of the City because of the Russian economical crisis so it is just me, Mark and Shaz. (*The Daily Telegraph*, Aug. 29, 1998, "Bridget Jones's Diary")[1]

---

1   This example, in fact, involves an important point: it is, in fact, possible that the synonymous use of the words *economic* and *economical* was fully intentional from the part of the author Helen Fielding, so that the variation was "in line" with Bridget Jones' overall character. Whether this is actually the case or not is impossible to say without consulting

One can also encounter cases where both forms are likewise used in the same text, but with different meanings, as in the following extract, in which the adjectives even have an identical referent (i.e. a car):

(2)   Ford Ka Step 1: turbocharged diesel capable of more than 100 mpg. Not economic for mass market production. [...] Mitsubishi Carisma GDI: one of the few cars in mass production. Fuel economy from gasolene direct injection goes up 20 per cent, making it as economical as diesel, or a 10 per cent improvement in power. (*The Daily Telegraph*, Apr. 25, 1998, "Lean, green, and very seldom seen")

In extract (2), the adjective *economic* may be regarded as having the sense 'profitable', relating to the viewpoint of the producer, whereas the ensuing *-ical* form pertains to the perspective of the consumer, and the adjective describing the car means 'not wasteful'.

The corpora examined contained a fairly large number of occurrences of the adjectives with the prefix *un-*, which will also be discussed in the present chapter. Special attention will be given to the meanings carried by *uneconomic* and *uneconomical* in relation to those established for the base forms.

1.   Etymology and early history of the pair

The origins of the pair *economic/economical* go back to the Greek adjective *οἰκονομικός*, Latin *oeconomicus*, and the French *économique*. The etymological information on *economic* in the *OED* s.v. includes the comment "[t]he Fr. *économique* is of earlier date [than the English *economic(al)*], and may have been the first source of the Eng. word". This remark is interesting in that similar comments do not appear in many entries for *-ic/-ical* words in the dictionary. The claim on French possibly being the immediate origin – which itself is an issue perhaps of minor importance only as regards the later developments in the use of the English adjectives – may be partly explained by the fact that the first citation of *economic* (nominal use, relating to 'housekeeping') from 1393 has the French *-ique* spelling rather than the Anglicized form. The first citations of the adjectives *economic* and *economical* date from 1592 and 1577, respectively, but Bailey

---

the author herself. The problem is also closely related to the notion of different levels of the narrative (both in works of fiction or non-fiction), as discussed in connection with the adjective pair *comic/comical* in Chapter 6. These instances illustrate one of the limitations of corpus analysis. Even though we may have a large number of authentic instances at our disposal for semantic analysis, the element of irony or the deliberateness in the use of anachronisms are features that inevitably escape the linguist, since determining their involvement often requires consulting the author. (I am very grateful to Professor Laurie Bauer for the discussion on these issues in connection with this example.)

(1978) s.v. gives an earlier instance of *economical* from circa 1485. According to the second edition of *Le grand Robert de la langue française* s.v. *économique*, the earliest recorded instance of the French word dates from 1371.[2] However, mere observations of the prior existence of the word or some of its uses in French should obviously not be regarded as sufficient evidence that French was the immediate source for the English adjectives.

The ultimate origin of the words is, of course, Greek, the adjective having been derived from the noun *οίκονόμος* 'steward', which itself consists of the parts *οίκό-ς* 'house' and *-νόμος* (derived from *νέμειν* 'to manage'; see e.g. the *OED* s.v. *economy*, or Liddell & Scott (1940) s.v. *οίκονόμέω*). Some of the present-day senses of the English *economic* and *economical* appeared already in Classical Greek: for example, according to Liddell & Scott's dictionary of Greek, *οίκονομικός* was used in the sense 'not wasteful' by e.g. the philosopher Xenophon.

Different aspects relating to things denoted by the original roots of the Greek word, namely, 'house' and 'to manage', have resulted in different types of uses of the adjectives in Greek, Latin, French, and English (cf. the numerous meanings of the noun *economy* listed in the *OED* s.v.). One problem in analysing the use of *economic/economical* has to do with interpreting the scope of reference, i.e. judging whether comments are being made on the management of an individual person, a household, family, community, village, town or a country, and whether the idea of management relates to financial aspects or management of affairs in general. For example, Aristotle's thesis *Οίκονομικός* is regarded by Liddell and Scott (1940) s.v. *οίκονόμέω* as dealing with 'public finance', whereas the *OED* s.v. *economic, sb*, sense 2, gives the quotation "Aristotle . . in his Œconomikes . . biddeth us to rise before the day" (from Cogan, *Haven Health* (1636, originally written in 1586), 16) under the sense 'the science or art of managing *a household*' (emphasis mine).

The mere notion of 'management', with its opposite relating to things which are not managed, arranged, or organized, has brought along an almost inherent sense of positive value judgement, which is more or less visible in some uses of the adjectives. For example, the Latin dictionary by Lewis and Short (1879) s.v. *oeconomicus* defines one meaning of the adjective with the paraphrase 'of or belonging to a proper (oratorical) division or arrangement; orderly;

---

2   Considering the individual meanings of *economic/economical*, it does not seem that the influence of French has been consistent since the first appearance of the English adjectives. That is, all of the senses of the French adjective *économique* do not seem to have appeared before they did for the English words – at least if we judge the matter by the first recorded senses of the words presented in dictionaries. For example, according to the *Robert* dictionary the sense 'careful; not wasteful' is first recorded for the word *économique* in 1690, while in a considerably earlier example quoted in Bailey (1978) s.v. *economical*, "he shewed to theym by his Informac[i]on the meanes & wayes[,] how they sholde brewe theyr drynke & make ale of barley thurgh ycomonycal prouysion and good husbondrye to make therof malte" (from John Skelton, *Diodorus* (tr.; c1485) book iv, folio 227r), *economical* seems to carry this very sense.

methodical'. The *OED* includes a more neutral-seeming sense 'pertaining to an organization' under the entry for *economical* (sense 5.b), but almost all the examples provided relate to the organization of heaven, which being divine could not be anything else than well-ordered and thus involving a positive value judgement. On the other hand, references to heaven, seen as "a house of God", would thus also involve the notion of pertaining to the management of a household. A positive attitude is similarly evident in the *OED* (s.v. *economical*, sense 1.a) quote "Oeconomicall science, that is . . the art of ruling a house *well*" (from T.B., tr., *The French Academie* (1586), I, 493; emphasis mine), although the *OED* definition under which it appears is itself more neutral, 'pertaining to a household or its management'. In present-day English, the use of *economical* in the sense 'not wasteful; careful' usually involves a positive value judgement, as noted by Evans and Evans (1957; s.v. *economical; thrifty; frugal; stingy; miserly*), with some exceptional ironic uses, as in "Were velvet to become as cheap as cloth, it would not be worn by the higher classes; its greater durability would make it too economical for them, and its adoption by the lower classes would render it vulgar" (John Rae, *Statement of Some New Principles on the Subject of Political Economy* (1834), Chapter XI).

As noted earlier, the nominal use of *economic*, in the sense 'the art or science of managing a household', preceded the adoption of the adjectives *economic* and *economical* (preceding also the noun *economy* in the same sense, first attested in an *OED* quotation dated 1530). The noun soon came to be used mostly in the plural form. Marchand (1969: 241) names *economic/economical* as an exception to his observation according to which the origin of the -*ical* suffix is in general "to be sought in adjectival derivations from names of sciences in -*ic*". As noted in Chapter 3, Marchand observed that many -*ical* adjectives preceded the -*ic* forms if there was an already existing noun ending in -*ic*. In the case of this particular word pair, Marchand's analysis of the *OED* seems to have been somewhat inaccurate, as even according to the dictionary, the form in -*ical* did indeed precede the adjectival -*ic* form. The relation between the nominal use of *economic(s)* and the two adjective forms is, however, a rather complicated issue: although the first citation of the nominal use dates from 1393, the second instance quoted in the dictionary is from 1586 (i.e. from roughly the same time when the two adjective forms are first attested), which raises some questions about the actual extent of the usage of the words, and about the nominal use having had any effect on the use of the -*ic*/-*ical* adjective forms.

Both the *Literature Online* texts and the non-fiction material culled from the Internet included only a few occurrences of *economic* and *economical* between the late sixteenth and early nineteenth century. The adjectives appeared more frequently in the non-fiction material considering the relative sizes of the corpora, as seen from Tables 27 and 28 below (representing the numbers of occurrences of *economic/economical* in different periods, with the numbers of authors given in parentheses).[3]

Table 27. *Economic/economical* in the prose section of the *Literature Online* corpus, 1550–1903.

	1513–1599	1600–1699	1700–1799	1800–1849	1850–1903
economic	-	1 (1)	-	6 (4)	11 (5)
economical	-	1 (1)	14 (8)	52 (20)	60 (20)
authors using both forms	-	1	-	4	3

Table 28. *Economic/economical* in the non-fiction texts examined (British authors), 1550–1899.

	1550–1599	1600–1699	1700–1799	1800–1849	1850–1899
economic	-	4 (3)	-	1 (1)	130 (6)
economical	-	5 (1)	10 (5)	51 (14)	50 (10)
authors using both forms	-	-	-	1	3

Considering the numbers of occurrences in Tables 27 and 28, it must be said that until the nineteenth century, the material does not provide enough instances of the two adjectives' use for drawing any far-reaching conclusions. However, as will be seen in subsequent sections, the nineteenth century material does include instances which are interesting as regards the developments in the adjectives' use. Of special interest are the differences between the fiction and non-fiction material, which partly reflect the fact that the late eighteenth century and the whole of the nineteenth century saw a significant boost in the overall conception of the science of economics in the sense that it is understood today. The "boost" is visible also in the fact that although the non-fiction material also contains seventeenth and eighteenth-century texts which deal with topics such as trade, taxation, and stability of currency (by writers like Edward Misselden, Dudley North, John Graunt, John Locke, and William Petty), the adjectives *economic* and *economical* were not used in the classifying sense 'relating to economics or the economy' to any notable extent until the nineteenth century. In Table 28, the

---

3   For example, in the period 1800–1849, the fiction material contained a total of 4.2 occurrences of *economic* and *economical* per one million words, whereas the non-fiction material contained 33.0 occurrences per one million words (in the texts by British authors), reflecting the fact that many of the non-fiction texts deal with economic subjects.

figures include the occurrences of *economic/economical* from all types of texts, although a great number are from books dealing with economic subjects. The use of the adjectives according to the subject matter and the British versus American aspect will be dealt with in more detail in the closer analysis of the material in subsequent sections.

Returning to the question of the nominal use of *economic(s)*, the *Literature Online* material does not include any such occurrences from the period 1513–1799, and only six occurrences from 1800–1903, while the non-fiction corpus includes four nominal instances of the word before 1799, nine occurrences in the nineteenth century material, and altogether 282 occurrences in the twentieth century material. Therefore very little can be said of the effect of the nominal use on the choice between *economic* and *economical* in the first centuries in the adjectives' history. From 1800 onwards, both adjective forms appear rather frequently, but it appears that the increasing nominal use certainly did not discourage people from using the shorter form as an adjective.

2.   *Economic/economical* in dictionaries and usage manuals

The earliest monolingual English dictionaries define *economic(al)* as relating to the affairs and management of a household. Interestingly enough, among the works consulted, *economic* makes its first dictionary appearance (Cawdrey 1604) before the form in *-ical*, contrary to many other cases of *-ic/-ical* adjectives. Among the seventeenth century dictionaries, Cawdrey's dictionary is also an exception in that it is the only one to include the *-ic* form of the adjective; in Cotgrave's French-English dictionary (1611), as well as in the monolingual dictionaries by Bullokar (1616), Cockeram (1623), and Blount (1656), only the *-ical* form is listed. Both forms are given as synonyms in Bailey (1721), Johnson (1755), Sheridan (1780), Walker (1791), Todd (1827), Richardson (1836), and Craig (1852). Since the eighteenth century, dictionaries include the sense 'frugal' as well; in Todd's second edition of Johnson's dictionary, all the examples of this sense have the *-ical* form.

The *OED* definitions of *economic* and *economical* resemble each other to a great extent; in fact, nearly all of the senses assigned to *economical* also appear under the entry for the *-ic* form. The only major difference between the definitions is the finer breakdown of the general sense 'relating to economics or the economy' in the case of *economic*, including more detailed definitions for phrases such as *economic man/rent/system/war(fare)/growth* (s.v. *economic*, senses 2.d–h). Comparing the definitions of the two forms, the groupings of the senses may be criticized for inconsistencies, as well as for having the potential to cause a certain amount of confusion. For example, the definitions seem inconsistent in the use of cross-references: *economical*, sense 2.b, includes a cross-reference to *economic*, 2.b, '[m]aintained for the sake of profit', whereas senses 1.a for both forms seem very similar, with no cross-references. *Economic*, sense 1.a reads '[p]ertaining to the management of a household, or to the ordering of private affairs' (marked obsolete), while the equivalent definition for *economical* reads '[p]ertaining to a household or its management; resembling what prevails in a household' (marked archaic), the examples provided not suggesting any evident difference between the meanings of the two forms.

Another curious detail in the *OED* definitions concerns *economic*, sense 3, '[t]hrifty, careful, saving, sparing' (marked obsolete), and *economical*, sense 3.a '[c]haracterized by, or tending to economy; of persons; saving, thrifty; opposed to *wasteful*'. The latter sense of *economical* is followed by sense 3.b for the phrase *economical man*, which includes a cross-reference to *economic*, sense 2.d, where the phrase *economic man* is explained as follows:

> **economic man**, a convenient abstraction used by some economists for one who manages his private income and expenditure strictly and consistently in accordance with his own material interests. Cf. *economical man*.

The organization of the sense groups of *economic* and *economical* in the dictionary are potentially misleading, as the phrase *economic man* is not defined in a subgroup under *economic*, sense 3, 'thrifty', in the same way as *economical man* appears in a subgroup under *economical*, sense 3, 'thrifty'. Instead, *economic man* appears as one of the senses 2.a–h, which generally relate to economics (on a scale larger than a household, e.g. communities or nations), or appear in phrases used in economic writing, or involve the notion of 'profitable'. The paraphrase for *economical*, sense 2.a, '[p]ertaining to, or concerned with, the development of material resources; relating to political economy', is very similar to that found under *economic*, sense 2.a, '[r]elating to the science of economics, relating to the development and regulation of the material resources of a community or nation'. As the senses 2.a and b of *economical* are for all intents and purposes identical with senses 2.a and b of *economic*, it appears questionable to present the phrases *economic man* and *economical man* under different "larger" sense divisions.[4]

The definitions of the adjectives in more recent dictionaries vary mainly in their subcategories of the general sense 'relating to economics or the economy', and in the extent to which the two forms are regarded as interchangeable (the

---

4   Considering the sense of the adjective in the phrase *economic(al) man* in the terminology used in economics, it seems that the adjective classifies the type of motivation affecting the actions of an individual, rather than describes the qualities or characteristics of man. In *The Theory of Economic Progress* by C.E. Ayres (fourth edition, 1996; first published in 1944), the concept is criticized with the comment "there is no 'economic man,' just as there is no 'theological man'", in which theological is likewise a classifier rather than an epithet. Therefore it would appear justifiable to categorize this special use of *economic(al)* under the major sense of 'relating to economics' rather than that of 'not wasteful; tending towards economy'.

form with a cross-reference to the other one usually being understood as being less frequent in the senses in question). Some works also distinguish between different notions of the sense 'not wasteful'. For example, the fifth edition of the *Oxford Advanced Learner's Dictionary* (1995; henceforth *OALD*) s.v. *economical* distinguishes the uses 'providing good service or value in proportion to the amount of money, time, etc spent', with the example *an economical car to run*, and 'using no more of sth than is necessary', as in *an economical style of writing*. The fourth edition of *Collins English Dictionary* (1998) s.v. *economical* groups these uses together in sense 1, but distinguishes them from the sense 'frugal, thrifty' (sense 2), with the example *she was economical by nature*. The different notions will be discussed in more detail in subsequent sections.

The overall picture of the use of *economic/economical* served to the readers of usage manuals is to a large extent similar to the one a reader would get from almost any of the recent English dictionaries, i.e. *economic* having the senses 'relating to economics' and 'profitable', and *economical* meaning 'not wasteful' (see e.g. Fowler 1926 s.v. *economic, economical*; Krapp 1927 s.v. *economic, economical*; Roberts 1967: 233). In that respect one wonders about the necessity for some dictionaries to provide an additional usage note after the definitions, one logical reason perhaps being the opportunity to provide typical example sentences to illustrate the differences.

One remark more likely to appear in usage manuals than in dictionaries, however, involves the use of *economical* in the sense of 'cheap' or 'inexpensive', which is often criticized, e.g. by Clark (1987) s.v. *economic, economical* and Alexander (1994) s.v. *economical, cheap, economic*. Some sources have no problem with the idea: for example, Howard (1993) s.v. *economic or economical* says that "[w]hen it's cheap at the price, or at least good value, use *economical*" (see also Todd 1997 s.v. *economic, economical*). The notion of being inexpensive is obviously related to the more general idea of not being wasteful – in this case, of money – and from this viewpoint it is not surprising to see examples grouped together which, strictly speaking, represent different facets of the wider sense. One instance of this kind of grouping is seen in the comment "[e]*conomical* means 'thrifty': *an economical housekeeper/meal*" (Greenbaum and Whitcut 1998 s.v. *economic, economical*; see also the quotations provided in the *OED* s.vv. *economic*, sense 3, and *economical*, sense 3.a). A housekeeper may be considered to be thrifty, while a meal itself is not thrifty, but by being inexpensive it is related to the idea of being thrifty.

3.   Different uses of *economic/economical*

In the following sections, some of the senses of *economic* and *economical* will be discussed in greater detail, with special attention to ones presenting most problems as regards their analysis in the corpus material.

3.1   'Relating to a household'

The classifying sense 'relating to a household', one of the first senses in which the adjectives *economic* and *economical* were used, is also a prominent one in the first centuries of the historical material studied. Instances of both forms were found representing this use:

(3)   a.   Quick was their pace in the dispatch of oeconomic or houshold-affairs,
             but slow in their Epicurean visits, or extravagant Gossipings. (Hannah
             Woolley, *The Gentlewoman's Companion* (1675), 37–38)

       b.   As soon as the Clock struck seven, the good Creature went down into
             the Kitchin, and began to exercise her Talents of Cookery, of which
             she was a great Mistress, as she was of every Oeconomical Office,
             from the highest to the lowest; [...] (Henry Fielding, *Amelia* (1752),
             190)

It is interesting that in the *OED*, the use of *economic* in this sense has been marked "obsolete", while that of *economical* is said to be "archaic". The latest quotations of the adjectives in this sense are not very helpful in determining the difference in the status of this use between the two forms, and in general it could be argued that one should hesitate about drawing conclusions from them. In fact, the latest quote for *economical* in this sense (1748) appears to be earlier than that for *economic* (1831). The latest recorded occurrences of words in the *OED* perhaps do not constitute a very reliable basis for drawing conclusions on usage, and the assignment of the labels "obsolete" and "archaic" from this viewpoint indeed does not seem coherent. However, the corpus material studied would seem to support the idea expressed in the *OED* labels, as the latest instances of *economic* in this sense were from earlier date than those of *economical*.

Considering examples (3a) and (3b), it would appear that rather than paraphrasing this use of the adjectives as 'pertaining to the management of a household', as in e.g. the *OED*, a mere reference to "household" is sufficient. This view is supported by the fact that the occurrences of the adjectives in this sense in the seventeenth century usually do not relate to financial matters, but to the household as a whole, as well as the things within it in general. It might therefore be better to consider instances relating to the handling of money and wealth under the category 'relating to economics and the economy', even if reference was made on the level of personal or household finance. This also seems sensible when one considers that it is nowadays possible to talk about *the economic situation/conditions of a household/family*, only in this case the reference to a household or family is made explicitly in the context, instead of being a semantic component of the adjective *economic(al)*. From this viewpoint, one might criticize the *OED* for categorizing the senses 1.b for both *economic* and *economical* (neither of which have been labelled obsolete or archaic), i.e., 'relating to private income and expenditure' and 'pertaining to pecuniary position', respectively, under the obsolete sense 'relating to a household' rather than under 'relating to economics'. In the *OED*, the sense 'relating to economics' involves cases referring to the handling of money, wealth, and other resources on a national level, although the word *economic* itself in both *the economic situation of a household* and *the economic situation of a country* would seem to carry exactly the same sense.

3.2   'Relating to economics or the economy'

Another classifying sense, 'relating to economics or the economy', is today considerably more often conveyed by *economic* than by the *-ical* form, although rare instances of the longer form are also found (and considered in the most prescriptivist usage manuals to be instances of misuse):

(4)   a.   However, it is, in this case, further apparent that Beijing simply cannot enforce law against intellectual piracy. Its authority in the provinces is extremely attenuated, particularly in matters economic. (*The Daily Telegraph*, Feb. 9, 1995, "Letter to the Editor: Why China's piracy will go on")

      b.   But apart from that, the Wilson years from the vantage point of 1995 look like a cul-de-sac, particularly in matters economical, ending with Britain achieving Third World status in an International Monetary Fund bail-out. (*The Sunday Telegraph*, May 28, 1995, "CITY COMMENT: Wilson's hidden business legacy")

In examples (4a) and (4b), we find *economic* and *economical* in the less usual post-modifying position, which in the analyses throughout the present study are categorized as attributive cases. The collocation in these cases has by no means affected the ordering of the adjective and the noun, and the phrase *economic matters* is, in fact, quite common in the material studied. As the sense of the adjectives in this case is a classifying one, they would not be expected to be used in a predicative position, but the corpus material shows that such instances are not at all uncommon or awkward:[5]

(5)   a.   The issues surrounding Italian political debate are, at the moment, wholly economic. (*The Daily Telegraph*, Feb. 13, 1995, "European Notebook: Fast cycle lane to power")

---

5   Some dictionaries, e.g. *OALD* (1995) s.v. *economic*, include specifications such as "attributive" in connection with this use of the adjective.

b. No one is in any doubt that the housing crisis is severe. But there is more than money at stake. This crisis is not just economic, it is political. (*The Sunday Telegraph*, May 28, 1995, "Focus on Negative Equity: Deep in debt and out for revenge")

As mentioned earlier, dictionaries vary as regards the distinction between the different aspects relating to economics and an/the economy. For example, *The New Penguin English Dictionary* (2000) s.v. *economic* distinguishes between the senses 'relating to economics or finance' (sense 1), 'of or based on the production, distribution, and consumption of goods and services' (sense 2), 'relating to an economy' (sense 3), and 'to do with practical or financial necessity' (sense 6). One can raise a question about the necessity for such a division, especially as the dictionary does not, unfortunately, provide examples of these uses of the word to illustrate the differences. Some dictionaries find it sufficient to refer to the different aspects by representing them all as one sense: for example, *Collins English Dictionary* (1998) s.v. *economic* settles for the paraphrase 'of or relating to an economy, economics, or finance', giving the phrases *economic development* and *economic theories* as examples.

Of the different aspects related to the handling, development, distribution, etc. of financial and material resources, some could arguably be presented as a separate group, e.g. those relating to the scientific aspects of economics. But even in that case, phrases such as *economic writers/writings/theories* may relate to the economy in general as well as the science investigating it, i.e. *economic writings* could be paraphrased as either 'writings about the economy (and/or its different aspects)' or 'writings within the field of economics'.

Some dictionaries and usage manuals note the significance of the level on which the handling of wealth and resources takes place in connection with the use of the adjectives. For example, Hardie (1991) s.v. *economic, economical* comments that "*economic* is used when talking about the management of money within *national* expenditure or industry" (emphasis mine). As noted earlier, the *OED* includes a separate subsense for things relating to the handling of money on the level of individual persons. A similar distinction is made in *Random House Compact Unabridged Dictionary* (1987) s.v. *economic*, sense 4, where one finds the paraphrase 'involving or pertaining to one's personal resources of money' and an accompanying example *to give up a large house for economic reasons*. As regards the analysis of the adjectives' use in the present study, it may be asked whether a distinction really needs to be made between instances such as *the government explained its decision with economic reasons* and *the man explained his decision with economic reasons*. In these two cases, it could be argued that whether reference is made to money matters either on a national or on a personal level becomes evident from the context rather than from the meaning of the adjective. In the latter sentence, the context is, in fact, insufficient, as the decision in question could have been made based on either the man's own economic situation or on that of the country or some other unit of society. Therefore it seems justifiable that as regards the sense 'relating to economics and the economy', occurrences of the adjectives will not in the present study be divided into subgroups according to the scope of reference.

3.3   'Not wasteful; sparing; careful', 'inexpensive'

The clearest examples of *economic(al)* in the descriptive sense 'careful with the handling of resources' or 'thrifty' appear when the adjective refers to people (although the word *thrifty* may have slightly different connotations from *economical*; see e.g. Evans and Evans 1957 s.v. *economical; thrifty; frugal; stingy; miserly*):

(6)   They possessed little property; but the one was enterprizing and industrious, the other careful and oeconomical; and both, with hearts glowing with affection for each other, saw cheering hope and fairy prospects dancing before their eyes. (Mary Hays, *Memoirs of Emma Courtney* (1796), 11)

Judging from the historical material studied, *economical* appears to have been the more common form in this sense when referring to people, the *OED* s.v. *economic* including the quote "We should be economic" (from Horace Walpole, *Memoirs of the Reign of George II* (1755), II.96) with the shorter form.

Apart from people, other things referred to as being *economical* may also be considered to contribute to sparing, or, as paraphrased in the *OED* s.v. *economical*, sense 3.a, to be 'characterized by, or tending to economy':

(7)   a.   The new Vicar is a teetotaller, miss, and a magistrate, and his wife has a deal of receipts for economical cooking, and is for making bread without yeast; [...] (Elizabeth Gaskell, *North and South* (1855), 283–284)

      b.   For someone so proud of her nimble fingers (she knits, embroiders and has illustrated half a dozen books), her gestures are few and economical. (*The Sunday Telegraph*, Apr. 9, 1995, "Food and Drink: A precise mix of drama and spice")

      c.   Miles was silent as the grave, but at once made up his mind that he would pass his autumn at some pleasant but economical German retreat, and that his autumnal retirement should be commenced within a very few days; – or perhaps hours might suffice. (Anthony Trollope, *The Way We Live Now* (1875), 268)

In some cases one may not be absolutely certain about what exactly it is that is entailed in the sense of the adjective. In (7c), the head word denotes a place, and *economical* might be understood as meaning 'inexpensive', but it might also mean that the retreat was not extravagant (it is also possible that both notions fit the description). In present-day English, both forms are found in cases where reference is made more or less directly to the low price of products, or to the low costs involved in their use (and thus providing good value for money). The sense 'frugal, not wasteful' is therefore in the more recent dictionaries usually assigned to *economic* as well:

(8) a. It would appear that our next small car should be an automatic with power steering. The car should be economic, with low maintenance costs. (*The Daily Telegraph*, Mar. 18, 1995, "Letter to the Motoring Editor: Moving On")

   b. Tesco, whose 'nature's choice' products provide a more economic alternative to organic food, says: 'We are always sensible to the need to change and improve things [...]' (*The Sunday Telegraph*, Jan. 15, 1995, "Focus: Animal Farming – Cruel or kind?")

   c. I would like a small/medium, economical and reliable car to a budget of £4,000. (*The Daily Telegraph*, Apr. 29, 1995, "Motoring: Stop/start")

   d. When recession hit in the mid-1970s, he championed Chinese food as an economical option for families on a budget. (*The Daily Telegraph*, Aug. 12, 1995, "Obituary of Kenneth Lo")

In the present study, no distinction is made between the senses 'inexpensive' and 'careful with the handling of resources': although in some cases *an economical car* means that the price of the car is low, whereas in others the adjective may refer to the low fuel consumption, it does not always become absolutely clear, even from a larger context, which sense of the two best describes the use of the word. For example, in the case of (8a), there is room for both interpretations.

The paraphrase 'inexpensive' does not appear as such in the *OED* definitions of either *economic* or *economical*, the explanation for the latter including the phrase "tending to economy", which would cover also cases such as (8c) and (8d). Interestingly enough, the *OED* sense for *economic*, 'thrifty, careful, saving, sparing' (sense 3), is accompanied by the label "obsolete", which in the light of examples (8a) and (8b) would clearly represent a case of misjudgement.

Another prominent use of *economical* relating to frugality is to be found in the expression *economical with the truth*, which may be regarded as a euphemism for providing only limited information on a given subject, intentionally withholding essential facts (see e.g. *Collins English Dictionary* s.v. *economical*; *CIDE* s.v. *economical*). According to the *OED* (see s.vv. *economic*, sense 5; *economical*, sense 4; *economy*, sense 6), this use stems from the concept of economy in theology, referring to '[t]he judicious handling of doctrine, i.e. the presentation of it in such a manner as to suit the needs or to conciliate the prejudices of the persons addressed' (*OED* s.v. *economy*, sense 6.a), later associated with the sense 'not wasteful' in the notion of "the economy of truth". From today's perspective, the use of *economical*, when appearing in the structure *economical with* + NP (e.g. *economical with the truth/actualité*/etc), often has a notably ironic or euphemistic tone, as in "A variety of water company spokesmen and even occasional Secretaries of State for the environment have been, shall we say, economical with their statistics during the present dry spell" (*The Sunday Telegraph*, Aug. 20, 1995, "The Weather: It's dry, damn dry and bloody statistics").[6]

One point worth noting is the fact that it is quite possible for the adjectives *economic* and *economical* to modify the same head word, but with different meanings. Considering the senses 'relating to economics and the economy' and 'not wasteful', Howard (1993) s.v. *economic* or *economical* presents the following rather humorous and imaginative examples:

> An *economic summit* is a conference of heads of states on the international economy; an *economical summit*, if one ever took place, would still be a gathering of presidents and prime ministers, but done on the cheap, with beer and sandwiches instead of champagne and banquets.

3.4   'Profitable'

In many dictionaries and usage manuals, the shorter form is also assigned the sense 'profitable', present in the following quotations:

(9)   a. The premium is £2.50 per annum per £1,000 of cover but there is a minimum premium of £300 so it is probably not economic for deposits of less than £150,000. (*The Sunday Telegraph*, Sept. 3, 1995, "Lorna Bourke's Family Finance Surgery: Investor cover")

       b. When negotiations on the treaty began, mineral prices were high – making undersea mining economic. But predicted shortages did not materialise and now the profits are not there for the taking – yet. (*The Sunday Telegraph*, Mar. 26, 1995, "Scope: The law splits ocean's spoils")

---

6   In his article on -*ic*/-*ical* adjectives, Ross (1998: 42) comments on the general shift towards the use of the -*ic* forms even with semantically differentiated pairs, and claims that "in the phrase 'very economic with the truth,' the lack of a final -*al* is already fairly widespread". This observation must be considered an overstatement, as no occurrences of the structure *economic with* + NP were found in the historical material studied, the *DTL* material, *BNC*, or the 56-million-word version of the *Bank of English* corpus (*Collins Wordbanks Online*), whereas instances of the pattern with *economical* were numerous.

c. Usually the surplus calves from the dairy herd are sold for veal production because they are mainly black and white Hostein-Friesians. Cows of the breed are renowned as the top milk-production animals of the world but the surplus bulls do not carry enough muscle to be economic beef animals. (*The Daily Telegraph*, Feb. 11, 1995, "Calf protests open a bull market for British beef stock")

Quite interestingly, *Collins English Dictionary* (1998) s.v. *economic* labels this use 'British', a comment which was not encountered in the other works studied. Some dictionaries distinguish between 'profitable' and 'having practical uses' (e.g. *The New Penguin English Dictionary* s.v. *economic*), and example (9c) could arguably fit in with the latter idea, although it is in some cases difficult to see any significant difference between the two senses.

The difference between the senses 'profitable' and 'not wasteful' has been illustrated with the phrases *economic rent* and *economical rent* e.g. by Fowler (1926) s.v. *economic, economical*, the former emphasizing the interests of "the landlord", the latter those of "the tenant".[7] In such cases, as well as in examples (9a–c), the sense of the adjectives is perhaps easily interpretable as either 'profitable' or 'not wasteful; frugal'. However, especially as far as companies and their interests are concerned, one might ask whether profitability and the desire to cut down expenses are, in fact, two sides of the same coin, as the expenses paid unavoidably have an effect on whether any commercial activity eventually makes a profit. In fact, the two senses become almost intertwined in the use of the prefixed form *uneconomic(al)*:

(10)   a. [...] it is inevitable that around 15 per cent of water will continue to run to waste. They say it is uneconomic to invest to reduce wastage below this level. (*The Daily Telegraph*, Aug. 26, 1995, "North West tops leak table by losing four out of ten gallons")

      b. No-one has a clue how much gas might be there or whether it is as uneconomical to extract as from most other holes off Ireland. (*The Daily Telegraph*, Aug. 18, 1995, "CITY: The Market – Uncertain dollar direction leaves equities rudderless")

In (10a) and (10b), the contexts involve doubts about the financial consequences of taking certain actions. The expenses of these actions are probably high for the companies in question, but it is not entirely clear whether the prefix *un-* is used to

---

7   In the terminology of economics, the phrase *economic rent* is also used to refer to "a payment to a factor of production (land, labour, or capital) in excess of that needed to keep it in its present use" (*Collins English Dictionary* s.v. *economic rent*). The everyday use relating to a payment of a dwelling is in *Collins English Dictionary* regarded as one encountered particularly in British English.

negate the sense more typically encountered with the *-ic* ('profitable') or the *-ical* form ('not wasteful'). Instead, the two perspectives into the issue are in such cases significantly similar to one another in that they share the idea of something that may not be altogether *wise* as far as either investing or spending money is concerned.[8] There are, however, some occurrences, sometimes with helpful lexical clues in the context as in (11a), which could more readily be interpreted as negating the sense 'profitable':

(11) a. Pennington guaranteed to get a rates reduction and said that if it failed to negotiate a cut the initial fee would be returned. That guarantee was in part the source of Pennington's downfall because it made the operation uneconomic. 'I think the business was inherently unprofitable – any business coming in paid a fee but that was subject to commission,' said Mr Henry. (*The Daily Telegraph*, Jan. 30, 1995, "Business Monitor: Rates cut guarantee that was too good to be true – Reassessments")

      b. I can assure the reverend gentleman that the high street travel agents in this area – not excluding Thomas Cook and Going Places in Hereford – ceased some time ago to offer railway booking services, probably on the grounds that the business was uneconomical. (*The Daily Telegraph*, Jan. 16, 1995, "Letter to the Editor: Not the ticket")

Howard (1993) s.v. *economic or economical* argues that "[t]he same distinction [existing between *economic* and *economical*] can apply to *uneconomic* and *uneconomical*, although both words usually mean the opposite of *economical*, that is to say wasteful or bad value for money", adding that "[*u*]*neconomic* is more applicable to important projects, *uneconomical* an everyday word for small matters". The problem of perspective can be brought up again, as for companies any actions that are not profitable are obviously wasteful

---

8   The notion of care and caution involved in the use of *economic(al)* in the sense 'not wasteful' (and, to some extent, in the sense 'profitable' as well) may cause some confusion in the interpretation of the adjective in cases where the head word itself denotes care and caution. For example, *Bloomsbury Good Word Guide* s.v. *economic or economical* gives the sentence "Buying a whole chicken makes economic sense" (from an advertisement in *Bejam* magazine, Autumn 1987) as an example where the unexpected form is used. In other words, the adjective in the phrase *economic sense* is considered to mean 'frugal; avoiding waste', while Todd and Hancock (1986) s.v. *-ic, -ical words* present a sentence with the same phrase as a typical example of the adjective in the sense 'relating to economics'. It would appear that the interpretation of Todd and Hancock is perhaps more accurate, as the adjective is of a classifying rather than descriptive type, denoting the kind of viewpoint from which the purchase makes sense. In the corpus material studied, not a single instance of the phrase *economical sense* was found (although conceptually it may not be entirely impossible), whereas *economic sense* was quite frequent.

and "bad value for money" as well. Considering Howard's additional comment, only a few instances of either *uneconomic* or *uneconomical* in the material studied actually related to the interests of individual persons (or their "small matters"). These cases, however, did appear more clearly to negate the sense 'not wasteful' or 'inexpensive', as, for example, in "'I suppose earls don't care tuppence that an electric fire is the most uneconomic way to heat a room,' came Giles's next gripe" (*The Sunday Telegraph*, Nov. 19, 1995, "Family Life: Giles enters into the spirit of stately life") and "Fortunately, most retailers will split packs for you if buying whole packs would be uneconomical" (*BNC*, A16 771).

Considering the occurrences of *uneconomic* and *uneconomical* in *The Daily Telegraph* material, it is interesting to note that the shorter form is clearly more common than the longer form, with 69 instances of the *-ic* and 15 instances of the *-ical* form. The overwhelming majority of the cases with *-ic* had to do with relatively large-scale business transactions, while only five cases related to individual persons or were otherwise perceived as having the sense 'wasteful' or 'expensive'. Of the *-ical* forms, only four instances emphasizing the individual perspective were found. This finding is in opposition to Howard's argument about both *uneconomic* and *uneconomical* usually negating the sense commonly identified with *economical*, most of the cases, in fact, either having the sense 'unprofitable' or involving both the idea of 'unprofitable' as well as that of undesirably high expenses.

4.   *Economic/economical* in the material studied

The following sections will present the uses of *economic/economical* in different periods in tabular form. This adjective pair was analysed in different types of historical and present-day English texts, including the prose fiction material in the *Literature Online* text collection, and the non-fiction texts culled from the Internet and already existing corpora containing non-fiction material. For the present-day use of the adjectives, *The Daily Telegraph* material (1995 issues) was examined, and additional searches were made in the *British National Corpus*, mainly in order to examine the differences in the relative frequency of the adjectives' use in different text types.

As mentioned earlier, *economic* and *economical* were not very numerous in the seventeenth and eighteenth century materials. As regards the seventeenth century, the *Literature Online* material contained one occurrence of each form, both appearing in the same text, and having the sense 'pertaining to a household'. The same sense was also carried by the adjectives in the non-fiction material from the same period, with four occurrences of each form. In one instance, *economical* was used to refer to a divine organization and management (in a text by John Milton; this occurrence was also the only predicative one).

The eighteenth century material is interesting in that only the *-ical* form was found in both fiction (14 occurrences, eight authors) and non-fiction works

(10 occurrences, five authors). The sense 'frugal, avoiding waste' was found in nine instances in the *Literature Online* material. In many cases of this type, the adjective modified words denoting people, and in four cases it appeared in the predicative position (as in *she learnt to be economical*). Five instances of *economical* had the sense 'pertaining to a household'. Of the ten instances of the adjective in non-fiction texts, seven carried the meaning 'frugal' (two of them in the predicative position), while three instances related to economics, the handling of wealth and other resources.

The nineteenth century material provides enough instances for a more detailed analysis, allowing a look into the development of the use of the adjectives in fiction and non-fiction texts in the two halves of the century (Tables 29 and 30).

Table 29. *Economic/economical* in the prose section of *Literature Online,* 1800–1849.

	economic	economical
1. a. 'relating to the economy, management of wealth and other resources'	2	13
b. 'relating to economics as a scientific discipline':		
~ *science*	-	1
2. 'not wasteful, frugal'		
a. people	-	21 (7)
b. others	4	17 (2)
total	**6**	**52 (9)**
# of authors:	4	20
# of authors using both forms: 4		

As can be seen from Table 29, *economical* was quite clearly the more frequently used form in all senses in fictional writings in the first half of the nineteenth century. Most often the *-ical* form was used in the sense 'not wasteful', but in the works of three authors, the adjective was also used in a sense relating to the possession, handling, or development of wealth and other resources.[9]

9   The picture one gets of the relation between different uses of *economical* may not be altogether accurate on the basis of the absolute figures, because of the 13 instances of *economical* in senses relating to money matters, as many as eight were found in texts by Benjamin Disraeli. Interestingly enough, Disraeli also used the adjective in the sense 'frugal'. One should therefore consider the figures in Table 29 with due caution, although one can safely make the overall conclusion of *economical* being the favoured form.

Table 30, presenting the occurrences of *economic/economical* in the non-fiction texts from 1800–1849, shows that in the same way as in fictional texts, *economical* was far more often used than its shorter counterpart in this period:

Table 30. *Economic/economical* in the non-fiction texts studied, 1800–1849 (British authors).

	economic	*economical*
1. a. 'relating to the economy, management of wealth and other resources'	1	28 (1)
b. 'relating to economics as a scientific discipline':		
~ *science/thinker/doctrine*	-	10
2. 'not wasteful, frugal'		
a. people	-	-
b. others	-	8 (3)
3. 'profitable, having practical uses'	-	5
total	**1**	**51 (4)**
# of authors:	1	14
# of authors using both forms: 1		

The figures in Table 30 include only those occurrences of the adjectives in texts by British authors; the small number of texts written by American authors from this period included only one occurrence of *economical*, having the sense 'frugal', while no instances of *economic* were found. Of the thirteen British authors using *economic(al)*, eight were economists. Therefore it is hardly surprising that the adjectives in question mostly related to economics and the economy, with collocations having to do with their scientific aspects presented as a subgroup in the table.

The uses of the adjectives in the latter half of the nineteenth century, presented in Tables 31 and 32, suggest that *economic* began to gain a firmer foothold when relating to economics and the economy, especially in British non-fiction texts, with still some variation between the two forms. The clear preference for *economical* seen in the first half of the century in this sense was no longer the norm in the latter half. However, there was no similar increase in the use of the shorter form in the sense 'not wasteful', for which *economical* became even more firmly established. This sense is also the only one where the adjective was used in a predicative position.

Table 31. *Economic/economical* in the prose section of *Literature Online*, 1850–1903.

	economic	economical
1. 'pertaining to a household'	-	1
2. a. 'relating to the economy, management of wealth and other resources'	9	7
b. 'relating to economics as a scientific discipline':		
~ *science*	-	-
3. 'not wasteful, frugal'		
a. people	-	19 (13)
b. others	-	33 (4)
4. 'profitable, having practical uses'	2	-
total	**11**	**60 (17)**
# of authors:	5	20
# of authors using both forms: 3		

Table 32. *Economic/economical* in the non-fiction texts studied, 1850–1899 (British authors).

	economic	economical
1. a. 'relating to the economy, management of wealth and other resources'	83	37
b. 'relating to economics as a scientific discipline':		
~ *science/thinker/doctrine*/etc.	44	6
~ *man*	2	-
2. 'not wasteful, frugal'	-	2 (2)
3. 'profitable, having practical uses'	1	5
total	**130**	**50 (2)**
# of authors:	6	10
# of authors using both forms: 3		

The numbers of authors being fairly low, especially in the case of the non-fiction material, it should be noted that the absolute numbers of occurrences of the adjectives in different senses are in themselves not very critical (although they are nevertheless suggestive of a general preference towards the use of the *-ic* form), considering the fact that some of the forms appeared several times in some texts. In other words, what is perhaps more significant and interesting than the fact that in the non-fiction material, *economic* appeared 129 times in the classifying sense, *economical* 43 times, is that there were, in fact, roughly the same number of authors using the forms in this sense.[10] Variation between the two forms when relating to economics and the economy was seen in both fiction and non-fiction material, and some writers used the *-ic* and *-ical* forms interchangeably:

(12)   a.   And very vaguely there came a suggestion towards the solution of the economic problem that had puzzled me.   (H.G. Wells, *The Time Machine* (1895), 80)

       b.   'Social triumphs, too, had been effected. I saw mankind housed in splendid shelters, gloriously clothed, and as yet I had found them engaged in no toil. There were no signs of struggle, neither social nor economical struggle. The shop, the advertisement, traffic, all that commerce which constitutes the body of our world, was gone [...]' (H.G. Wells, *The Time Machine* (1895), 52)

       c.   Allusion was made in an earlier page to the passion for jewels which distinguishes the men of the East from the men of the West, and this form of the desire of wealth has sprung mainly from the absence for many ages of the conditions essential to general prosperity, economic progress, and the accumulation of wealth in really useful forms. (T.E. Cliffe Leslie, *On the Philosophical Method of Political Economy* (1876))

       d.   It is an assumption equally ill-founded with respect to both the extremes of economical progress, the earliest and the most advanced; to the former, because there is no regular labour, no calculation of gain, and no exchange between individuals [...] (T.E. Cliffe Leslie, *On the Philosophical Method of Political Economy* (1876))

The low numbers of authors notwithstanding, one may nevertheless note some of the parallels in the use of the adjectives in the fiction and non-fiction material. As noted earlier, there is an overall preference for the *-ical* form in the eighteenth century texts. Especially in the second half of the nineteenth century, furthermore, the use of *economic* increases in the classifying sense in relation to that of *-ical*.

------

10   As regards the sense 'relating to economics', the American non-fiction material from 1850–1899 is not significantly different from the British material, instead pointing also towards a degree of variation between the two forms, with three authors using *economic*, and five using *economical*. The *-ical* form was more frequent in the American material (24 occurrences, as opposed to four of *economic*), being used in the senses 'frugal' and 'profitable' as well.

The majority of all the non-fiction texts from 1900–1961 culled from the Internet are writings by American authors. The differentiation between the two forms in these texts is very clear indeed:

Table 33. *Economic/economical* in the non-fiction texts studied, 1900–1961 (American authors).

	economic	*economical*
1. a. 'relating to the economy, management of wealth and other resources'	745 (10)	1
b. 'relating to economics as a scientific discipline':		
~ *science/theory/research*/etc.	103	-
~ *man*	9	-
2. 'not wasteful, frugal'		
a. people	-	-
b. others	-	8 (7)
3. 'profitable, having practical uses'	-	6 (3)
total	**857 (10)**	**15 (10)**
# of authors:	23	7
# of authors using both forms: 5		

As can be seen from Table 33, the shorter form is exclusively used in the classifying sense, whereas nearly all the occurrences of *economical* are descriptive. All the authors using both *economic* and *economical* assigned the two forms different senses.[11] The differentiation again shows the decreasing significance of the absolute numbers of occurrences, *economic* being overwhelmingly more often used than *economical*, but its meanings being almost completely different from those of the latter. In texts by English authors in the same period, which were considerably fewer in the whole material, *economic* was used by only three authors, mostly in the classifying sense, as well as twice in the phrase *economic rent*. *Economical* was found in texts by two authors (one of them also using the shorter form), with a few cases being classifiers, and one instance having the sense 'not wasteful'.

On the basis of the historical fiction and non-fiction material, it seems that *economical* was the dominant form in the eighteenth century, and continued to be so well into the nineteenth century. The earliest detectable signs as to the major

---

11   Of the 23 authors using *economic*, 12 were economists, and those authors' texts also included most of the occurrences of the adjective, e.g. by Frank Knight (319 instances), Edwin Seligman (269), and Allyn Young (47).

division between the two forms, along the lines of classifying versus descriptive, are to be seen in the latter half of the nineteenth century. One of the likely historical factors behind the division is the birth of the modern concept of economics as a science, studying the "laws" affecting the production, distribution, and consumption of wealth or other resources or goods. Sometimes also referred to as political economy, this new field of scholarly thought could be considered to have been started in the late eighteenth century, with works by writers such as James Stewart and Adam Smith, continued in the nineteenth century by David Ricardo, among others – later referred to as the "classical school" of economics (for further information, see e.g. *Encyclopædia Britannica, Macropædia Vol. 6* (1974) s.v. *economics*). Obviously, further impetus for this new type of thinking resulted from the onset of the industrial revolution.

It seems that the longer form, which for some time had been more common than the shorter one, was also at first used in the new classifying sense, but gradually a distinction started to develop between the two forms. By the twentieth century, the differentiation had only become sharper, and exceptions to the recently established "rule" in the use of the adjectives were already quite rare, as reflected in e.g. Fowler's (1926) comments on the pair. It could be argued that the assignment of the new sense eventually to the shorter form is in line with the general tendency in favour of the forms in -*ic*, seen in most of the cases where one of the forms was becoming extinct.

The same general distinction is visible in the use of the adjectives in the 1995 issues of *The Daily Telegraph*, presented in Table 34 below:

Table 34. *Economic/economical* in the 1995 issues of *The Daily Telegraph*.

	economic	*economical*
1. a. 'relating to the economy, management of wealth and other resources'	3854 (18)	2
b. 'relating to economics as a scientific discipline':		
~ *science/theory/doctrine*/etc.	29	-
~ *man*	1	-
2. 'profitable, having practical uses'	19 (12)	1
3. 'not wasteful, frugal'		
a. people	-	9 (4)
b. others	20 (15)	132 (62)
c. ~ *with* + NP (ironic)		
1. *the truth*	-	24 (24)
2. others	-	5 (5)
total	**3923 (45)**	**173 (95)**

When it comes to the extent of overlap between the two forms, the distinction between *economic* and *economical* is indeed quite sharp, so much so that comments on the two forms being frequently confused seem almost totally unjustified. However, the figures in Table 34 do provide support for Crystal's (1991) observation of the greater likelihood of the shorter form being used more often in the sense 'not wasteful' than the longer form being used as a classifier. The descriptive uses of the adjectives are interesting in that both forms are used to carry two distinct descriptive senses, with *economic* being clearly more common in the sense 'profitable'. In the sense 'not wasteful', *economical* is the more frequently used form, but the number of instances of *economic* in this sense is also remarkable, and one can easily consider these occurrences enough to merit inclusion in a dictionary. A thing worth noting, however, is that *economic* is not used in this sense to describe people. Instead, only *economical* is used in such cases. Also remarkable in the uses of *economic* in descriptive senses is the fact that a great majority of these cases appear in a predicative position (the number of predicative instances of *economical* also being quite large).

The preference for the *-ic* form in the sense 'profitable' is one for which no significant, visible signs were to be seen in the historical material, although comments tho that effect were already made by Fowler in 1926. It would therefore appear that this use has become more frequent and grown in importance during the twentieth century.

Having acknowledged the lines of distinction between *economic* and *economical*, the status of the words in the English lexicon could be further investigated, for example, by examining their relative frequencies of use in different types of texts. Presented in Table 35 are the numbers of occurrences of the adjectives in the different written and spoken domains in the *British National Corpus* (the figures in parentheses denoting the number of texts including the adjectives):[12]

---

12   It must be noted that the figures in Table 35 also include those cases where the adjectives appeared as a part of a proper name, whereas such instances were excluded from the analysis and the tabular presentation of *The Daily Telegraph* material. In Table 35, such instances have a greater effect on the figures for *economic*, which appears more often in proper names than *economical*. However, the inclusion of such cases in the figures is not likely to cause significant distortion as regards the conclusions drawn on the overall use of the adjectives in different domains of written and spoken language.

Table 35.   *Economic/economical* in different domains of written and spoken
language in the *British National Corpus*.

A = # of occurrences
B = # of occurrences per 1 million words

	economic		economical	
	A	B	A	B
Written domains:				
1. Imaginative	102 (52)	6.2	32 (28)	2.0
2. Natural and pure sciences	447 (51)	118.1	30 (22)	7.9
3. Applied sciences	900 (193)	126.7	65 (45)	9.1
4. Social sciences	5282 (298)	379.8	75 (53)	5.4
5. World affairs	10609 (393)	619.3	51 (40)	3.0
6. Commerce and finance	3659 (210)	504.2	73 (44)	10.0
7. Arts	488 (108)	74.8	43 (28)	6.6
8. Belief and thought	328 (63)	109.1	13 (11)	4.3
9. Leisure	436 (142)	35.8	87 (53)	7.1
Spoken domains:				
1. Educational/informative	203 (37)	124.3	5 (4)	3.0
2. Business	80 (26)	62.2	2 (2)	1.6
3. Public/institutional	214 (42)	129.3	8 (7)	4.8
4. Leisure	40 (17)	25.6	5 (4)	3.2
total	**22788 (1632)**	**244.0**	**489 (341)**	**5.2**

Considering the figures in Table 35, it can be observed that *economic* is in
present-day English a word of great prominence, with more than 600 occurrences
per one million words in the written domain "World affairs", in which it appears
most frequently. Also speaking of the importance of the economy for people's
everyday lives is the fact that *economic* occurs relatively often in the spoken
domains as well. It is interesting to observe that the frequency of the -*ic* form is
clearly at its lowest in the "Imaginative" domain, consisting of fiction texts, in
which classifying -*ic*/-*ical* adjectives are, in general, perhaps less frequently used
than in other types of texts. *Economical* is considerably less frequent in all of the
written and spoken domains, but its status in the English lexicon today may
nevertheless be considered reasonably stable. References to frugality through the
use of *economical* were apparently most common in the domain of "Commerce
and finance", very probably reflecting the prominent concerns in this field,
having to do with issues such as economic feasibility and marketability.
      As regards prefixed forms of *economic(al)*, variation – as well as semantic
overlap – was to some extent encountered with the prefix *un-*. In the historical

material, the occurrences of prefixed forms of the adjectives were so few that any far-reaching conclusions cannot be drawn on the basis of them. Apart from the prefix *un-*, all the prefixed forms of *economic* in *The Daily Telegraph* material were classifying, the same observation also applying to neo-classical compounds (e.g. *socio-economic*, *politico-economic*) as well as other compound structures (e.g. *political-economic*). It is also interesting to note that derivatives with *un-* were in all cases descriptive, whereas those with *non-* were classifiers (e.g. *non-economic questions* 'questions not relating to the economy').

As noted in connection with the use of *uneconomic(al)*, the prefixed forms did not seem to have been used to negate the distinct senses commonly assigned to *economic* and *economical*, respectively. Instead, the notions of not making a profit and wastefulness appeared, in many cases, to be mixed together in the use of both the *-ic* and *-ical* forms. In other words, *economic* and *economical*, on the one hand, and *uneconomic* and *uneconomical*, on the other, differ as to the extent to which the meanings of the two forms have been separated. *Economic* is clearly favoured in the sense 'profitable', and *economical* in the sense 'not wasteful', but in the prefixed forms the two senses are intertwined and difficult to separate from one another. Therefore it is difficult to argue conclusively that the tendency towards favouring shorter forms manifests itself here, although *uneconomic* occurs more frequently than the *-ical* form.

5. General remarks

The present-day situation in the use of *economic/economical*, at least as regards the written material analysed, seems to correspond quite well with the generalisations made in dictionaries and usage manuals. Some of the arguments based on such observations, however, may be considered somewhat questionable, as e.g. that of Marchand (1969: 242) on the general semantic differentiation between the forms in *-ic* and *-ical*:

> The word *economical* today has the meaning 'thrifty', whilst *economic* means 'belonging to the science of economics'. This characterizes the general tendency of differentiation: as derivatives in *-ic* are, morphologically speaking, derivatives from the basic substantive, they have notionally also a direct connection with the idea expressed by the root.

Looking at the historical aspects of *economic/economical*, this statement raises some suspicions in that it is, first of all, etymologically inaccurate: the Greek adjective was observed to be a combination of words meaning 'house' and 'to manage', and the first uses of the adjectives in English related to 'a household' and the activities within it. Marchand's idea seems incomplete because it is made from the viewpoint of the present-day situation, and does not necessarily reflect the diachronic developments accurately (as observed in general in Chapter 3).

The historical evidence provides several instances contradicting his theory: for example, if it could be argued that the original uses of the adjectives, i.e. having the sense 'pertaining to a household' were, in fact, closest to the original idea of the root, the form in *-ical* would have been more likely to lose this sense. Instead, this use eventually died out altogether. Moreover, it was the *-ic* form that disappeared before the *-ical* form in this sense.

Similarly, in his attempt to distinguish semantic elements typically assigned to one of the forms in pairs ending in *-ic/-ical*, Marsden (1985) considers *economical* to be the form including a positive value judgement. Marsden's analysis is unfortunately insufficient, as he fails to include among the present-day uses of the adjectives the sense 'profitable', which also involves this very notion. As this sense is used almost exclusively with the form in *-ic*, it also breaks the general pattern as regards the distinction Marsden claims exists between *-ic* and *-ical* forms, since with this pair, senses involving a value judgement are assigned to both forms instead of just one of them.

Rather than attempting to measure the "semantic distance" between the meaning of the adjectives and the meaning of the root, it is perhaps more fruitful to examine the changes in the adjectives' use over a long period of time. The historical material indicates that while *economical* appears to have been the more common form in the eighteenth and early nineteenth century, a clear change can be seen in the use of the adjectives in the latter half of the nineteenth century, eventually resulting in *economic* being preferred in the classifying, and *economical* in the descriptive sense. The historical non-fiction texts in electronic form also proved useful in the analysis of this adjective pair, as the uses of the adjectives in the material largely correspond with those in the fiction texts in the *Literature Online* corpus, one corpus thus validating the observations made on each other.

It appears that although *economic* is today used considerably more often than *economical*, the use of the longer form in the sense 'not wasteful' is one that does not involve or cause any significant contradictions or confusion as regards its semantic function. In fact, the sense that has developed for the adjective in *-ical* is semantically and lexically viable, explaining its survival through centuries. It would seem that *economical* continues to have a fairly secure place in the English lexicon in the future as well. The only possible question marks as concerns its future have to do with the sense 'profitable', which seems to have become relatively well-established, nowadays expressed by means of the *-ic* rather than the *-ical* form. It will be interesting to see whether the two descriptive senses 'profitable' and 'not wasteful' will merge, as was seen in the negated prefixed forms *uneconomic/uneconomical*, to denote in a less specific sense something regarded as wise or sound from an economic point of view. Another possibility is that the sense 'not wasteful' remains intact, but that *economic* becomes increasingly popular in this sense as well.

Chapter 8

Shocks, sparks and excitement vs. engineering: *electric/electrical*

Together with *magic/magical*, the adjective pair *electric/electrical* represents something of a "lower level" among the *-ic/-ical* pairs manifesting differentiation, as far as the number of entries in usage manuals and special usage notes in dictionaries are concerned. This word pair does not seem to have rated as "important" or worthy of special attention as, for example, *classic/classical* or *historic/historical*. Moreover, the usage notes that there are often tend to clarify the semantic difference between *electric/electrical* and *electronic* rather than between *electric* and *electrical*. One reason for this may be the fact that the two forms have not developed meanings so far apart from each other that the use of one form in place of the other would lead to any serious misunderstanding. This feature applies, of course, to *classic/classical* and *historic/historical* as well, but it could nevertheless be argued that the different uses of *electric/electrical*, in comparison, have not diversified from the original notion to the extent that has happened with the other two pairs.

It is not at all uncommon to find cases where both forms have the same head word, the adjectives having identical meanings, as in the following citations containing the phrases *electric(al) current* and *electric(al) cables*:

(1)   a.   The device is said to be an alternative to facelift surgery, involving toning facial muscles with a small electric current. (*The Daily Telegraph*, July 6, 1995, "CITY: Amstrad lift")

      b.   The device stimulates the facial muscles with a small electrical current applied to the skin through hand-held probes. (*The Daily Telegraph*, Oct. 3, 1995, "Innovations: Now they can process your words. . .and your wrinkles")

      c.   They also noted hazards including bare wires on light fittings in the bathroom; unprotected electric cables outside many apartments; [...] (*The Daily Telegraph*, Sept. 16, 1995, "Travel: Compensation for holiday on 'building site'")

      d.   Every so often, too, he gives you a snippet from his fund of London secrets, such as the existence of the ravens' grave at the Tower (in the middle drawbridge moat, next to some electrical cables). (*The Sunday*

Telegraph, Oct. 29, 1995, "Travel: Show me the way to the raven's grave")

In the same vein as in examples (1a–d), dictionaries are not in agreement over which forms of the adjectives are used in different collocations, either. For example, *electric* is the form given in collocation with the word *charge* in the *OED, LDEL* (1991), and *COBUILD* (2001), whereas e.g. *The Concise Oxford Dictionary of Earth Sciences* (1990) and *A Dictionary of Electronics* (1971) refer to an *electrical charge*.

The comments made on the adjectives also vary as concerns the extent to which the two forms are regarded as having distinguishable uses. For example, according to Evans and Evans (1957) s.v. *electric; electrical*, excluding the figurative sense 'exciting' or 'thrilling', the two forms are "synonymous". A different view on the uses is presented by Roberts (1967: 233), who includes *electric/electrical* (together with *economic/economical* and *historic/historical*) among those *-ic/-ical* pairs which "differ importantly in meaning", providing example sentences with the phrases *electric current* and *electrical engineer*. However, Roberts does not elaborate on the semantic difference which he claims to perceive.

Electric/electrical is, in fact, a pair manifesting various forms of differentiation, some of which are peculiar to the pair, and separate it from the other "major" *-ic/-ical* pairs (being perhaps closest to *magic/magical*). In addition to the two forms having some clearly distinct meanings, the choice of *electric* or *electrical* is in some cases also governed by the head word of the phrase. The most prominent instance is the use of the adjectives when referring to machines – usually household appliances – which are powered by electricity, the specific head words appearing with the shorter (e.g. *electric iron/kettle/oven*), general terms with the longer form (e.g. *electrical appliances/devices/goods*). As noted in Kaunisto (1999: 349), the semantic difference in this case does not manifest itself in the adjectives themselves, but in the whole phrases through the head words.

It could be argued that the features which can be regarded as unique in the use of each *-ic/-ical* pair very often have to do with the semantic aspects of the adjectives themselves. This claim also applies to the pair *electric/electrical*. As observed in Kaunisto (1999), one has first to acknowledge the fact that the adjectives in question relate to a natural phenomenon our knowledge of which has increased along with developments in science and technology. It is therefore obvious that what is commonly meant by different phrases including *electric/electrical* has likewise changed in the course of time. New phrases are continuously being coined, whilst others have become obsolete. One example of a phrase perhaps only seen in old scientific writings is *electric fluid*, which, according to the *OED* s.v. *electric*, sense 2.b, was the term originally used by Benjamin Franklin for a "subtle, imponderable, all-pervading fluid, the cause of electrical phenomena". Nowadays phrases such as *electric(al) current* and *electric(al) charge* perhaps come closest to the meaning of the phrase coined by

Franklin. As regards phrases like *electric(al) machine/apparatus*, today most likely understood as referring to appliances powered by electricity, they were in the late nineteenth century used of "the various instruments and machines necessary for the illustration of the laws of electric action", as stated in *The Royal Dictionary-Cyclopædia* (1862–1867), s.v. *electrical apparatus*.

In line with the overall tendency for preferring the forms in *-ic* in most recent coinages, Marsden (1985: 29) suggests that the more modern the invention denoted by the phrase *electric(al) X*, the more likely one is to see *electric* rather than *electrical* used as the modifier. By examining dictionaries and usage manuals alone, one could make a case for a few instances of shifts in the preferred adjective form in some phrases, most often indeed from *electrical* to *electric*. For example, *The Royal Dictionary-Cyclopædia* (1862–1867) and the first (as well as the second) edition of the *OED* include the phrase *electrical eel*, whereas the more recent British dictionaries e.g. *The Chambers Dictionary* (1993), *The Concise Oxford Dictionary of Current English* (1990), *Collins English Dictionary* (1998), and *The New Penguin English Dictionary* (2000) usually refer to the animal as an *electric eel*. In the *OED*, *electrical eel* is presented as a notable exception, most "phraseological combinations" listed under *electric* 2.b tending to favour *electric*. This shows that preferences in collocational variation may change, and thus should not be too hastily equated with fixedness.

Another feature peculiar to this adjective pair is the fact that in some phrases, especially in those relating to the physical characteristics of electricity, it is possible to actually omit the adjective. For example, when referring to electric(al) currents, the adjective is often not needed, because the idea becomes evident from the context, as in "the quantity of electricity which passes each second in a current of one ampere" (from the article "Of the 'Electron,' or Atom of Electricity" by George Stoney (1894)). In fact, some dictionaries, e.g. *Collins English Dictionary* (1998), have separate entries for phrases such as *electric charge/circuit/current/discharge*, the definitions of which are mere cross-references to the head words along the lines "another name for charge (sense 25)", "another name for circuit", and "another name for current (sense 8)". This feature is possibly a significant factor explaining the variation between the adjectives in such phrases, as, in fact, there would have been less natural impetus to separate between two items verging on the redundant.

1.   Etymology and early history of the pair

The Latin word *electricus* was coined from the word *electrum* (being in turn an adoption of the Greek word ἤλεκτρον), meaning 'amber', as the phenomenon of electricity was at first connected with the static force produced by rubbing amber.[1] As noted by Heller, Humez and Dror (1983) s.v. *electric, electron*, "[e]ventually the meaning of the term lost its connection to rubbing amber and focused on the current, however produced". In the modern sense of 'relating to the phenomenon of electricity', *electricus* is first recorded in writing in 1600, in a groundbreaking book by an Englishman, namely the scientist William Gilbert in his treatise *De Magnete* (*OED* s.v. *electric*; *Le Grand Robert de la langue française*, second edition, s.v. *électrique*).

The first uses of the English forms *electric/electrical*, however, have not been attributed to William Gilbert. Under the entry for *electric* in the *OED*, the first citation of the acclimatized version is from Sir Thomas Browne's 1646 work *Pseudodoxia Epidemica* (also known as *Vulgar Errors*), although an instance from twenty years earlier can be found in the dictionary under the entry for *attraction*, namely "The Drawing of Amber and Iet, and other Electrick Bodies, and the Attraction in Gold of the Spirit of Quick-silver" from Sir Francis Bacon's *Sylva* (1626), §906. The first citation of *electrical* in the *OED* is from Nathaniel Carpenter's *Geography delineated forth in two bookes*, published in 1635. The meaning of the adjectives can be paraphrased as 'possessing the property of developing electricity when excited by friction or by other means' (*OED* s.v. *electric*, sense 1.a).

The coinage of both *electric* and *electrical* may be considered another result of the mistakenly perceived "pattern" of Latin adjectives ending in *-icus/-icalis*, as a form such as **electricalis*, according to the reference works studied, did not exist in Latin. The eagerness in applying affixes to produce new words in the Early Modern English period, as well as the strong – sometimes arguably too strong – influence of Latin, is furthermore shown by the fact that *electric* and *electrical* also had a rival coined with *-al*, i.e. *electral* (*OED* s.v.). Similarly to the sometimes erroneous idea of English formations in *-ical* representing Latin words ending in *-icalis*, misconceptions on the existence of words ending in *-alis* prompted English coinages. According to the *OED*, the nowadays obsolete adjective *electral*, used in the same senses as *electric/electrical*, was formed as if there had been an equivalent Latin word **electralis*, with the suffix *-alis* added to *electrum*. Interestingly enough, *electral* appears to have been coined after *electric/electrical*, the first citation in the *OED* dating from 1673. This word, however, apparently never seriously threatened the position of its *-ic/-ical* counterparts. Not a single instance of the word was found in the corpora studied, nor of the likewise obsolete adjective *electrine* (from Latin *electrinus*), sometimes used in the sense of *electric/electrical*, as in "They

---

1   Apart from relating specifically to the electric(al) properties of amber, *electricus* was also used in Latin in the sense 'of amber' or 'amber-like', and e.g. Latham (1965) in his *Revised Medieval Latin Word-List from British and Irish Sources* records a use of the adjective in this sense from as early as 1267. Another adjective form, *electrinus*, was also used in this sense (as well as in the sense 'made of amber', see *Oxford Latin Dictionary* 1982, Lewis and Short 1879 s.v.).

supposed it to contain an Electrine Principle in it" (from Henry More, *Divine Dialogues* (1713, originally published in 1668), 560; *OED* s.v. *electrine*, sense 1).

It would seem that in the early years of the pair *electric/electrical*, the adjectival use of *electric* was not significantly affected by the nominal use of the same form. In the historical corpora studied (with texts from early sixteenth century to mid-twentieth century), only one nominal occurrence of *electric(s)* was found. Considering the numbers of occurrences of the two forms in historical corpora, presented in Tables 36 and 37, it appears that since the eighteenth century, *electric* has been used more often, both as regards the authors using the forms and the absolute numbers of occurrences.[2]

Table 36. *Electric/electrical* in the prose section of the *Literature Online* corpus, 1750–1903.

	1750–1799	1800–1849	1850–1903
electric	14 (6)	36 (15)	111 (35)
electrical	14 (6)	8 (5)	22 (12)
authors using both forms	2	5	9

Table 37. *Electric/electrical* in the non-fiction texts examined (British and American authors), 1750–1961.

	1750–1799	1800–1849	1850–1899	1900–1961
electric	13 (4)	23 (9)	136 (23)	121 (23)
electrical	6 (3)	6 (3)	53 (18)	33 (15)
authors using both forms	1	3	15	10

The historical developments in the use of *electric* and *electrical*, however, go much deeper than can be detected from Tables 36 and 37. One point which can be raised involves the figurative use of the adjectives, as in the following:

(2)   a.   The want of veneration, too, made him dead at heart to the electric delight of admiring what is admirable; it dried up a thousand pure

---

2   In Table 37, the occurrences from different types of genres have been combined, as have the uses in texts by British as well American authors. The overall tendencies as seen in the figures were the same in e.g. texts on psychology and chemistry, and no difference could be perceived between British and American authors, either. In the more detailed tabular presentations of the different uses of the adjectives, British and American texts are presented separately (the tables representing the uses by American authors are given in Appendix B).

sources of enjoyment; it withered a thousand vivid pleasures. (Charlotte Brontë, *Shirley* (1849), 62)

b.   The joy of that moment was sudden and electric! (Mary Robinson, *Walsingham* (1797), III, 11)

c.   And then they came together, and there was wit and repartee suitable to the electrical atmosphere of the dancing-room, on the march to a magical hall of supper. (George Meredith, *The Egoist* (1879), 24)

d.   The mention of the bishop was electrical; it produced an immediate and miraculous change in the countenance of the reverend Enoch Ellis. (Thomas Holcroft, *The Adventures of Hugh Trevor* (1794–1797), 19)

Although both forms have been used figuratively, as illustrated in (2a–d), this function was and is carried considerably more often by *electric*, and thus the mere observation of the absolute numbers of occurrences of the two forms is clearly not sufficient, but a more in-depth examination is needed. Moreover, in some cases, the same head word may be modified by *electric/electrical*, but the referents may relate to electricity in different ways, as with the phrases *electric/electrical service* in (3a) and (3b) below:

(3)   a.   Willesden to Broad Street, half-hourly from 6.15 a.m. to 6.50 p.m., connecting with the Euston Watford electric services. (*The Times*, May 7, 1926, "Train Services Improving")

b.   All cabins have private baths, with shower, and 110-volt electrical service, the standard American voltage, to handle hair dryers, electric razors, and small travel irons. (Martha Shirk and Nancy Klepper, *Super Family Vacations – Resort and Adventure Guide* (1989))

In example (3a), culled from *The Changing Times* CD-ROM, *electric service* relates to the electrically powered railway service, whereas in (3b) (from *Collins Wordbanks Online*, usbooks/09, text B9000000475), *electrical service* refers to the supply of electricity. Considering the possibility that changes in the use of the adjective forms may have developed according to the different kinds of relations to electricity, examples (3a) and (3b) above show that although the role of collocates in the choice of the adjective form may in some circumstances be considered remarkable, a close semantic analysis is necessary in order to avoid misrepresentations of the issue as a whole.

2.   *Electric/electrical* in dictionaries and usage manuals

In the seventeenth century English dictionaries consulted, neither *electric* nor *electrical* were listed, and in those included in the *EMEDD* database, the adjectives did not appear in any definitions, either. The first occurrences of words beginning with *electr-* were found in Blount (1656), with entries for *electriferous* 'that yeelds Amber', *electricity* 'the power to attract strawes or light bodies, as Amber doth', and *electrine* 'pertaining to, or that is made of Amber'. Of the *-ic/-ical* forms, *electrical* seems to have been the form appearing in dictionaries first, being included in Bailey (1721) with the definition 'that attracts like Amber'. In later eighteenth and nineteenth century dictionaries, both forms are usually given, with no explicit indication of difference in meaning, as, for example, in Johnson (1755), Sheridan (1780), Walker (1791), Todd's edition of Johnson (1827), Richardson (1836), and Craig (1852).

The early twentieth-century perceptions on the use of *electric/electrical* are well exemplified by Fowler's (1926) comments on this pair:

> The longer form, once much the commoner (the OED quotes *electrical shock, battery, eel,* & *spark,* never now heard), survives only in the sense *of* or *concerning electricity,* & is not necessarily preferred even in that sense except where there is danger that *electric* might mislead; e.g. *had no electrical effect* might be resorted to as a warning that 'did not alter the state of the atmosphere as regards electricity' is meant, & not 'failed to startle'; on the other hand the difference between the 'electric book' that gives one shocks & the 'electrical book' that improves one's knowledge of science is obvious.

In addition to the rather strained example phrases *electric(al) book*, Fowler's comments are unfortunately not as clear as possible: one cannot be absolutely certain whether the reference to *electrical* being "more common" earlier relates to overall frequency (possibly not) or to a wider distribution as regards its semantic functions. Based on Tables 36 and 37 above, it is evident that as far as mere frequency is concerned, *electrical* has not dominated over the shorter form at any stage. Equally unclear is Jespersen's (1942: 392) view (possibly based on the first edition of the *OED*), according to which *electrical* is 'the ordinary word', while *electric* appears "in many set phrases" such as *electric arc/charge/spark*. The "ordinariness" again perhaps suggests the idea of *electrical* being used most often in the broader sense 'of or having to do with electricity' instead of it being more usual than *electric* in general.

Jespersen's comment gives reason to assume that of the two forms, *electric* has been more prone to form fixed phrases than the longer form. This is also the impression one might easily get by examining dictionary entries of phrases including *electric* or *electrical*, because the ones with the shorter form far outnumber those with *electrical*. In the second edition of the *OED*, as many as 89 different "phraseological combinations" with *electric* plus a noun are listed s.v.

electric, sense 2.b, while only four equivalent phrases with *electrical* are given under the corresponding section (sense 2) of the longer form. A similar tendency is almost the norm in the more recent dictionaries of present-day English: for example, *The Chambers Dictionary* (1993), *Webster's Third New International Dictionary* (1993, 1st edition 1961), *Collins English Dictionary* (1998), and both the British and American editions of *Encarta World English Dictionary* (1999) include a considerably greater number of separate entries for phrases with *electric* (e.g. *electric blanket/field/guitar*, to name but a few) than for those with *electrical* (only *electrical engineer/engineering*). In the *OALD* (1995) and *The New Penguin English Dictionary* (2000), only phrases with *electric* have been separately defined.

The question of fixed or "set" phrases and their inclusion in dictionaries is, in fact, a complex one, and a well-known problem in dictionary-making (see e.g. Benson, Benson and Ilson 1986: 252–256; Ivir 1988; Landau 1989: 239). When can a phrase with *electric/electrical* be regarded as fixed, and what exactly are the reasons for dictionaries assigning separate entries to such phrases? Probable factors may be their frequency of occurrence and/or opaqueness. The issue of the frequency of particular phrases, however, can be highly dependent on the subject matter or the overall genre of the discourse. On the other hand, the selection of the phrases in relation to their opaqueness can also be puzzling: on the face of it, with no context, why would phrases such as *electric razor* or *electric jazz* merit inclusion in a dictionary more than, say, *electrical accessories* or *electrical contractor*? And why define *electric razor* separately, but not *electric iron*? Moreover, the dictionaries' practice to give considerably more separate entries to phrases with *electric* is not supported by the sheer number of different collocates in the corpora studied: for example, the 1995 issues of *The Daily Telegraph* included 194 different collocates following *electric* and 144 following *electrical*. Although the number is greater for the different phrases with the *-ic* form, the relation does not correspond with that of the entries in dictionaries.

Considering the definitions of *electric* and *electrical* in the *OED* in greater detail, the situation is more straightforward than in the case of other differentiated *-ic/-ical* pairs. For most uses of *electrical*, i.e. 1.a, 1.b, and 3, a crossreference is given to the corresponding sense divisions of *electric*. The definitions of the adjectives in the dictionary, which are identical in both the first and the second edition (the latter contains some additional quotations) are presented in the following:

> *electric*
> 1. a. Possessing the property (first observed in amber) of developing electricity when excited by friction or by other means.
>   b. Charged with electricity, excited to electrical action.
> 2. a. Of the nature of, or pertaining to, electricity; producing, caused by, or operating by means of, electricity.
>   b. Forming phraseological comb. with sbs., esp. in many names of instruments for developing, measuring, illustrating, or applying

electricity, and of machines, etc. in which electricity serves as the motive or controlling power [...]
3. *fig.* Chiefly with reference to the swiftness of electricity, or to the thrilling effect of the electric shock; also in obvious metaphorical uses of the phrases in 2 b.
4. *electric blue*: a trade name for a steely-blue colour used for textile fabrics; also, a brilliant light blue; also in extended use and *ellipt.* electric green = *electric blue*.
5. *Comb.* as †*electric-magnetic* = ELECTRO-MAGNETIC.

electrical
†1. a. = ELECTRIC A. 1 a. *Obs.*
　　b. = ELECTRIC A. 1 b.
2. (The usual modern sense.) Relating to or connected with electricity; also, of the nature of electricity. Sometimes used in the combinations mentioned under ELECTRIC A. 2 b, in most of which, however, *electric* is more usual; exceptions are *electrical machine, electrical eel*; [...]
3. *fig.* Cf. ELECTRIC 3.
†4. Skilled in the science of electricity. *Obs. rare.*

As mentioned earlier, under *electric* 2.b and *electrical* 2, some phrases containing the adjectives are separately defined (e.g. *electric battery, electric circuit, electrical engineering, electrical precipitation*). It is perhaps slightly confusing that there should be two separate subsenses 2.a and 2.b for *electric*, while the corresponding use of *electrical* is presented under one sense group. This can only be explained by the possible desire to emphasize the fact that *electric* appears in fixed phrases considerably more often than *electrical*. No suggestion is made to the effect that there is a semantic difference between instances under *electric* 2.a and b; in fact, 2.a includes the following additional note:

> Except in the phrases in b, ELECTRICAL *a.* is now more usual in this sense. In some cases the choice between the two adjs. is somewhat arbitrarily restricted by usage: thus we usually say 'an *electrical* machine', but 'an *electric* battery'.

Sense 4 of *electrical*, exemplified by the single quote "The author, having no electrical friend whose sagacity he could confide in" (from E. Darwin in *Philosophical Transactions* (1757), L, 240), could equally well be interpreted as having the sense 'relating to electricity', and the quote could have been included under sense 2.

Compared to the *OED*, one difference – which is an improvement – in the definitions of *electric/electrical* in some of the recent dictionaries is the more detailed classification of the uses of the adjectives. Some of the different ways in which the referents relate to electricity are actually mentioned in the *OED*, e.g. 'producing electricity', 'caused by electricity', or 'operating by means of electricity', but unfortunately they have been grouped together (*electric* 2.a). A fact worth noting is that *electrical*, sense 2 does not include specific paraphrases such as 'caused by electricity', but is instead defined with the vaguer phrases 'relating to' and 'of the nature of' (which are included under *electric* 2.a). The quotations provided for *electrical* 2 generally include phrases like *electrical experiments/books/engineering*, which may suggest a more "remote" connection with electricity than the ones under *electric* 2.a, e.g. *electric virtue/power/action*, which in turn can be seen as relating more directly to, or even being, the phenomenon. However, *electrical* 2 is also exemplified by some quotes with *electrical shock*, which could be thought of as having the more specifically definable meaning 'caused by electricity'. It is therefore difficult based on the *OED* to make judgements on preferences in the use of the adjectives in these senses, let alone on the historical developments in this respect.

OALD (1995) s.v. *electric*, senses 1.a–d assigns four different non-figurative senses to *electric*: 'using electrical power' (e.g. *an electric oven*), 'used for carrying an electric current to an appliance, etc.' (e.g. *an electric plug*), 'produced by electricity' (e.g. *an electric current*[3]), and 'producing electricity' (e.g. *an electric generator*). For *electrical*, however, equally detailed paraphrases have not usually been provided. Instead, *electrical* is often defined with the vague description 'of or pertaining to electricity', *electrical engineering/ appliances* being the typical examples. This reflects the existing consensus on the differentiation between the two forms, according to which *electric* has a closer relation to electricity, whereas, in the words of Crystal (1991) s.v. *electric, electrical*, "[e]*lectrical* is more loosely related to the physical power of electricity, and is mainly used to characterize general concepts associated with the subject, or the people and activities involved in its study". The same view is also present in the comments by e.g. Tennant (1964) s.v. *electric, electrical*, Greenbaum and Whitcut (1988) s.v. *electric(al), electronic*, and Howard (1993) s.v. *electric or electrical*, as well as in the *Modern Dictionary of Electronics* (1977), in which the definition of *electrical*, quite interestingly, reads '[r]elated to, pertaining to, or associated with electricity *but not having its properties or characteristics*' (emphasis mine).

It is possible that the vague, sometimes one-line definitions of *electrical* in dictionaries, with no other uses given, are to some extent due to the principles employed in the compilation of the dictionaries so as to include the most prominent uses of words. However, the study by Kaunisto (1999) showed that there is considerable overlap in the use of the two forms when relating to the physical properties of electricity (e.g. *electric(al) charge/power*) or to its transmission (e.g. *electric(al) cable/wire*; see also Hann (1992) s.v. *electrical/*

---

3   Instead of using the paraphrase 'produced by electricity' for phrases such as *electric(al) charge/conductivity/current/voltage,* in the present analysis they are classified as relating to the physical aspects of electricity, with the paraphrase 'caused by electricity' being used for cases like *electric(al) shock*, and 'produced by (means of) electricity' used for e.g. *electric(al) stimulation/treatment.*

electronic equipment, and the usage note '*electric* or *electrical*?' in *The New Penguin English Dictionary* (2000)). With some senses and some head words, *electrical* even seemed to be favoured over *electric*. Among the dictionaries consulted, *COBUILD* (2001; the earlier editions of 1987 and 1995 including a similar treatment of the adjective) is a refreshing exception in that instead of including only one vague definition for *electrical*, it lists four different major uses, as presented below (the taxonomy of *electric* in *COBUILD* (2001) resembles that of *OALD* (1995) discussed above):

> *Electrical* goods, equipment, or appliances work by means of electricity. *...shipments of electrical equipment. ...electrical appliances.*
> *Electrical* systems or parts supply or use electricity.
> *Electrical* energy is energy in the form of electricity.
> *Electrical* industries, engineers, or workers are involved in the production and supply of electricity or electrical goods.

All in all, the description of the use of *electric* and *electrical* in dictionaries and usage manuals could be said to manifest the influence of the availability of large corpora, the more recent sources (from approximately the early 1990s onwards) showing promising signs of more detailed and accurate accounts of the perceivable differences between the two forms. The role of the collocates in illustrating the different uses of the forms is obvious, and it is to be hoped that more attention will in the future be paid to their placing in the dictionary entries, to avoid giving false implications on which phrases are fixed and which are not.

3.   Different uses of *electric/electrical*

The following sections will discuss some of the uses of *electric/electrical*, from both a historical and a present-day viewpoint. Particular attention will be paid to instances presenting problems in the analysis of the corpus material, including both adjectival and nominal uses of the words.

3.1   'Having the potential to develop electricity', 'charged with electricity'

The earliest use of *electric/electrical*, relating to the potential of a substance to develop electricity through friction, is one of which very few instances were encountered in the corpora studied. No occurrence of the type exemplified by "[e]lectricall bodies drawe and attract not without rubbing and stirring vp of the matter first" (*OED* s.v. *electrical* 1.a; from Nathaniel Carpenter, *Geography delineated forth in two bookes* (1635) I. iii, 54) was found in present-day material of either adjective form. One may therefore ask whether the label "obsolete" in the *OED* should perhaps be assigned to *electric* as well as *electrical* in this sense.

Electric/electrical in the sense 'charged with electricity' was likewise rarely attested in either historical and present-day corpora, one nineteenth-century instance being "Stiller and stiller grew Nature, as at the meeting of two electric clouds" (George Meredith, *The Ordeal of Richard Feverel* (1859), 266).[4] As observed in Kaunisto (1999: 350), a more idiomatic expression in present-day English is *live* (e.g. *the rail he fell on was live*). The relative infrequency of this use is in line with the observation concerning the awkwardness of Fowler's example *an electric book*. The sense 'electrically charged' is, however, still viable in figurative uses, as in *the atmosphere was electric*, where the adjective is actually interchangeable with the word *charged*.

The sense 'charged with electricity' is one which characteristically describes the quality of the thing modified by the adjective, rather than denoting a class to which the referent belongs. It is no surprise then that all the examples of *electrical* in this sense given in the *OED* have the adjective in a predicative position, e.g. "The smoke and vapour of volcanoes are highly electrical" (from Robert Bakewell, *Introduction to Geology* (1815), 313).[5]

3.2   'Relating to electricity as a physical phenomenon', 'producing or carrying electricity'

As noted earlier, there is some variation between *electric* and *electrical* when referring to the physical aspects of electricity, typical head words being *current*, *charge*, *field*, *force*, and *power*. It is rather easy to find instances where an author uses both forms in free variation. In the following examples, (4a) and (4b) are from two articles written by Roger Highfield, the Science Editor of *The Daily Telegraph*, while (4c) and (4d) come from a 1916 article by Gilbert Lewis:

(4)   a.   Then an electric field is used to shift the whole microparticles to obscure or reveal the black dye in the microcapsules; this principle can be used to build an image. (*The Daily Telegraph*, July 30, 1998, "Connected: Electronic ink could hold volumes and save trees")

---

4   One could argue for the inclusion of instances of *electric(al) battery* among those of the sense 'charged with electricity', but in the case of batteries the semantic relation with electricity is notably different from the original idea of an object being electrically charged so that one could get an electric shock by touching it.

5   Interestingly enough, the second edition of the *OED* gives no actual quotations of *electric* in this sense, although the corresponding use of *electrical* (sense 1.b) instead of a definition proper contains a mere cross-reference to *electric*.

    b.   Sulphur dioxide venting from the volcanoes is energised by the charged particles from the electrical fields and results in the gas glowing in a brilliant blue. (*The Daily Telegraph*, Oct. 15, 1998, "Jupiter's blue moon puts on an electric light show")

    c.   Electric forces between particles which are very close together do not obey the simple law of inverse squares which holds at greater distances. (Gilbert Lewis, "The Atom and the Molecule" (1916), 768)

    d.   Ever since the first suggestion of Helmholtz, numerous efforts have been made to explain chemical combination by the assumption that in the formation of a compound some of the different charged parts of the molecule thus produced are held together by electrical forces. (Gilbert Lewis, "The Atom and the Molecule" (1916), 771)

Among the head words modified by the adjectives relating to electricity, different semantic groups can be distinguished. While some words denote specific features of the phenomenon, e.g. *current* and *charge*, others have by nature a more general reference, as, for example, *electric(al) activity/ condition/state*. In the historical corpora studied, instances of both forms are found in connection with the latter type of head words, but in present-day English, there seems to be quite a strong tendency to favour *electrical*, especially when modifying the word *activity*[6]. Another distinct group involves the study of the phenomenon, with head words such as *science*, *study*, *research*, and *experiments*. It appears that *electrical* has been and remains the preferred form in such cases, although occasionally *electric* is found as well, as in (5a):

---

6   One very interesting observation has been made by Ian Gurney (personal communication), who suggested that *electrical* could more likely be used when referring to an activity or currents which are very low, in which case the additional *-al* ending might carry something of a diminutive shade in it when compared to the *-ic* form. This idea has also been suggested by Quirk et al (1985: 1554) in connection with the pairs *atheistic(al)* and *egotistic(al)*, exemplified by the sentences *His views are (rather) atheistic/egotistic* and *His views are (slightly) atheistical/egotistical*. This distinction, if it truly exists, is also most fascinating in the light of Marchand's (1969) idea of adjectives in *-ic* having a closer relation than those in *-ical* with the root of the word, as discussed in Chapter 3. As regards *electric/electrical*, many instances of the phrase *electrical activity* in the material have to do with activity in the brain or muscles. However, the total number of instances of *electric/electrical* in connection with words such as *current(s)* and *charge(s)* in the corpora studied are too low for looking into this argument in greater detail. As was seen in examples (1a) and (1b), both forms were found in phrases of the type *a small ~ current*, i.e. where the size was explicitly mentioned. The difference in the use of the forms in cases without explicit reference to the size, but where it would nevertheless be implied in the context (e.g. by phrases like *in the brain*) remains an interesting possibility for further investigation by means of a larger corpus.

(5)   a.   But the great differences in the disruptive and luminous effects, when the forces are too strong for electric equilibrium, presented by the two modes of electrification, which have been known from the earliest times of electric science, show physical properties not touched by the mathematical theory. (Lord Kelvin (William Thomson), "Aepinus Atomized" (1902))

       b.   Let me tell you, my friend, that there are things done to-day in electrical science which would have been deemed unholy by the very men who discovered electricity. (Bram Stoker, *Dracula* (1897), 195)

One difficulty in the analysis of the corpus material and the assignment of the occurrences into different categories involves the occasional omission of certain words in the phrases containing the adjectives. For example, it would intuitively seem sensible to distinguish instances having the word *power* as the head from those where the adjective modifies words such as *generator*, *plant*, or *company*, which pertain to the production or distribution of electricity rather than relate to the phenomenon directly (or actually *are* electricity). However, there are also instances of *electric(al) power generator/plant/company*, where the phrase *electric(al) power* could be regarded as modifying the head word *generator*, *plant*, or *company*, i.e. [[*electric(al) power*]$_{NP}$ *company*]$_{NP}$. What makes the issue even more complex is that in cases of this type, one also encounters phrases like *power company* and *power plant* without the adjective. From a present-day point of view, the structural analysis [*electric(al)* [*power company*]$_{NP}$]$_{NP}$ seems less attractive, because by common custom, the phrase *power company* – almost without any surrounding context – already implies that the company produces electricity rather than some other kind of power (e.g. thermo-dynamic or manual, as those kind of companies do not exist; *a nuclear power plant*, on the other hand, is a kind of electric(al) power plant). It is uncertain, however, whether compounds such as *power company* or *power plant* have been formed independently or from phrases such as *electric(al) power company* via omission of the adjective.

Considering the present analysis, it would seem strange to categorize instances such as *electric(al) power generator* and *electric(al) generator* differently. On the other hand, it would perhaps not be well judged to present instances of *electric(al) power* and *electric(al) generator* within the same group. That might obscure the possibility that the adjective forms may have developed separate preferences in connection with particular kinds of words which represent different semantic groups. Therefore the occurrences of *electric/electrical* in these cases are categorized according to the ultimate head word, but for the sake of clarity, the numbers of cases with and without the word *power* are also given separately (see also p. 167 for discussion on the analysis of the phrase *electrical (goods) retailer*, and cf. Table 49).

    In addition to instances pertaining to the production of electricity, one can distinguish cases which have to do with the transmission of electric(al) power, e.g. *electric(al) cable/cord/wire*, or its supply, as in *electric(al) plug/socket*. In connection with this type of head words as well, one can encounter instances such as *electric(al) power cable/cord*, complicating the analysis somewhat. The presentation of such cases in the present analysis follows the policy adopted for *electric(al) company/plant* (with the numbers of occurrences with and without the word *power* given separately, cf. Tables 3 and 4 in Appendix B).[7]

    When relating to electricity as a physical phenomenon, or denoting objects which carry electricity, the adjectives *electric* and *electrical* have a characteristically classifying function, and are therefore very rarely seen in a predicative position.

3.3 'Relating to the design, construction, or installation of electric(al) supplies, equipment or other applications of electric(al) power'

As noted earlier, *electrical* is today preferred in phrases relating to the scientific study of the phenomenon of electricity, e.g. *electrical experiment/ research*. The preference for the longer form seems to have become established fairly early. This use of *electrical* is also likely to have influenced its preference later in connection with the practical work relating to the various applications of electricity, the most prominent phrases today being *electrical engineer* and *electrical engineering*. It could be argued that electrical engineering should not be considered separate from the science of electricity: in fact, instead of beginning with inventors such as Morse, Edison, or Siemens, numerous accounts of the history of electricity also describe the pioneering work into the nature of the phenomenon by e.g. Gilbert, Franklin, Ampere, Davy, and Faraday, to name but a few. However, one may claim that the increase in the number of practical applications of electricity in the latter half of the nineteenth century – for example, electrically powered means of transportation, communication, as well as lighting – brought along a whole new field of profession not necessarily concerned with research into the physical properties of electricity.

    Veering away from a strictly scientific or experimental line of work, *electrical* is today also preferred when modifying words such as *contracting*, *services*, and *work* (including e.g. installations), as well as other professional titles apart from engineer, e.g. *designer, draughtsman*, and *technician*. In the same way as with the relation to the physical properties of electricity, *electrical*

---

7   Conceptually it would perhaps not be an altogether impossible idea to suggest that in some cases, *electric(al)* is actually short for *electric(al) power*. It must be noted, however, that all words modified by *electric(al)* do not equally readily allow the inclusion of the word *power*: whereas instances of *electric(al) power cord/switch* can be found (sometimes without the adjective), *electric(al) power wire* somehow seems less likely, not to mention *electric power iron/toothbrush*.

here functions as a classifier, and thus it mostly occurs in an attributive position, although predicative instances are not altogether impossible, e.g. "The only difference is that this time the scope of our work is civil, mechanical and electrical" (*BNC*, HP4 876).

3.4   'Powered by electricity'

As noted in Kaunisto (1999), one of the most interesting areas where one finds a distinction between *electric* and *electrical* has to do with devices or systems that use electricity as their source of power. The uses of *electric* and *electrical* manifest a distinction along the lines of specific versus general: in practice, *electric* is more commonly used when modifying words such as *iron*, *kettle*, *toothbrush*, and *whisk*, while in connection with *appliance*, *device*, *equipment*, *goods*, *machines*, and so on, *electrical* is usually preferred. Some exceptions to this pattern can occasionally be found, as in the following cases:

(6)   a.   Matsushita Electrical Industrial is the world's largest maker of electric appliances and video tape recorders as well as one of the biggest users of assembly robots. (*BNC*, B7B 600)

   b.   But I have never held that all inventions are evil. Some, though not many, are actually beneficial. Bicycles, refrigerators, typewriters, electrical orange squeezers, anaesthetics are a few that come to mind. (*The Sunday Telegraph*, June 18, 1995, "Way of the World: Fax")

The earliest observations on this distinction between the adjective forms can probably be linked with the introduction and study of large, computer-searchable text corpora. Among the works consulted, the earliest comment to this effect – relating particularly to devices – was found in the *Bloomsbury Good Word Guide* (1988) s.v. *electric, electrical*. The more elaborate distinction along the lines of specific versus general has later been suggested e.g. by Swan (1995: 256).[8] In

---

8   Greenbaum and Whitcut (1988) s.v. *electric(al), electronic* also advocated the idea of *electric* being favoured with specific, and *electrical* with general terms, considering all the uses of the adjectives: "Systems that use electricity as a direct source of power are *electric*: *an electric plug/clock*. *Electrical* expresses a rather less direct and more general connection with electricity: *electrical appliances*; *an electrical engineer*; *electrical fault in the system*." Obviously aiming at a neat and useful generalization on the main differences between *electric* and *electrical*, Greenbaum and Whitcut are perhaps too liberal in combining different facets of the uses of the adjectives in their glosses. *An electric plug* does not actually *use* electricity, but merely connects a device to an electric(al) supply. Another inaccuracy has to do with *electrical appliances*, a phrase which in most cases relates to things which do "use electricity as a direct source of power". From the viewpoint of the present analysis, though, the words *appliance*, *device*, and *goods* are slightly

some sources, the distinction is not spelt out explicitly, but is implied through the examples given (see e.g. Hann (1992); *OALD* (1995) s.vv.), while some miss it out altogether, using the phrases *electric device/machine/appliance* with general reference in their definitions or commentary (e.g. Urdang (1988) s.v. *electric/electrical/electronic*; *COBUILD* (2001) s.vv.).

Based on the historical corpora and the quotations including *electric/electrical* in the CD-ROM version of the *OED*, the first phrases with the adjectives denoting electrically powered things include *electric telegraph/bell/light/tramway/heater*. For these phrases with specific reference, the use of which began to develop and increase since electricity became commercially available (from around the mid-1800s onwards), *electric* seems to have been the preferred form from the very beginning.[9] The historical material also provides interesting new information considering Marsden's (1985: 29) comment according to which the strong foothold of the phrases *electrical goods/appliances* in present-day English "might owe its origin to the very early days of electric power". While the overall more general references to electricity in the use of *electrical* may stem from earlier times, the first uses of the adjectives with words such as *appliance*, *device*, and *goods* appeared after those with a specific reference, i.e. phrases of the type *an electric bell* are older than ones like *electrical equipment* (at least when the equipment does not mean machines producing electricity by friction). This itself is hardly surprising, as one would logically expect superordinate terms to have developed after the subordinate ones. The increase in the number of general references is probably most significantly linked in time with the surge of electrically powered household appliances into everyday use, the greatest increase of which is likely to have occurred in the twentieth century.

The development of the preference for *electrical* in connection with general terms in the sense 'powered by electricity' is particularly fascinating, because it goes against the overall tendency among *-ic/-ical* adjectives to favour the forms in *-ic* in more recent coinages. Also of interest is the type of the distinction between the two adjective forms, because it is a mixture of collocational restriction and semantic differentiation. Semantically, the basic meanings of both *electric* and *electrical* are practically the same ('powered by electricity'). The specific or general reference to items, manifested in the collocating head words, affects the choice of the adjective form. The effect of the

---

problematic in that strictly speaking, their reference can also include objects such as plugs and adaptors, which are not powered by electricity, whereas *an electrical apparatus/machine* always is. This minor semantic detail notwithstanding, the use of the adjectives in connection with the general terms *apparatus, appliance, device*, etc. are all categorized in the sense group 'powered by electricity'.

9   One notable exception is the phrase *electric(al) telegraph*: the *OED* includes three quotations with the phrase *electrical telegraph*. Interestingly enough, all of these instances deal with the early experiments on the application of electricity into telegraphy, and they precede the introduction of the apparatus invented by Samuel Morse in 1837, using techniques which became the first widely accepted standard throughout the world. No instances of *electrical telegraph* were found in the material studied dating from after 1834.

semantic element, i.e. the type of reference, however, seems to be stronger than that of the collocating noun, for there are instances where *electric* collocates with superordinate terms without being exceptional as in (7). These cases include ones where the superordinate term is used as a pro-form, substituting a previously mentioned specific word, usually with an explicit contrast made with comparable devices not powered by electricity:

(7)   For extensive hedging with thick, springy growth such as beech, hawthorn, hornbeam, yew or evergreen Lawsonia and leylandii cypresses, petrol trimmers are recommended. Electric machines cope well with box, cotoneaster, privet and smaller-leaved types for shaping or topiary. (*The Daily Telegraph*, Sept. 23, 1995, "Gardening: They crunch and they shred: the tools of the trade")

Example (7) includes the phrase *electric machines*, although one would expect the word *machines* as a superordinate term to select *electrical* instead. In the extract above, *machines* acts as a pro-form to avoid repetition of the word *trimmers*, retaining the specific nature of the reference. The specificity is similarly retained when using *one(s)* as the pro-form, as in "In effect, this is a small boiler which will run more cheaply than an electric one and will reduce dependence on a single fuel" (*BNC*, HH6 1590).

Electric is also the preferred form when there is an intervening modifier specifying the function of the apparatus, as in *an electric cooking appliance* or *an electric espresso/knitting/milking machine*. Interestingly enough, it appears that in connection with superordinate terms, the specificity must become evident from the very phrase modified by the adjective (as noted, through the use of a pro-form or by means of an intervening modifier); in cases where the function or purpose of the device is explicitly stated, but outside the phrase, the longer form tends to be used more often:[10]

(8)   Amstrad is launching itself into the beauty products market with a £2m advertising campaign for its Ultima 'face care system', an electrical device for toning facial tissue to reduce wrinkles and sagging. (*The Daily Telegraph*, Sept. 29, 1995, "CITY: Amstrad joins beauty parade")

The shorter form is also used more often when referring to musical instruments and vehicles powered by electricity. In the case of musical instruments, the amplification or production of the sound of the instrument is done by using electricity, or, more specifically, by electronic means. In addition to specific words such as *guitar*, *organ*, and *drums*, on the one hand, and *car*,

---

10   It must be noted that cases such as (8) are relatively rare, and the observation on the preference for *electrical* is based on the study of the *BNC*, the 1993 and 1995 issues of *The Daily Telegraph*, as well as the use of the adjectives in the quotations in the *OED*, which, added together, bring out the distinction between the two forms.

train, and *van*, on the other, *electric* is used with the superordinate terms *instrument* and *vehicle*. As mentioned in Kaunisto (1999: 352), these terms are not entirely comparable to terms such as *appliance*, *device*, and *gadget*, being in fact more specific. The function of *vehicle* (used for transportation) is understood without any context, and one of the meanings of *instrument* is "a device used to produce music" (*LDEL* s.v.). *Electric* is also used of the electrically produced or amplified music itself, as in "The staging of the Crucifixion, accompanied by John Tam's wonderful electric folk music, is almost unbearable in its graphic depiction of human suffering" (*The Daily Telegraph*, Oct. 19, 1995, "The Arts: Beyond doubt a marvellous piece of work").

Relating to the commercial distribution of electrical goods and appliances, *electrical* is the preferred form when modifying words such as *retailer*, *retailing*, *shop*, and *store* (i.e. *electrical retailers* refers to ones who sell electrical goods). In fact, one can encounter occurrences of the type *electrical goods retailer* as well as *electrical retailer*. Considering the organization of categories in the analysis of the material, the situation here resembles that of *electric(al) power generator* and *electric(al) generator*. In this case, however, it is justifiable to include instances of *electrical goods retailer* in the same category as those of *electrical goods*, because the phrase *goods retailer* does not usually appear by itself (and even if it did, one would not naturally interpret the goods to be electrical ones). Instead, *goods* is normally modified by a classifier, e.g. *electrical/sporting/fishing goods*.[11]

Referring to electrically powered devices, some instances of the adjectives in a predicative position can be found (although they are far from ordinary), slightly more often than when referring to electricity and its properties.

---

11   The British and the American editions of *Encarta World English Dictionary* (1999) differ interestingly in their definitions of *electric/electrical*. Sense 3 of *electrical* in the British edition includes a crossreference to sense 3 of *electric*, 'powered or operated by electricity', followed by the example phrase *electrical goods*. While the American edition also gives this sense to *electric*, it has not been assigned to *electrical*. One reason may be that the phrase *electrical goods* is not commonly used in American English (at least when compared to British English): in the 1994 edition of *The Washington Post*, no instance of this phrase was found. Instead, the phrase *electrical equipment* seems to be used in those cases where the British would often use *electrical goods*, e.g. *electrical equipment company/manufacturer/salesman* (less frequently found in *The Daily Telegraph*) as opposed to *electrical goods distributor/retailer/shop* (commonly found in British English). Although the phrase used as the example in the British edition is less common in American English, one would still expect the sense 'powered by electricity' to be included under *electrical* in the American edition of the dictionary, too, as the distinction between specific and general terms appears to exist in both variants of the language.

3.5   Figurative uses

Another major difference between the two adjective forms today is the clear preference for *electric* when used figuratively, one apt paraphrase being 'full of tension' (other equivalents including 'exciting', 'thrilling' and 'tense'), which those usage manuals including a note on *electric/electrical* usually also comment on (e.g. Evans and Evans 1957 s.v. *electric; electrical*; Urdang 1988 s.v. *electric/electrical/electronic*). Only a few of the present-day sources consider the two forms interchangeable in such functions, among them the eighth edition of *The Concise Oxford Dictionary of Current English* (1990), *Webster's Third New International Dictionary* (1961/1993), and Howard (1993), some of them nevertheless mentioning that the longer form is now less common.

In the late eighteenth century and the nineteenth century, both forms were used figuratively (the descriptive nature explains the numerous occurrences in a predicative position), as illustrated earlier in examples (2a–d). In the *OED*, the first quotation of *electrical* in this sense dates from 1775, that of *electric* from 1793. Although figurative uses of the longer form are rarely found in present-day English, this meaning of *electrical* in the *OED* is not labelled obsolete or archaic.

The *OED* definition of the figurative use (s.v. *electric*, sense 3) reads 'Chiefly with reference to the swiftness of electricity, or to the thrilling effect of the electric shock; also in obvious metaphorical uses of the phrases in 2 b' ("2 b" containing the numerous "phraseological combinations" discussed earlier). It is possible that the figurative uses of *electric* and *electrical* actually stem from different kinds of literal notions, including those observed in the definition in the *OED*. Some instances mostly suggest the result or effect, which is likened to that of an electric(al) shock, e.g. *the effect was electric(al)*, while others may have the literal equivalent of 'electrically charged', as in *the atmosphere/mood was electric(al)*. Yet other cases may emphasize the speed of the action or effect in question, most clearly when the head word relates to this very characteristic, e.g. *electric(al) rapidity/speed/swiftness*, as in "Storm and sunlight swept, one after another, with electrical rapidity at all times through her vivid changeful temper" (Ouida, *Under Two Flags* (1867), 250). The different notions involved in the figurative uses have also been noted in dictionaries, e.g. *The Concise Oxford Dictionary of Current English* (1990) s.v. *electric* which describes the use with the paraphrase 'causing or charged with sudden and dramatic excitement'.

For the tabular presentations of the present analysis, however, it is not feasible to attempt a detailed categorization of the different aspects of meaning of the figurative uses according to the literal equivalents. Some instances can, in fact, be ambiguous in this respect: in *the atmosphere in the room was electric*, the atmosphere may be regarded as both 'exciting' as well as 'charged' (or 'excit*ed*'). Similarly, speed or swiftness itself may be considered exciting or thrilling apart from being merely likened to that of electricity, and the extent of the causal element (i.e. causing excitement) in the use of the adjective is impossible to measure conclusively from any instance. Although there are also cases which are less ambiguous, in the present analysis the figurative cases are placed into two groups: ones where reference is made to the speed observed, and others.[12]

3.6   Nominal uses of *electric/electrical*

Although the nominal uses of *electric/electrical* will not in the present study be subjected to a close analysis, a few comments on them can be made, paying attention to the different kinds of uses generally noted as well as the issue of determining whether the word should be regarded as a noun or an adjective in particular instances. As observed in section 1, the nominal uses of *electric* and *electrical* have been considerably less common compared to their adjectival use, and few nominal instances of the words came up in the material studied. The use of the forms as nouns cannot be said to have influenced the adjectival uses in any remarkable way, least of all leading towards a situation in which one of the forms would be used solely as a noun, the other as an adjective. On the contrary, the nominal uses are likely to have been modelled to a great extent after the different adjectival ones.

Electric/electrical is a remarkable pair of words ending in *-ic/-ical* in that both forms have adjectival as well as nominal functions. According to the *OED*, *electric* was the first of the two forms to have been used as a noun, namely to designate a substance that develops electricity if excited by friction. *Electric* has also been used as a noun to refer to devices such as the electric lamp and the electric guitar, or vehicles such as the electric train, this use often being labelled informal in dictionaries (see e.g. *Collins English Dictionary* (1998) s.v.). Both forms are used nominally of electric(al) circuitry and cabling in the plural, as in "Check that you won't sever electrics or plumbing" (*The Daily Telegraph*, Feb. 10, 1996, "Property: DIY") and "Hall busied himself with the 'dry trace' (woodwork, electricals, plumbing)" (*The Sunday Telegraph*, Feb. 19, 1995, "Have-a-go heroes: The house that Ron Hall built"). According to some dictionaries, *electrics* is also used of electrical appliances (e.g. *Collins English Dictionary* (1998); the British edition of *Encarta World English Dictionary* (1999)). In CD-ROM editions of *The Daily Telegraph*, however, *electrics* appears to relate more often to systems of electric(al) circuits and wires, while *electricals* is mostly used as a general term for electrical appliances, which is quite logical, considering the specific vs. general distinction between the adjectives in relation to electrically powered machines.

---

12   Figurative uses of *electric(al)* which are better paraphrased as 'emotionally charged' than 'exciting' include cases where the adjective is followed by the preposition *with* + NP, as in *the atmosphere was electric with expectation*. Such instances are used as examples in e.g. *The American Heritage Dictionary of the English Language* (2000) and *The New Penguin English Dictionary* (2000), which distinguish between the senses 'exciting, thrilling' and 'tense, charged'.

Electricals is also often used of companies manufacturing or selling electrical appliances, the material studied including the following interesting set of *electrical(s) (goods) retailer*:

(9)   a.   Dixons, the electrical goods retailer, has become one of the main suppliers to the 'property crime industry', Mr Stanley Kalms, chairman, said [...]. (*The Daily Telegraph*, June 30, 1993, "£20m stolen from Dixons stores")

      b.   At 42, Mr Corbett will be the youngest member of Grand Met's board. He joins after six years at Redland. He has also worked for Dixons, the electrical retailer. (*The Daily Telegraph*, Dec. 15, 1993, "City: Grand Met brings in Redland Man")

      c.   Dixons, the electricals retailer, has appointed Peter Morris as president of Silo, its loss-making American subsidiary. (*The Daily Telegraph*, Feb. 3, 1993, "City: Dixons post new chief to US offshoot")

Based on (9a–c), it could actually be asked whether *electrical* in collocation with words such as *retailer* is in fact a noun, representing the nominal phrase *electrical goods* in the same way as *electricals*. Differing views are also to be seen in the interpretation of *electric* in the phrase *electric bill*. In the second edition of the *COBUILD* dictionary, *electric* in the example sentence "An average electric bill might go up $2 or $3 per month" is classified as a noun, the description of the use reading "The *electric* is the supply of electricity to a house or other place; an informal use". Apart from the supply of electricity, *electric* is sometimes used nominally to refer to electricity or electric(al) power itself, as in "he took a good five-second dosage of electric before he was dramatically knocked to the floor" (*The Daily Telegraph*, Dec. 23, 1995, "Racing Diary: Under orders at the 'Crown'"). On the one hand, interpreting *electric* as a noun in *electric bill* would seem reasonable considering the fact that the phrase *electricity bill* is also commonly used. On the other hand, however, it is not impossible to find instances of *electrical bill* either: a search of the phrase with the *Google* Internet search engine produced a number of web pages including the phrase, e.g. "we want to save money on our home electrical bill by using less electricity" (from the Green and Growing Education Projects web site, http://www.gatewest.net/~green/its/lElectric3.html, last accessed on July 5, 2003). Quite interestingly, the third edition of *COBUILD* includes the same example sentence with *electric bill* as in the previous edition, but with *electric* now defined as an adjective. As regards the analysis of the corpora, instances of both *electric bill* and *electrical retailer* have been included in the tabular presentations.

4.   *Electric/electrical* in the material studied

The following section surveys the uses of *electric* and *electrical* in the historical and present-day corpora studied. The historical corpora include the prose section of the *Literature Online* text collection and the non-fiction corpus culled from the Internet. As these corpora included relatively few occurrences of the adjectives from the seventeenth and eighteenth centuries, all instances of the adjectives appearing in the quotations of the *OED* from these periods were also examined from a CD-ROM version of the dictionary.

To investigate the use of the adjectives in present-day British English, their occurrences in the 1995 issues of *The Daily Telegraph* were analyzed. In Kaunisto (1999), an analysis was made on *electric/electrical* in the 1993 issues of the same newspaper, and the results here – with some minor changes in the categorizations of different uses – will be compared to the earlier ones. To supplement the analysis as far as a number of particular collocations are concerned, references will also be made to the adjectives' use in the *British National Corpus*.

As regards non-fiction, the fact that *electric* and *electrical* relate to a scientific phenomenon means that greater attention has to be paid to the use of the adjectives in question in different scientific fields than, for example, in the case of the inherently "non-scientific" pair *comic/comical*. Electricity has been approached and applied in many different ways according to the scientific discipline, and different types of references to electricity may be perceived in the use of the adjectives in texts relating to e.g. psychology and chemistry.

Judging from the corpus materials from the seventeenth century and the first half of the eighteenth century, no remarkable differences in the use of the two adjective forms can be noted. In fact, only a few authors used the adjectives in the fiction and non-fiction corpora, as well as in the *OED* quotations.[13] As regards the corpus texts from the latter half of the eighteenth century, the numbers of occurrences of *electric* and *electrical* are likewise rather low, as can be seen

---

13   One author of interest in this period, however, is Robert Boyle, who in the extract from *Electricity & Magnetism* (1675–1676) included in the *Helsinki Corpus* was found using *electric* exclusively as a noun (i.e. a substance which possesses the property of developing electricity by means of friction), while reserving *electrical* for the adjectival function. In the 36 occurrences of *electrical*, Boyle used the adjective in references to materials having the property of developing electricity by means of friction (e.g. *electrical bodies*), as well as in relation to research into electricity (as in *electrical experiments*).

from Tables 38 and 39.[14] The figures are too low so as to suggest any clear differences in the use of the two forms.[15]

Table 38.   *Electric/electrical* in the prose section of *Literature Online, 1750–1799.*

	electric	electrical
1. 'having the property to develop electricity'	-	1
2. 'having to do with electricity as a physical phenomenon'	1	2
3. 'caused by electricity': ~ *shock/stroke*/etc.	5	8
4. figurative: 'full of tension', 'exciting'		
a. ~ *rapidity*	-	1
b. others	8 (2)	2 (2)
total	**14 (2)**	**14 (2)**
# of authors:	6	6
# of authors using both forms: 2		

Table 39. *Electric/electrical* in the non-fiction texts examined, 1750–1799.

	electric	electrical
1. 'having the property to develop electricity'	1	-
2. 'having to do with electricity as a physical phenomenon'		
a. research: ~ *experiment*	-	2
b. ~ *machine*	-	1
c. general terms: ~ *virtue*	-	1
3. 'caused by electricity': ~ *spark*	12	2
total	**13**	**6**
# of authors:	4	3
# of authors using both forms: 1		

---

14   The sense 'caused by electricity' includes cases such as *electric(al) shock/stroke/ spark*, which in the present analysis are regarded as "by-products" of electric(al) activity, and are therefore separated from more intentional actions and processes powered by electricity (e.g. *electric(al) recording/stimulation*), although in some cases, e.g. the production of electric(al) shocks, definite intention can sometimes be involved.

15   The phrase *electric(al) machine* in the previous centuries usually related to machines used in scientific experiments to develop electricity.

As for individual phrases, there were no perceivable signs of fixedness in relation to the adjective form used; instead, variation between the forms was seen even when used by the same writer (as in the case of examples (4a–d) above):

(10)   a.   In the earthquake at Jamaica, June 7, 1692, in which several thousands perished, it is certain, that not only many houses, and a great number of people, were intirely swallowed up; but that, at many of the gapings or openings of the earth, torrents of water that formed great rivers, issued forth [...] Now to me the electrical stroke does not appear sufficient to produce these things. The power of electricity, to be sure is vast and amazing. (Thomas Amory, *John Buncle* (1756–1766), 170–171)

       b.   [...] or, the water of the great abyss is with such violence moved, that it shakes the arches of the earth, and where infinite wisdom directs, is enabled by Almighty Power to open the globe with tremendous noises, and pour forth vast torrents of water, to cover a land where once a flourishing city has stood. The electric stroke cannot be more dreadful than such exertion of omnipotence. (Thomas Amory, *John Buncle* (1756–1766), 179)

       c.   In a paper, printed in the last volume of the Philosophical Transactions, in which I gave my reasons for thinking that the diminution produced in atmospheric air by phlogistication, is not owing to the generation of fixed air, I said it seemed most likely, that the phlogistication of air by the electric spark was owing to the burning of some inflammable matter in the apparatus [...] (Henry Cavendish, "Experiments on Air" (1785))

       d.   This being premised, we may safely conclude, that in the present experiments the phlogisticated air was enabled, by means of the electrical spark, to unite to, or form a chemical combination with the dephlogisticated air, and was thus reduced to nitrous acid, which united to the soap-lees, and formed a solution of nitre; [...] (Henry Cavendish, "Experiments on Air" (1785))

Although the quotations in the *OED* do not as such constitute a corpus with a clear structure or organization, the occurrences of *electric/electrical* in them are rather interesting. In the quotations from the first half of the eighteenth century, no occurrences of *electric* were found, whereas seven authors used the *-ical* form. Quotations from the latter half of the century, however, included ones in which 28 different authors used *electric*, while eight used *electrical* (of these authors, three used both forms). Considering the fact that *electrical* was the first of the two forms, it is possible that the longer form indeed may have been at least slightly more common until the mid-eighteenth century, the latter half of the century witnessing a relative increase in frequency of the shorter form. The uses of the adjective forms in the quotations, including those instances for which the author was specified, are presented in Tables 40 and 41 below.

Table 40. *Electric/electrical* in the *OED* quotations, 1700–1749.

	electric	*electrical*
1. 'having the property to develop electricity'	-	3 (1)
2. 'having to do with electricity as a physical phenomenon'		
a. research: ~ *experiment*	-	1
b. ~ *machine*	-	1
c. ~ *battery*	-	1
d. others: ~ *fire/force*/etc.	-	12
3. 'caused by electricity':		
~ *shock/attraction*	-	3
total	**-**	**21 (1)**
# of authors:	-	7

In Table 40, eleven instances in group 2.d are of the phrase *electrical fire* (used in the same sense as *electric(al) fluid*) from texts by Benjamin Franklin, who in his later writings used both forms in connection with the word *fire*. Examining Table 41, it can be seen that in phrases with head words such as *flash*, *shock*, and *stroke*, in which the use of the adjective may be paraphrased as 'caused by electricity', only *electric* was used, although in Tables 38 and 39, both forms were used in phrases carrying this sense. Considering the numbers of authors using *electric/electrical* in phrases of this type, combining the fiction and non-fiction corpora as well as the *OED* quotations from the eighteenth century, 15 authors used *electric*, and four used *electrical* (two of these authors used both forms), indicating a slight preference for the shorter form in this sense. One phrase with which a similar analysis can be made is *electric(al) fluid*, with ten authors using *electric*, and three using *electrical*.[16]

---

16   Group 8 ('others') contains instances which would have required a larger context in order to have been placed into any of the other groups.

Table 41. *Electric/electrical* in the *OED* quotations, 1750–1799.

	electric	electrical
1. 'having the property to develop electricity'	7	4
2. 'having to do with electricity as a physical phenomenon'		
a. ~ *machine*	1	2
b. ~ *jar*	-	1
c. others: ~ *fire/fluid*/etc.	19	7 (1)
3. 'charged with electricity'	1	-
4. 'carrying electricity': ~ *circuit*	1	-
5. 'caused by electricity': ~ *flash/shock/stroke*/etc.	11	-
6. figurative: 'full of tension', 'exciting'	1	-
7. ~ *eel*	1	-
8. others	2	1
total	**44**	**15 (1)**
# of authors:	28	8
# of authors using both forms: 3		

As far as can be concluded from the material studied, the eighteenth century use of the two adjective forms would seem to suggest an increase in the use of *electric*. During this period, knowledge of electricity and its applications increased through research by scientists like Benjamin Franklin, Henry Cavendish, Joseph Priestley, and Richard Watson, whose uses of the adjectives are also represented in the texts studied. In fact, the occurrences in Tables 39, 40 and 41 are, for the most part, found in texts by scientists examining the nature of electricity. While some of the scientists' uses of *electric* and *electrical* suggest a preference for one or the other form in some collocations, it is, however, notable that there was a considerable amount of variation between the two forms, in some cases even with one and the same author.

Tables 42 and 43, presenting the uses of *electric/electrical* between 1800 and 1849 in the *Literature Online* prose section and the non-fiction texts, respectively, give a very similar picture of the adjectives' use to the one emerging from the *OED* material for the latter half of the eighteenth century. The most common phrases relating to the physical characteristics of electricity, e.g. ~ *fluid/current*, show a preference for *electric*, as do instances paraphrasable as 'caused by electricity'. References to devices powered by electricity make their first entrance in the material studied with *electric telegraph*.

Table 42. *Electric/electrical* in the prose section of *Literature Online*, 1800–1849.

	electric	*electrical*
1. 'having to do with electricity as a physical phenomenon'		
a. ~ *machine*	-	2
b. ~ *battery/jar*	2	-
c. others: ~ *fluid*/etc.	10	-
2. 'caused by electricity': ~ *shock/spark*	9	-
3. 'powered by electricity': ~ *telegraph*	1	-
4. figurative: 'full of tension', 'exciting'	14 (1)	6 (3)
total	**36 (1)**	**8 (3)**
# of authors:	15	5
# of authors using both forms: 5		

Table 43. *Electric/electrical* in the non-fiction texts examined, 1800–1849.

	electric	*electrical*
1. 'having to do with electricity as a physical phenomenon'		
a. general terms: ~ *action/condition*/etc.	1	5 (1)
b. others: ~ *fluid/current*/etc.	16	-
2. 'caused by electricity': ~ *shock/light*/etc.	2	1
3. 'powered by electricity': ~ *telegraph*	1	-
4. figurative: 'full of tension', 'exciting'	3	-
total	**23**	**6 (1)**
# of authors:	9	3
# of authors using both forms: 2		

All occurrences of the adjectives from this period in the non-fiction texts are from texts by British authors. The seven texts in which the adjectives were used deal with different kinds of topics, e.g literary criticism (Shelley and Coleridge), economic thinking (Bagehot), and the nature of electric(al) phenomena (Faraday).

Given the fact that the number of absolute occurrences of *electric/electrical* in Tables 42 and 43 is again relatively low, the *OED* quotations were examined from this period as well, and the uses of the adjectives are presented in Table 44 below. The results are generally parallel to the ones in Tables 42 and 43. Considering the period as a whole, *electrical* seems to have been the preferred form when referring to machines used in scientific experiments to develop electricity. The preference for *electric* in connection with the words *fluid* and *current* finds further support from the quotations in the *OED*, with six occurrences of the phrase *electric fluid* (all by different authors), and 14 of *electric current* (by eight authors). Although not a single corresponding phrase was found with *electrical*, there was some variation in connection with certain other words, e.g. *force*. In the case of the sense 'caused by electricity', the shorter form was favoured by a number of different authors in connection with *shock* and *spark*.

Table 44. *Electric/electrical* in the *OED* quotations, 1800–1849.

	electric	*electrical*
1. 'having the property to develop electricity'	-	1
2. 'having to do with electricity as a physical phenomenon'		
a. research: ~ *experiment*/etc.	-	3
b. ~ *machine*	-	7
c. ~ *battery/jar*	2	2
d. general terms: ~*action/state*/etc.	2	4
e. others: ~ *current/fluid*/etc.	24	5
3. 'charged with electricity'	1	2 (2)
4. 'carrying electricity': ~ *wire*/etc.	3	-
5. 'caused by electricity':		
a. ~ *shock*	6	-
b. ~ *spark*	6	1
c. others	2	3
6. 'powered by electricity':		
~ *telegraph*	3	1
7. figurative: 'full of tension', 'exciting'	9 (2)	2
8. others	3	3
total	**61 (2)**	**34 (2)**
# of authors:	43	23
# of authors using both forms: 9		

The uses of the adjectives in the *Literature Online* material in 1850–1903, presented in Table 45, show one striking development, namely the increasing number of references to electrically powered devices (group 5). All of the collocates were specific terms, i.e. specifying the function of the object in question, including *telegraph, light, bell, lamp*, and *furnace*. It is particularly interesting to observe that only *electric* was used in these expressions, and that superordinate terms modified by the adjectives in the corresponding sense did not occur at all in the material from this period.

Table 45.   *Electric/electrical* in the prose section of *Literature Online*, 1850–1903.

	electric	electrical
1. 'having to do with electricity as a physical phenomenon'		
a. research: ~ *science*/etc.	-	2
b. ~ *machine*	2	-
c. ~ *battery*	1	-
d. general terms: ~ *condition*	-	1
e. others: ~ *current/force*/etc.	10	-
2. 'charged with electricity'	1	-
3. 'carrying electricity': ~ *wire*/etc.	8	-
4. 'caused by electricity':		
a. ~ *shock*	19	1
b. ~ *spark*	1	-
c. ~ *flame*	1	-
5. 'powered by electricity':		
a. appliances, specific ~ *telegraph/light/bell*/etc.	28	-
b. transportation systems ~ *tramway/railway*	2	-
c. actions, processes, illumination, etc.	6	2
6. others: ~ *eel*	1	-
7. figurative: 'full of tension', 'exciting'		
a. ~ *rapidity/velocity*/etc.	4	1
b. others	27 (4)	15 (7)
total	**111 (4)**	**22 (7)**
# of authors:	35	12
# of authors using both forms: 9		

Another detail worth paying attention to is the fact that compared to the form in *-ic*, the material contained relatively few instances of *electrical* in literal senses. It could be regarded as indicative of a fairly established use of *electrical* at the time that the rare literal instances found include cases such as *electrical science/experiment*, i.e. collocates with a semantic nuance (research on electricity) which was in earlier periods already observed to show signs of preference for *electrical*. In the latter half of the nineteenth century, the longer form also had a fairly strong standing as regards figurative uses.

As regards the non-fiction corpus from this period, the uses of *electric/electrical* by British authors were found mostly in texts by scientists, e.g. Ernest Rutherford, J.J. Thomson, George Stoney, and Charles Darwin. The results, presented in Table 46, seem to be in line with the observations made on the developments so far, suggesting a general preference for the use of *electric*.

Table 46. *Electric/electrical* in the non-fiction texts examined, 1850–1899 (British authors).

	electric	electrical
1. 'having to do with electricity as a physical phenomenon'		
a. research: ~ *experiment*/etc.	-	4
b. ~ *machine*	1	2
c. ~ *battery*	2	1
d. general terms:		
~ *action/properties*/etc.	2	4
e. others: ~ *field/force*/etc.	58	23 (2)
2. 'having to do with the supply of electricity': ~ *supply*/etc.	3	1
3. 'caused by electricity': ~ *spark/flame*/etc.	9	-
4. 'powered by electricity':		
a. appliances, specific ~ *telegraph/lamp*	8	-
b. actions, processes: ~ *excitation*	-	1
5. others		
~ *fish*	1	-
~ *organs* (of fish)	8	-
6. figurative: 'full of tension', 'exciting'	3	-
total	**95**	**36 (2)**
# of authors:	11	10
# of authors using both forms: 8		

It must be noted, however, that the uses of the adjectives in both the fiction and non-fiction corpora are quite dispersed, often with only a few occurrences per semantic group or collocation. Although *electric* was used more often in phrases denoting different facets of electricity as a physical phenomenon (group 1), little can be said about the preferences in the case of individual collocations.[17] For example, of the 58 occurrences of *electric* in group 1.e, fourteen were used in connection with *field*, while there were no instances of *electrical field*. The fourteen instances of *electric field*, however, appeared in texts by only two authors, Thomson and Rutherford. Similarly, all occurrences of *electric organ(s)* in the table are from Charles Darwin. Comparing Tables 45 and 46, it can be noted that scientists' uses of the adjectives included a considerably smaller number of references to practical applications of electricity outside scientific work, while the prose fiction works perhaps reflect better the significance of the introduction of new inventions for the average person.

Examination of the works from the first half of the twentieth century in the non-fiction corpus, as seen from Table 47, produces results very similar to the ones in Table 46, the greatest difference between the forms being the more frequent occurrence of *electric* in connection with words such as *field* and *force*. In the same way as in the previous 50-year period, most of the authors using the adjective forms in the non-fiction corpus were chemists and physicists.

Table 47. *Electric/electrical* in the non-fiction texts examined, 1900–1947 (British authors).

	electric	electrical
1. 'having to do with electricity as a physical phenomenon'		
a. research: ~ *experiment*/etc.	1	-
b. ~ *machine*	1	-
c. general terms:		
~ *action/properties*/etc.	2	1
d. others: ~ *field/force*/etc.	29	3
2. 'caused by electricity':		
~ *attraction.*	2	-
3. 'powered by electricity':		
~ *method*	-	1
4. figurative: 'full of tension', 'exciting'	1	-
total	**36**	**5**
# of authors:	5	3
# of authors using both forms: 2		

---

17   As regards individual collocations with *electric/electrical*, the only combination in the *OED* quotations between 1850 and 1899 that manifests a clear preference for either form is ~ *current(s)*, which was modified by *electric* in the quoted extracts by 23 different authors, while the phrase *electrical current* appeared only once.

Although the present study does not aim at comparing the use of *-ic/-ical* adjectives between British and American English, the non-fiction corpus also includes texts by American authors. The uses of *electric/electrical* in these texts are presented in two tables in Appendix B (the first table covering the period 1850–1899, the second 1900–1961). The majority of the authors using the adjectives are psychologists (referring to e.g. stimulation by means of electricity, and various equipment used in the experiments), but the overall differences between the uses of the two forms are remarkably similar to the ones observed in British materials with a heavier emphasis on chemistry and physics.

The present-day use of *electric/electrical*, examined in the 1995 issues of *The Daily Telegraph* and presented in Table 48, shows interesting developments that took place during the twentieth century. It could be said that the eighteenth and nineteenth century materials give an impression of *electric* becoming increasingly dominant over the longer form, gaining ground as the clearly preferred form particularly with new kinds of referents, most prominently when used of electrically powered devices. *Electrical* appears to have been somewhat competitive, but still the less frequent form in most uses, except perhaps for phrases relating to the scientific study of electricity.

Table 48. *Electric/electrical* in the 1995 issues of *The Daily Telegraph*.

	electric	*electrical*
1. 'having to do with electricity as a physical phenomenon'		
a. research: ~ *pioneer*/etc.	-	2
b. general: ~ *activity*/etc.	-	13
c. others: ~ *current/power*/etc.	31	42
d. producing electricity: ~ *power station* etc.	5	7
2. 'having to do with the transmission of electricity':		
a. 'carrying electricity': ~ *cable/wire*/etc.	23	26
b. 'having to do with the supply of electricity': ~ *plug/socket*/etc.	13	14
c. ~ *resistance/insulation*/etc.	-	5
d. relating to disruptions in the transmission of electricity: ~ *fault*/etc.	-	33
3. 'caused by electricity':		
a. ~ *shock*	39	-
b. others	5	1

	electric	*electrical*
4. 'powered by electricity':		
a. appliances, specific		
~ *mixer/whisk/*etc.	281 (1)	12
a'. *motors/engines/*etc.	20	3
a''. ~ *chair/fence*	95	-
b. appliances, general (pro-forms)	3	-
c. appliances, general		
~ *appliances/devices/goods/*etc.	7 (1)	139
c'. relating to the manufacturing and trade of electrical appliances:		
~ *department/retailer/store/* etc.	-	121
d. vehicles	88 (1)	1
e. music or musical instruments	57 (3)	1
f. actions, processes, illumination, etc.		
1. ~ *light/lighting*	16	-
2. others	16	10
g. ~ *parts/components/systems/*etc.	-	31
5. relating to the design, construction, and installation of electric(al) supplies and applications of electricity:		
~ *engineer(ing)/work/*etc.	1	93
6. others:		
~ *blue/green*	9	1
~ *age*	1	1
~ *grammar*	-	1
~ *safety*	-	1
~ *eel*	2	-
~ *organs* (of fish)	1	-
~ *biorhythms*	-	1
~ *nerve centre*	-	1
~ *response*	-	1
~ *rubbish/waste* (appliances)	-	2
~ *signal*	1	3
~ *storm*	4	6
7. figurative: 'full of tension', 'exciting'		
a. ~ *pace/speed*	2	-
b. others	51 (25)	-
total	**771 (31)**	**572**

During the twentieth century, general references to devices powered by electricity increased dramatically. In this function, *electrical* is now almost the standard form, modifying words such as *accessories*, *appliances*, *goods*, *devices*, and *machines*, which is also reflected in its use with words like *retailer*, *shop*, *store*, and *wholesaler*. Similarly, *electrical* is overwhelmingly the preferred form in phrases relating to the professional aspects, such as the design and construction of practical applications of electricity, as in *electrical engineer(ing)/contractor/ contracting/work*, phrases which were not, in fact, very common in the earlier centuries.

The changes as regards *electrical* being preferred in the "new" contexts raises the question of why the *-ical* form should have been used instead of *electric*. As suggested earlier, one possibility is that the distinction along the lines of specific versus general had its earliest manifestations in the preferred use of the longer form when relating to research into electricity, and the preference was subsequently "passed on" to the corresponding concept of engineering. In the *OED* quotations, the first instances of *electrical engineer(ing)* date from the 1880s. Considering the use of the adjectives with words such as *apparatus* and *machine*, in the latter half of the nineteenth century most instances probably still related to machines used for generating electricity, and both *electric* and *electrical* were used in such contexts. The use of the longer form when referring to electrically powered devices appears to have become increasingly more common during the twentieth century, reinforcing the "specific versus general" distinction.

Table 48 also shows *electrical* to be the preferred form today in phrases denoting disruptions in the transmission of electricity (group 2.d), as in *electrical fault/problem/short circuit*. This is very likely a twentieth century development as well, because no occurrences of this kind were found of either adjective form in the nineteenth century texts studied. The preference for *electrical* in such contexts can be seen as being somewhat parallel to the specific/general distinction. In addition to Marchand's (1969: 242) idea on the difference between the forms, according to which "an engineer is *electrical*, as he has to do with electric things, but current is *electric*, is the thing itself", it could be argued that *electrical* in some cases (though perhaps not always) involves some kind of distance from electricity 'the phenomenon' or 'the source of power', or, as in connection with words like *failure*, *fault*, and *problem*, actually designates an out-of-the-ordinary lack of electricity.[18]

The use of *electrical* when modifying general terms likewise becomes evident in it being preferred over the *-ic* form when modifying words such as *parts*, *components*, and *systems*, referring to elements in electrically powered machines. These elements, the function of which usually remains unspecified, may either carry electricity or they may be powered by electricity (and could, in

18   I would like to thank Ian Gurney (personal communication) for his comments on *electrical fault/problem*/etc.

fact, be categorized into either of the latter sense groups). The preference for *electrical* in such cases has also been noted in *COBUILD* (2001) s.v. *electrical*.

As regards *electric*, Table 48 further shows that it is clearly more often used in connection with specific terms for electrically powered devices, e.g. *iron*, *kettle*, and *toothbrush*, and, correspondingly, when referring to electrically powered musical instruments and vehicles. Thus the distinction that began to develop around the mid-nineteenth century has since become even more firmly established. The same sharpening of the distinction also applies to the figurative uses, the shorter form nowadays being practically always the one used in such cases.

The figurative uses of *electric* are also the most typical cases in which the adjective is seen in a predicative position. This is hardly surprising, since it is practically the only use of the adjective in present-day English in which it may be regarded as having a descriptive meaning. In the classifying (or "limiting") uses the adjectives are less common in a predicative position, although it is possible to say *the cooker/car/train was electric*.[19] Also worth noticing is the fact that *electrical* was not found in a predicative position at all.

Interestingly enough, there are also groups of head words with which there seems to be considerable variation between the two forms. These groups deserve a more detailed analysis in order to examine whether variation exists in connection with all collocates, or whether some of the individual phrases show greater levels of fixedness than others. As further data for the analysis, the adjectives in the corresponding collocates in the *British National Corpus* were also examined.

In Table 48, groups 1.c and 1.d are among those which show variation in the use of *electric/electrical*. Examining the collocates in detail (see Table 49) reveals that apart from a few instances, there is notable variation even in the case of individual collocates.

---

19   As a classifying adjective, *electric* seems to be less awkward in the predicative position when used of electrically powered devices. With other kinds of head words, the predicative position of the adjective seems rather strange, as in ?*the current/charge/field was electric*. With some collocates in group 2.a, the predicative use would suggest a descriptive meaning rather than a classifying one; for example, in the case of *the cable/wire was electric*, instead of referring to the function of the object, transmitting electricity, the phrases are more likely interpreted as conveying the sense of the object being live.

Table 49. *Electric/electrical* in the 1995 issues of *The Daily Telegraph* (semantic groups 1.c and 1.d).

	electric	electrical
1.c		
~ arc	1	-
~ charge	7	6
~ current	8	10
~ discharge	-	2
~ energy	-	4
~ field	2	4
~ impulse	-	2
~ polarity	-	1
~ potential	-	2
~ power	11	7
~ pulse	1	-
~ voltage	-	1
~ wave	1	3
1.d		
~ company	1	3
~ plant	-	1
~ power company	1	-
~ power generation	-	1
~ power giant	-	1
~ power partner	-	1
~ power station	2	-
~ utility	1	-

The numbers of occurrences of *electric/electrical* in connection with the head words in Table 49 are, for the most part, parallel to the ones in the 1993 issues of *The Daily Telegraph*, examined in Kaunisto (1999), with the exception of *current*. Eight occurrences in the 1993 issues were found modified by the *-ic* form, while the material did not include a single instance of *electrical current*. Therefore an examination of the most frequently occurring phrases with a corresponding relation to electricity in the written domains of the British National Corpus sheds more light on the issue. The results are presented in Table 50, with the figures in parentheses denoting the number of texts including the phrase.

Table 50.   *Electric/electrical* in the *British National Corpus* (semantic groups 1.c and 1.d).

	electric	electrical
1.c		
~ charge	50 (24)	35 (24)
~ current	80 (61)	31 (20)
~ discharge	5 (5)	16 (14)
~ energy	-	28 (16)
~ field	200 (37)	21 (9)
~ force	7 (4)	14 (8)
~ impulse	2 (2)	28 (18)
~ potential	3 (3)	16 (9)
~ power	38 (28)	32 (26)
~ pulse	9 (8)	6 (5)
1.d		
~ company	1 (1)	1 (1)
~ generator	4 (3)	4 (4)
~ plant	-	1 (1)
~ power plant	2 (2)	1 (1)

Based on the figures presented in Tables 49 and 50, it could be argued that *electric* is preferred over *electrical*, at least to some extent, when modifying the words *current* and *field* (corresponding to the findings in nineteenth century materials). *Electrical*, on the other hand, seems to be used more often in connection with *discharge*, *impulse*, and, most prominently, *energy*. Other phrases in the table show no striking inclinations towards a preference for either form, the most interesting collocates being *charge* and *power*, with roughly equal numbers of absolute occurrences as well as texts in which the phrases were used.

Considering groups 2.a and 2.b in Table 48, relating to cables, cords, and similar objects carrying electricity or functioning as the supply of electricity (including objects used in controlling the supply, e.g. plugs and switches), both forms again appear to be used with an almost equal frequency. As the numbers of absolute occurrences of *electric/electrical* in phrases of this type in *The Daily Telegraph* material were relatively low, the most common corresponding phrases were examined in the *BNC* as well. A more detailed breakdown of the use of the adjectives in individual collocations, presented in Appendix B (Tables 3 and 4), shows that in many cases both forms are used. Some tendencies to prefer either form in certain collocations are quite astonishing, defying logical explanation: for example, *electric* is somewhat more common in connection with *cable*, whereas when modifying *wire* and *wiring*, *electrical* is more frequently found. As regards the head words *plug*, *socket*, and *switch*, there is a very slight tendency to favour *electric*, while *electrical* appears to go more often with *supply*.

The obvious question that arises from the results is: what could explain the variation between *electric* and *electrical* in certain phrases, when in some other cases (e.g. electrically powered devices) one can observe quite a strong tendency to use one form only? The only explanations that suggest themselves are rather insufficient. One factor potentially having an effect on the matter could be the relative infrequency of the phrases in question, i.e. phrases which are not all that often used have not had the opportunity or the natural impetus, as it were, to become fixed as to the choice of the adjective form. Moreover, the possibility of omitting the adjective may also have slowed down the processes of differentiation. These points, however, only serve to explain why variation exists to begin with, but not why some phrases do show stronger levels of fixedness. Considering, for example, the head words *charge*, *power*, and *energy*, the combined occurrences of *electric charge* and *electrical charge* (as well as those of *electric(al) power*) in the corpora of different periods always outnumbered those of e.g. *electrical energy*.

Considering instances of *electric/electrical* with an attached prefix or initial combining form, the forms ending in *-ic* are considerably more frequent in the 1995 material from *The Daily Telegraph*. The most frequent word of this type found was *hydro-electric(al)*, with 28 occurrences ending in *-ic* and only two in *-ical*. As such this result would seem to support the idea of prefixed forms of *-ic/-ical* adjective pairs tending to favour the shorter forms, according to the principle of economy. On closer examination, only *hydro-electric* was used to modify words with which the base forms *electric/electrical* showed variation, e.g. *generator/power/ station*. Interestingly enough, the two occurrences of *electrical* with an initial combining form or prefix appeared with collocates which would normally also select the form in *-ical*, namely *hydro-electrical engineer* and *non-electrical goods*. Although the numbers of occurrences of this type are quite low, it may nevertheless be considered a possibility that in the case of certain phrases, the strength of the fixedness of the form in *-ical* would override the effect of the tendency towards economy when a prefix is added.

5.   General remarks

Examination of the uses of *electric/electrical* in both historical and present-day corpora shows this pair to be an intriguing one, in some ways manifesting developments parallel to those of many other *-ic/-ical* pairs, but, significantly, also showing types of change which appear quite unique. As regards the mere frequency of use, *electric* seems to have overtaken its longer counterpart in the eighteenth century. This development could be viewed as being concurrent with the gradual ousting of the *-ical* forms in several *-ic/-ical* pairs, also affecting the figurative applications of the adjectives, which ultimately came to favour the form *electric*. The distinction between *electric* and *electrical* as to the figurative, descriptive use, paraphrasable as 'full of tension or excitement', is in present-day English one of the clearest instances of differentiation, as the longer form in this function may be considered a deviation from the norm.

As regards the classifying use of the adjectives, basically having the function of associating the referent with the domain of electricity, other forms of differentiation are to be detected. As a significant backdrop to these developments, one must acknowledge the influence of the historical achievements in both basic research into the nature electricity and the resultant practical applications, as the new inventions without exaggeration led to radical changes in the everyday lives of the people in the whole Western civilization. It is noteworthy, therefore, that the most drastic changes in the uses of the adjectives have taken place in the nineteenth and twentieth centuries.

The classifying uses manifest a distinction between the uses of the two adjective forms along the lines of specific versus general, most clearly visible in connection with devices powered by electricity. Quite fascinatingly, the distinction becomes evident through the head words that the adjectives modify (or through the combination of the adjective and the noun), *electric* being preferred with specific (e.g. *kettle, toothbrush*), and *electrical* with general (e.g. *appliances, devices*) terms. The preference for the shorter form in connection with specific terms became firmly established as early as in the nineteenth century. The use of *electrical* in connection with general terms became established in the twentieth century, which led to a sharper differentiation between the two forms.

Electrical has also become the preferred form when modifying words which instead of denoting any of the types of electrical phenomena themselves, relate to the activities of people associated with the application of electric(al) power, including *engineering, design, contracting*, and, most basically, *work*. This use may be considered to support Marchand's view of the forms in *-ical* having a more remote connection with the basic semantic concept designated by the adjective. The earliest signs of this use, which has become increasingly more prominent in the language since the late nineteenth century, are most likely visible in the preference for *electrical* in relation to research into electricity.

Signs of distinction between the forms according to the principle of *electrical* being preferred with general terms can also be seen in cases relating to electricity as a phenomenon. *Electrical* is the more common form when modifying words such as *phenomenon, condition, property*, and *quality*. With these kinds of referents, however, the overall process of differentiation may actually be regarded as being incomplete, because both *electric* and *electrical* are used with specific terms, and *electric* is by no means always the preferred form. Instead, in some cases there is notable overlap even with the same head word, as in *electric/electrical charge*. As regards the possible developments affecting the use of *electric/electrical* in the future, these kinds of collocates are most interesting to observe, the logical assumption of future changes being that *electric* will become the preferred form.

Chapter 9

The past and the important things in it: *historic/historical*

> People think of history in the long term, but history, in fact, is a very sudden thing.
> (Philip Roth, *American Pastoral* (1998))

Together with the pairs *classic/classical* and *economic/economical*, the adjective pair *historic/historical* has been thought to manifest the sharpest and clearest differentiation between the two forms in present-day English. Whenever books on language use comment on the semantic differences between adjectives ending in *-ic* and *-ical*, it is usually these pairs that are given as examples. But again, it is not to be expected that when investigating the actual use of *historic/historical,* the findings would be in complete accordance with the statements made in such books, nor that native speakers of English are necessarily aware of *any* semantic difference between the variants. In fact, it comes as no surprise that the closeness in form of the two variants, as well as their sometimes nuance-like semantic differences, can occasionally confuse people in their choice between *historic* and *historical*. Confusion can even occur when the adjectives are used in proper names (where no variation is normally to be expected), and even within two consecutive sentences, as happens in the following example:

(1)   With its frills, flounces and great swathes of tartan it looks like the sort of garment that the late lamented Sir Nicholas Fairbairn, chairman of Historic Scotland, loved to wear. Historical Scotland's predecessor, the Historic Buildings Council for Scotland, put Winton very high on its list of grant priorities. (*The Daily Telegraph*, 8 Apr., 1995, "Travel: Intimate on a grand scale – Special Opening")

As regards the present-day use of *historic* and *historical,* this pair is the most polysemous of all adjective pairs ending in *-ic* and *-ical*, alongside *classic/classical*. As with the latter pair, the various functions of these adjectives, as well as the complexities that can be observed in their use, are for the most part due to the multifarious ways of approaching the very concept that underlies the words, in this case *history*. In fact, in the *OED* definition of *history* s.v., the word is given as many as nine different senses, some of which also have several subglosses (i.e. 4.a, 4.b, etc.), reflecting the different viewpoints one can have to the idea of history. Therefore it would appear only natural that the derived adjectives should correspondingly have a great number of semantic nuances.

1.   Etymology and early history of the pair

Corresponding to many other *-ic/-ical* adjective pairs in English, the origins for *historic* and *historical* in English are to be found in three languages: the Greek word ἱστορικος and the Classical Latin word *historicus*, as well as the French *historique*. A fascinating detail to be observed is that neither *historic* nor *historical* was the first adjective in English relating to the concept of history: the *OED* gives the nowadays obsolete adjective *historial*, the first citation s.v. being from 1382 and the last from 1649. This adjective was a direct adoption of the French word *historial*, which in turn was an adoption of the Late Latin adjective *historialis*. In English, *historial* may thus be considered a forerunner for the *-ic/-ical* forms, as its uses were to a great extent similar to *historic* and *historical* later on: the *MED* s.v. *historial* gives it the senses 'belonging to history, authentic, true', 'of historical importance', and 'dealing with history'. The influence of the perceived pattern of Latin words ending in *-icus* and *-icalis* eventually led to the ousting of *historial*, which was, in fact, etymologically a more logical and "correct" adjective than *historical*, as Latin apparently never had an adjective such as **historicalis* (nor a noun such as **historica*).

As with many other *-ic/-ical* adjective pairs, the longer form came into use before the shorter: the first recorded instance of *historical* in the *MED* (s.v. *historical*) is from 1475. As regards *historic*, Bailey's (1978) collection of antedatings offers the quote "What's here? / Poetique fury, and Historique stormes?" (s.v. *historic*) from Jonson's *Volpone*, published in 1607, which represents an antedating to the first recorded instance of *historic* in the *OED*. However, the Early English Prose Fiction database (1513–1699) of the Chadwyck-Healey *Literature Online* contains one occurrence of the *-ic* form (with the *-ique* spelling) which actually antedates Jonson's use of the word:

(2)   [...] when an high-pac'd Muse treading a lofty march, leades honor enchained in an Epique pen, grac'd with the furtherance of historique Clio, or treate the tragical tropheyes of the cothurnate Muse, [...]   (John Dickenson, *Arisbas* (1594), 53)

In the *Literature Online* text collection, *historic* is in all prose databases considerably less common than *historical*. The same relation in the figures can be seen in the non-fiction texts examined. The numbers of occurrences and authors using these adjectives in the corpora are presented in Tables 51 and 52 (the figures in parentheses denoting the number of authors):

Table 51. *Historic/historical* in the prose section of the *Literature Online* corpus, 1550–1903.

	1550–1599	1600–1699	1700–1799	1800–1849	1850–1903
historic	1 (1)	-	7 (2)	15 (5)	65 (18)
historical	4 (3)	22 (15)	51 (23)	105 (23)	146 (30)
authors using both forms	-	-	2	5	16

Table 52. *Historic/historical* in the non-fiction texts studied (British authors).

	1550–1599	1600–1699	1700–1799	1800–1849	1850–1899	1900–1947
historic	-	-	5 (1)	1 (1)	6 (4)	1 (1)
historical	20 (2)	22 (13)	21 (13)	14 (7)	62 (13)	42 (5)
authors using both forms	-	-	-	-	2	1

It can be observed from the tables that *historical* has been the dominant form for centuries, with *historic* gradually gaining more ground from the eighteenth century onwards. As regards the eighteenth century texts, *historic* was to a great extent used in the same senses as *historical*, and some writers at times used the words interchangeably, including Henry Fielding in the following passages from his 1749 book *Tom Jones*:

(3) a. [...] for while some are, with M. Dacier, ready to allow, that the same Thing which is impossible may be yet probable, others have so little Historic or Poetic Faith, that they believe nothing be either possible or probable, the like to which hath not occurred to their own Observation. (Henry Fielding, *Tom Jones* (1749), 3, 140)[1]

  b. For he is obliged to record Matters as he finds them; though they may be of so extraordinary a Nature, as will require no small Degree of historical Faith to swallow them. (Henry Fielding, *Tom Jones* (1749), 3, 144)

Based on the occurrences in the *Literature Online* material, the most significant increase in the use of *historic* in relation to the longer form seems to have taken

---

1 In the *OED* s.v. *historical, historical faith* (now obsolete) is defined as 'that concerned only with historical facts; intellectual belief or assent, as distinct from faith that is practically operative on conduct'.

place in the latter half of nineteenth century. In the non-fiction texts, occurrences of *historic* were few in number even in the latter half of the nineteenth century and the first half of the twentieth century. As far as mere numbers of occurrences are concerned, the use of *historic* in relation to *historical* appears to have increased dramatically during the latter half of the twentieth century: for example, the 1995 issues of *The Daily Telegraph* contained altogether 1004 occurrences of *historic* and 899 of *historical*. However, as will be seen in subsequent sections, the semantic differentiation between the two forms reduces the informational value of the total frequencies of the two forms. The relations between the absolute frequencies of *historic* and *historical* today appears to vary according to text type. The differences reflect the semantic separation between the two forms, with some types of texts including e.g. a relatively greater number of references to the research of history, which results in a greater number of uses of *historical* than *historic*. In contrast, those domains which to a greater extent involve assessment and evaluation of the importance or value of things from a viewpoint of history (e.g. *a historic event/occasion*) also include a relatively greater number of occurrences of *historic*.

2.   *Historic/historical* in dictionaries and usage manuals

As *historical* appeared before the -*ic* variant in English, it was naturally also the first of the two to appear in dictionaries. Among the first English dictionaries where the word appeared were those of Cawdrey (1604) and Bullokar (1616). Samuel Johnson's dictionary (1755) was one of the first to include both forms, and like most -*ic*/-*ical* adjectives, they were given under the same entry, a practice which prevailed in dictionaries well into the twentieth century. This would suggest that the two forms were considered by Johnson to be synonymous, with the meanings 'containing or giving an account of facts and events', and 'pertaining to history or narrative' (s.v.). When the adjectives later developed other meanings and functions, dictionaries to a great extent still merely listed the different senses without especially assigning any of them to either form: for example, *Chambers's English Dictionary* s.v. *historic, historical* in 1914 gives the senses 'pertaining to history', 'famous in history', and 'authentic' under a joint entry for both variants. This is understandable given that earlier the forms were used interchangeably, as observed, for example, in the 1993 edition of *The Chambers Dictionary*.

As such the fact that the differences in the use of the two forms are nowadays noted more often would give the impression that the division is today more clear-cut and that there is less interchangeability than before. But such an argument would not be very well-founded if based solely on the comments found in dictionaries of different times, especially when considering the development of new linguistic research tools, which have changed the overall approach to dictionary-making as a whole. In addition, some dictionaries published in the

1990s do state that for some senses, both forms are used – sometimes this information is given explicitly, and sometimes by using cross-references (e.g. *LDEL* and *Encarta World English Dictionary*). Barber's (1964: 114) comments on *historic* and *historical* even lead one to assume that the differentiation between the two forms is beginning to disappear, partly because of analogous pairs in *-ic/-ical* where both forms are used synonymously.

In the *OED,* some of the cross-references have supplementary comments as regards which of the forms is the more common in current use. The overall presentation of the different meanings of *historic* and *historical* in the *OED* is, however, somewhat unclear, particularly in the case of those definitions which do not include a cross-reference, but which are still very close in content to the glosses listed under the other variant. For example, sense 1 of *historic* reads 'of or belonging to history; historical; esp. of the nature of history as opposed to fiction or legend'. Firstly, in this gloss attention is caught by the word *historical*: as *historical* has been given seven different senses under its own entry, its use in the definition of *historic* can be confusing, as it might easily suggest that *historic* is, or has been, freely used in all of the senses in which *historical* has been used. When one examines the definitions of *historical* more closely, sense 1 seems to be very similar to *historic* 1, and it is given in two parts, 1.a 'of or pertaining to history; or the nature or character of history, constituting history; following or in accordance with history', and 1.b 'of, pertaining to, of the nature of history as opposed to fiction or legend'. The absence of a clear cross-reference in these definitions would suggest that the meanings of *historic* 1 and *historical* 1.a and b are different, although the examples provided include very similar instances of the two words, e.g. "The sort of difficulty against which simple historic truth has to struggle" (from John Freeman, *Historical Essays I* (1871), i), and "The bulk and gross of his narration was founded upon mere historical truth" (from Sir Walter Raleigh, *The History of the World* III (1614), ii, §3). One also wonders why there is no division into 1.a and 1.b with *historic* resembling that found under *historical*. The picture of the adjectives' use does not become much clearer even in cases where cross-references are used: *historic* 3 reads 'conveying or dealing with history; recording past events; = HISTORICAL (which is the usual prose equivalent)', leaving the cross-reference unspecified, which is all the more unfortunate as none of the senses of *historical* explicitly refers to *historic* 3.

The presentation of the use of these adjectives in the *OED* therefore needs to be approached with a certain amount of caution, considering furthermore that the division into different senses dates from as early as 1928, as it remained largely unchanged in the second edition of the dictionary. It could be argued that as some uses have become obsolete or old-fashioned, while new ones have developed, it is the changes in the use of the adjectives themselves and thus the difficulty to present the old and the new together that may have caused complexities (from the viewpoint of present-day English) in the *OED* definitions. Nevertheless, considerably clearer presentations of the adjectives' use are to be found in some of the more modern dictionaries.

As regards the description of the use of *historic* and *historical* in usage manuals, the sources consulted are largely in agreement which each other. Some of the differences observed will be discussed in the following sections on different uses of the adjectives. Considering the general line of differentiation between the two forms, Fowler's comments (1926; s.v.; Fowler's italics) are worth quoting in full:

> The DIFFERENTIATION between the two forms has reached a stage at which it may fairly be said that the use of one in a sense now generally expressed by the other is a definite backsliding. The ordinary word is *historical*; *historic* means memorable, or assured of a place in history; *historical* should not be substituted for it in that sense; the only other function retained by *historic* is in the grammarians' technical terms *historic tenses, moods, sequence, present*, &c., in which it preserves the notion *appropriate to narration of the past* of which it has been in general use robbed by *historical*.

Gowers' edition (1965) of Fowler's book s.vv. *historic, historical* also has the further comment on *historic* "now in common use as an epithet for buildings worthy of preservation for their beauty or interest". A good example of the comments usually found in dictionaries and usage manuals on *historic/historical* in the latter half of the twentieth century is provided by *LDEL*'s additional usage note after the definitions, s.vv.:

> In current usage, *historic* usually means 'memorable' or 'famous or important in history'. *Historical* is the normal adjective meaning 'having the nature of history' or 'belonging to the past', often in the senses 'having really existed; not fictional or legendary' <*it is still debated whether Robin Hood was a historical figure*> and 'because of past events' <*for historical reasons the boundary runs down the middle of the stream*>. This distinction, although artificial, is desirable to prevent ambiguity < '*Yes, sir, "an extinct case of purely historic concern", sir' Strickland went on. ... 'Historical', Lacon corrected him irritably. 'Not historic concern. That's the last thing we want!'* – John Le Carré>.

One peculiar detail in the above quote is the claim that the distinction between the two forms is "artificial". This can mean either that the distinction does not really exist, but is only considered by language purists to be desirable, or that the prescriptivists are responsible for the differentiation in present-day English. Neither claim seems very plausible, and would be quite difficult to prove, which leaves one to wonder why the comment on artificiality was made in the first place.

3.   Different uses of *historic/historical*

The following sections will deal with the different senses in which *historic* and *historical* have been and are used. The order of presentation is meant to reflect both the chronological sequence of the uses of the adjectives, and the centrality of the senses from the viewpoint of present-day English. Therefore the first sections will deal mostly with uses for which *historical* is now the preferred form, although the shorter form has also been used in these senses. The examples illustrating the various uses of the adjectives have been culled mostly from the *Literature Online* material and the 1995 issue of *The Daily Telegraph*.

3.1   'Having to do with history', 'pertaining to history'

As pointed out earlier, Fowler considered *historical* to be "the ordinary word", the longer form being the usual one for the central, classifying sense 'having to do with history', 'relating to history' or 'from the viewpoint of history', as in *historical knowledge/perspective/considerations*, linking the referent to the general domain of history or the past. It must be admitted that such a definition is quite vague, as are 'of history' or 'pertaining to history', which are often found in dictionaries. The almost unavoidable problem with these definitions is that in their vagueness they are not exclusive of the other senses of the words, i.e. they could potentially be applied to all instances of *historic* and *historical*: for example, the phrases *a historic event, a historic building, historical knowledge, the historical Jesus* and *a historical play* all in one way or another have to do with or relate to history and are thus 'of history'. In some dictionaries and usage manuals it has been considered sufficient to express only the most noticeable semantic difference between the *-ic* and *-ical* forms, without specifying any individual uses for *historical* apart from 'having to do with history' (e.g. Room 1985 s.vv. *historic, historical*).

The classifying nature of *historic(al)* in this sense can be observed from the fact that when used in coordination with other adjectives, these conjoints are most typically classifying, not descriptive (cf. Bache and Davidsen-Nielsen 1997: 457), as in (4a) and (4b):

(4)   a.   Also published this month is *Anne Frank beyond the Diary* (Puffin, £6.99), a poignant photographic record of the family's life before the war, alongside political and historical background to the Holocaust. (*The Daily Telegraph*, Apr. 1, 1995, "Children's Books: From hippos to the Holocaust's horror")

        b.   Opposition to new development is often driven by this very fear of environmental dilution – of characterless, bland design that pays no attention to local topography, building styles and materials, or to the

host of other historical, geographical and cultural factors that give
each village its unique identity. (*The Daily Telegraph*, Apr. 22, 1995,
"Property: A place in the country?")

This sense is the first one that the adjectives were used in, and in the corpora
examined, it was also the most common sense for both forms. In present-day
English, *historic* is still occasionally used in this sense (as in (5a) and (5c)
below), although it is usually considered to be less common than the longer form:

(5)   a.   In spite of this distinguished support, it is hard to see how Millenium
             City will fulfil its aims of raising historic awareness, celebrating
             cultural diversity and generating national pride.   (*The Daily
             Telegraph*, Jan. 4, 1995, "The Arts: Blurred visions of the future")

        b.   In his forthcoming book, *In the Fifties* (to be published by John
             Murray in April), Peter Vansittart singles out Sybille Bedford for these
             travel pieces. He praises her 'particular historical and political
             awareness, sensory immediacy, or the pause for the odd or grotesque,
             the delight in the human scale, contempt for the immoderate or
             vogueish'. (*The Daily Telegraph*, Feb. 4, 1995, "Books:
             Unconventional pieces of a jigsaw")

        c.   Fletcher's slap-happy use of a Shakespeare concordance as a historic
             source-book involves him in crashing blunders; [...] (*The Sunday
             Telegraph*, Oct. 29, 1995, "Books: The gender study industry")

        d.   The writer was P.S. O'Hegarty, a veteran Fenian, and his book, *The
             Victory of Sinn Fein*, was published in 1924: it is considered by some
             historians a valuable historical source book because of the writer's
             close association with Arthur Griffith, the founder of Sinn Fein, and
             Michael Collins. (*The Sunday Telegraph*, Mar. 12, 1995, "Deadlier
             than the male – as ever")

As a classifying adjective, *historic(al)* in this sense is considerably more common
in the attributive position, but instances of predicative use can also be found:

(6)   The reason that Jews are light drinkers is more historical than religious.
        (*The Daily Telegraph*, May 28, 1995, "A Jewish drinking problem")

In some rare cases, the adjective is found as the head of the noun phrase:

(7)   Eco-tourism has had other spin-offs. Roland Barthes pointed out the
        middle-class tourist's obsession with the historical and the picturesque.
        (*The Sunday Telegraph*, Jun. 4, "Travel: Save our planet from the ego-
        tourists")

Dictionaries and language usage manuals often distinguish between 'relating to the study of history', as in *historical method/research/studies* and the more general sense 'having to do with history' (e.g. Krapp 1927: 315; Alexander 1994 s.v. *historical*; *COBUILD* 2001 s.v. *historical*). Some of the sources examined even give paraphrases such as "having to do with the historian" (Phythian 1979 s.v. *historical*) and "suitable for study by historians or using their methods" (Ebbitt and Ebbitt 1990 s.v. *historical*). Obviously the more detailed the division that is made between the different shades of meaning or fields of use, the better the chances to detect the differing uses of the forms in -*ic* and -*ical*. In this case such a division can be regarded as successful, because when referring to things pertaining to the study of history, *historical* seems to have always been the preferred form, i.e. there has been less variation between the two forms in this more clearly defined sense than in the wider sense. The *OED* does not record any instances of *historic* as dealing specifically with the study of history, and in the corpora examined, no occurrences of *historic* were found in this sense.[2] There are, however, some problems with the division into the general and the more specified sense, particularly with collocations such as ~ *knowledge/perspective/ information,* which can all be seen as relating to the study of history. It is obvious that one does not have to be a historian to consider things or evaluate them from a historical perspective, let alone have historical knowledge about something, and certainly not all information of the past is necessarily studied by scholars. It is more sensible therefore to consider such more generally interpretable collocations to be examples of the more general sense, and assign only the clearest cases such as ~*research/treatise/scholar* to their own subgroup. Another subgroup sometimes given separately is 'the study of a subject based on an analysis over a period', as in *historical linguistics* (e.g. *Oxford Dictionary and English Usage Guide* 1996 s.v. *historical*).

Similarly, some dictionaries distinguish between the more general sense and 'having to do with the recording of history', the obvious example being *historical record(s)*. In this case, both the shorter and the longer form have been used (both in the concrete sense of records as actual physical artefacts and to convey the more abstract idea of the whole recorded history):

(8)   a.   [...] appears like the earth-born myrmidons of Deucalion, for they certainly have no human origin; bear no connexion with the history of their country; are neither to be found in the poetic legend nor historic record of Scotland, and are even furnished with appellations which the

---

2   Some occurrences of *historic* in this sense can be found elsewhere, as in "I have sometimes thought that historic research would be easier for me if sometimes I knew what men did before I was forced to understand why they did it; [...]" in Winifred Margaretta Kirkland's *The Joys of Being a Woman and Other Papers* (1918), found in the Modern English Collection of the University of Virginia Electronic Text Center (http://etext.lib. virginia.edu).

Caledonians neither previously possessed nor have since [...] (Lady Morgan, *The Wild Irish Girl* (1806), 75)

b. At what time (as the Historicall Records of auncient Anualls make mention) the King of Tunis, through the attempting brauados of some insulting Rebels, held the holde of his royall seate in hazard, as daily awaiting his downe-fall, drawne through ciuil warres, and warlike mutinies: [...] (Robert Kittowe, *Loues Load-starre* (1600), 7)

c. Mr Metcalfe, who describes the building as no more than a 'heap of rubble', has been told he can demolish for safety reasons part of a wall which overhangs a public footpath, but the rest must stay as a valuable historic record. (*The Daily Telegraph*, July 17, 1995, "Farmer's ruin saved as 'very fine house'")

d. The historical record confirms that huge sea level changes are possible. (*The Daily Telegraph*, Aug. 11, 1995, "Waterworld vision of the future is sunk by scientists")

Variation between the two adjectives is also encountered in collocation with the word *document(s)*:

(9) a. Krips's fleet tempos draw crisp playing from the VPO but, with papery mono sound and a pinched, uncertain Pedrillo, this set is more of a historic document than a best buy. (*The Daily Telegraph*, Mar. 25, 1995, "Classical Budget Cds: Keeping up with the action")

b. I still use Herald Two almost every day. It looks shabby from most angles. The hood is a historical document in itself, a drooping patchwork of splits and patched repairs. (*The Daily Telegraph*, July 26, 1995, "Motoring: Slightly seedy, but a triumph of make do and mend")

As illustrated by examples (8a–d) and (9a) and (9b), the artefacts in question may or may not have been produced for the specific purpose of recording events of the time, but in their own ways they tell us something about the past.

Sometimes the division into different senses has been exaggerated somewhat: for example, in the quote from the usage note in *LDEL, historical* is said to have the sense 'because of past events', modifying the word *reasons* in the example. In fact, this is a collocation which manifests some variation between the two forms in both *The Daily Telegraph* material and the *British National Corpus*, although the longer form is more common:

(10) a. Unlike other European countries it's not yet possible in the UK to walk into the local branch of a high street bank and ask to see the latest eurobonds on offer. That is partly for historic reasons: British investors have traditionally shown more appetite for shares than bonds. (*The Daily Telegraph*, Sept. 20, 1995, "Special Report on Corporate Bond Peps: Low interest rates give eurobonds a real shine")

b. Although the principle seemed not unfair, the practicalities of introducing such a system proved to be complex, not least because for historic reasons unit costs vary very considerably between one institution and another. (*BNC*, GUV 268)

c. Compared to Europeans, Americans take a relatively indulgent view of new arrivals. This is partly for obvious historical reasons, but also because each new wave of immigrants reassures Americans that they still live in the land of opportunity. (*The Daily Telegraph*, Feb. 17, 1995, "Clinton acts to end illegal immigration")

d. According to Pflug, this is for historical reasons -- during the 1980s, organisations focussed spending on mission-critical applications to the detriment of the less exciting back-office kit, but 'this is now coming back to haunt the industry'. (*BNC*, CPP 66)

Here the paraphrase 'because of past events' seems to correlate with the whole phrase *historic(al) reasons* rather than with the adjective only; it would be normal to say *reasons that have to do with past events*, but **reasons because of past events* is ill-formed. Variation between the forms in this collocation has also been noted e.g. by Gowers (1973) s.v. *historic* and Howard (1993) s.vv. *historic, historical*, who, based on the general differentiation between the adjectives, writes: "'For historic reasons', commonly heard, should be 'for historical reasons' (for reasons related to history)." The gloss 'because of past events' would seem to better suit collocations such as ~ *responsibilities*, where again variation is found:

(11) a. The momentum for Nato expansion is probably unstoppable. Bonn officials argue that Germany has a historic responsibility to usher the Central Europeans into Western institutions. (*The Daily Telegraph*, Dec. 11, 1995, "They've little to applaud")

b. A BJP vice-president said India had a 'historical responsibility' to welcome Bangladeshi Hindus, whereas 'some of the Muslim migrants are part of the larger design of Bangladesh against India's stability'. (*BNC*, CR9 833)

In (11a), *historic* can be seen to suggest a notion of importance as well, but the interpretation 'due to history', as in (11b), seems nevertheless more likely. As regards the question whether this should be considered a subgroup of its own here, paraphrasing the phrase *historic(al) responsibility* as 'responsibility that has to do with the past' without an explicit reference to the causal relationship between the adjective and the noun does not leave out anything essential, and thus instances of the type are placed in the large group 'having to do with history'.

3.2   'Based on history'

One sense distinguishable from 'having to do with history' is 'based on history', used mainly of literary works with a story line set in the past. Such instances of *historic(al)* could arguably be considered to actually mean 'having to do with history' (i.e. a play, book, film etc. that has to do with history), and several usage manuals do indeed give the phrase *historical novel* as an example of the general sense (e.g. McKaskill 1977 s.vv. *historic, historical*; Swan 1995: 256). In this function the adjectives nevertheless form phrases which constitute a perceivably distinct idea of its own, which speaks for a separate definition. This is also the approach taken in many dictionaries, e.g. *COBUILD, NODE,* and *Encarta World English Dictionary.* Judging from the *Literature Online* material and the *OED*'s presentation of the adjectives in question, it seems that this sense has been among the first uses of the words, the earliest recorded instance of *historical* in this sense going back to 1590. Considering the meaning of the adjectives, this "new" use was not radically different from the original one, and here, too, the adjectives clearly have a classifying function, separating the referent from other types of narrative works. *Historical* has always been the more common form in this use, occurrences of the shorter form – as in examples (12a) and (12b) – being few in both the historical and the present-day material:

(12)   a.   This introductory Chapter, he says, is the best Mark of Genius, and surest Criterion of an Author's Parts; for by it the most indifferent Reader may be enabled to distinguish what is true and genuine in this historic kind of Writing, from what is false and counterfeit: [...] (Francis Coventry, *Pompey the Little* (1751), 126)

       b.   The trend back to paved streets and decent street 'furniture' which would not look out of place on a historic film set is, conservationists argue, long overdue. (*The Sunday Telegraph*, Apr. 2, 1995, "Cobbles bring heritage clash to the surface")

       c.   In precedent times when elocution with poesie joying their rivall, Juned, Invention bedicious wits, with their workes were patronized; And Historicall fictions received favour in the royall Palace of greatest Princes: so hereditarily descending from the Poets are in these our times applauded, [...] (Alexander Hart, *Alexto and Angelica* (1640), 2-3)

d. Before inventing the 'medieval whodunnit' she wrote conventional crime thrillers and historical novels, and made excellent translations from Czech. (*The Daily Telegraph*, Oct.16, 1995, "Obituary of Edith Pargeter")

This use of *historical* is also extended to the authors and artists who have produced works set in history, as in *historical novelists/writers*. The *OED* (s.v. *historical*, senses 3.a and 3.b) makes a distinction between those works of art with history as their setting, which are usually narrative works, and those which represent past events, most typically pictorial works, such as paintings and photographs. Similarly, *The Chambers Dictionary* (1993) assigns separate definitions to the phrases *historical novel* 'a novel having as its setting a period in history and involving historical characters and events' and *historical painting* 'the painting of historic scenes in which historic figures are introduced'. Again, the latter sense can be extended to the artists as well:

(13) "[...] These are persons of consequence, I tell you." "Who are they?" inquired Sheppard. "Why, first," rejoined Austin, "there's Sir James Thornhill, historical painter to his Majesty, and the greatest artist of the day. Those grand designs in the dome of St. Paul's are his work [...] (William Ainsworth, *Jack Sheppard* (1839–40), Vol. III, 127)

The *OED*'s presentation of this sense, however, is quite confusing. The examples for the *OED*'s sense 3 for *historic* appear very similar to the first ones given for *historical* 3.a and 3.b, all of which include phrases with head words such as *poetry*, *poet*, *poems*, *painter*, *painting* etc. The glosses for both adjectives include the phrase 'dealing with history', and it is possible that the unspecified cross-reference in *historic* 3 actually relates to these senses of *historical*. In *historic* 3, however, the aspect of *recording* history is also mentioned, but it is not explicitly given under either *historical* 3.a or 3.b, the former having the specified notion of 'using history as its basis'. This would then suggest that *a historic painter*, as in "John Freeman, An historic painter, was a rival of Fuller" (*OED*, s.v. *historic*, sense 3, from Horace Walpole, *Anecdotes of painting in England*, edited by G. Vertue (1786), III, 12), makes paintings of current subjects and thus records history, whereas *a historical painter* makes paintings of past events, representing something already recorded. Such a fine differentiation between *historic* and *historical* existing in the sixteenth and seventeenth centuries seems unlikely, and this reading is rather the result of the dictionary-makers' difficulties in clearly defining first of all what they consider as constituting the general classifying sense, and secondly distinguishing the different sub-senses. Instead, phrases such as 'connected with history' and 'dealing with history' and 'relating to history', all very similar to one another, appear in the glosses for almost all of the senses listed under *historic* and *historical*, and then in the case of *historic* 3, both the sub-senses 'based on history' and 'recording history' seem to have been merged together.[3]

3.3   'Existed in history'; 'belonging to the past'

A distinction can be made between the uses of *historical* in the following examples:

(14)   a.   But despite this, Foucault's essay on The History of Sexuality does offer a most stimulating challenge to traditional historical accounts, partly because of its undermining of conventional approaches, partly because it is an aspect of a much wider intellectual effort, whose implications are likely to be of major importance. (*BNC*, EEN 83)

b.   One of the more fascinating aspects of Roman Britain is the interweaving of the evidence recovered from archaeological discovery and that from the surviving historical accounts. (*BNC*, EB7 480)

In the case of (14a), the phrase *historical accounts* refers to accounts that first and foremost have to deal with history and are *about* history, and in this analysis, *historical* in the phrase would be placed into the 'having to do with history' sense group. In (14b), however, the accounts are ones that were produced in the past and are thus from history or the past, and could thus be considered to "belong to the past". Similarly, instead of suggesting a connection with history as a concept or with the past in a more general sense, the phrases *historical events/ figures/periods* would in most cases seem to represent a use of the adjective comparable to the one in (14b). In the *Literature Online* material, the earliest instances of this use, which could be paraphrased as 'existed or happened in the past' or 'belonging to the past', were found in a text dating back to 1635:

(15)   Histories which containe great varietie of mournfull and memorable Accidents, Historicall, Morall, and Divine, very necessary to restraine and

---

3   It is not impossible to imagine dictionary-makers struggling for suitable definitions for all the various uses of *historic/historical,* when even in cases where phrases with the same adjective form and the same head word can mean two different things, depending on the context. But it is obvious that in previous times, for instance, a poem or a painting, and nowadays a film may have different functions as regards their relation to history. There are old poems which have actually recorded history, and also ones that have been based on historical events. A film such as *Titanic* is 'based on history', as it uses historical events in the setting of its storyline, whereas a documentary film on the American Civil War is about history, and in such a case *historical* in the phrase *historical film* would be better categorized as 'having to do with history'.

deterre us from this bloodie Sinne, which in these our dayes makes so ample, and large a Progression. (John Reynolds, *The Triumphs of Gods Revenge* (1635), IV, 1)

Historical seems to have been at all times the preferred form in this sense, with only a few occurrences of *historic* found in the corpora examined:

(16) a. Except that, when a particular hurricane is so destructive that it becomes a major headline-grabber, the name is replaced in subsequent years. This is to ensure that there is no confusion between historic hurricanes. (*The Sunday Telegraph*, May 28, 1995, "The Weather: Wind of change hits hurricane names")

    b. This has provided the closest match yet between what we know of historic greenhouse gas emissions and this century's uneven 0.5C temperature rise – and hence made the most reliable forecasts of impending climate change. (*The Daily Telegraph*, Apr. 3, 1995, "Britain sets the pace in war on global warming")

Many dictionaries published in the late twentieth century make a distinction between the senses 'having to do with history' and 'existed in history' (e.g. *Collins English Dictionary*). The *OED* with its vague definitions is again less than useful as regards this use of *historical*. It appears that the use of the word in this sense in some fairly common phrases, e.g. *historical event,* totally escaped the dictionary-makers, and no example of any similar instance is given.

In the case of this classifying sense, quite often a distinction is made between things belonging to the past and those which are contemporary, as in (17a) and (17b):

(17) a. The medium does not easily lend itself to exploring delicate shades of behaviour, whether contemporary or historical. (*The Daily Telegraph*, Aug. 9, 1995, "Leading Article: Balancing act")

    b. Undeniably, too, the private lives of some of our great historical figures look somewhat suspect under a microscope, just as the private lives of some of our great contemporary ones do; but such activities are not normally the most important feature of great historical events. (*The Daily Telegraph*, Sept. 19, 1995, "Leading Article: The case for heroes")

Some instances of *historical* in this use were found in a predicative position:

(18) What a difference 50 years makes. Many of these professions now seem quaintly historical - locomotive fireman, organ-grinder, chamois seller, navvy - and the clothes are fixed in an age of sackcloth and leather. (*The*

204 The past and the important things in it: *historic/historical*

Sunday Telegraph, Feb. 5, 1995, "The Arts: Flick of the darkroom switch")

3.4 'Existed in history, as opposed to fictional or legendary'; 'authentic'

Related to the sense 'existed in history', *historic(al)* can also be used in the sense of 'having really existed in the past' with an emphasis on the genuine and actual existence and characteristics of the referents, as opposed to their fictional representations or legendary qualities. The clearest instances of such a use of *historic(al)* are those referring to people, with the pattern *the + historic(al) +* the name of a person, as in examples (19a) and (19b):

(19) a.   Could not the 'real Jesus' or, as later generations were to term him, the 'historical Jesus', conceivably have been quite a different sort of figure from the Christ who was subsequently preached and described in the terms of the Nicene Creed as God made man? (*BNC*, CL6 244)

b.   '[...] Many music experts maintain that we know a lot about the historical Farinelli, when in fact we know only a few details.' (*The Daily Telegraph*, Nov. 3, 1995, "The Arts: A cut above the rest")

This function of the adjective is not restricted to the pattern seen above, but is found, for example, in "*The Historical Figure of Jesus* by E. P. Sanders, Penguin, £7.99" (*The Daily Telegraph*, Nov. 26, 1995, "Books: Paperbacks"). In these instances, a contrast is made between what is truly known to have existed and what is only legendary. They differ from the usual instances of the sense 'existed in history': for example, such a contrast is not present in examples (20a) and (20b):

(20) a.   The latest survey of Oxbridge students reveals that the historical figure they most admire is Jesus and their favourite book is the Bible. (*The Daily Telegraph*, Dec. 24, 1995, "The Arts: Westward leading, still proceeding")

b.   Wagner is already the subject of more books than any historical figure bar Jesus Christ [...] (*The Daily Telegraph*, Apr. 10, 1995, "The Arts: Twilight of the couch potatoes")

Instead, these sentences and the use of *historical* in them does not at all question the actual existence or the historical accuracy of the attributes commonly assigned to Jesus. From this viewpoint, the use of the adjective in (20a) and (20b) is neutral in the sense that the issue of truthfulness is not the centre of attention, being regarded as a fact. However, the question of actual existence can be thrown into relief, as in examples (21a) and (21b):

(21) a. Although most scholars now tend to accept that St George probably was a historical figure, solid facts about our patron saint are hard to come by. (*The Sunday Telegraph*, Apr. 23, 1995, "The West bank, England and St George")

      b. Though the legend has no basis, he [St Giles] was certainly a historical figure. (*The Sunday Telegraph*, Aug. 27, 1995, "Sunday Comment: Saints and sinners")

It could be argued, then, that in these instances *historical* simply means 'existed in history', and that it is the syntactic context (e.g. *X was a historical figure*) that brings up the question of contrast between the actual and the legendary. In many dictionaries and usage manuals no overt distinction is necessarily made between the sense 'having really existed in history' and the more neutral 'existed in the past' or 'belonging to history', although at the same time, the contrast to fictional or legendary status is emphasized. The examples used to illustrate the matter in many cases resemble examples (21a) and (21b), as in the following extract:

> A **historical** event is one that belongs to history, so that it actually took place: King Arthur is generally believed to be a historical figure, though some regard him as legendary. (*The Hutchinson Concise English Usage*, s.v. *historic, historical*)

Similarly, in the *MED* definition of *historial*, these senses are grouped together in the same gloss, which reads 'Belonging to history, authentic, true'. In some other sources consulted, a distinction is made, e.g. *Random House Compact Unabridged Dictionary* s.v. *historical* gives the senses *historical* 3 'having once existed or lived in the real world, as opposed to being part of legend or fiction or as distinguished from religious belief', accompanied by the example 'a theologian's study of the historical Jesus', and *historical* 4 'narrated or mentioned in history; belonging to the past'. The contrastive use of *historical* is also given in the *OED*.

There are also some instances of *historical* which could be regarded as borderline cases between these two very closely related senses:

(22) a. Sir – I am afraid that Bruce Anderson is confusing the historical Richard III with the exotic ogre who was conjured up by Shakespeare out of the fevered imaginings of such writers as Thomas More (article, Nov. 8). This is hardly surprising, of course, when one considers the theatrical artifices of Francis Urquhart, which owe something to Laurence Olivier's portrayal of Richard; but any resemblance to the historical figure, who seems to have pardoned too often and too leniently, is less than convincing. (*The Daily Telegraph*, Nov. 9, 1995, "Letter to the Editor: King besmirched")

b.   In hindsight, the mythologised Drake of patriotic legend was to be far more influential than the historical man. (*The Sunday Telegraph*, Oct. 1, 1995, "Books: The patriotic pirate")

In (22a) and (22b), the phrases *historical figure* and *historical man* could be regarded as having the neutral sense 'existed in history'. In these cases, the question of the existence of the persons is irrelevant as there is no argument about it, but in the context, a contrast is made between the dramatic and legendary characterisations and what is actually known about the two men from history. One could also claim that the words *figure* and *man* only serve as replacements for the names Richard and Drake, as it would be perfectly correct to say "the mythologised Drake of patriotic legend was to be far more influential than the historical Drake", in which case we would have a clearer instance of *historical* with the contrastive function.

Considering some of the examples presented, which may present problems as to definitions of *historic(al)*, it is easy to understand why some dictionaries would choose to have only one sense group along the lines of 'existed in history, as opposed to fiction or legend'. In the analysis here, all those instances of *historical* which suggest any kind of notion of 'authentic' or 'true' or a contrast to a legend, even if this becomes evident from the context rather than from the collocating word only, are placed into a group of their own.

In the light of the *OED* presentation of *historic* and *historical*, this use would seem to have developed in the nineteenth century, the first citation dating from 1843. But considering that the sense 'authentic, true' is given for *historial* in the *MED*, it appears possible that this use for *historical* is of earlier origin. Compared to the other uses of the adjectives in question, the occurrences with a clear contrast to fiction or legend have probably been rather few before the nineteenth century. In the corpora examined, only a few instances of the adjectives in this particular meaning can be found in the nineteenth century texts:

(23)   This was not the same building of which the stately ruins still interest the traveller, and which was erected at a later period by the Lord Hastings, High Chamberlain of England, one of the first victims of the tyranny of Richard the Third, and yet better known as one of Shakspeare's characters than by his historical fame. (Walter Scott, *Ivanhoe* (1819), 212)

Only one instance of *historic* in this sense was found in the corpora; none of the dictionaries consulted assigned the sense 'authentic' to the shorter form.

3.5   'Famous or important in history'

The central meaning of *historic* today is 'famous or important in history' or 'making history', most commonly used of events and actions, as exemplified by the following passages:[4]

(24)   a.   When the American Bob Beamon smashed the world long jump record in 1968, his leap of 8.90m was, in athletics terms, equivalent to Neil Armstrong's historic steps on the moon the same year. (*The Daily Telegraph*, June 27, 1995, "Athletics: Edwards can take giant leap towards centre stage")

          b.   Of course Heath has consoled himself with the thought that he had led Britain into Europe, and that this was an historic achievement and his legacy to an ungrateful people. (*The Sunday Telegraph*, June 18, 1995, "Sunday Comment: Ted Heath: still sulking 25 years on")

Occasionally *historical* is also used in this sense, although it is considerably less common than the shorter form:[5]

(25)   a.   New York's Dow Jones share index yesterday broke above 5000 for the first time amid 'whistles and whoops' as traders celebrated the historical moment in dealing rooms across the city. (*The Daily Telegraph*, Nov. 21, 1995, "CITY: Dow Jones passes 5000 after US budget pact")

          b.   Today he captains Northamptonshire in one-day battle in the NatWest final against Warwickshire and a historical double remains within his grasp if the leaders falter in the County Championship race. (*The*

---

4   Because of the many aspects that things relating to history can be viewed from, arriving at the most suitable paraphrases for the different uses of *historic* and *historical* is not at all a simple task. In dictionaries and usage manuals, the same phrases are sometimes used in the definitions of different senses of the adjectives. For example, we find the phrase "part of history" in Bryson (1984) s.vv. *historic, historical* ("Something that makes history or is part of history . . . is historic") and *COBUILD* (2001), s.v. *historical* ("Historical people, situations, or things existed in the past and are considered to be a part of history"), clearly referring to different uses.

5   In some dictionaries this sense is given for the longer form as well as the shorter: for example, *Webster's New Encyclopedic Dictionary* (1993) gives the sense 'famous in history' for *historical*, with *historical personages* as an example. This particular example seems like a poor choice, as the aspect of being famous or important is already included in the word *personage*. The meaning of the adjective in such cases is better paraphrased as 'existed in history'.

Daily Telegraph, Sept. 2, 1995, "Cricket: Lamb the laughing cavalier")

In addition to important events, *historic(al)* in this sense can also be used of persons, places, or objects:

(26) a.   As he announced the final tally – 8,348,700 votes in favour of Saddam out of 8,357,560 voters – Mr Ibrahim praised the president variously as a historic and wise leader, a great warrior, a beacon to all Arabs, the rightful heir [...] (*The Daily Telegraph*, Oct. 17, 1995, "Saddam's victory hailed by gunfire")

      b.   Roy Campbell, the South African poet, was once put out when, on the Riviera, observing an ample form under a large hat, he took it for a much-loathed decadent and pinched the broad behind – only to find himself faced with the historic features of Sir Winston gazing in mute reproach. (*The Sunday Telegraph*, May 7, 1995, "Books: Between the war and the Sixties")

      c.   'Owen died a year later. I didn't realise then what a historical picture I had taken,' Chapman recalls. (*The Daily Telegraph*, May 6, 1995, "Outdoors: Bones and stones of a disappearing Dartmoor")

In the *OED*, the first recorded instances of *historic* in this sense precede those of *historical* (first instance of *historic* being from 1794, that of *historical* from 1834). Interestingly enough, according to the *MED* (s.v.), *historial* was much earlier also used in this sense, as seen from the example "Boþe two as in her writyng Ne varie nat but in litel þing Touching mater, as in special, þat is notable or historial" (from John Lydgate, *Lydgate's Troy Book*, edited by H. Bergen (1420), 5.3338). The quotation is the only example given of the sense, and it seems possible that this use of the adjective was relatively rare. Quite correctly, however, the *OED* s.v. adds in its definition of *historical* in this sense that the shorter form "is now the usual word". The definition of *historic*, sense 2 reads 'Forming an important part or item of history; noted or celebrated in history; having an interest or importance due to connexion with historical events', and it is something of a surprise to notice that instead of events all the examples refer to places (e.g. *historic spot*), although nowadays the most common instances of *historic* have to do with important events. The examples of *historical* in this sense also include places and objects (e.g. *historical ship*), and what from the viewpoint of present-day usage would seem like odd uses of the adjective, for example "It has become an historical fact [...] that 'Childe Harold' and the 'Bard of Memory' met at Pisa" (from Thomas Medwin, *The Angler in Wales* (1834) I, 25).

In the corpora studied, the first instances of *historic* involving the notion of 'famous or celebrated in history' were found in the nineteenth century works, suggesting that the increase of this use did indeed take place during this period:

(27) a. How could he think of himself who had done nothing, accomplished nothing, so long as he brooded on the images of signal Englishmen whose names were historic for daring, and the strong arm, and artfulness, all given to the service of the country? (George Meredith, *Beauchamp's Career* (1876), 19)

      b. A man who inherits a historical name owes something to his forefathers, and has no right to risk the reputation of his family by humouring his own whims. (William Black, *A Daughter of Heth* (1871), 94)

      c. Another voice was that of the Corn Law convert, whose phantom he had just seen in the quadrangle with the great bell. Jude thought his soul might have been shaping the historic words of his master-speech: [...] (Thomas Hardy, *Jude the Obscure* (1896), 97)

      d. Even if, instead of following the dim daybreak, our imagination pauses on a certain historical spot, and awaits the fuller morning, we may see a worldfamous city, which has hardly changed its outline since the days of Columbus, seeming to stand as an almost unviolated symbol, [...] (George Eliot, *Romola* (1863), 2–3)

It could be postulated that before becoming more common, this sense of *historic(al)* was first used mostly of famous names, words, or places having a connection with important events, and possibly in the second half of the nineteenth century, the adjectives – especially *historic* – came to be used of such events themselves.

As regards their function, in this sense the adjectives are descriptive: they can be coordinated with other descriptive adjectives, as in "The RSPCA described its success as an amazing and historic victory against sadists" (*The Daily Telegraph*, July 15, 1995, "Wild animal 'sadists' face jail"). It is therefore quite common to find *historic* in a predicative position, as in the following example:

(28) He knew others, armed with statistics and a sense of tradition, were describing the victory as historic, but he preferred to portray it as 'the ultimate training run' for next weekend's Lucerne Regatta. (*The Daily Telegraph*, July 3, 1995, "Rowing: Redgrave yet to prove he can pass through retirement barrier")

There are instances of words which can be modified by both *historic* in the sense now discussed and *historical* in another sense. Such instances are quite often found in usage manuals as illustrations of the difference between the two forms, as in the following passages (see also Follett 1966 s.v. *historic, historical*):[6]

> *A historic voyage*, for example, is contrasted with one that is of no lasting significance, whereas *a historical voyage* is contrasted with one that never took place: the voyage of Christopher Columbus to the New World was both *historic* and *historical*. (*Bloomsbury Good Word Guide* 1988 s.v. *historic, historical*)
>
> A historical novel is based on, or dealing with, history; a historic novel is a literary landmark, one that makes history. (Copperud 1964 s.v. *historic, -al*)

An interesting relation between the uses of *historic* and *historical* when modifying the same word can be seen in the following examples:

(29)   a.   Readers will be interested to know that Mr Mant, now in his 90th year, has also recently had published a book on the fall of Singapore in 1942, another historic event to which he was witness. (*BNC*, FT9, 437)

      b.   [...] state of things I have thought it necessary to premise for the information of the general reader, who might be apt to forget, that, although no great historical events, such as war or insurrection, mark the existence of the Anglo-Saxons as a separate people subsequent to the reign of William the Second; yet the great national distinctions betwixt them [...] (Walter Scott, *Ivanhoe* (1819), 6–7)

While a clear difference can be observed in the meanings of *historic* and *historical* in phrases like *a historic event* ('an event that is important in history') and *a historical event* ('an event that occurred in the past'), it could be argued that the actual semantic content of the phrases *a historic event* and *a great historical event* in (29a) and (29b) is almost exactly the same. In this case, where both events have clearly occurred in the more or less distant past, the latter could even

---

6   Some of the sources consulted attempt to illustrate the difference between the use of *historic* and *historical* simply by giving examples of words typically collocating with each form. This may not be the best way to approach the issue with this adjective pair, because, as already noted, many words can be used with both forms, even though the forms were used in different meanings. For instance, Greenbaum (1996: 455) gives the collocation ~ *events* as an exemplary collocating word for *historic,* although *historical* is also very commonly used in connection with this particular word.

be regarded as a "periphrastic" version of *a historic event.*[7] In other words, the greatness of the event in question is in the first instance included in the adjective *historic*, whereas it is not contained in *historical* in the latter phrase.

In his analysis of *historic/historical,* Marsden (1985: 29) considers the shorter form to be the "marked" member of the pair, as it expresses value judgement, whereas *historical*, lacking this particular semantic component, is in his view the more neutral form. Because of the presence of value judgement, the meaning 'important in history' often results in rather immediate and subjective uses of *historic*.[8] This is evident considering the fact that *historic* is nowadays very often used of events that are taking place at the moment or immediately prior to the utterance, as in *This is a historic event*, when referring e.g. to a peace agreement. The word can also be used of prospects in the future, as in "Their whole attitude is so professional that, with the right preparation, they could pull off another historic victory for league" (*The Daily Telegraph*, Dec. 26, "Talking Rugby League: Different leagues, but worth a try"). Some dictionaries and usage manuals have understandably chosen to paraphrase such uses of the adjective as 'likely to be important in the future' (e.g. Greenbaum and Whitcut (1988), *Collins English Dictionary,* and *OALD*, s.v. *historic*). It is possible that the element of tentativeness in the paraphrase is a reaction to the "looser" or "cheaper" use of the word as an expression of enthusiasm. However, it could be argued that subjectivity in the use of *historic(al)* in this sense is almost unavoidable, and the addition of "likely to be" or toned-down expressions such as "important enough to be noted in history" (see e.g. McKaskill 1977 and Bremner 1980 s.v. *historic, historical*) are somewhat unnecessary.

3.6 'Having a long history'

Only a few present-day dictionaries and usage manuals distinguish between the senses 'important in history' and 'having a long history'. Of the works consulted,

---

7   It is not entirely uncommon, however, to find constructions such as *great* + *historic* + noun, where the adjective *great* has an emphasizing function. For example, in Edgar Rice Burrough's *The Lost Continent* (1916), 73 (from the electronic version included in the Modern English Collection of the University of Virginia Electronic Text Center), we find the passage "There were mural paintings, too, depicting great historic events of the past". In this case, *historic* is most likely used in the sense of 'important in history', as the reference to the past is made explicitly in the sentence, although the entire expression may admittedly seem slightly awkward.

8   Of course, *historic* in the sense 'important in history' can also be used from an objective viewpoint; the writer's own positive value judgement or high degree of enthusiasm towards the thing referred to is not always present. In fact, the situations and events themselves may be considered regrettable, as in "the historic surprise raid [in Pearl Harbor] by Japanese aircraft dropping bombs and torpedoes" (*The Sunday Telegraph*, Aug. 13, 1995, "Travel: The bombs that began the war").

Wood (1962) s.v. *historic, historical* is the first to do this, assigning both senses to *historic*, with the examples "Historic cities such as York and Chester" and "A fund for the preservation of historic buildings". In more recent works, this distinction is still rarely made (found e.g. in Crystal 1991, and Turton and Heaton 1996 s.v. *historic, historical*). One reason for this may be that very often things are considered important *because* they have a long history: for example, McKaskill (1977) gives the paraphrase 'having a long and important history' (with the examples *historic city/castle*), while still separating such instances from historic events and occasions.

The usual examples of the present sense are *historic buildings/cities/ houses*. One difficulty in analysing the meaning of *historic(al)* in such phrases is that it is often virtually impossible to determine whether the writer has wanted to convey the notion of importance or the fact that the referent has a long history, or both. Furthermore, exactly why e.g. a building is regarded as *historic* can depend on different factors: to quote Morris and Morris (1985) s.v. *historic*, "A *historic* building is usually one in which important events took place or one whose architecture is such a prime example of a particular era as to be worth preserving". To fulfil the second "requirement", a building would not necessarily even have to be an old one – although they usually are relatively old – as long as it exemplifies a distinguishable architectural style. The age of the buildings can also be the primary decisive factor: on the web site of the Dallas branch of the Building Owners and Managers Association (BOMA), the "entry requirements" for histori*cal* buildings include "must be at least 50 years old with the original design maintained" (http://www.bomadallas.org/historic.htm). All in all, it can be said that when referring to buildings, towns, and physically existing entities in general, importance as a semantic component is present in this use, in some cases more prominently than in others.

Although *historic* is usually considered to be the more common form in this sense, sometimes similar instances of both forms were found in *The Daily Telegraph* material, as in (30a–d):

(30)   a.   However, the economic pressures that now dominate football have penetrated even the most proud and historic football clubs. (*The Daily Telegraph*, Dec. 18, 1995, "Letter to the Sports Editor: Everton 'family' values come under scrutiny")

       b.   In Castleford on Wednesday, a group called Rugby League Fans United will meet to co-ordinate resistance to the new Super League. Their flier, handed out at Wembley, declares: 'Three weeks ago, the so-called rugby league representatives autocratically decided to sell our game to a multinational corporation, carve it up, lose several historical clubs in the process, and change from a winter sport to summer. The fans were not consulted.' (*The Daily Telegraph*, May 1, 1995, "Rugby League: Past takes on the future in Wembley collision")

    c.   The majority of the top Australian players signed with Murdoch's new Super league but the Australian RL hierarchy, contracted to Murdoch's historic rival Kerry Parker until 1999, refused to switch. (*The Sunday Telegraph*, Oct. 1, 1995, "Rugby League: England can cash in on gold rush chaos")

    d.   [the subheader:] Atmosphere of hostility towards FIFA president as historical rivals battle to host 2002 tournament
        [the actual text:] Any of the 21 members of FIFA's executive committee, who vote for the Koreans instead of historic rivals Japan in June next year, will be identified as supporters of a nascent democratic movement. (*The Daily Telegraph*, Sept. 29, 1995, "Soccer: Havelange's powerbase is challenged by Korean bid"[9])

Some variation – or, vacillation – between *historic* and *historical* appears to occur when the adjectives modify words such as *monument, site* or *sight*.[10] Both forms can be found, for example, in names of associations: on the web site of The Royal Commission on the Ancient and Historical Monuments of Wales – in which case the form with *historical* seems to be the official form – both variants of the adjective are used in the text when referring to the commission (http://www.rcahmw.org.uk). *The Daily Telegraph* material also provides us with the names *Cornwall Historic Church's Trust* and *The Norwich Historical Church Trust*. It is possible that the older the association, the more likely its name to include the form *historical* rather than *historic,* showing that *historic*, nowadays with stronger connotations of positive value judgement than the longer form, has become a fashionable form in more recent times. Given the connotations and the fashionableness of the shorter form, it is understandable for a town with a long history to advertise itself as *historic* rather than *historical*, even if nothing spectacularly important ever happened there.

    The adjectives in the present sense can also be used in connection with abstract ideas, often coming close to the notion of 'traditional':

(31) a.   Even today, far too few engineers are accepted as advisers and managers because of our historic respect for brilliant scientists. (*The Daily Telegraph*, Dec. 22, 1995, "Letter to the Editor: Our neglected engineers")

---

9   It is possible that the subheader and the article itself, with their variation of *historic rivals* and *historical rivals*, were not written by the same person.

10   In some cases, *historic(al)* in connection with *monument/site/sight* can of course mean 'important in history'. Because of the difficulty in determining whether the adjectives were used in this particular meaning or in the sense 'having a long history', those cases where the context clearly implied that the referent was important in history were the only ones where the adjective was analysed as having that sense.

b. Mr Morris was also the most prominent opponent of Mr Blair's scrapping of Labour's historic commitment to public ownership of the economy's commanding heights. (*The Daily Telegraph*, May 23, 1995, "Left behind by a Right turn: Morris")

c. The unilateral ceasefires of autumn 1994 have given hundreds of thousands of people outside the extremist camps a fragile hope that the promise can set aside its historical distrust and create a lasting settlement. (*The Daily Telegraph*, Sept. 5, 1995, "Special Report on Northern Ireland: A matter of clinging to small beginnings")

d. This helps explain the increasing militancy of nurses as seen in the past few weeks, with the Royal College of Nursing's anger over the pay awards and their threat to drop their historical opposition to taking strike action. (*The Sunday Telegraph*, May 21, 1995, "No-frills angels come down to earth")

There are also cases where the referent, having a long history, is not regarded in a positive light, as in "the Government's belated efforts to remedy Britain's historic neglect of vocational education have gone seriously wrong" (*The Daily Telegraph*, Aug. 21, 1995, "Leading Article: Slow to learn") or "Corruption is a historic Italian practice" (*The Daily Telegraph*, Sept. 7, 1993, "Days of Laughter in the Dark").

One group of words with which the use of *historic* is preferred to the longer form is old vehicles, and phrases such as *historic cars* could even be considered fixed expressions. It is possible that contributing to the fixed nature of the use of *historic* in such cases is the fact that the phrase itself was most often used by car enthusiasts, in a way almost becoming a part of the jargon. As with *classic cars*, there are possibly several different views as to what exactly constitutes a historic car, the essential factor nevertheless being its old age. In some cases, in a modifying function, the word *car* is omitted, but nevertheless understood, as in "The awesome pre-war Mercedes GP cars would be beaten in modern historic racing by lesser but more highly developed machinery – but at Goodwood, the 'hod rods' are kept away" (*The Daily Telegraph*, Mar. 4, 1995, "Motoring: Hotfooting it to glorious Goodwood").

In the sense now examined, the adjectives may often be considered to have both descriptive and classifying functions; some of the most common phrases with *historic(al)* in the sense 'having a long history' have become more or less fixed expressions, as e.g. *historic buildings/cars*. As such things are often thought of and referred to as designating a separate class of buildings or cars, the adjective denotes a particular type or class. It is quite usual then that the phrase is modified by a descriptive adjective without a comma being inserted (e.g. *great historic buildings/houses*). Thus the adjective *historic* would have a clear classifying feature, while at the same time it does have a specific descriptive function as well. In cases such as (31a–d), however, the function of the adjective seems descriptive rather than classifying.

In the *American Heritage Dictionary* (2000), a separate category in the definition of *historical* has been adopted when referring to artefacts used in the past (s.v. *historical*, sense 1.c.), with the examples *historical costumes* and *historical weapons*. Instances of both *historic* and *historical* can be found modifying such words, as in the following examples from *The Daily Telegraph* material:

(32) a. Housed in a former workhouse, the museum will incorporate a comprehensive exhibition of historic medical equipment, conference facilities and an education department for medical students. (*The Daily Telegraph*, Nov. 24, 1995, "Trust wins £4.9m for Capability Brown park")

      b. Wallpaper and fabrics group, Walker Greenbank, has acquired one of the largest archives of historic wallpapers in the world, with the acquisition of traditional wallpaper manufacturer John Perry and distributor Cole & Son in a £1.5m deal. (*The Daily Telegraph*, Feb. 3, 1995, "CITY: Greenbank asset")

      c. Sir Anthony Grant, Tory MP for Cambridgeshire SW, hopes to reform Britain's law on treasure trove to maximise the prospects of historical artefacts remaining in museums in Britain rather than being sold abroad. (*The Daily Telegraph*, Dec. 5, 1995, "MP tries to reform treasure trove law")

While cases such as (32a–c) obviously invoke a contrast to contemporary things and are thus classifiable under the sense 'belonging to the past', the referents could also be regarded as having a long history, especially since as existing physical artefacts they still have current relevance. Additionally, in cases where the artefacts are put on display in exhibitions, the notion of prestige very easily becomes prominent, which explains the occasional tendency to use *historic* as well as *historical*. In addition to the paraphrase 'having a long history', the simple paraphrase 'old' is not altogether impossible either (the use of the word *old* itself in such cases may have obvious negative connotations, which itself is some motivation to use the more "respectable" word *historical*). Thus the adjective in phrases like *historical photographs* could also be placed in this category, although as artefacts photographs were not "used" in the same sense as the items in examples (32a–c). Artefacts such as the ones mentioned are very often exhibited in museums, so by extension of this particular use – again with an evident contrast to contemporary things – the adjectives are correspondingly used to modify more general terms, e.g. *art* and *exhibitions*, in connection with which there is also variation between the two forms. In fact, both examples (33a) and (33b) are by the same writer, John McEwen:

(33) a.   While they sanction these revisionist shows on the one hand, on the other they reduce the historic collection to a minimum in favour of modern art. (*The Sunday Telegraph*, Oct. 22, 1995, "The Arts: Glum parade of the great and good")

     b.   Mixing contemporary and historical art is a dodgy business, as Michael Craig-Martin's enjoyable *Drawing the Line* at the Whitechapel Gallery (until September 10) demonstrates [...] The surprises are in the historical selection: the extraordinarily modern-looking *Puzzle – Construction of Hollow Boxes* by Leonardo; [...] (*The Sunday Telegraph*, July 30, 1995, "The Arts: Sell-out of the true avant-garde")

3.7   Other uses

The following sections will examine some other functions of the adjectives *historic/historical*. These functions represent uses which are more or less exceptional compared to the general uses, or which pertain to specialized domains of writing and thought.

3.7.1   *Historic/historical* in the terminology of economics and statistics

Economics is one specific field which has been singled out as manifesting a use of *historic/historical* which does not conform to the norm. Similarly to the use of the adjective in *historic cars*, the use of *historic* in the field of economics may be considered almost jargonistic. For example, Howard (1993) s.v. *historic, historical* notes that "the financial world refers to *historic cost* (the cost of an item at the time it was produced), an incorrect use which is accepted – for *historical* reasons". *Collins English Dictionary* (1998), on the other hand, has a separate entry for *historical-cost accounting*, defined as 'a method of accounting that values assets at the original cost'. *The Chambers Dictionary* (1993) notes that both forms are sometimes used, with *historic* (or *historical*) *cost* s.v. being defined as 'the actual price paid'. This use of the adjectives, which also suggests the notion 'original', could be classified into the sense group 'belonging to history', but as the use of the two forms in the field of economics seems to differ from other types of texts, the instances relating to economics or statistics are here discussed and classified separately.[11]

---

11   Some texts on economic matters in the material studied did include some more "regular" uses of *historic(al)*, instead of being suggestive of language especially used in this field. Therefore cases such as *a historic decision*, although appearing in an article dealing with financial matters, would be classified into the sense group 'making history or

Some other notions can also be involved in the use of *historic(al)*, such as 'being the record level in history', as in *historic lows* in example (34):

(34)   Further support came from strong bond markets (gilts, up 1/4 at the long end, came off their highs after some light profit-taking) and sterling's relative stability after scraping historic lows earlier in the week. (*The Daily Telegraph*, Dec. 2, 1995, "CITY: The Market – Inflation index puts equities in top gear")

This kind of use of *historic* could also be regarded as suggesting the semantic aspect of 'making history'. It is possible that instances such as example (34), where the use of the *-ic* form perhaps does not seem too awkward, actually may have partly influenced some of the "nonconformist" uses of *historic* in the economics terminology in general.

3.7.2 *Historic/historical* collocating with *importance/interest/significance*/etc.

Variation between *historic* and *historical* can often be seen when the adjectives modify words such as *importance*, *interest*, *merit*, *significance*, and *value*, i.e. words which themselves suggest a (positive) value judgement:

(35) a.   In a letter to a national newspaper, Mr Carter wrote: 'With misgivings, I created a clause which made it an offence to alter a listed building in such a way as to 'affect its quality as a building of architectural or historic importance'.' (*The Daily Telegraph*, Jan. 11, 1995, "Property: Owners on the 'style police' blacklist")

      b.   Land of scenic, scientific or historical importance: this may include parks and gardens, and land which includes archaeological sites, etc. (*The Sunday Telegraph*, Oct. 22, 1995, "Guide to Lottery Funding: How it could be you")

      c.   Alarm bells rang when conservationists realised the tunnel was not even statutorily listed as a structure of special architectural or historic interest, and on March 24 the tunnel was 'spot' listed just days before builders were due to move in. (*The Sunday Telegraph*, Oct. 29, 1995, "Property: Brunel's Thames Tunnel – Wreck of the Week")

      d.   More than 1,000 properties of architectural, historical and cultural interest will open to the public free on the weekend of Sept 16–17. (*The Daily Telegraph*, Sept. 6, 1995, "Open house")

---

important in history', whereas uses as part of a term in economics, such as *historic(al) cost/prices/earnings*, are classified as a separate group.

As regards their adjectival function, in (35a–d), both *historic* and *historical* are classifying adjectives, used in the sense 'having to do with history'. The classifying function becomes evident from the fact that the adjectives in question are used in coordination with other classifiers (*architectural, scientific, cultural*). Considering the general differentiation between the two forms, *historical* would be the expected form in these examples. This is also the view held by Ilson and Whitcut (1994) s.v. *historic, historical*, who regard the sentence "The battle of Hastings was of great historic importance" as ill-formed, adding that "**a great historic importance* is like saying 'great important importance'". A similar comment on the variation is made by Burchfield (1996) s.v. *historic*. It would seem likely that the main reason for the variation between the two adjective forms in such instances is the idea of value judgement in the words *importance/significance/interest*. As regards the overall semantic aspects of the two forms, *historic* is strongly associated with value judgement, which could be one factor explaining why the writers have chosen to use the shorter form instead of *historical*. Such a choice is understandable considering the fact that very often examining things from the viewpoint of history almost unavoidably involves having to make evaluations of different factors, including e.g. their importance.[12]

3.7.3   *Historic(al) present*

Both *historic present* and *historical present* have been used of a narrative style in which the present tense is used of things that have happened in the past, as in "Anyway, I'm in the pub with my friends and a bloke comes up to me and asks if I want to buy a stereo" (*CIDE* s.v. *historic*). *The Daily Telegraph* material included only one occurrence of the phrase (with the *-ical* form), but dictionaries, grammar books, and usage manuals show no clear preference for either form. Fowler (1926) s.v. *historic, historical* presents the phrase *historic present* as one exception where – in his opinion – the otherwise incongruous use of *historic* is permitted. It is possible that the use of *historical* has gained ground since Fowler's days, but neither form finds conclusive support in the dictionaries published over the last 15 years. The shorter form in this phrase is given, for example, in *NODE, OALD, CIDE*, and *Macmillan English Dictionary*, whereas *Encarta World English Dictionary*, *The Chambers Dictionary*, and *Collins English Dictionary* give *historical present* as the headword.

---

12   Moreover, there are some native English-speaking informants who are not opposed to the use of the phrases *historic significance* or *historic importance*. This is perhaps because in the case of *importance* and *significance* one is more likely to expect a descriptive adjective as its modifier (for example, typical collocations for *importance* include *of considerable/great/growing/huge/real importance*), whereas *interest* is often preceded by a classifier, an adjective denoting the type of interest in question.

4.   *Historic/historical* in the material studied

As observed in section 1 of the present chapter, *historical* was the more frequent form in the corpus texts from earlier centuries. In the latter half of the sixteenth century, only a few authors represented in the corpora used either *historic* or *historical*. In the non-fiction texts, twenty occurrences of *historical* were found (used by two authors). Most of these instances related to writings describing an event in history or having an earlier period of history as its setting (e.g. *a historical poem*).

In the seventeenth century texts, *historical* was the only form found, both in the fiction and non-fiction material examined. The adjective was most frequently used in the general classifying sense 'having to do with history'.

Table 53. *Historic/historical* in the prose section of *Literature Online*, 1600–1699.

	historic	*historical*
1. a. 'having to do with history'	-	17 (1)
b. 'having to do with the recording of history'	-	1
2. 'based on history' (writing)	-	2
3. 'belonging to history', 'existed in the past'	-	2 (1)
total	**-**	**22 (2)**
# of authors:	-	15

Table 54. *Historic/historical* in the non-fiction texts examined, 1600–1699.

	historic	*historical*
1. 'having to do with history'	-	14
2. 'based on history'		
a. writing	-	3
b. painting	-	3 (3)
3. 'belonging to history', 'existed in the past'	-	2 (1)
total	**-**	**22 (4)**
# of authors:	-	13

The adjectives in the eighteenth century texts, as seen from Tables 55 and 56, were more numerous, no doubt partly owing to the material being somewhat larger in size. The number of occurrences of *historic* are greater than in the previous century material, but the form in *-ical* is nevertheless the commoner form in all senses in which the adjectives were used.

Table 55. *Historic/historical* in the prose section of *Literature Online*, 1700–1799.

	historic	*historical*
1. a. 'having to do with history'	5	37
b. 'having to do with the recording of history'	-	1
2. 'based on history'		
a. writing	2	6
b. painting	-	5
3. 'belonging to history', 'existed in the past'	-	1
4. 'genuinely existed or occurred in the past', 'authentic'	-	1
total	**7**	**51**
# of authors:	2	23
# of authors using both forms: 2		

Table 56. *Historic/historical* in the non-fiction texts examined, 1700–1799.

	historic	*historical*
1. a. 'having to do with history'	4	16
b. 'having to do with the recording of history'	-	2
c. 'having to do with the research of history'	-	2
2. 'based on history' (writing)	1	1
total	**5**	**21**
# of authors:	**1**	**13**
# of authors using both forms: 1		

In the 1800–1849 *Literature Online* material, the situation as regards the uses of *historic* and *historical* was very similar to that in the eighteenth century, as shown in Table 57. The adjectives are most often used in the general sense 'having to do with history', but the meaning 'belonging to history' or 'existed in the past' has also gained a firmer foothold. The number of the different senses in which the adjectives are used seems also to have increased. The first occurrences of the words denoting things regarded as famous, important, or otherwise notable in history are encountered.

Table 57. *Historic/historical* in the prose section of *Literature Online,* 1800–
    1849.

	historic	historical
1. a. 'having to do with history'	11	49 (1)
b. 'having to do with the recording of history'	1	5
c. 'having to do with the research of history'	-	4
2. 'based on history'		
a. writing	-	12
b. painting	-	7
3. 'belonging to history', 'existed in the past'	1	20 (2)
4. 'important or famous in history'	2	1
5. 'genuinely existed or occurred in the past', 'authentic'	-	4
6. 'having a long history'	-	3
total	**15**	**105 (3)**
# of authors:	5	23
# of authors using both forms: 5		

The non-fiction texts from the same period included only a few occurrences of
historic or *historical* (one and fourteen, respectively), most of them used in the
general sense 'having to do with history'.

The *Literature Online* prose texts dating from 1850–1903 (see Table 58)
show a continued increase in the use of *historic* in relation to the number of
occurrences of the longer form.[13] In some of the more recently introduced
meanings, 'important in history' and 'having a long history', *historic* appears to
have been quite "competitive" with *historical*; as regards the sense 'important or
famous in history', the instances of *historic* even outnumber those of *historical* in
this period. This suggests that the introduction of a new sense has at quite an
early stage – if not right at the outset – led to differentiation between the two
adjective forms, there being a clear tendency for this new sense to be assigned to
the shorter form rather than to the one carrying the more conventional meanings.
In other words, *historic*, being until then the less frequently used, practically
synonymous variant of *historical*, was "available" for a previously unattested
sense. Additionally, the significance of the novelty of the sense 'important in
history' has to be emphasized, this usage being descriptive instead of classifying,

13   It is also interesting to note that the use of both *historic* and *historical* became
more frequent during the nineteenth century, even when considering that the size of the
Literature Online material between the years 1800 and 1903 is more than three times that
of the period 1513–1699, and more than twice that of 1700–1799.

thus changing the fundamental semantic and functional status of this adjective pair. It could be postulated, then, that had there not been such a novel sense introduced, *historic* eventually might have begun to disappear from use. This, rather than the *-ic* form slowly becoming the favoured form, would perhaps have been more likely, since *historical* had already become fairly well established.

Table 58. *Historic/historical* in the prose section of *Literature Online*, 1850–1903.

	historic	*historical*
1. a. 'having to do with history'	33	91 (7)
b. 'having to do with the recording of history'	1	2
c. 'having to do with the research of history'	-	2
2. 'based on history'		
a. writing	2	12 (1)
b. painting	1	5
3. 'belonging to history', 'existed in the past'	2	18
4. 'important or famous in history'	19 (4)	5 (2)
5. 'genuinely existed or occurred in the past', 'authentic'	1	6 (2)
6. 'having a long history'	6	5
total	**65 (4)**	**146 (12)**
# of authors:	18	30
# of authors using both forms: 16		

In the case of 'having genuinely existed, authentic', *historical* was the favoured form, probably because it is semantically rather close to the sense 'existed in the past, used in instances where the existence is not questioned. In all the remaining senses, too, *historical* is more or less clearly preferred. In the non-fiction texts written by British authors (Table 59) from this period, the increase in the use of *historic* is not visible to the same extent. It must be noted, however, that the numbers of authors using the adjectives are also rather small. Interestingly enough, the non-fiction material by American authors from this period includes a greater number of instances of *historic/historical*, and the figures indicating their uses (presented in Appendix C, Table 1) correlate to some extent with the ones for the *Literature Online* material in Table 58 (i.e. *historic* appears to have a stronger foothold in the senses 'important in history' and 'having a long history').

Table 59. *Historic/historical* in the non-fiction texts studied, 1850–1899 (British authors).

	historic	historical
1. a. 'having to do with history'	3	39 (2)
b. 'having to do with the research of history'	-	9
2. 'based on history' (writing)	-	2
3. 'belonging to history', 'existed in the past'	1	7
4. 'important or famous in history'	2	-
5. 'genuinely existed or occurred in the past', 'authentic'	-	2
6. 'having a long history'	-	3
total	**6**	**62 (2)**
# of authors:	4	13
# of authors using both forms: 2		

The rather small number of British non-fiction writings from the first half of the twentieth century did not contain many instances of *historic* and *historical* (one and 42, respectively). The more numerous American texts from 1900–1961 show a tendency in the use of the adjectives similar to the one observed in the late nineteenth century texts, with *historical* being the preferred form in the older, classifying meanings, and *historic* being more usual than *historical* in the more recent, descriptive senses. The results gained from the British and American twentieth century non-fiction material are presented in Appendix C, Tables 2 and 3, respectively.

The different uses of *historic/historical* in the 1995 issue of *The Daily Telegraph*, excluding those instances where the adjective was part of a proper noun, are presented in Table 60 below. The ordering of the senses (1, 2, 3, etc.) in the table is a rough approximation of the order in which they were introduced into English.

Table 60. *Historic/historical* in the 1995 issues of *The Daily Telegraph.*

	historic	historical
1. a. 'having to do with history', 'relating to or about history'	48	429 (12)
a'. collocations indicating importance or value:		
~ *import/importance*	8	19
~ *interest*	16	12
~ *merit*	1	2
~ *significance*	4	11
~ *value*	-	6
b. 'having to do with the recording of history'	6	17
c. 'having to do with the research of history'	1	57
2. 'based on history, using history as the setting': novels, plays, etc.	1	83 (1)
3. 'belonging to history', 'having happened or existed in the past'	16 (1)	132 (3)
4. 'genuinely existed or occurred in the past', 'authentic', opposed to fictional or legendary	2	19 (1)
5. 'important or famous in history', 'making history'	362 (19)	15 (1)
6. '(important through) having a long history', 'traditional', 'used in the past'		
a. large man-made constructions, e.g. buildings, castles, etc. (also, organisations relating to them)	199 (4)	13
b. other physical artefacts	18	16
c. art, architectural styles, exhibitions, etc.	6	4
d. places, areas, and towns	102	12
e. clubs, institutions, etc.	16	2
f. cars (also ~ *car racing*)	26	-
f'. other vehicles	14	-
g. abstract ideas, activities over a long period of time	106 (3)	41
7. relating to economics and statistics: ~ *cost/high/low*/etc.	52	8
8. others: ~ *present*	-	1
total	**1004 (27)**	**899 (18)**

It can be seen from Table 60 that *historical* is in present-day English more common than its shorter counterpart in nearly all of those senses in which *historical* was likewise favoured in earlier centuries in the fiction and non-fiction material. In the major classifying senses, 'having to do with history' (sense 1.a) and 'existed in history' (sense 3), *historical* is clearly more common than *historic*. Among the most frequent collocating words in sense 1.a were *context* (21 occurrences with *historical*, none with *historic*), *reasons* (17 vs. 6), and *accuracy* (17 vs. none). For sense 3, the most frequently found collocates included e.g. *figure* (21 occurrences with *historical*) and *event* (18 occurrences with *historical*). Interestingly enough, in those cases where the collocates indicate importance or value (group 1.a'), the margin of difference is narrower, but adding the figures together, *historical* is in such cases used slightly more often. Similarly, a narrower difference is seen in sense 1.b, 'having to do with the recording of history'.

The longer form is also preferred when the adjectives are used in the meaning 'having genuinely existed in history' (sense 4). An even greater preference for *historical* can be perceived in references to the research of history (sense group 1.c) or to novels, plays, films, etc. which are either based on history or which use history as their setting (sense 2).

Historic is clearly preferred to *historical* for conveying the sense 'famous or important in history' (sense 5). Similarly, *historic* is used more often than its longer counterpart when referring to buildings, houses, castles, etc. which have a long history (sense 6, group a). The most prominently appearing head words of the adjectives in this group include *building(s)* (55 with *historic*, 1 with *historical*) and *house(s)* (39 vs. none). The shorter form is likewise far more frequent in connection with places, areas, and towns (sense 6, group d) with 32 instances of *historic towns/cities*, as opposed to a mere one of *historical town*. The rivalry was more even with the collocate *site(s)*, ten times used with *historic*, and five times with *historical*. The shorter form is also more common when used of "traditional" clubs or institutions, as well as old cars and other vehicles. In the case of physical artefacts and objects used in the past (sense 6, group b), as exemplified in (32a–c), both *historic* and *historical* were used in the newspaper texts with roughly the same frequency. "Traditional" activities or ideas (sense 6, group g), as in examples (31a–d), seem to show a preference for *historic* (106 occurrences), but *historical* is also used relatively often in similar instances. In specialized phrases used in relation to economics, statistics, and accounting, *historic* is the preferred form (e.g. *historic cost/earnings*).

The results from *The Daily Telegraph* material suggest that in cases where the function of the adjective is more clearly classifying, *historical* is the preferred form, whereas *historic* is significantly more common when the adjective has a descriptive function. The existence of some "problem areas", showing a more balanced distribution of the two forms, can be explained by the potentially "confusing" semantic aspects of the collocating words or by the possibility to view the matter from different viewpoints. When the head word itself denotes importance or value, for instance, the sense 'important in history' may lead the speaker or writer to use *historic* instead of *historical* even if the function is clearly classifying. Variation is also seen in the case of the sense 'having a long history', especially when the adjective refers to things used in the past, art and artistic styles from previous times, as well as long-term activities. In such instances, the speaker or writer may either link the idea of old age with importance or significance, or have a more neutral attitude towards the thing in question, simply making the connection between age and the notion 'of the nature of history'. Such variation, then, is quite understandable, considering the fact that the word *traditional* itself may have either positive or neutral connotations.

A few observations can also be made on the overall frequencies of *historic* and *historical*. The slightly greater absolute frequency of *historic* in the 1995 issues of *The Daily Telegraph* is also seen in other yearly issues of the same newspaper (e.g. the 1993 and 1994 issues). The frequency band notations in *COBUILD* (2001) s.vv. *historic*, *historical* are also in agreement with this finding: both adjectives are included in the same frequency band (indicating approximately 1500 words in the *Bank of English* text corpus). A similar relation between the frequencies of the two forms was furthermore seen in the 1994 issues of *The Washington Post*. However, the matter is surrounded with complexities: the relation between the frequencies of the two adjective forms very likely depends on the type of text in question. In contrast with *The Daily Telegraph* material, the *British National Corpus* includes altogether 2311 occurrences of *historic*, and as many as 5558 occurrences of *historical*. An examination of the frequencies of the adjectives in different domains of writing and speech reveals that the 50-50 relation does not apply to all areas of language use. The results with the numbers of occurrences of the adjectives are presented in Appendix C, Table 4 (the figures inside parentheses denote the number of texts in which the adjectives were used). It turns out that in most of the written domains of the corpus, *historical* is used much more often than *historic*, both as regards the absolute frequencies and the numbers of texts including the adjectives. In only one domain, "Leisure", *historic* was more frequent than *historical*.

As mentioned earlier, however, the differences in the absolute frequencies in different domains of writing and speech probably reflect the semantic differentiation established between the two forms. In other words, considering the extent of the semantic differentiation between *historic* and *historical* in *The Daily Telegraph* material, it seems highly unlikely that the same lines of differentiation would not emerge in other types of texts (save texts on economic matters). Instead, those domains which are more likely to include classifying references to history (rather than descriptive or qualitative ones regarding the importance of the referents) are also more likely to include a relatively greater number of occurrences of *historical* than *historic*. In fact, it is intuitively quite plausible to assume that newspaper articles characteristically include a relatively great number of assertive evaluations and analyses on the implications and effects of actions and events that are reported on. What is also important to note is the difference between the *BNC* and *The Daily Telegraph* material as far as they represent the language as a whole. There are obviously some areas of language use that are probably not represented in newspapers to the same extent as they are in the *BNC*.

5.   General remarks

It has been observed in the previous sections that throughout their existence in the English vocabulary, the adjectives *historic* and *historical* have carried a number of different uses. In the same way as in connection with e.g. *classic/classical*, the numerousness of the nuances involved in the adjectives' use reflects the possibility of viewing the basic concept and core meaning – in this case, history – from a variety of angles. Among the semantic components mixed in the uses of the adjectives discussed in this chapter are the abstract idea of history, the past in general, authenticity, old age, tradition, and prestige. The semantic differentiation between the two forms has developed so far that when modifying the same word, the two phrases can have entirely different meanings, as in the case of *a historic event* ('an event important in history') and *a historical event* ('an event that took place in the past').

Until the semantic division between the two variants, *historical* appears to have been the dominant form. Well into the eighteenth century, *historic* was the less frequent variant, practically synonymous with *historical*. When a new use of the words emerged, which added the notion of importance to the basic meaning, and thus made the function of the adjective descriptive rather than "merely" classifying, the shorter form gradually began to gain ground. Eventually *historic* became the favoured form in the descriptive senses, while *historical* remained the preferred variant in the older uses, denoting the type or class, i.e. connecting the referent with the domain of history. The changes, however, did not result in *historic* ultimately taking over all of the senses carried by the two forms, with *historical* becoming obsolete. Instead, the level of the previous dominance of the longer form, as well as the apparently stark difference between the descriptive and classifying uses, help to explain why both forms have survived and have been assigned senses different from each other, the differences being often pointed out and emphasized in dictionaries and usage manuals today.

Some degree of variation between the two forms can still be seen. In addition to the variation caused by the obvious proximity of appearance of *historic* and *historical*, the semantic features present which in some cases promote the use of one of the forms instead of the other, can sometimes be interpreted as supporting the use of both forms. Instances where both forms are often used include cases where the head word itself suggests prestige, e.g. *importance, interest, significance*, and *value*. Similarly, some variation between the forms is seen in connection with old buildings and cities. It appears that the contrast between the notions of 'having a long history' and 'having to do with history' has not in all cases become firmly established. As observed by Ross (1998: 42–43), it is possible that the present-day tendency to favour *historic* in such instances is partly a result of a slow shift towards the use of the forms in *-ic* even in the case of semantically differentiated *-ic/-ical* pairs. However, it is notable that the particular instances where variation is seen most today are also ones which are semantically most "vulnerable" in this respect. It remains to be seen whether variation between the two forms will increase in cases where *historical* is now clearly the preferred form.

Chapter 10

From supernatural powers to exciting football games: *magic/magical*

Although *magic/magical* is usually listed among those *-ic/-ical* adjective pairs subject to semantic differentiation, it is also that pair among the ones studied with which writers of usage manuals tend to lean towards descriptivism rather than taking a firm prescriptivist stance. It is this adjective pair that writers of usage manuals would most readily admit as showing a degree of semantic overlap, even interchangeability, of the two forms, while maintaining that more or less clear distinctions of usage can nevertheless be perceived. As with other *-ic/-ical* pairs in present-day English, one can find instances of slips or inconsistencies in the use of *magic* and *magical* by one and the same writer, as in the "fixed" expression *Magic(al) Sense* in examples (1a) and (1b), where the phrase approximates the status of a proper name (notice the capital letters). The examples are found in the same text, which explains the rules of a fantasy card game (*Magic(al) Sense* being a feature of one of the characters on the cards):

(1)   a.   Characters cannot rely on skills such as Magical Awareness and Magic Sense to show this, since the whole of this room radiates magic. (*BNC*, CLK 1453)

        b.   The masks are clearly magical, as any character with Magical Sense may realize. (*BNC*, CLK 761)

In some cases "true" free variation between the two forms can be detected, as in example pairs (2a) and (2b) (again from fantasy game instructions), and (2c) and (2d), all from the *British National Corpus*:

(2)   a.   It draws magic power from the War Altar and glows with a green inner light. (*BNC*, CN1 2293)

        b.   It draws magical power from the War Altar and passes it into the Grand Theogonis [...] (*BNC*, CN1 2302)

        c.   In this myth Isis was a woman who longed to increase her magic powers and join the gods in order to rule over them. (*BNC*, EVR 249)

        d.   Osiris was dead, but Isis had great magical powers and she had the body of her husband. (*BNC*, EVR 300)

Still considering the general remarks on *-ic/-ical* adjectives made by various writers, one more thing that makes *magic/magical* stand out from the others is that there is a syntactic factor alleged to affect the use of the two forms. According to Fowler (1926), and the *OED* (s.vv. *magic, magical*), *magic* can only be used attributively, whereas *magical* can be used in both attributive and predicative positions. This element has been downplayed in dictionaries in recent years, largely because of the informal British English use of *magic* in the sense of 'excellent', often appearing in predicative position, as in *It was really magic*. In addition, the importance of collocation in the choice of *magic* or *magical* has been pointed out, especially in the case of *magic* appearing in some fixed expressions. At this point it seems worth quoting in full Burchfield's (1996) comments on these adjectives s.v. *magic, magical*, illustrating the main points of interest:

> Until recently *magic* was normally used only in the attributive position (*magic carpet, magic circle, magic spell*) when the sense was the normal one of 'of or pertaining to magic'. In this position, except in fixed phrases like *magic lantern* or *magic square*, it vied with *magical* (*the magical word 'democracy'*; *a magical effect on the economy*). The words were not freely interchangeable in this position but no clear-cut rule can be stated. Perhaps *magical* tended to be used mainly in contexts of high approbation, and *magic* in contexts of enchantment, but the line between them has always untidily been drawn. In the second half of the 20c. *magic* has come to be used colloquially in the attributive [sic] position or by itself (*Magic!*) as a term of enthusiastic commendation, simply meaning 'wonderful, exciting', e.g. *It's magic!*; *The food* (or *concert, exhibition*, etc.) *was magic*. Doubtless, except in fixed phrases, the two words will continue to vie with each other in the years ahead, esp. in figurative, extended, and weakened senses, both in the attributive and the predicative positions.

1.   Etymology and early history of the pair

The models for the English words *magic* and *magical* are to be found in the Latin noun *magia* (in late Latin also *magica*), and the Latin adjective *magicus* (which had some nominal uses as well), which in turn have their origins in the Greek noun μαγεία and the adjective μαγικός. Most likely the immediate "source" for the word *magic* in English, however, was the Old French word *magique*, which functioned as both a noun and an adjective. In modern French, however, *magique* is only used as an adjective, and *magie* as the noun, a development in most

Romance languages, which did not manifest itself in English, where the use of the same word was retained in the two functions (see the *OED* s.v. *magic*).

Apart from other features already mentioned, the pair *magic/magical* differs from the other "major" *-ic/-ical* adjective pairs in that the longer form may be considered to have been formed by adding the suffix *-al* to an already existing word ending in *-ic* (while *magic*, in turn, has no potential base word to which the suffix *-ic* could have been added). This is because *magic* – as both a noun and an adjective – was used in English much earlier than *magical*. It appears that more or less right from the start, *magic* was used as both a noun and an adjective: the first recorded instances of the word in both functions in the *MED* and the *OED* are from the late fourteenth century. The first citation of *magical* in the *OED* s.v. *magical* dates from 1555, but there is, in fact, an earlier occurrence of the word in the same dictionary under the entry for *curious* (sense 5.c): "That Citie was full of Curiouse menne, and such as were geuen to magicall artes" (from Nicolas Udell, et al., *The first tome or volume of the paraphrase of Erasmus upon the Newe Testament*, published in 1549).

As regards the semantic aspects of the two forms, the addition of *-al* in itself did not originally introduce anything new, as *magical* was used in the same sense as *magic*, i.e. 'of or pertaining to magic', the most common phrase containing the adjectives being *magic(al) art(s)*. The idea of simply adding *-al* onto the *-ic* form (as mentioned in the *OED* s.v. *magical*) may be questioned, for one would then expect *magical* to have been a secondary adjective form to *magic*, with clearly separate semantic or syntactic uses, but this obviously was not the case at the point when the longer form was created.[1] Alternatively, the formation of *magical* could be linked to the general uprise of *-ical* endings towards the end of the sixteenth century. As observed in Chapter 4, some adjectives ending in *-ical* came into existence even though there already were synonymous adjectives ending in *-ic*.

Magic as the earlier adjectival form remained in use, and even dominated to some extent over the longer form for centuries, as far as relative frequency of use is concerned. This can be seen from the numbers of occurrences of the two adjectives in the *Literature Online* material, presented in Table 61 below. The figures inside parentheses indicate the numbers of authors using the adjectives (where relevant, a second number denotes the number of books by anonymous writers).

---

1   The simple assumption that *magical* is a secondary form to *magic* is rather easy to make, considering some descriptions of the present-day use of the adjectives which suggest that *magical* has undergone more semantic extensions than *magic*. For example, in *Oxford Dictionary and English Usage Guide* s.v. *magic, magical*, the longer form is assigned more senses: *magic* is paraphrased as 'of magic', whereas *magical* has the gloss 'of magic; resembling, or produced as if by, magic; wonderful, enchanting'.

Table 61. *Magic/magical* in the prose section of the *Literature Online* corpus, 1513–1903.

	1513–1599	1600–1699	1700–1799	1800–1849	1850–1903
magic	50 (6/2)	13 (6/1)	72 (15)	100 (21)	178 (28)
magical	7 (4/1)	19 (8/6)	18 (9)	55 (16)	64 (20)
authors using both forms	2/1	-	6	10	12

In almost all periods, *magic* is used more frequently than *magical*, with the exception of the seventeenth century, but the numbers of authors using the adjectives are fairly low especially in the first two periods examined. The relation between the numbers of authors and the numbers of occurrences also suggests that those authors using the word *magic* tended to use it more often compared to those who used *magical*. For example, in Richard Jefferies's *Bevis* (1882), *magic* as an adjective appears 34 times, whereas *magical* crops up only twice. Additionally, it has to be noted that the figures denoting the absolute numbers of occurrences lose some of their significance as the differentiation between the two forms becomes more and more established, i.e. the "dominance" in frequency is less important when the two forms are used in different meanings.[2]

2.   *Magic/magical* in dictionaries and usage manuals

Examining the treatment of *magic* and *magical* in early English dictionaries provides no great surprises: as both adjectives were at first synonymous, and the dictionaries – from today's point of view – do not exactly represent the apex of accuracy and consistency, all kinds of presentations are found. In *EMEDD*, the adjective *magic* is recorded first in Palsgrave's (1530) English/French dictionary. Both adjective forms are found in Mulcaster (1582) and Florio's (1598) Italian-English dictionary. Cockeram (1626, second edition) has an entry only for *magic* as a noun, although both forms of the adjectives appear in definitions elsewhere in the book. In some dictionaries only *magic* is given as the adjective (Bullokar 1680, sixth edition), while in others, *magical* is the sole adjective form (e.g.

---

2   *Magic* and *magical* were not very frequent in the non-fiction texts examined; only a few authors per century were found using the adjectives. Therefore the occurrences of the adjectives in these texts are referred to only cursorily. In fact, considering that the adjectives relate to actions and practices involving supernatural powers, it could be argued that the use of these words is not drastically different between fiction and expository writing. The adjectives found in the *OED* citations are mostly from fictional texts (many of them being also included in the *Literature Online* collection), and they will likewise be commented on just briefly.

Kersey 1702).[3] In Bailey (1721), *magic* and *magical* are treated as synonyms. The senses usually given are along the lines of 'of, or belonging to, magic' and 'enchanting, conjuring'.

In Johnson's dictionary (1755), the two forms are given separate entries, but the paraphrases are quite close to each other: *magic* is defined as 'acting or doing by powers superior to the known power of nature', while *magical* has the sense 'acting, or performing by secret and invisible powers'. *Magic* is given the additional paraphrases 'enchanted; necromantick' and 'done or produced by magic', and *magical* that of 'applied to persons using enchantment', but the meanings beginning with 'acting...' are virtually identical, unless the intended difference between the forms lies in the degree or the actual origin of the power in question. Practically the same treatment of the words is found in the dictionaries by Sheridan (1780) and Barclay (1819), the similarity suggesting that Johnson's definitions clearly served as a model. In the nineteenth and early twentieth century, however, it was not uncommon to present the two forms as synonyms, as in e.g. Richardson (1836), Craig (1848), and *Chambers's English Dictionary* (1914). In some cases where *magic* and *magical* are grouped in the same entry – often with the minimalistic comment "also *magical*" under the main entry for *magic* – it is the examples that suggest the different senses carried by the two forms, although nothing to this effect is explicitly mentioned the definitions themselves, as in Webster (1828):

MAGIC,
MAGICAL, *a.* Pertaining to magic; used in magic; as a *magic* wand; *magic* art.
2. Performed by magic, the agency of spirits, or by the invisible powers of nature; as *magical* effects.

The definitions of the two adjective forms in the *OED* are also very much alike, although differences can be perceived as well. For the senses 1.a–c of *magical*, the *OED* gives cross-references to those of *magic*. Sense 1.a for both reads 'of or pertaining to magic', the definition of the shorter form having the additional note "Also, working or produced by enchantment. Not in predicative use." Sense 1.b involves physical objects which are enchanted or are used in sorcery (the examples including *magic wand*, *magic mirror*, and *magic(al) glass*), with the comment that often such references are made figuratively. For *magical*, this sense has been marked as obsolete, in the same way as sense 1.c, 'addicted to magic', given as an obsolete sense for *magic* as well. As regards the predicative uses of the adjectives in the senses relating to sorcery, *magical* was in the corpora

---

3   In some instances, it is difficult to say whether *magic* is definitely presented as a noun or an adjective (or both). The definition of *magicke* in Cawdrey (1604), 'inchaunting, conjuring', can arguably be interpreted as standing for both functions, while the paraphrase given for the word by Bullokar (1616), 'Inchantment, sorcerie', suggests that the word is a noun.

examined more numerous than *magic*, but some occurrences of the shorter form in this position were found, as in "As for the burning of those Ephesian books by St. Pauls converts, tis reply'd the books were magick, the Syriack so renders them" (John Milton, *Areopagitica* (1644), 12).[4]

The second senses assigned to *magic* and *magical* in the *OED* are also very similar to one another, although this time there is no cross-reference. Sense 2 for *magic* reads 'producing wonderful appearances or results, like those commonly attributed to sorcery', while for *magical*, sense 2 reads 'resembling magic in action or effect. Also, produced as if by magic.' Most of the examples for *magic*, sense 2 include fixed phrases such as *magic box*, *magic carpet*, and *magic marker*, but there are example sentences under each adjective form that point to an overlap in usage, such as "Water at all times is a magic word in a sultry climate like Palestine" (from Cunningham Geikie, *Life and Words of Christ*, xlix (1879), 589) and "Ile humbly signifie what in his name, That magicall word of Warre we haue effected" (from William Shakespeare, *Antony and Cleopatra* (1606), III, 31).

The *OED* gives separate glosses for phrases such as *magic square*, *magic circle* (sense 3; *magical circle/square* also given as obsolete phrases under *magical*, sense 3), and *magic stitch* (sense 4), and also explains the use of the word in expressions in nuclear physics (sense 5). However, the meaning of the *adjective* in such phrases is not paraphrased, but the connection of the referent with the concept of magic varies from one phrase to another. Finally, the *OED* mentions the function of *magic* (sense 6) 'in weakened use as an enthusiastic term of commendation: superlatively good, excellent, 'fantastic'', as in "'Oh, aye,' said Jock graciously, 'he's magic with that mashie'" (from *The Scotsman* (Weekend Supplement), 24 Dec. 1976, 5/1). Somewhat surprisingly, unlike most dictionaries, the *OED* does not include the sense 'enchanting or thrilling' for *magical* (e.g. *the magical beauty of the scene*). Although the *OED*'s quotations are not exactly of this type, it is possible that this sense is thought to be already included in *magical* 2 'resembling magic in action or effect'.

In usage manuals, the figurative uses of *magic* and *magical*, especially the ones suggesting great enthusiasm, receive the oft-seen criticism of overuse. After commenting on the loose use of *magic* as a noun, Shaw (1975) s.v. *magic*, *magical* observes the dangers involved in the use of the adjectives:

> As an adjective, *magic* means much the same as *magical*, but here again exaggeration is usually apparent: "The lovers spent a magical (or magic) night" and "This baritone has a magic (or magical) range to his voice" are examples of overemphasis. Recommendation: use

---

4   This particular instance was found in an electronic version of the book downloaded from the Internet, at http://www.dartmouth.edu/~milton/reading_room/areopagitica/part_1/index.html; retrieved on February 14, 2001, and checked against the page image files of the original work at http://www.octavo.com/collection/mltare.html; retrieved on May 24, 2001.

both adjectives sparingly and always place *magic* directly before the word it modifies: "magic number," "magic square," "magic lantern," "magic artistry." If this can't be done, use *magical*.

Although in the passage above *magic* and *magical* are considered to a large extent interchangeable, the usual view held in usage manuals is that *magic* tends to be used of things more directly relating to sorcery or witchcraft, whereas *magical* more often deals with things that merely resemble magic (see e.g. Clark 1987, Manser 1988, Alexander 1994, and McGlynn 1995), an idea which, as seen earlier, is also to be seen in the *OED*'s entry for *magical*. Marsden (1985), who regarded imitation as one of the most prominent separating elements between the forms ending in *-ic* and *-ical*, also emphasizes its role in connection with this adjective pair. Additionally, the extended, metaphorical senses are generally regarded as more descriptive of the referent rather than just classifying the thing as belonging to the domain of sorcery. This has been said to explain the greater "flexibility" of *magical*, which, having both classifying and descriptive functions, appears more easily in attributive and predicative positions. These kind of comments can be found in e.g. Evans and Evans (1957) s.v. *magic, magical*:

> *Magical* is more versatile, since it can be used to describe attributes or characteristics (*a magical transformation*) and to stand predicatively (*The reaction was magical*). *Magic*, on the other hand, is now used chiefly to identify (*magic lantern, Magic Flute*).

The question of the functions of *magic* and *magical* is, however, somewhat problematic, especially as regards the analysis of the corpus material. Consider, for instance, the following examples:

(3)   a.   If hit by a magic weapon, the Crystal Cloak is immediately dispelled but no damage is suffered from that hit and the magic weapon which inflicted the hit will be destroyed on the D6 roll of a 3 or more. (*BNC*, CN1 2541)

       b.   Those who fail see, at the far end of this room, something which they most wish to see – be it gems and gold, a magical weapon, a religious icon, a powerful Grimoire. (*BNC*, CLK 1626)

If the phrase *a magic weapon* can be likened to the phrases *a magic lantern* and *a magic flute*, where the adjective, according to Evans and Evans, is a classifier (or an "identifier"), should then *magic* and *magical* in (3a) and (3b) be analyzed differently, the former as having a classifying (denoting the type of the referent) and the latter a descriptive function? Such a decision in this case does not seem very sensible, as the fundamental meaning of the adjectives in both (3a) and (3b) is 'possessing supernatural powers' or 'enchanted'. To tease out the difference of the adjectives as regards their function, one can try to consider them in corresponding predicative positions. While all native speakers of English would probably find nothing grammatically wrong with the sentence *The weapon was magical*, opinions might differ in the case of *The weapon was magic,* some having no problem with it, whereas some might consider it less likely than the version with *magical*. Considering the examination of the corpora, then, it would be very difficult, almost impossible, to try to incorporate different functions of the adjectives into the tabular presentations of the uses of *magic* and *magical*. Such a practice would be questionable especially in the case of historical corpora, as evaluations of the acceptability of test sentences to tease out the functional differences between the adjectives would have to be made on the basis of present-day intuition of the language. It seems more reasonable to pay attention to the different semantic nuances and the types of words that the adjectives are used to modify, recording the numbers of occurrences of the adjectives in attributive and predicative positions, and *then* to postulate on the extent of the functional differences between the two forms.

3.   Different uses of *magic/magical*

The following sections will discuss the different uses of *magic* and *magical* in more detail. The main division has to do with the relation to sorcery, whether the adjective involves this element or not. The cases lacking this element are further divided into subcategories according to the different nuances they suggest. The division is not altogether straightforward, and in the course of the analysis of the material some compromises proved inevitable. The reasons for making particular decisions are also discussed.

3.1   'Relating to sorcery or supernatural powers'

In the classifying sense 'of or about magic' or 'having to do with magic', the shorter form was in earlier centuries the more common form, especially in the phrase *magic art(s)*, but in present-day English, *magical* seems to be favoured in many collocations (e.g. *beliefs*, *knowledge*, etc.):

(4)   a.   This frier Laurence of whom hereafter we shal make more ample mention, was an aucient Doctor of Diuinitie, of the order the friers of Minors, who bisides the happy profession which hee had made in studie of holie writ, was very skilful in Philosophy, and a great searcher of nature secrets, & exceeding famous in Magike knowledge, and other hidde and secret sciences, which nothing diminished his reputation, bicause he did not abuse the same. (William Painter, *The Palace of Pleasure, Tome 2* (1567), 470–471)

  b. This is the greatest repository of magical knowledge in the world, compiled down the centuries by High Elf mages and scholars, who dedicate their lives to the accumulation of magical lore. (*BNC*, CM1 230)

In connection with words such as *power*, *force*, *quality*, and *property*, denoting the idea of the supernatural phenomenon itself, both adjective forms are used, today with a slight preference for *magical*. This observation would seem to go against comments such as "The adjective *magic* is more closely related to the art or practice of magic than *magical*" in *Bloomsbury Good Word Guide* (1988) s.v. *magic, magical*. However, when referring to specific actions or rituals performed in sorcery, *magic* has indeed been used more often, the most typical example phrases being *magic spell/charm/rite*, for which *magical* is occasionally found as well:

(5) a. But when the wicked Nigromances Osmond perceiued, that his Magicke spels tooke small effect, and how in despite of his Inchauntments the Christians got the better of the day, he accursed his Art, [...] (Richard Johnson, *The seuen Champions of Christendome, Part 1* (1608), 211)

  b. "Were it not well, brethren," said the Grand Master, "that we examine something into the former life and conversation of this woman, specially that we may discover whether she be one likely to use magical charms and spells, since the truths which we have heard may well incline us to suppose, that in this unhappy course our erring brother has been acted upon by some infernal enticement and delusion? [...]" (Walter Scott, *Ivanhoe* (1819), 248)

  c. She was a mantri, a person who knew certain magic incantations, and was reputed to be able to cure sick animals. (*BNC*, BNU 156)

  d. At this stage it is evident that the legend was employed as a magical incantation to protect the body of the king and prevent any desecration. (*BNC*, EVR 228)

In addition to rituals and other actions of sorcery, the shorter form is more common when referring to physical objects which are either used in sorcery or are enchanted and thus possess supernatural powers. Again, there are collocations which have in the course of time become more fixed than others, including *magic wand* and *magic mirror*, for which *magical* is rare. The tendency to prefer the shorter form is, however, fairly strong in general for all collocations denoting objects, whether they are instruments used by sorcerers (a wand, a glass) or not (e.g. an armour, a sword).[5] This preference may in part be due to the nowadays obsolete use of the noun *magic* to refer to such items, as in "There are diuers kindes of these Magicks, whereby they bragge and boast that they are able to do any thing, and that they know hereby all things" (from Lodowick Lloyd, *The Pilgrimage of Princes* (1573), 37; cited in *OED*, s.v. *magic, sb.*, sense 1.c).[6]

These observations lead one to consider the distinction between *magic* and *magical* along lines somewhat similar to the findings on *electric* and *electrical* (cf. Gries 2001: 96). It would seem that the semantic aspects of the collocating words play a role in the choice of the adjective: the more "remote" words representing the classifying sense 'having to do with magic', e.g. *knowledge*, appear more often with *magical*, whereas the words denoting more "immediate", concrete or visible things, such as actions of conjuring or enchanted objects, tend to select the shorter form of the adjective. In phrases denoting the idea of the phenomenon itself, *magical* is used more often, which contrasts with the assumption that a closer semantic connection with the basic or original sense of the adjective would generally show as a preference for the *-ic* form. It can be argued, then, that the selection of either *magic* or *magical* according to the head word follows the lines of concrete versus abstract or immediate versus remote. As was seen earlier, such a distinction could also be seen to some extent with the pair *electric/electrical*, where the longer form is preferred in senses with a more remote connection with electricity, as in *electrical engineering*. In the sense 'powered by electricity', the selection of the adjective was governed by the head word through an opposition of specific versus general (*electric kettle* vs. *electrical appliances*). This type of drastic distinction, however, cannot be observed in the case of *magic/magical* with head words such as *artefacts, items, objects,* etc., with which both forms are found in the material studied, in spite of the head word clearly signifying concrete things:

(6)   a.   His feet were firmly placed upon the road to power when he uncovered a magic artefact, the Crown of Sorcery, in the subterranean ruins of the daemon-haunted city of Todtheim on the edge of the Northern Wastes. (*BNC*, CMC 200)

       b.   Teclis is the greatest sorcerer of this age of the world, a mage so powerful that spells and magical artefacts are named after him. (*BNC*, CM1 2113)

---

5   In the non-fiction material studied, a text by Ebenezer Sibly, an 18th century astrologer, included a number of instances of both *magic* and *magical* when denoting rituals and, rather exceptionally for the form *magical*, even objects having supernatural powers (e.g. *magic(al) rites/wand*). In fact, Sibly appears to have preferred the use of *magical*: in the extract from *A New and Complete Illustration of the Occult Sciences* (1795), *magic* as an adjective was used nine times, and *magical* as many as 42 times.

6   The first citation of *magic* as a noun denoting an object having supernatural powers in the *OED* dates from as early as 1386; the last citation is from 1813.

Some explanations as to why such a fairly clear-cut distinction as was seen with *electric/electrical* does not apply in this case, do suggest themselves. When referring to objects, the use of a superordinate term with *magic/magical* does not produce a similar effect of semantic distancing as regards the function or purpose of the thing in question: for *electrical appliances, devices*, etc., the specific function may be unknown, whereas the phrase *magic(al) artefacts* still refers to ones used in sorcery.[7] On the other hand, it is possible that such phrases are simply not used in any type of texts frequently enough so as to develop such fine semantic distinctions in the adjectives' use.

Considering the possibility that *magic/magical* could, after all, manifest a semantic distinction along the lines of 'specific versus general' in the same way as *electric/electrical* when denoting objects, the analysis of *magic/magical* raises the problem involving the decision not to distinguish between the senses 'enchanted; possessing supernatural powers' and 'used in magic'.[8] These senses could be thought to promote different adjectival functions in phrases, i.e. the former having a descriptive focus and the latter being classifying. It would be possible, then, to hypothesize that one of the phrases, *magic artefacts* or *magical artefacts*, relates more often to things which are thought to be enchanted, while the other phrase tends to be used in a classifying sense to denote paraphernalia used in magic(al) rites. As regards examples (6a) and (6b), the latter could perhaps be more readily be regarded as having a classifying function, whereas in (6a), the adjective could arguably be analyzed in both ways. What makes the issue even more problematic is the fact that the two senses are intertwined, as objects that one might consider to be characteristically used in sorcery (e.g. wands) would also be thought of as having supernatural powers, almost by definition. In addition, it would be very difficult to draw a clear line between those things that are used by magicians in their rites and those which are (merely) referred to as being enchanted. Although in some cases it obviously may be easier to say whether the adjective's function is more descriptive or classifying, there are not many practical arguments that would speak for attempting to distinguish between the senses 'enchanted' and 'used in sorcery'. For example, it would not seem particularly reasonable to categorize occurrences of the phrases *magic mirror* or *magic ring* according to whether the context involves specific actions of sorcery or not, as the adjectives can be equally ambiguous in either type of context. This feeling is further emphasized by the fact that with head words

---

7   One is reminded of the phrase *electric instruments*, denoting a musical instrument, where the function is also known, although the head word is a superordinate term. There was no variation between the two adjective forms in this case. The situation is not, however, exactly identical to the case of *magic(al) artefacts/paraphernalia*/etc., as with the latter it is the whole phrase rather than the head words themselves that suggests the function of the object in question.

8   It is not surprising to observe that sense 1.b of the adjective *magic* in the second edition of the *OED* includes both 'employed in magic rites' and 'endued with magic powers'.

denoting concrete items specifically, e.g. *wands*, *swords*, etc., *magic* clearly tends to be the preferred form anyway.

When in a predicative position, however, the adjectives are more easily interpreted as carrying the descriptive sense 'possessing supernatural powers'. In such instances, *magical* is the usual form:

(7)   And she drew the weapon from behind the altar. "Take it. It is yours now. It is magical. Whoever smites with it, need never smite again [...]" (Charles Kingsley, *Hereward the Wake* (1865), 127)

As noted earlier, some instances of *magic* in this sense can occasionally be found in a predicative position, but these may seem slightly odd in some native speakers' opinion:

(8)   He took his spear and drew a circle on the platform of sand. "Come inside this. There, that's it. Now stand still here. A circle is magic, you know." (Richard Jefferies, *Bevis* (1882), 74)

The strangeness of *magic* in cases such as example (8) noted today may have less to do with the meaning of the adjective than the fact that *magic*, as observed in the *OED* note s.v. *magic*, sense 1, is not used predicatively, at least not very often. It is possible that this, in turn, stems from the earliest functions of *magic* as a classifier (or identifier). On the other hand, it could be asked whether native speakers' reactions become emphasized simply as a result of asking about such occurrences, and drawing attention to the *-ic/-ical* variation. Without such an "imposed" viewpoint, perhaps *magic* in the following present-day example would seem perfectly normal:

(9)   'Are you sure that's a real spell?' said the girl. 'Well, it's not very good, is it? I've tried a few simple spells just for practice and it's all worked for me. Nobody in my family's magic at all, it was ever such a surprise when I got my letter, but I was ever so pleased, of course, [...] (J.K. Rowling, *Harry Potter and the Philosopher's Stone* (1997), 79)

Relating to sorcery, some uses of *magic* and *magical* can also be paraphrased as 'produced by magic', as in example (10):

(10)   There was a gem in the brain of the dragon, Philostratus told us, and "by the exhibition of golden letters and a scarlet robe" the monster could be thrown into a magical sleep, and slain. (Oscar Wilde, *The Picture of Dorian Gray* (1891), 202)

3.2   'Resembling magic'; figurative uses

There are uses of *magic* and *magical* which, instead of implying that sorcery, witchcraft, or supernatural powers are involved, suggest that the thing in question in some way resembles magic. It can be observed that such cases also include common expressions going back to the idea of sorcery. Compare, for instance, examples (11a) and (11b):

(11)   a.   He believed in the magic powers of the witch Brandon; and he asked Torfrida, in his simplicity, whether she was not cunning enough to defeat her spells by counter spells.   (H. Rider Haggard, *King Solomon's Mines* (1885), 193)

      b.   There were rich men there. There were men there who could confidently place fabulous figures on cheques; and yet they did not seem to know what a magic power they possessed. (William Black, *A Daughter of Heth* (1871), 50)

In (11a), there is a definite relation with sorcery, whereas in (11b), there is not, and the sentence might as well read *they did not seem to know what a magic-like power they possessed*. However, one might ask whether *magic* in (11b) is merely a figurative use of the word in the sense 'of magic', or is there actually a separate sense 'resembling magic'? The question is highly relevant as regards the distinction between *magic* and *magical*, as in dictionaries it is usually *magic* which is said to have figurative functions under definitions that suggest a closer relation to "magic proper", while *magical* "merely" resembles magic (e.g. *OED* s.v. *magic*, senses 1.b and 2; *magical*, sense 2).

    The question of figurative use and the sense 'resembling magic', which is important for analysing the research material, especially when setting up the categories into which the different uses of *magic* and *magical* will be divided, can be approached by considering the comments on the phrase *a magic word* to be found in the *CIDE* s.v. *magic*:

> A magic word is a word said by someone performing a trick to help it work successfully: I'll just say the magic word and the rabbit will disappear – Abracadabra! (fig.) Like most mothers, she always asks her small children "What is the magic word?" when they haven't said 'please' or 'thank you'.

The phrase *magic word*, then, can be understood to denote an expression used in magic, and in the example sentence on figurative usage the words *please* and *thank you* are likened to such a function. However, the same phrase can also have different kinds of nuances:

(12) a. My dear mother, quoth the novice, coming a little to herself,--- there are two certain words which I have been told will force any horse, or ass, or mule, to go up a hill whether he will or no; be he never so obstinate or ill-will'd, the moment he hears them utter'd, he obeys. They are words magic! cried the abbess, in the utmost horrour --- (Laurence Sterne, *Tristram Shandy* (1760), 82)

    b. "Who is it?" roared Sam again. Once more was a joint reply returned; and though the words were inaudible, Sam saw by the motion of the two pairs of lips that they had uttered the magic word "Pickwick." (Charles Dickens, *Pickwick Papers* (1836–1837), 253)

    c. "But never fear, my lady; we will fight to the last gasp. Hollo, lads, here is a battle for you!" At that magic word, all the Irishmen clubbed their sticks, and ran forward. (E.S. Barrett, *The Heroine* (1813), 80)

    d. "A sail! A sail!" But a minute before I had felt so utterly prostrated, that I should not have believed myself capable of taking half-a-dozen steps without a long rest between each. Yet these magical words sent me rushing up the companion ladder with as much speed and energy as I should have been capable of after a long night's refreshing slumber. (William Clark Russell, *The Wreck of the Grosvenor* (1877), 166)

In (12a), *magic* may be thought to have the descriptive sense of 'possessing supernatural powers', possibly more so than the sense 'used in magic', but both *the magic word 'Abracadabra'* and *words magic* in (12a) suggest a clear intention or possibility to cause something to happen by the use of the words. In (12b), while not relating to sorcery, the word *Pickwick* either may or may not be something that is specifically intended to produce a desired effect: it can be regarded as having a function similar to that of *please* or *thank you* in the earlier case, or it may be thought to involve the notion of '(excitingly) special', having a mysterious quality about it. In (12c) and (12d), the words in question are clearly not ones intentionally uttered to produce the particular effect that nevertheless does occur. In some cases, it may be impossible to determine even from the context whether the word has a power (in the figurative sense) to cause a certain effect or is implied to have an enchanting or a thrilling quality: for instance, in the earlier cited example from Burchfield (1996), *the magical word 'democracy'*, could have both interpretations (although as an example, Burchfield probably intends it as one having the potential to produce a desired effect). Owing to such complexities, all instances of *magic* and *magical* referring to words are placed in the same category under the heading 'special', except for those which can be clearly classified into the sense group 'enchanting' (e.g. *the magic(al) words of Shakespeare*).

One can also find similar semantically complex instances of *magic/magical* with other collocating words:

(13) a. "If you would be kind enough, sir," suggested Mrs. Armytage, "to sit as far away on that side"---indicating the one opposite to her---"as you can; and if you'd just pull the window down; and,---yes, thank you, if you wouldn't mind my---it's so very refreshing this warm weather."
On hearing the two magic syllables "refresh", the dull eye of the young man brightened up, and he grinned fawningly.   (George Augustus Sala, *The Seven Sons of Mammon* (1862), 40)

      b. However this may be, certain it is, that all offices about the Court and connected with the army [...] can only be filled by the nobility; nor can any person who has the misfortune of not inheriting the magical monosyllable von before his name, which, as you know, like the French de, is the shibboleth of nobility, and the symbol of territorial pride, violate by their unhallowed presence the sanctity of Court dinners, [...] (Benjamin Disraeli, *Vivian Grey* (1826–1827), 145)

In these examples, the most accurate way to paraphrase *magic* and *magical* again seems to be 'special' or 'having an effect resembling magic'.

Rather than attempting to distinguish between figurative uses and the sense 'resembling magic', a more practical solution is simply to categorize instances of *magic* and *magical* according to whether or not they relate to magic as a phenomenon or to the practice of sorcery. As support for this decision, sense 2 for the noun *magic* in the *OED* can be cited: '*fig.* A secret and overmastering influence resembling magic in its effects', joining both facets of the word's use together. It could be asked, then, whether dictionaries' remarks on the figurative uses of the adjective *magic* serve any purpose at all. While it has been observed that as far as the *magic/magical* distinction is concerned, the note 'often figurative' for *magic*, and assigning the sense 'resembling magic' only to *magical* causes unnecessary confusion (which is why some newer dictionaries employ additional usage notes), there are figurative uses of *magic* in certain collocations which would not fit the description 'resembling magic'. For example, in "She had heard of inaccessible truths brought to light by the magic wand of alcohol" (George Meredith, *Evan Harrington* (1861), 244), it is the phrase *magic wand* rather than just the adjective that is used figuratively. The same goes for other largely fixed phrases, e.g. *magic spell*. In such cases, the head word itself often relates to sorcery (outside of the domain of magic, the word *wand* alone is rarely used); therefore these combinations are not here analysed separately according to whether the context suggests the involvement of supernatural powers or not. On the other hand, the phrase *magic word*, as has been seen, can be regarded as a borderline case, because there are instances where the adjective may have a clearly descriptive function. The latter phrase is therefore analyzed according to the division outlined above.

The sense 'special' may be considered a subgroup of the wider sense 'resembling magic'. This characterization fits well when reference is made to numbers or figures, especially when representing levels which are considered remarkable. Both *magic* and *magical* are used in this function:

(14)   a.   If a new drama series on ITV or BBC1 gets six or seven million viewers, it's deemed to be only a partial success. The magic 10 million is the real aspiration – whether quoted or not. (*The Daily Telegraph*, Aug. 26, 1995, "The Arts: Ideas sacrificed to numbers: Edinburgh")

     b.   Life continues: invitations to make guest appearances and speaking engagements fill her diary, and at the end of next month she will realise a long ambition with an appearance on BBC Television's *A Question of Sport*. Other aspirations include reaching the magical figure of 250 caps and winning a medal at the European Cup. (*The Daily Telegraph*, Feb. 24, 1995, "Hockey: Ramsay on record trail after private upheaval")

Instances such as those in examples (14a) and (14b) are especially common in present-day English. As in the case of *magic(al) words*, they stem from uses relating to sorcery:

(15)   "Some conjurers say that number three is the magic number, and some say number seven. It's neither, my friend, neither. It's number one." (Charles Dickens, *Oliver Twist* (1837–1839), 116)

The meaning 'special or important' has been separately given in some dictionaries, e.g. *OALD*. Other frequently occurring collocations where this sense is present include *ingredient*, *formula*, and *solution*, which, however, differ somewhat from cases such as those in examples (14) and (15) in that they more explicitly denote things that have the power to produce certain effects. In fact, they are to a great extent like figurative uses of the phrase *magic wand*, and could equally well be categorized in the same way. Of the two adjective forms, *magic* is more commonly used in this sense:

(16)   a.   'The business will continue in exactly the same way in the future as in the past with the added magic ingredient that the investment team will now be the owners.' (*The Daily Telegraph*, Oct. 27, 1995, "CITY: Management buys CINVen")

     b.   Privatisation, of itself, is no magic formula for all our ills, any more than nationalisation is the bureaucratic disaster the critics would have us believe. (*The Daily Telegraph*, Sept. 1, 1995, "Letter to the Editor: Right managers")

3.3   'Enchanting, wonderful'; 'excellent'

The adjectives *magic* and *magical* are also used in the descriptive sense 'enchanting' or 'wonderful', exemplified in the following passages:

(17)   a.   Yes, perhaps it was just another Nutcracker, but for its audience and for this critic it was an opportunity to respond afresh to Tchaikovsky's magic score and the lure of good dancing, the pleasure that any classic superlatively well danced can recreate all over again. (*The Sunday Telegraph*, Dec. 24, 1995, "The Arts: Even turkeys strut their stuff")

        b.   Having the orchestra on stage gave Britten's magical instrumentation more prominence than usual, but with Colin Davis at the helm this was a Dream to remember. (*The Daily Telegraph*, Dec. 12, 1995, "The Arts: Dream for all seasons")

The native speakers consulted have been unanimous in their reactions to the above instances, and considered the adjectives to have the same meaning. This sense has been paraphrased in many different ways in dictionaries, including 'wonderful', 'enchanting', 'charming', 'exciting', 'beautiful', and 'delightful', among others. The sources examined mostly assign this sense to *magical*, but some include it in the definitions of both forms, e.g. *CIDE*, *Random House Compact Unabridged Dictionary*, and *Collins English Dictionary*.

In the *OED*, however, this use of the adjectives is not given. For *magical*, sense 2, 'resembling magic in action or effect', the examples provided are more of the type seen in the previous section. In fact, some instances of *magic* and *magical* in that section could be paraphrased as 'wonderful', 'enchanting' or 'mysterious' as well, 'special' as an attribute not being too far away, either. Moreover, the sense 'enchanting' certainly fits in with the description 'resembling magic'. The distinction between the two uses is indeed very fine, but it can nevertheless be justified: as regards the use of the two adjective forms, the cases dealt with in section 3.2 show preferences in the choice of the adjective forms similar to comparable instances with a direct relation to supernatural powers. The cases discussed here, however, usually involve a description of the appearance of the thing referred to, or of the feeling it has aroused, and *magical* is clearly used more often in such instances than *magic*. The following examples perhaps justify the categorization further:

(18)   a.   When they carped about his style and 'almost sensual instinct for an opportunity', she defended him. 'What's wrong with that? Many people are too obtuse to choose the magic moment!" (*The Sunday Telegraph*, May 14, 1995, "Sunday Matters: The Midas touch behind Michael")

b.   Francis, apparently, is wont to talk of how an error-ridden game which includes the odd flash of genius is preferable to one in which there are no mistakes or magic moments. (*The Daily Telegraph*, Jan. 16, 1995, "Five Nations Championship: Admiring glances at male (role) models")

c.   There are one or two magical moments, but the film seems to give up the ghost halfway through, and not even some mouth-watering Tuscan landscape can revive it. (*The Sunday Telegraph*, Apr. 2, 1995, "The Arts: How high do wannabes have to jump?")

In (18a), the moment is notably "special" in the same way as magic(al) figures, levels, or marks are in that they are known to have a remarkable quality about them. In this case, one could also talk about "the right moment", for which there is even the possibility of choice, albeit apparently requiring some "special" awareness. In contrast, in (18b) and (18c) the adjectives *magic* and *magical* describe a slightly different kind of remarkable quality, including – as in most cases of the adjectives used in this sense – a strong element of positive value judgement.

The first citation of *magical* in the sense 'resembling magic' in the *OED* is from 1606, but it is difficult to estimate when the sense 'enchanting', 'wonderful', as described in other dictionaries, appeared in English. The first occurrence analysed as having this sense in the material examined dates from the seventeenth century:

(19)   As soon as he found himself alone, and that his first Astonishment had given his Reason the leisure to examine this strange and magical Adventure, he sometimes thought himself not so unfortunate as he imagin'd before, and at other times he had such an amazing prospect of his destiny, as almost run him into Despair: [...] (Anonymous, *The Rival Mother* (1692), 104)

According to some French dictionaries consulted, e.g. Robert (1959) s.v. *magique*, the figurative sense of *magique* (with the examples *l'effet magique* and *spectacle magique*) developed in the eighteenth century, which suggests the possibility that this use appeared in English earlier than in French.

Apart from positive value judgement, the adjectives in this sense sometimes describe darker, mysterious features as well:

(20)   But *The Park*, first seen in 1983, is an extraordinary piece – strange, frightening and magical. (*The Daily Telegraph*, Sept. 14, 1995, "The Arts: A dream of a nightmare")

According to many recent dictionaries, *magic* is nowadays also used to express approval, as in *the show was absolutely magic*. Dictionaries usually label this use of the adjective informal, colloquial, or non-standard, as well as chiefly British English.[9] The use in question presents some problems in the corpus analysis of *magic* and *magical*, because it is in many instances practically indistinguishable from the sense 'enchanting', which often implies a notion of approval or pleasantness as well.[10] Looking at written material, it is not possible to state when the use of the adjectives is informal or colloquial, especially when we are not talking about brief exclamations such as "It's magic" or "Magic!". The basic question therefore is whether or not the "colloquial" use of *magic* and the "standard" use of *magical* involve two separate senses, that is, 'excellent' as opposed to 'enchanting'. If not, then the basic meanings of the two forms in such instances are identical, with only the level of formality being the differentiating feature.

As regards the corpora examined, it seems that especially for *magic*, many of the cases involving a notion of great approval appear in quotations of spoken language, but variation between the two forms can also be seen in plain written reportage:

(21)   a.   And so we must be at the Oval – who is going to take it upon themselves to bowl that magic delivery and take that stunning catch to get the West Indies No 3 out? (*The Sunday Telegraph*, Aug. 20, 1995, "Cricket: Self-confidence the key to team's series success")

       b.   Allcock survived a tough challenge from Scotland's Hugh Duff, who fought back from two sets down to level at 2–2. But he could not stop Allcock playing a handful of magical deliveries to win 7–1, 7–3, 4–7, 3–7, 7–6. (*The Daily Telegraph*, Feb 24, 1995, "Bowls: Hard sell almost backfires on Thomson")

As far as the categorizations in the present analysis are concerned, instead of attempting to force a distinction between the senses 'enchanting', as in *the magic(al) beauty of the scenery*, and the "colloquial" sense traditionally described as 'wonderful' or 'excellent', the policy adopted here is to place such occurrences in the same group. This does not, of course, deny the possibility of a subjectively perceivable existence of this kind of semantic distinction.[11]

---

9   This use of *magic* is also given in the second edition of the *OED* (with the label "colloquial"), the first citation dating from 1956. Somewhat surprisingly, *CIDE* s.v. *magic* considers this use as "dated".

10   In fact, considering examples (17a) and (17b), one could argue that *magic* and *magical* are not synonymous at all, but *magic* in the phrase *magic score* merely shows approval, whereas *magical* in *magical instrumentation* describes the mysterious, enchanting qualities (while showing approval at the same time).

11   The decision not to distinguish between these senses does have an effect on the numbers of occurrences in the tabular presentation, although only marginally, as *magical* is clearly the favoured form. One possibility would be to present separately those

Contrary to the statements in many dictionaries, it appears that the use of *magic* in the sense of 'enchanting' or 'excellent' is not attested solely in British English, but instances of the adjective in this use can be found in American sources as well:

(22)   Redskins fans have seen horrors, they've looked into the maw of despair, they've lived through years they wish they could forget. (Last year, for instance.) But they've also seen good years, great years, magic years they'll hold forever in sweet memories. (*The Washington Post*, Sept. 4, 1994, p. 14, "Skins Deep", by Peter Carlson)

3.4   Other uses

In addition to the uses discussed in the previous sections, *magic* and *magical* have some other senses and functions. While there are numerous cases of further semantic nuances, only those which were encountered in the material examined (most likely representing the most common cases) are discussed here. One of the oldest fixed collocations is *magic lantern*, a projector of magnified images, for which the longer form of the adjective does not appear in the material studied or in any of the dictionaries consulted. Equally fixed is the phrase *magic mushroom*, referring to mushrooms containing hallucinogenic substances. A *magic bullet* is an expression used of especially effective medicines (or ones that are being developed) for specific purposes. Apart from having the sense 'possessing supernatural powers', the phrase *magic circle* also denotes "a small group of people privileged to receive confidential information or make important decisions" (*NODE* 1998 s.v. *magic circle*). The abovementioned uses may, in fact, also be regarded as instances of the sense 'resembling magic'.

Some variation occurs between *magic realism* and *magical realism* (and, by extension, *magic(al) realists*), fairly recent terms referring to a literary style combining elements of realism and fantasy:

(23)   a.   A lot of writers use magic realism as a sentimental trick. (*The Daily Telegraph*, Dec. 16, 1995, "The Arts (Interview): From Mambo Kings to the miraculous")

         b.   The 'magical realism', which is the hallmark of modern Latin American fiction, is pretty much the way she has always looked at the

---

positively loaded instances of *magic* and *magical* appearing in sports articles, and thus to get closer to the uses of the adjectives in the sense of 'excellent'. The results would probably show relatively more occurrences of *magic*. Such a categorization, however, would be highly questionable, as it would suggest that for sports fans, the performances in the field are not as enchanting, thrilling or magic-like as comparable performances in the concert hall are to their audiences.

world, long before she became a famous novelist. (*The Sunday Telegraph*, Sept. 10, 1995, "Interview: My country, my child, my passion – Isabel Allende")

The variation can also be seen in dictionaries, some of which use the *-ic* form, others opting for the *-ical* variant.

4.   *Magic/magical* in the material studied

Some difficulties in the analysis of the corpus material were caused by merely determining whether *magic* in certain collocations is, in fact, an adjective or a noun (cf. Marsden 1985: 29). For example, some informants might regard *magic* in the phrase *magic tricks* as a noun, while others would not hesitate about its being an adjective.[12] More straightforward to interpret are the phrases *a magic show* or *a magic act* (both referring to a magician's performance), where *magic* is more easily recognizable as a noun. Similar problems arise when *magic* is found in a predicative position: in the sentence *It's magic*, one cannot be entirely certain whether the word is a noun or an adjective (in some cases, there may be a helpful adjective or an adverb modifying the word, e.g. *It was absolute magic/It was absolutely magic*). In *The Daily Telegraph* material, all of the ten cases of *magic* in a predicative position are ones where the word could, in fact, be interpreted in either way. As regards single-word exclamations (*Magic!*), which present a similar problem, the four cases in the newspaper material were left out of the analysis altogether.

In the *Literature Online* material, during the period 1513–1599, *magic* is the dominant adjective form, but it mostly appears in the phrase *magic art*, as can be seen from Table 62. In the seventeenth century, as seen from Table 63, *magical* was somewhat surprisingly more often used than *magic*, and was used in a wider spectrum of senses. It must be noted, however, that the overall number of occurrences of the adjectives, as well as that of the authors using them, is fairly low.[13] One observation worth noting is that between 1513 and the end of seventeenth century, most of the occurrences of both adjective forms relate to sorcery, with only a couple of instances of metaphorical uses.

---

12   *Magic* in the phrase *magic tricks* is in the present analysis treated as an adjective, but in the statistical presentations these occurrences are given separately, which is also appropriate as the expression is firmly fixed with the *-ic* form.

13   Interestingly enough, the seventeenth century occurrences of *magical* outnumbered those of *magic* also in the *OED* citations (with an approximately similar relation between the frequencies of the two forms), while *magic* was the more frequent form in the citations from the sixteenth and eighteenth centuries. The uses of the adjectives (again rather low in number) as regards different senses resembled the *Literature Online* results as well.

Table 62. *Magic/magical* in the prose section of *Literature Online*, 1513–1599.

	magic	magical
1. 'of or being magic'		
a. ~ *art*	31	1
b. others	2	1
2. 'enchanted, possessing supernatural powers'		
a. actions, spells, rites, etc.	11	2
b. people	4	1
c. objects	2	-
3. 'produced or done by magic'	-	1
4. 'resembling or working like magic'	-	1
total	**50**	**7**
# of authors (+ anonymous):	6 (2)	4 (1)
# of authors using both forms: 2 (+ 1 anonymous book)		

Table 63. *Magic/magical* in the prose section of *Literature Online*, 1600–1699.

	magic	magical
1. 'of or being magic'		
a. ~ *art*	3	-
b. others	-	3
2. 'enchanted, possessing supernatural powers'		
a. actions, spells, rites, etc.	10	4
b. people	-	2
c. objects	-	5
d. others	-	2
3. 'produced or done by magic'	-	1
4. 'resembling or working like magic'	-	1
5. 'enchantingly beautiful', 'wonderful'	-	1
total	**13**	**19**
# of authors (+ anonymous):	6 (1)	8 (6)
# of authors using both forms: -		

The eighteenth century material in the *Literature Online* collection, presented in Table 64, shows the slightly stronger position of *magic*, which is generally preferred in all senses of the adjectives, except for the collocate *effect*, which, as can be seen in subsequent tables, has at all times shown a preference for the longer form. The adjectives are increasingly used figuratively, although the majority of the occurrences still have to do with sorcery or the suggested presence of supernatural powers. The first instance of the sense 'special' (*magical words*) also appears, as well as the earliest recorded predicative use of *magical*.

Table 64. *Magic/magical* in the prose section of *Literature Online*, 1700–1799.

	magic	*magical*
1. 'of or being magic'		
a. ~ *art*	9	-
b. others	9	1
2. 'enchanted, possessing supernatural powers'		
a. actions, spells, rites, etc.	11	4
b. places	2	-
c. people	1	1
d. objects	6	2
e. ~ *circle*	5	-
f. others	6	2
3. 'resembling or working like magic'		
a. ~ *power/force*/etc.	4	1
b. ~ *effect*	-	2
c. actions (e.g. ~ *touch*)	3	1 (1)
d. objects	1	-
4. 'special, as if having a supernatural effect'	-	1
5. 'enchantingly beautiful', 'wonderful'	8	3
6. others: ~ *lantern*	7	-
total	**72**	**18 (1)**
# of authors:	15	9
# of authors using both forms: 6		

In the first half of the nineteenth century, *magic* continues to be used more often than *magical*, although the relation of the numbers of occurrences does not match that of the authors using the forms. The shorter form dominates over the longer one in almost all senses, except for the sense 'enchanting', for which both forms are used (with a slight preference for *magical*), as in the following examples:

(24)   a.   The sun had only broken forth at its setting; and it now glittered from its western pyre over the dripping hedges, and spread a brief, but

magic glow along the rich landscape around; [...] (Edward Bulwer-Lytton, *Eugene Aram* (1832), 139)

  b. I saw several young persons dressed as I was, so was under no embarrassment from the singularity of my habit, and only rejoiced, as I hung on my uncle's arm, at the magical splendour of such a scene, and at his goodness for procuring me the pleasure of beholding it. (Walter Scott, *Redgauntlet* (1824), 242–243)

Table 65. *Magic/magical* in the prose section of *Literature Online*, 1800–1849.

	magic	*magical*
1. 'of or being magic'		
a. ~ *art*	5	2 (1)
b. others	4	9
2. 'enchanted, possessing supernatural powers'		
a. actions, spells, rites, etc.	9	1
b. places	3	-
c. people	-	1
d. objects	11	3
e. ~ *circle*	16	-
f. others	6	3
3. 'produced or done by magic'		
a. ~ *effect*	-	1
b. others	1	1
4. 'resembling or working like magic'		
a. ~ *power/influence*	10	5
b. ~ *effect*	-	4 (2)
c. actions (e.g. ~ *touch*)	4	1
d. objects	4	-
e. manner of action	2	4
f. others	-	2
5. 'special', 'mysterious', 'as if having a supernatural effect' (words, numbers, etc.)	11	1
6. 'enchantingly beautiful', 'wonderful', 'thrilling'	10	17 (5)
7. others: ~ *lantern*	4	-
total	**100**	**55 (8)**
# of authors:	21	16
# of authors using both forms: 10		

In the group 'resembling magic', some variation between the two adjective forms is seen when referring to actions and manners of action:

(25)   a.   Esther felt vexed with herself that her heart was suddenly beating with unusual quickness, and that her last resolution not to trouble herself about what Felix thought, had transformed itself with magic swiftness into mortification that he evidently avoided coming to the house when she was there, though he used to come on the slightest occasion. (George Eliot, *Felix Holt* (1866), 57–58)

       b.   The loud knocks at the door which announced the arrival of company, were signals that operated punctually upon her associations; and to this species of conventional necessity her most violent passions submitted with magical celerity. (Maria Edgeworth, *Belinda* (1801), 115)

Comparing *magic/magical* in examples (25a) and (25b) with those in examples (24a) and (24b), it could be asked whether it would be possible to place all of them in the same semantic category. It is true that they can all be described as 'resembling magic' or 'produced as if by magic'. Moreover, they all seem to include a sense of approbation. While it must be admitted that the classification of such cases is by no means a simple task, in (25a) and (25b), however, it can be argued that rapidity is one of the attributes commonly assigned to magic, so the quality in these cases is 'magic-like'. The instances belonging to the group 'enchanting' mostly involve cases which appear to emphasize the emotional reactions to beautiful (often visually) or mystifying things.

Considering the period 1850–1903 (Table 66), *magic* is the more common form in senses relating straightforwardly to sorcery or the presence of supernatural powers, enchanted things, and "special" words, names, and numbers, whereas variation between the two adjective forms occurs in senses to do with magic-like characteristics.[14] One notable feature is the still increasing distinction between the two forms as regards predicative uses, *magical* appearing more often in this position. Most of the predicative uses relate to the 'magic-like' senses, which, in a way, can be seen as an indication of a further functional differentiation between *magic* and *magical* along the lines of classifying versus descriptive, with the shorter form relating to supernatural powers in a literal sense, and *magical* being used of things resembling magic.

---

14   The figure for *magic* when referring to enchanted objects includes as many as 22 instances from books by Charles Kingsley alone, but one can be fairly safe in the conclusion on the preference for *magic* in such cases even if the 22 occurrences were excluded. It is interesting to note, however, that Kingsley used *magical* in reference to enchanted objects twice, in both cases in a predicative position, suggesting a degree of consistency or a clear distinction in his use of the two adjective forms.

Table 66. *Magic/magical* in the prose section of *Literature Online*, 1850–1903.

	magic	magical
1. 'of or being magic'		
a. ~ *art*	4	1
b. others	18 (1)	4
2. 'enchanted, possessing supernatural powers'		
a. actions, spells, rites, etc.	12	5
b. places	7	1
c. people	1	2
d. objects	53	4 (2)
e. ~ *circle*	7 (1)	-
f. others	17	2 (1)
3. 'produced or done by magic'		
a. ~ *effect*	-	2 (1)
b. others	1	4
4. 'resembling or working like magic'		
a. ~ *power/influence*	3	5
b. ~ *effect*	1	7 (4)
c. actions (e.g. ~ *touch*)	1	2
d. objects	1	2
e. manner of action	5	2
f. others	1	9 (5)
5. 'special', 'mysterious', 'as if having a supernatural effect' (words, numbers, etc.)	18	1
6. 'enchantingly beautiful', 'wonderful', 'thrilling'	16	11 (5)
7. others: ~ *lantern*	12	-
total	**178 (2)**	**64 (18)**
# of authors:	28	20
# of authors using both forms: 12		

    Taking a leap of nearly one hundred years forward, and considering the uses of *magic/magical* in *The Daily Telegraph* of 1995, an interesting observation emerging from Table 67 is that the numbers of occurrences for *magic* and *magical* are almost equal. The main division into different senses is again made according to whether or not the adjective has to do with sorcery or enchantment through supernatural powers. In many cases, the analysis involved examining the larger context where the adjective was used. Other words relating to sorcery, e.g. *conjuring*, if appearing in the immediate context, did not as such justify the inclusion of *magic* or *magical* into sense groups having to do with sorcery or supernatural powers in a literal sense, as such terms can be used figuratively as well; for example, *magical* in the sentence "The russet, rustic sets designed by Christiane Kubrick conjure up a magical atmosphere" (*The Daily Telegraph*, Dec. 29, 1995, "The Arts: Spellbinding fairy-tale") would be categorized as having the sense 'enchanting', 'exciting', or 'thrilling' instead of 'having to do with magic' or 'produced by magic'.

In the classifying sense 'of or having to do with magic', *magic* would seem to have lost some of its ground to the longer form, although in collocations denoting concrete actions relating to sorcery (*incantations*, *spells*, etc.), *magic* continues to be the more common variant. To some extent, the choice of the adjective form appears to be governed by the collocation: in connection with words such as *power*, *quality*, *property*, *force*, and *effect*, *magical* is used more often, especially when considering the metaphorical uses of the words as well. When referring to physical objects, *magic* is the preferred form, with only two occurrences of *magical*.

Table 67. *Magic/magical* in the 1995 issues of *The Daily Telegraph*.

	magic	*magical*
1. 'of or being magic'		
a. ~ *art*	-	2
b. ~ *tricks*	7	-
c. ~ *power/quality/property*	2	5
d. others	2	9 (2)
2. 'enchanted, possessing supernatural powers'		
a. actions, spells, rites, etc.	7	1
b. places	-	6
c. people, animals, etc.	4	3
d. objects		
1. *wand*	20	-
2. *carpet*	7	-
3. others	19	2
e. medicines, potions, etc.	9	-
f. ~ *circle*	1	-
g. others	15 (1)	3
3. 'produced or done by magic'		
a. ~ *effect*	1	-
b. others	-	1

	magic	*magical*
4. 'resembling or working like magic'		
a. ~ *power/quality/property*	1	15
b. ~ *effect*	1	9 (2)
c. actions (e.g. ~ *touch*)	11	4
d. objects	13	-
e. medicines, drugs, etc.	2	6
f. others	9	4
5. 'special', 'mysterious', 'as if having a supernatural effect'		
a. numbers, figures, levels	19	4
b. words, names	9	2
c. moment, time	3	1
d. ~ *ingredient*	9	1
e. ~ *formula*	11	-
f. ~ *recipe*	2	-
g. ~ *solution*	2	-
h. others	6	1
6. 'enchantingly beautiful', 'wonderful', 'thrilling'	45 (8)	196 (27)
7. of a style of fiction:		
~ *realism*	19	4
~ *fantasists*	-	1
8. others:		
~ *bullet*	1	-
~ *circle* (group of people)	9	-
~ *lantern*	2	-
~ *mushroom*	9	-
total	**277 (9)**	**280 (31)**

Considering the group 'resembling magic', and the subclasses therein, the adjective forms seem to behave to a large extent in the same way as they do when referring to 'magic proper', i.e. magic is preferred in connection with actions and objects, while magical is the more common form with *power*, *quality*, and *effect*. In the group entitled 'special', the collocations *ingredient, formula, recipe*, and *solution* show the clearest preference to *magic*. These collocations are also ones which present clearly figurative uses, involving the notion of an ability to produce a certain effect. The other collocations may have other nuances, especially in the case of numbers, as seen earlier. But in these cases as well, *magic* is considerably more frequent than *magical*.

The figures for the group 'enchanting', 'wonderful' show that *magical* is the more common form in this sense. The number of occurrences of *magical* here is striking in that it is by far the most common meaning in which this form is used in general, displaying also the largest number of predicative uses. Considering *magic* in this sense, the adjective actually appears quite often compared to the other usages of the word, although the figure admittedly may include instances which might be regarded by some as representing a colloquial use of the word in the meaning 'excellent'. As regards the other semantic groups, *magic* tends to be the favoured form, with slight variation between the phrases *magic realism* and *magical realism*, and their derivatives.

Considering the developments that have taken place during the larger part of the twentieth century, not represented in the corpus material for the present study, it would seem that the situation witnessed in Table 66 already shows the direction of the differentiation between *magic* and *magical*. The most significant differences seen today were already to some extent established in the latter half of the nineteenth century. The most remarkable development since that period has been the increase in the use of *magical* in the sense 'enchanting', bringing the overall number of its occurrences at a level with *magic*, at least in *The Daily Telegraph* material. Another important finding is that in uses other than 'enchanting', certain collocations with *magical*, i.e. *power, influence, effect*, etc. are becoming fixed, some of them at this stage being more established than others. This is an interesting development, especially in the light of comments usually assigning the feature of forming fossilized phrases to *magic* (e.g. Swan 1995: 256).

5.   General remarks

As has been observed in the present chapter, the difference between the adjectives *magic* and *magical* is on many occasions a matter of mere nuance. The line of distinction between the two forms appears to be a mixture of different kinds of factors. On the one hand, the forms are to some extent divided as regards their function: *magic* tends to be the more usual form as a classifier, relating to sorcery or supernatural forces, while *magical* describes more often than classifies. The most significant increase in the use of *magical* in the corpora examined can be linked with its use in the sense 'enchanting', which became more frequent particularly in the nineteenth century. However, *magical* is not completely void of classifying uses. There is evidence of the collocate influencing the choice of the adjective form, with the longer form being preferred in connection with abstract words such as *power, force, quality*, and *knowledge*, while *magic* is more frequent when denoting objects or actions involved in sorcery. The latter preference for *magic* is already visible in the texts from the eighteenth century; as for the head words with abstract reference, further data is needed to determine the timing of the changes in more detail.

Considering the results concerning the use of the adjectives in the corpora in general, there is perhaps less interchangeability today than one would expect from the comments referred to in the introductory paragraphs of this chapter. One feature that is often stressed in usage manuals is the "freer" or less restricted use of *magical* in both attributive and predicative positions in the sentence. When one examines the numbers of predicative uses of *magic* and *magical*, a difference in favour of magical can be observed, but the difference is numerically perhaps not as striking as one would have expected. This itself may not be entirely surprising, because usage manuals have a tendency to pay attention to questions of acceptability, which are not necessarily directly reflected in actual frequencies of use.

As far as possible future developments in the use of *magic/magical* are concerned, perhaps the most crucial meaning where changes are likely is the descriptive sense 'enchanting'. The notion of approval, which is increasingly signalled through the word *magic*, may be linked more closely to the use of both adjective forms in this sense. Given the direction of change in most semantically differentiated *-ic/-ical* pairs, one might assume that *magic* eventually becomes the more frequent form in the descriptive sense as well, as in the case of *electric/electrical*, and that the choice between the two forms will be governed even more strongly by the collocating words.

Chapter 11

Obsolescence of one of the forms

This chapter examines those adjective pairs ending in *-ic* and *-ical* where one of the forms has become extinct or considerably rarer than its rival form at some stage in the history of English. As it would not be feasible to examine the uses of all *-ic/-ical* adjectives occurring in the corpora, the study must concentrate on the pairs with a reasonably high frequency of occurrence. The study was limited to those pairs of which the less frequent form occurred at least twenty times in either the prose section of *Literature Online* or the non-fiction texts. Some thirty pairs came up, and of these, the more prominent ones were chosen to illustrate the process of obsolescence. Pairs with lower numbers of occurrences may not yield sufficient evidence of the nature of the competition between the two forms. As regards the two collections of texts, the adjective pairs meeting these requirements were slightly different, to some extent because of differences in genres, but also simply because of the smaller size of the collection of non-fiction texts studied. In many cases, the two corpora nevertheless showed similar developments in the uses of the pairs, as will be seen below. To further complement the examination of some of the adjective pairs, their occurrences in the *OED* citations were studied. The previous chapters, which described semantically differentiated *-ic/-ical* pairs, involved a prolific use of examples from the corpora. The role of semantic differentiation, however, is less prominent in the case of the adjective pairs discussed here, and examples of authentic use are also somewhat fewer.

1.   Obsolescence of the forms in *-ical*

When we study the use of the *-ic/-ical* pairs in the corpora examined, some of the pairs show a notable shift in preference in the use of the two forms during the seventeenth century. In the case of pairs such as *heroic/heroical* and *majestic/majestical*, the forms in *-ical* were more frequent in the latter half of the sixteenth century. The longer forms also entered the English lexicon before those in *-ic*, judging from the first citations of the words in the *MED* and the second edition of the *OED* (*heroic* 1549, *heroical* ca. 1475; *majestic* 1601, *majestical* 1579).[1] The figures indicating the numbers of occurrences of these adjective pairs are parallel in both the fiction and non-fiction corpora (see Tables 68–71; the

---

[1]   An antedating to the first citation under the entry for *majestic* in the *OED* can be found elsewhere in the dictionary citations: "Mercie, whose maiestick browe Should be vnwrinckled" (*Sir Thomas More* (1592), iii.i., 172) s.v. *unwrinkled*.

figures in parentheses denote the numbers of authors using the forms). In the seventeenth century, the relative frequencies of the forms in *-ic* increased, while the variants ending in *-ical* eventually became archaic, if not altogether obsolete (the *BNC* includes two occurrences of *heroical*, and one occurrence of *majestical*).

Table 68. *Heroic/heroical* in the prose section of *Literature Online*.

	heroic	heroical	number of authors using both forms
1550–1599	5 (2)	31 (12)	-
1600–1649	27 (8)	13 (6)	5
1650–1699	80 (17)	65 (8)	6
1700–1749	67 (8)	3 (1)	1
1750–1799	146 (22)	4 (4)	4
1800–1849	223 (27)	6 (5)	5
1850–1903	280 (43)	19 (4)	4

Table 69. *Heroic/heroical* in the non-fiction texts studied.

	heroic	heroical	number of authors using both forms
1550–1599	7 (2)	12 (4)	2
1600–1649	8 (3)	15 (6)	2
1650–1699	68 (11)	6 (6)	3
1700–1749	12 (10)	3 (2)	1
1750–1799	30 (10)	-	-
1800–1849	7 (3)	-	-
1850–1903	5 (5)	-	-
1900–1949	3 (1)	-	-

As regards *heroic/heroical*, the figures in both Tables 68 and 69 show a preference for the use of the form in *-ical* in the latter half of the sixteenth century. The same kind of preference is evident in the early English dictionaries (monolingual or bilingual) in *EMEDD*: *heroical* is found in the definitions in Thomas (1587), Florio (1598), Cotgrave (1611), and is assigned an entry of its own in Cawdrey (1604), while *heroic* appears for the first time in Bullokar (1616), after which both forms are found. The uses of the two forms in the seventeenth century – during which "co-existence", and thus the heaviest "contest" between the forms, can be observed – were remarkably similar in the corpora studied, with no obvious difference in meaning. Many of the authors used both forms synonymously:

(1) a.   This grave Senator had a Sonne who bearing his name, disagreed not from his properties, but punctually had his Fathers heroicke inclinations, which made him as happy as meritorious, and was no lesse honoured of all men [...] (Alexander Hart, *Alexto and Angelina* (1640), 19–20)

     b.   [...] Sandrico for the better satisfaction of his friend and himselfe, begun to enquire and demand of the Inhabitants what they could informe him concerning the heroicall inclination of this Roman Goddesse, [...] (Alexander Hart, *Alexto and Angelina* (1640), 56)

In the latter half of the seventeenth century, *heroic* was used by a greater number of authors than *heroical*, and in subsequent centuries the position of the form in *-ical* became increasingly weaker. The pattern as regards the shifts in preference observable in Tables 68 and 69 parallels the occurrence of the two forms in the *OED* citations (see Appendix D, Table 1).

The historical behaviour of the pair *majestic/majestical*, as noted above, is notably similar to that of *heroic/heroical*. Although the numbers of occurrences are considerably lower in the non-fiction texts, the general patterns in both Table 70 and 71 show a similar tendency, and resemble the frequencies of the two forms in the *OED* citations between 1550 and 1749 (Appendix D, Table 2).

Table 70. *Majestic/majestical* in the prose section of *Literature Online*.

	majestic	*majestical*	number of authors using both forms
1550–1599	1 (1)	14 (10)	-
1600–1649	15 (7)	19 (8)	2
1650–1699	67 (15)	10 (3)	1
1700–1749	33 (7)	-	-
1750–1799	79 (21)	1 (1)	1
1800–1849	224 (29)	4 (4)	4
1850–1903	190 (30)	2 (2)	2

Table 71. *Majestic/majestical* in the non-fiction texts studied.

	majestic	*majestical*	number of authors using both forms
1550–1599	-	2 (2)	-
1600–1649	5 (2)	5 (2)	-
1650–1699	11 (5)	4 (2)	1
1700–1749	16 (7)	-	-
1750–1799	6 (4)	-	-
1800–1849	9 (7)	-	-
1850–1903	6 (5)	-	-
1900–1949	1 (1)	-	-

The occurrences of *majestic/majestical* in the dictionaries in *EMEDD* likewise speak in favour of an initial preference for the form in *-ical*: the longer form is found in earlier works as a headword and/or in the definitions, e.g. in Florio (1598) and Cotgrave (1611), while *majestic* appears for the first time in Blount (1656). No significant semantic difference could be observed in the use of the two forms, which were both used in classifying ('pertaining to a majesty or majesties', e.g. *majestic(al) duties*) and descriptive senses ('powerful, beautiful', 'being like or befitting a majesty', e.g. *majestic(al) grace*). The majority of the instances in the corpora represent the latter use.

One can observe the "fashionableness" of forms ending in *-ical* in the sixteenth century (especially in the latter half) with pairs other than *heroic/heroical* and *majestic/majestical*. In some cases, the shorter form actually preceded the form in *-ical*, but even with these pairs the *-ical* form gained ground for a while, to be later replaced by the shorter form. For example, as concerns the pairs *angelic/angelical* (the first citations in the *MED/OED* dating from ca. 1390 and 1500, respectively), and *authentic* (1340)/*authentical* (1531), the shorter forms were at first more frequent as far as the *OED* citations are concerned, as shown by Tables 72 and 73 below:[2]

2 The evidence from the *OED* is more illuminating for the early history of these pairs than the fiction and non-fiction corpora because the latter do not stretch so far back in time. As for the later history of the words, the figures presented in Tables 72 and 73 stretch until those periods in which one can unquestionably observe the preference for the use of the forms in *-ic*; the last occurrence of *angelical* and *authentical* in the *OED* citations date from 1864 and 1861, respectively. In present-day English, both *angelical* and *authentical* are obsolete.

Table 72. *Angelic/angelical* in the *OED* citations, 1450–1899.

	angelic	angelical
1450–1499	3	-
1500–1549	3	5
1550–1599	6	11
1600–1649	7	14
1650–1699	17	17
1700–1749	9	4
1750–1799	5	2
1800–1849	9	4
1850–1899	25	3

Table 73. *Authentic/authentical* in the *OED* citations, 1350–1799.

	authentic	authentical
1350–1399	3	-
1400–1449	3	-
1450–1499	9	-
1500–1549	6	3
1550–1599	12	11
1600–1649	26	17
1650–1699	26	5
1700–1749	17	2
1750–1799	28	-

The uses of the adjectives in the *Literature Online* and the non-fiction corpora also show initial variation in the use of the forms (see Tables 74–77), after which the shorter forms gradually begin to dominate over the longer ones. The dominance seems to have become established slightly earlier in the case of *authentic/authentical*; with *angelic/angelical*, the period of the variation seems to have continued longer. As for *authentic/authentical*, the fiction and non-fiction corpora, quite interestingly, yield opposite patterns as regards the period 1550–1599, but the numbers of occurrences and the authors using the forms are rather low.

Table 74. *Angelic/angelical* in the prose section of *Literature Online*.

	angelic	angelical	number of authors using both forms
1550–1599	3 (3)	20 (12)	1
1600–1649	1 (1)	6 (2)	-
1650–1699	4 (4)	37 (8)	1
1700–1749	38 (8)	1 (1)	1
1750–1799	88 (24)	-	-
1800–1849	121 (26)	9 (3)	3
1850–1903	69 (28)	20 (6)	5

Table 75. *Angelic/angelical* in the non-fiction texts studied.

	angelic	angelical	number of authors using both forms
1500–1549	1 (1)	-	-
1550–1599	-	-	-
1600–1649	1 (1)	6 (3)	-
1650–1699	3 (3)	62 (9)	3
1700–1749	4 (2)	12 (2)	1
1750–1799	3 (1)	5 (1)	1
1800–1849	1 (1)	-	-
1850–1903	2 (1)	-	-
1900–1949	1 (1)	-	-

Considering *angelic/angelical*, the majority of instances found in the texts represented the descriptive sense 'graceful, beautiful', but both forms were also occasionally found in the classifying meaning 'of or pertaining to angels' (e.g. *angelic(al) choir/vision*). In the nineteenth-century novels we find some authors using both forms synonymously: for instance, in the passages below we find William Thackeray using *angelic* and *angelical* with the same head word:

(2)   a.   If her mother would but have omitted that chorus, which she cackled perseveringly behind her daughter's pretty back: about Rosey's angelic temper; about the compliments Signor Polonini paid her; [...] (William Thackeray, *The Newcomes* (1854), Vol. II, 172)

       b.   He may have treated the woman ill, I suspect he has not an angelical temper: but in this matter he has not been so bad, so very bad as it would seem. (William Thackeray, *The Newcomes* (1854), Vol. I, 294)

Table 76. *Authentic/authentical* in the prose section of *Literature Online*.

	authentic	*authentical*	number of authors using both forms
1550–1599	-	12 (6)	-
1600–1649	5 (3)	11 (6)	-
1650–1699	25 (12)	6 (3)	-
1700–1749	18 (6)	-	-
1750–1799	13 (10)	-	-
1800–1849	50 (16)	-	-
1850–1903	47 (15)	-	-

Table 77. *Authentic/authentical* in the non-fiction texts studied.

	authentic	*authentical*	number of authors using both forms
1550–1599	6 (4)	-	-
1600–1649	11 (4)	5 (4)	-
1650–1699	10 (5)	4 (2)	1
1700–1749	6 (6)	-	-
1750–1799	30 (12)	-	-
1800–1849	8 (5)	-	-
1850–1903	8 (5)	-	-
1900–1949	5 (2)	-	-

Another pair manifesting a shift similar to the previous pairs, both as regards the early history, the timing and direction of the changes in the preference for one of the forms, is *domestic/domestical*.[3] The first citation of *domestic* in the *MED* (ca. 1425) is of an earlier date than that of *domestical* (1459). The *Literature Online* material (Table 78) again shows a notably greater frequency of the form in -*ical* in 1550–1599, followed by a decline in its use, with *domestic* gaining ground.[4] It is interesting to note that in the *OED* citations (Table 79) the

---

3   The occurrences of *domestic/domestical* in early dictionaries also reflect the preference for *domestical* in the latter half of the sixteenth century: *domestical* is the sole form appearing in definitions or as a headword in Thomas (1587), Coote (1596), Cawdrey (1604), and Cotgrave (1611), both forms being listed in Bullokar (1616), Cockeram (1623), and Blount (1656).

4   As regards the non-fiction texts examined, the sixteenth century material contained only one occurrence of *domestic* and *domestical* each; in the texts from later periods, *domestic* was the more frequent form. No instances of *domestical* were found in the material from the first half of the seventeenth century onward.

period of "popularity" of the form in -*ical* was preceded by variation between the forms until the middle of the sixteenth century.[5]

Table 78. *Domestic/domestical* in the prose section of *Literature Online*.

	domestic	*domestical*	number of authors using both forms
1550–1599	1 (1)	32 (11)	1
1600–1649	13 (9)	2 (2)	1
1650–1699	54 (13)	3 (1)	-
1700–1749	75 (10)	-	-
1750–1799	349 (29)	-	-
1800–1849	736 (32)	-	-
1850–1903	798 (41)	-	-

Table 79. *Domestic/domestical* in the *OED* citations, 1450–1650.

	domestic	*domestical*
1450–1499	-	1
1500–1549	6	5
1550–1599	-	19
1600–1649	27	14
1650–1699	26	4

This pair differs from the previously mentioned ones, however, in that *domestic* also had a nominal use derived from the adjective, denoting a household servant, earlier also a member of the household (the figures in the tables, however, present only the adjectival instances). The *OED* notes that *domestical* has also had this function, but instances of this type were not found in the material studied. The nominal use of the shorter form nevertheless did not lead to a distinction between the two word forms along the lines of nominal versus adjectival function. Instead, the longer form eventually became increasingly rarer, with *domestic* being the form used for both functions. The same observations can, to a great extent, also be made on *rustic* and *rustical* (see Appendix D, Table 3).

As regards the shift in preference from the forms in -*ical* to those in -*ic* in the seventeenth century or the first half of the eighteenth century, the corpora studied show a similar shift taking place with the adjective pairs *extrinsic/ extrinsical*, *intrinsic/intrinsical*, and *prophetic/prophetical*. The numbers of occurrences of these adjectives were fairly low, and the total number of occurrences of the rarer form were in some cases fewer than twenty in the fiction or non-fiction corpus. However, together with their occurrence in the *OED*

---

5   The last citation in the *OED* containing *domestical* dates from 1856.

citations and the early English dictionaries, one can observe a weakening in the position of the forms in *-ical* between 1600 and 1749. Below the cut-off level of twenty occurrences of the less frequent form, variation between the two forms between 1550 and 1749 could also be seen with *aromatic/aromatical, harmonic/harmonical, magnetic/magnetical, monastic/monastical, pathetic/pathetical,* and *seraphic/seraphical.* The *OED* citations again included more occurrences of the forms in *-ical* in the late sixteenth century, but in the course of time, the longer forms gradually became obsolete.

It appears that shifts in usage in favour of the forms in *-ic* have occurred at all times since the beginning of the seventeenth century. In other words, not all shifts took place in the seventeenth century, but during the centuries following. For example, the uses of *emphatic/emphatical* in the prose fiction works in the *Literature Online* text collection (Table 80) show the two forms having a roughly equal standing until the end of the eighteenth century, after which *emphatic* became the more frequently used form (*emphatical* being nowadays obsolete).

Table 80. *Emphatic/emphatical* in the prose section of *Literature Online*.

	emphatic	*emphatical*	number of authors using both forms
1550–1599	-	-	-
1600–1649	2 (1)	-	-
1650–1699	-	1 (1)	-
1700–1749	-	5 (2)	-
1750–1799	33 (9)	17 (10)	4
1800–1849	120 (23)	4 (4)	1
1850–1903	154 (25)	-	-

According to the *OED*, *emphatical* preceded *emphatic* in the English lexicon, and this also becomes evident from the occurrence of the forms in early English dictionaries, with the form in *-ical* appearing first in Florio's Italian-English dictionary (1598), and *emphatic* being first "caught" by the lexicographers – but presented alongside *emphatical* – in Bailey (1721). As regards the earlier periods represented in Table 80, the frequencies of the adjectives are fairly low, and therefore it is convenient at this juncture to present the occurrences of the adjectives in the *OED* citations, which yield a similar chronological pattern. Table 81 indeed suggests that the shorter form did not become the dominant one until the first half of the nineteenth century:[6]

---

6   The last citation in the *OED* containing *emphatical* dates from 1864.

Table 81. *Emphatic/emphatical* in the *OED* citations, 1550–1989.

	emphatic	emphatical
1550–1599	-	3
1600–1649	-	12
1650–1699	-	10
1700–1749	3	8
1750–1799	8	7
1800–1849	24	6
1850–1899	35	1
1900–1949	18	-
1950–1989	12	-

Some adjective pairs in the material studied show a tendency to favour the longer forms well into the nineteenth century, which suggests that the final shift to the forms in -*ic* did not occur until the twentieth century. This appears to be the case with, for example, *enigmatic/enigmatical*, the works for the last period of the *Literature Online* material still including more instances of *enigmatical* (see Table 82). The longer form has now disappeared from common use: in the *BNC* it occurs only twice, while the corpus includes altogether 266 instances of *enigmatic*. Similarly, the 1995 issues of *The Daily Telegraph* contain 134 instances of *enigmatic*, but not a single occurrence of the form in -*ical*.

Table 82. *Enigmatic/enigmatical* in the prose section of *Literature Online*.

	enigmatic	enigmatical	number of authors using both forms
1550–1599	-	-	-
1600–1649	-	3 (2)	-
1650–1699	1 (1)	3 (3)	-
1700–1749	-	1 (1)	-
1750–1799	-	10 (6)	-
1800–1849	1 (1)	8 (5)	1
1850–1903	19 (5)	25 (12)	5

The uses of *enigmatic/enigmatical* in the *Literature Online* in the latter half of the nineteenth century do not suggest any striking lines of semantic differentiation. All of the five authors using *enigmatic* also used the longer form; for instance, George Meredith used the two forms in very similar phrases, as shown in the example below.

(3)   She had much to do: the arrangements to dismiss her servants, write to house-agents and her lawyer, and write fully to Emma, write the enigmatic

farewell to the Esquarts and Lady Pennon, Mary Paynham, Arthur Rhodes, Whitmonby (stanch in friendship, but requiring friendly touches), Henry Wilmers, and Redworth. He was reserved to the last, for very enigmatical adieux: he would hear the whole story from Emma; must be left to think as he liked. (George Meredith, *Diana of the Crossways* (1885), Vol. III, 252)

As regards those adjectives in the material studied which manifest a shift from the use of the forms in -*ical* to those in -*ic*, the timing of the shift is presented pair by pair in Table 83 below. The table includes those -*ic/-ical* pairs with the greatest numbers of occurrences: the pairs given in bold type are ones for which the total number of occurrences of the rarer form exceeded twenty in either the fiction or the non-fiction corpus. The pairs with lower total frequencies of the rarer item, but which nevertheless appear to indicate a shift (supported by the occurrences in the *OED* citations), are given unbolded.

Table 83.   The -*ic/-ical* adjectives manifesting a shift in preference from -*ical* to -*ic*, according to period of shift.

1600–99:	*aromatic/aromatical*	1800–99:	*academic/academical*
	authentic/authentical		***aristocratic/aristocratical***
	domestic/domestical		***emphatic/emphatical***
	heroic/heroical		***epidemic/epidemical***
	intrinsic/intrinsical		***misanthropic/misanthropical***
	majestic/majestical		***poetic/poetical***
	prophetic/prophetical		***tragic/tragical***
	seraphic/seraphical		
1700–99:	***angelic/angelical***	1900–99:	***enigmatic/enigmatical***
	democratic/democratical		***ironic/ironical***
	extrinsic/extrinsical		*pragmatic/pragmatical*
	magnetic/magnetical		*problematic/problematical*
	sarcastic/sarcastical		***symbolic/symbolical***
	sympathetic/sympathetical		

The placing of a pair in a particular chronological group was determined on the basis of the first fifty-year period during which the form in -*ic* was used by a greater number of authors. As for the unbolded pairs in the group 1900–1999, i.e. *pragmatic/pragmatical* and *problematic/problematical*, the forms in -*ical* were more frequent in both the historical fiction and non-fiction corpora throughout, but with the numbers of occurrences of *pragmatic* and *problematic* increasing somewhat (nevertheless below twenty) in the latter half of the nineteenth century.

Since nowadays the forms in -*ic* are more frequently used than the -*ical* variants, the shift may be assumed to have occurred in the twentieth century.[7]

The main function of Table 83 is to show that adjective pairs have differed as regards the timing of the shift from -*ical* to -*ic*. It is interesting to observe that the timing of the shift is not directly connected to the etymology of the pair, i.e. there are cases where a relatively "old" pair has undergone a shift significantly later than other pairs coined at roughly the same time. For example, a shift in favour of the shorter form is seen in the seventeenth century usage of *majestic/majestical* and *seraphic/seraphical*, but in the case of *enigmatic/ enigmatical*, *ironic/ironical*, and *problematic/problematical*, a similar change appears to have occurred as late as the twentieth century, although all of these adjectives date from the late sixteenth or the early seventeenth century (with the -*ical* form occurring first). One must obviously acknowledge that with even larger corpora, a more detailed picture of the temporal aspects of the shifts could be achieved, not to mention the inclusion of a far greater number of -*ic/-ical* pairs. It is also possible that examination of large collections of texts representing different genres might reveal significant differences due to the type of text.

Considering the adjective pairs in Table 83, it is tempting to look for semantic components common to the words that would explain why these particular pairs behaved in the same way with respect to the shift from -*ical* to -*ic*. As observed in Kaunisto (2001), one feature that does suggest itself is the semantic component of nobility or grace, which is present in the meanings of *angelic(al)*, *heroic(al)*, and *majestic(al)*, and might also be regarded as being related to the basic meanings as well as the connotations of *authentic(al)*, *prophetic(al)*, and *seraphic(al)*. This observation brings to mind the idea presented by Elphinston (1765: 323–324) of -*ic* as the foreign ending being preferred on "solemn" occasions, and -*ical* as the domestic ending being used in "familiar" contexts. With his comment "[s]o we say almost only *majestic*, *miltonic*, from *majesty*, *Milton*, &c. and *whimsical*, *finical*, from *whimsy*, *fine*, &c.", Elphinston also suggests that there was a connection between the basic meaning of the word and the ending that most often is used.[8] Based on the current data, however, one should perhaps not draw too far-reaching conclusions on the significance of this perceivable "group" of adjectives in terms of their constituting a driving force or model in the shift from -*ical* to -*ic* among all -*ic/-ical* adjective pairs. While it does indeed seem to be the case that the -*ic* ending is preferred with adjectives with the semantic component of nobility or grace, there are other pairs, such as *domestic/domestical*, which manifest a similar

---

7   The 1995 *DTL* material contained 221 occurrences of *pragmatic*, but none of *pragmatical*. *Problematic* occurred 85, and *problematical* 18 times.

8   As Elphinston (1765: 328) suggests, the fact that -*ic* is preferred to -*ical* in adjectives formed from peoples' names can be regarded as being related to the idea of the solemn nature of the base word resulting in the choice of the ending -*ic*. The connection is easy to make, since the people from whose names adjectives were derived were obviously important, respected, powerful, or legendary.

shift without having this semantic feature. Moreover, there are also adjectives ending in -*ic* which involve a completely opposite notion, e.g. *demonic, despotic, idiotic*, and *parasitic*. According to the *OED*, these adjectives had corresponding forms ending in -*ical* (most of them nowadays obsolete or rare) coined before those in -*ic*. It is nevertheless intriguing to perceive Elphinston's intuitive comments, made in the late eighteenth century, find at least partial validation in large historical corpora.

Other tempting generalisations based on the adjectives in Table 83, although relating to a lower number of pairs, would be that the shift in favour of the forms in -*ic* could be seen in adjectives relating to forms of government (e.g. *aristocratic/aristocratical, democratic/democratical*) and literary genres (*poetic/ poetical, tragic/tragical*). As regards *aristocratic(al)* and *democratic(al)*, it would seem that rather than considering adjectives relating to forms of government constituting a group of their own, it is more accurate to regard the behaviour of these pairs as corresponding with that of other adjectives ending in -*cratic/ -cratical* (including e.g. *autocratic* and *theocratic*).[9] Although there are -*ic/-ical* adjectives denoting forms of government without the -*crat* element, with the form in -*ic* being nowadays prevalent (e.g. *anarchic/anarchical* and *despotic/ despotical*), some adjective pairs of this kind do not conform to the pattern. For example, *monarchical* and *tyrannical* are today more common than *monarchic* and *tyrannic*.[10]

Adjectives relating to literary genres include a number of pairs in -*ic/-ical* where the form in -*ical* is nowadays rare, if not totally obsolete. Examples of such pairs are *dramatic/dramatical, epic/epical*, and *prosaic/prosaical*. One could likewise make a case for the gradual disappearance of *comical* (see Chapter 6). However, there is one exception to the pattern, namely the pair *satiric/satirical*, where the longer form has been dominant over *satiric* since the latter half of the sixteenth century (more details on the pair given in the following section). It therefore seems that although it is possible to perceive groups of adjectives with a reasonable amount of semantic similarity with each other, there are also

---

9   The shift in the preference from the forms in -*ical* to -*ic* also becomes evident when we examine the numbers of first citations of adjectives ending in -*cratic/-cratical* in the *OED*. The dictionary includes three first citations of adjectives ending in -*cratical* from 1550–1599, but none of those ending in -*cratic*. Between 1600 and 1799, the numbers of first citations for both endings are roughly equal, but after 1800 the new formations in -*ic* clearly outnumber those in -*ical* (in 1800–1989, 34 first citations with the -*ic* ending, as opposed to five ending in -*ical*).

10   One could suggest that the form in -*ic* is in general favoured when the underlying noun denotes a person or a creature, whether it is typically viewed in positive or negative terms, thus including quite a large number of instances like *angelic, demonic, despotic, heroic, idiotic, majestic, parasitic, prophetic, seraphic*, as well as e.g. *Aristotelic, Byronic, Ciceronic, Miltonic*, and *Satanic*. Apparently exceptional instances such as *monarchical* and *tyrannical* could be explained as relating to the nouns *monarchy* and *tyranny* instead of to *monarch* and *tyrant*, respectively.

exceptional cases, which rather suggests that the shifts in preference for either form may not have been strictly governed by the semantic aspects of the adjectives themselves. On the other hand, as exceptions they do not entirely exclude the possibility of semantically coherent groups of words behaving in the same way. The issue remains one which would undoubtedly benefit from further research into larger corpora.

Some of the adjective pairs in Table 83 deserve closer attention. *Poetic/poetical* is a pair which is relatively often commented on in usage manuals today. Attempts have been made to suggest a semantic difference between the two forms: for example, Bailie and Kitchin (1988) s.v. *poetic, poetical* claim that while the forms are largely interchangeable, *poetical* is "a more neutral word [which] may simply mean 'of or pertaining to poetry'", as in *poetical works*. *Poetic*, on the other hand, is more readily useable with a descriptive meaning, suggesting "the charm or qualities characteristic of poetry", exemplified by the phrases *poetic feeling/licence/justice*. This idea was probably first suggested by Fowler (1926) s.v. *poetic(al)*, who says that "*poetical* labels, while -*ic* admires". Krapp (1927) s.v. -*ic*, -*ical* reiterated Fowler's comment, presenting the phrases *a poetic composition* and *a poetical composition* as examples with a different meaning (the form in -*ic* describing the nature or quality of the work, *poetical* denoting the form or style). However, other manuals, such as Hardie (1991) s.v. *poetic, poetical, poetics, poesy*, present the two forms as synonymous. This is the view held by Burchfield (1996) s.v. *poetic, poetical*, who also adds that *poetic* is fixed in phrases modifying the words *diction*, *justice*, and *licence*, while the longer form is fixed in the expression *the poetical works of X*.

As regards the uses of *poetic/poetical* in the *BNC* and the 1995 issues of *The Daily Telegraph*, *poetic* is considerably more common whether relating to poetry or poets in the classifying sense (e.g. in phrases such as *poetic achievement/career/skill/texts/writings*, as well as in references to Coleridge's 'poetic creativity') or describing something as sublime or beautiful (as in *the poetic beauty of the landscape*). Furthermore, the use of *poetical* in the present-day material was not restricted to the classifying sense. In fact, the majority of the instances were descriptive, which thus undermines Fowler's argument on the semantic distinction between the two forms. The *BNC* includes altogether 717 occurrences of *poetic*, and 52 of *poetical*, the corresponding figures in the *DTL* material being 261 versus 11. The numbers of occurrences of the adjectives in the *Literature Online* and the non-fictional texts studied are presented in Tables 84 and 85 below, both indicating an overall shift from the use of *poetical* to *poetic*, with the longer form having a strong foothold well into the nineteenth century. Considering the present-day situation, the latest change in favour of *poetic* must have taken place in the late nineteenth or early twentieth century. Further support for these observations can be found from the numbers of occurrences of the adjectives in the *OED* citations (presented in Appendix D, Table 4). It is therefore reasonable to assume that the form in -*ical* in this case is gradually disappearing from the language.

Table 84. *Poetic/poetical* in the prose section of *Literature Online*.

	poetic	*poetical*	number of authors using both forms
1550–1599	-	25 (13)	-
1600–1649	2 (1)	13 (7)	-
1650–1699	9 (4)	35 (8)	3
1700–1749	7 (5)	35 (7)	4
1750–1799	20 (10)	87 (20)	8
1800–1849	65 (15)	140 (23)	14
1850–1903	117 (27)	126 (26)	17

Table 85. The numbers of occurrences of *poetic/poetical* in the non-fiction texts studied.

	poetic	*poetical*	number of authors using both forms
1550–1599	-	43 (5)	-
1600–1649	1 (1)	12 (6)	-
1650–1699	3 (3)	25 (7)	2
1700–1749	2 (2)	24 (8)	1
1750–1799	7 (5)	28 (13)	2
1800–1849	25 (3)	26 (8)	3
1850–1903	28 (7)	20 (3)	2
1900–1949	6 (1)	17 (2)	1

Until the nineteenth century, *poetical* was more frequently used than *poetic*, and it was used in both the classifying and descriptive senses. In the nineteenth century texts, as earlier, *poetical* was considerably more common when modifying the words *justice* and *licence*, which nowadays form fixed phrases with *poetic*. As can be observed from Table 84, the shorter form became increasingly more common compared with *poetical*, and in the nineteenth century, many authors used both forms. For example, Disraeli uses both *poetic* and *poetical* in connection with the word *feeling*, Anthony Trollope has both forms in similar senses modifying *justice*, and Thackeray writes of persons of *a poetic(al) turn*. The texts studied show no signs of evident semantic differentiation between *poetic* and *poetical* concomitant with the increase in the use of *poetic*. In the late nineteenth century, Sweet (1891: 490) also presented the pair as an example where the two forms are "often used almost indifferently".[11]

11　Both the historical and present-day corpora contained very few instances of the phrase *poetic(al) works (of)*, with the exception of book titles (usually with the form in

However, in the nineteenth century, the longer form was more frequently used in a predicative position. In the *Literature Online* texts from 1750–1799, there was no great difference as to the numbers of predicative uses of the two forms (*poetic* none, *poetical* 2). The texts published in 1850–1903, on the other hand, contained seven predicative occurrences of *poetic*, while *poetical* was found in this position 28 times. This difference is also noted by Fowler (1926) s.v. *poetic(al)*, who illustrated the idea with the examples *An idea more true than poetical* and *A no less true than a poetic idea*. As regards the present-day situation, the prevailing form, *poetic*, is quite usual in a predicative position as well.

Another pair where the *-ical* form started to show signs of weakening in the nineteenth century is *tragic/tragical*. Fowler (1926) s.v. *tragic(al)* was ready to consider the longer form "dead", at least as regards "serious" uses of the word. Few usage manuals include any comments on the pair, while some recent dictionaries still give *tragical* as a rare variant of *tragic*. The numbers of occurrences of the two forms in the prose works of the *Literature Online* collection are presented in Table 86 below:

Table 86. *Tragic/tragical* in the prose section of *Literature Online*.

	tragic	*tragical*	number of authors using both forms
1550–1599	15 (6)	71 (19)	5
1600–1649	18 (8)	61 (11)	6
1650–1699	13 (8)	51 (18)	4
1700–1749	20 (4)	34 (9)	4
1750–1799	37 (9)	54 (16)	7
1800–1849	103 (14)	34 (15)	9
1850–1903	232 (33)	51 (13)	11

As can be observed from Table 86, *tragic/tragical* fits the pattern seen in connection with other *-ic/-ical* adjective pairs discussed in the present section: the longer form was dominant in the latter half of the sixteenth century, after which the use of the form in *-ic* began to increase. As opposed to pairs such as *heroic/heroical* or *majestic/majestical*, however, the decline in the use of *tragical* did not begin until much later.

The numbers of authors using both forms overall in Table 86 are notably high in relation to authors using only one of the forms. In the descriptive sense paraphrasable as 'sorrowful', 'sad', 'dreadful', or 'fatal', both forms were used by many authors in free variation: e.g. *tragic(al) catastrophe/end/event/misfortunes*. However, *tragic* was earlier the preferred form in the classifying sense 'of or pertaining to tragedy', as in *tragic(al) actor/muse/poem/poet(ry)/writer*, relating

---

-ical, which may partly explain the comments made by Bailie and Kitchin referred to above), making it difficult to estimate the degree of fixedness of either form in this case.

to the genre of tragedy rather than describing the quality or nature of the referent. This was also noted by Krapp (1927) s.v. -*ic, -ical*; in the definition of *tragical* in the *OED*, the sense 'of tragedy' is marked obsolete, while the label is not assigned to other senses. As regards the historical corpora studied, instances of the adjectives in the classifying sense were in general quite few in number. Some instances of this type of both *tragic* and *tragical* were found in the sixteenth and seventeenth century texts. In the *Literature Online* texts, the preference for the use of the shorter form when modifying words such as *actor, actress*, and *poet* was not particularly noticeable until the latter half of the eighteenth century. One can nevertheless argue that the developments in the use of pair *tragic/tragical* involved a certain degree of semantic differentiation. Interestingly enough, the differentiation between the forms was not of a lasting nature, as the change in favour of *tragic* when used in the classifying sense was not counterbalanced by a similarly growing preference in the use of *tragical* in the descriptive sense. Instead, the shorter form gained ground in all functions (no significant difference was seen in the attributive or predicative uses of the forms), and *tragical* began to disappear from use altogether. The *BNC* includes six, and the 1995 issues of *The Daily Telegraph* two occurrences of *tragical* (the corresponding figures for *tragic* being 1202 and 561, respectively). The historical changes in the use of this pair resemble to a great extent – both as regards the assignment of the classifying sense to the -*ic* form and the weakening of the -*ical* form – those observed in connection with *comic/comical*, a pair discussed in more detail in Chapter 6.

2.   Obsolescence of the forms in -*ic*

In contrast with the adjective pairs discussed in the section above, there are pairs where one can perceive a relative increase in the use of the forms in -*ic* beginning in the seventeenth century, but the longer form has nevertheless eventually prevailed. The clearest example of such a case is *tyrannic/tyrannical*:

Table 87. *Tyrannic/tyrannical* in the prose section of *Literature Online*.

	tyrannic	*tyrannical*	number of authors using both forms
1550–1599	-	28 (8)	-
1600–1649	1 (1)	3 (2)	1
1650–1699	7 (4)	46 (13)	1
1700–1749	8 (4)	18 (6)	2
1750–1799	10 (9)	50 (20)	7
1800–1849	13 (7)	62 (17)	5
1850–1903	3 (3)	52 (20)	2

As can be seen from Table 87, indicating the uses of *tyrannic/tyrannical* in the *Literature Online* texts studied, the form in *-ical* – as with many other *-ic/-ical* pairs discussed earlier – was the dominant form in the second half of the sixteenth century. The seventeenth century witnessed a rise in the use of *tyrannic*, but the use of the shorter form never outnumbered that of *tyrannical*. No signs of semantic differentiation between the two forms are evident in the historical texts studied. For example, in his novels Walter Scott used phrases such as *tyrannic power* and *tyrannical power* in contexts suggesting no difference in meaning. Considering the competition between the two synonymous forms, on the basis of Table 87 it could be argued that from the mid-seventeenth century until the mid-nineteenth century the position of the shorter form was fairly "promising", even though *tyrannical* was more frequently used. Contrary to *enigmatic/enigmatical* or *poetic/poetical*, however, the latter part of the nineteenth century did not witness a major increase in the use of *tyrannic*. On the contrary, *tyrannic* only became weaker.[12] In the *BNC*, only two occurrences of the shorter form can be found (as opposed to 70 instances of *tyrannical*), while the 1995 issues of *The Daily Telegraph* include no occurrences of *tyrannic* (42 of *tyrannical*).

The longer form can also be seen as having prevailed in the case of *satiric/satirical*. The numbers of occurrences of the two forms in the *Literature Online* prose section are presented in Table 88 below.

Table 88.   *Satiric/satirical* in the prose section of *Literature Online*.

	satiric	*satirical*	number of authors using both forms
1550–1599	-	5 (4)	-
1600–1649	-	-	-
1650–1699	1 (1)	8 (7)	-
1700–1749	1 (1)	16 (5)	1
1750–1799	-	51 (16)	-
1800–1849	5 (3)	54 (17)	1
1850–1903	22 (6)	95 (22)	5

Considering the *OED* first citations of the two forms, that of *satiric* is of an earlier date (1509 versus 1520 for *satirical*). The longer form, however, seems to have become the dominant variant, with *satiric* never exceeding it in usage. Fowler (1926) s.v. *satiric(al)* claimed that *satirical* is mostly used in the descriptive senses 'addicted to, intending, good at, marked by satire' (exemplified by *a satirical rogue; you are pleased to be satirical; with satirical comments; a*

---

12   The non-fiction corpus studied included a smaller total number of occurrences of *tyrannic/tyrannical*, the longer form being clearly preferred in all of the fifty-year periods between 1500 and 1950. Only four occurrences of *tyrannic* were found in the non-fiction material, as opposed to 67 occurrences of *tyrannical*.

satirical glance), while in the classifying sense 'of or belonging to satire' (e.g. *the ~ poems of Pope*; *the Latin ~ writers*) both forms are found, with *satiric* being more common. However, the existence of this kind of distinction between the two forms – which could be perceived in the uses of *comic/comical* (see Chapter 6) and, to some extent, *tragic/tragical* (see previous section) – does not find support from the *Literature Online* texts, in which *satiric* was less frequent than *satirical* in all senses.[13] In the texts from the nineteenth century, some writers used both forms with identical meanings:

(4) a. While Hobson Newcome made these satiric and facetious remarks, his half-brother paced up and down the glass parlour, scowling over the panes into the bank where the busy clerks sate before their ledgers. (William Thackeray, *The Newcomes* (1854), Vol. II, 149)

     b. [...] when the Caledonian giant uttered satirical remarks against the assembled company, averring that they were a parcel of sneaks, [...] Clive slipped off his fine silk-sleeved coat in an instant, invited Mr. M'Collop into the back yard [...] (William Thackeray, *The Newcomes* (1854), Vol. I, 169)

Instead of being an accurate description of current usage of *satiric/satirical*, the distinction pointed out by Fowler was one that he rather considered desirable. This becomes evident from Fowler's own comment that "[the] differentiation might well be hastened by deliberate support; but the line of demarcation between the two groups is not always clear." The idea has apparently not received enough support since Fowler made his remark, as the shorter form is still the less common one, whether the word is used in a classifying or a descriptive sense. The *BNC* includes 21 occurrences of *satiric*, and 183 of *satirical*. The corresponding figures in the 1995 issues of *The Daily Telegraph* are 14 and 141, respectively. However, the two forms seem to have differed as to their predicative use: of the 22 instances of *satiric* in the *Literature Online* texts from 1850–1903, only one had the adjective in a predicative position, whereas 21 out of the corresponding 95 instances of *satirical* were predicative. In the present-day corpora studied, the numbers of predicative cases of *satiric/satirical* largely reflect the overall relative frequency of their use. Recently published usage manuals usually do not comment on any kind of semantic differentiation between the two forms; the remarks rather tend to suggest that *satiric* is disappearing from the lexicon (e.g. Bailie and Kitchin 1998 s.v. *satiric, satirical*).[14]

---

13 Based on the *OED*, the adjective pair *farcic/farcical* resembles *satiric/satirical* as regards the preference for the longer form. The adjective *farcic* appears to have been considerably rarer than *farcical* at all times; no occurrences of the shorter form were found in the historical corpora studied.

14 Burchfield (1996) s.v. *satiric, satirical* notes that *satiric* and *satirical* are largely synonymous, quoting Fowler's comment on the unclarity of the "demarcation" between

The adjective pairs *tyrannic/tyrannical* and *satiric/satirical* seem to have behaved in a way opposite to a number of pairs in *-ic/-ical* discussed in the previous section. There does not appear to be any immediately evident factor in the etymological background or syllable structure of the pairs, for example, that would explain why the form in *-ical* should have become the dominant form. As observed in the previous section, the uses of adjective pairs semantically comparable to these two – e.g. *despotic/despotical*, as well as *poetic/poetical* and *tragic/tragical* – have in general changed so as to favour the shorter forms. One observation could be made on *satiric/satirical* as a possible explanation, albeit somewhat unconvincing, of the dominance of the *-ical* form. According to the *OED*, *satiric* originally had a nominal function, referring to satirists. The first citation of the noun dates from 1387, whereas that of the adjective is from 1509. This could then be argued as having resulted in the preference to use the form in *-ical* as the adjective, in the same way as with the noun-adjective pairs *logic/logical* and *rhetoric/rhetorical* (see Marchand 1969: 241). However, the weakness of this argument lies partly in the fact that as far as the corpora studied are concerned, the noun *satiric* does not seem to have been particularly frequent compared to the adjectives *satiric/satirical*. Secondly, the first citation of *satirical* in the *OED* is from 1529, i.e. twenty years later than that of the adjective *satiric*. In addition, the prominent nominal uses of e.g. *magic* and *comic* did not result in the adjectival function being reserved exclusively to the *-ical* forms.

As regards the historical corpora studied, there were some other *-ic/-ical* pairs, however, where one can observe a gradual weakening of the adjectival use of the forms in *-ic*, this function being almost entirely carried by the longer form. In such cases the form in *-ic* has a nominal use. One pair of this type is *hysteric/hysterical*, of which both forms were at first used as adjectives. Many authors in the eighteenth and nineteenth century texts used the two forms interchangeably in phrases such as *hysteric(al) fit/laughter/tears*. According to the *OED* s.vv. *hysteric, hysterical*, both forms have also been used as nouns, denoting medicines used to treat hysteria and people suffering from this ailment. The plural forms *hysterics/hystericals* were also used in the same sense as hysteria, or, more specifically, of hysteric(al) fits or laughter. In the historical corpora, however, the form in *-ic* was considerably more frequent than *-ical* in the nominal function. As can be seen from Table 89, which gives the numbers of adjectival uses in the *Literature Online* texts, *hysteric* appears to have been more

the forms. However, Burchfield suggests that while *satirical* is today the commoner form in British English, the reverse might hold in American English. The uses of the adjectives in the 1994 issues of *The Washington Post*, however, do not wholly confirm this theory, as *satiric* was used on 49, and *satirical* on 67 occasions. It nevertheless appears that although *satirical* is the slightly more frequent form, *satiric* does indeed have a firmer stand in American English, and the "competition" between the two forms is still "unresolved". The uses of the adjectives showed no significant differences as regards the meanings, as both forms were used for different types of referents, e.g. relating to authors of satires, or describing a style or attitude (*satiric(al) bite/edge/look*).

frequent than *hysterical* in the latter half of the eighteenth century, but the following century witnessed a drastic shift in favour of the longer form.

Table 89. *Hysteric/hysterical* in the prose section of *Literature Online*.

	hysteric	hysterical	number of authors using both forms
1550–1599	-	-	-
1600–1649	-	-	-
1650–1699	1 (1)	-	-
1700–1749	2 (2)	-	-
1750–1799	21 (11)	11 (5)	2
1800–1849	16 (7)	70 (17)	5
1850–1903	15 (8)	157 (33)	8

The 1995 issues of *The Daily Telegraph* include only two instances of *hysteric* as an adjective (and seven occurrences of the singular nominal form, denoting a hysterical person), while the adjective *hysterical* appears 169 times.

Another -*ic*/-*ical* pair developing a more clear-cut noun-adjective distinction through the centuries is *mechanic/mechanical*. As can be observed from Tables 90 and 91, representing the numbers of the adjectives in the *Literature Online* material and the non-fiction corpus, respectively, the adjectival uses of *mechanic* became rare in the nineteenth century.

Table 90. *Mechanic/mechanical* in the prose section of *Literature Online*.

	mechanic	mechanical	number of authors using both forms
1550–1599	1 (1)	7 (2)	1
1600–1649	1 (1)	4 (4)	-
1650–1699	10 (5)	3 (3)	1
1700–1749	4 (2)	4 (1)	1
1750–1799	8 (6)	43 (16)	3
1800–1849	4 (3)	81 (21)	3
1850–1903	5 (4)	226 (38)	4

Table 91. *Mechanic/mechanical* in the non-fiction texts studied.

	mechanic	mechanical	number of authors using both forms
1550–1599	1 (1)	5 (2)	-
1600–1649	2 (2)	6 (5)	2
1650–1699	7 (5)	24 (9)	2
1700–1749	10 (2)	9 (3)	1
1750–1799	8 (5)	35 (10)	3
1800–1849	3 (1)	141 (14)	1
1850–1903	-	45 (16)	-
1900–1949	-	10 (5)	-

Apart from the senses prevalent today, *mechanic* and *mechanical* were in earlier centuries used in a number of different senses (see *OED* s.vv.), some of them now obsolete. Until the mid-eighteenth century, the numbers of occurrences of *mechanic/mechanical*, as well as those of authors using the adjectives were too low in the texts in the corpora so as to suggest any clear preference for either form in any particular sense. For example, both forms were used in the sense of 'vulgar', 'low', or 'base', derived from the use of the adjectives relating to manual labour or people engaged in manual labour (see *OED* s.vv. *mechanic* 2, *mechanical* 2.a):

(5)   a.   And so, that which probably makes me obnoxious to the censures of the multitude, as it hath to the hatred of my new Relations, is the low spiritedness, and pityful ignorance of such Mechanick and base people. (Anonymous, *The Case of Madam Mary Carleton* (1663), 49)

        b.   [...] the Mantles which had served his former old wife were too much out of fashion to be used now [...] and a new one must be bought; and not one would serve the turn, but several there must be; [...] there must be one costly one, wherin the Child must be dressed to be Christened in; (for it is too mechanical and base to use that of the Midwives) [...] (Richard Head and Francis Kirkman, *The English Rogue*, Part IV (1671), 295)

Some authors were found using both forms in identical meanings, as in examples (6a) and (6b) below:[15]

---

15   As regards the meaning of the adjective in the phrase *mechanic(al) philosopher*, when relating to 'theories and their advocates', *mechanic(al)* have been used in the sense of 'explaining phenomena by the assumption of mechanical action' (*OED* s.vv. *mechanic*, 7; *mechanical*, 6).

(6) a. But the greatest of all the particular Phaenomena is the Formation and Organization of the Bodies of Animals, consisting of such Variety and Curiosity; that these mechanick Philosophers being no Way able to give an Account thereof from the necessary motion of Matter, unguided by Mind for Ends, prudently therefore break off their System there when they should come to Animals, and so leave it altogether untouch'd. (John Ray, *The Wisdom of God Manifested in the Works of Creation* (1717), 44)

b. But now their Gravity unites and binds them up fast, hindring the Dispersion of their Parts, I will not dispute what Gravity is; only I will add, that, for ought I have heard or read, the Mechanical Philosophers have not as yet given a clear and satisfactory Account of it. (John Ray, *The Wisdom of God Manifested in the Works of Creation* (1717), 62)

In the nineteenth century texts, writers of both fiction and non-fiction appear to have been considerably less inclined to use *mechanic* as an adjective, regardless of the meaning to be conveyed, opting for the form in *-ical* instead.

Considering that the word *mechanics* was used of the construction of machines as well as the science of motion as early as the seventeenth century (*OED* s.v. *mechanics*), the behaviour of the adjectives *mechanic/mechanical* ultimately resembles that of some other pairs which have a corresponding noun ending in *-ic(s)* denoting a scientific field, theory, or method of action. This generalisation, observed by Marchand (1969: 241), is perhaps best exemplified by *mathematic/mathematical*, along with e.g. *logic/logical*, *practic/practical, rhetoric/rhetorical,* and *tactic/tactical*. In the historical corpora studied, the shorter forms of these pairs were rare (the total number of occurrences not exceeding the level of twenty), and the preference for the use of the forms in *-ical* appears to have been established at a relatively early stage.

In the case of *heretic/heretical*, the longer form is likewise preferred in the adjectival function (see Appendix D, Table 5). The analysis of the pair is problematic as regards some instances of *heretic*, which could be analysed either as representing an attributive use of the noun or as being adjectival, as in *a heretic leader* (see also the *OED* s.v. *heretic*). But even if all those problematic cases of *heretic* were analysed as adjectives, the preference for the use of *heretical* would be obvious. A pair more easily analysable is *fanatic/fanatical*, with which the use has been developing along the lines of noun-adjective distinction, i.e. the adjectival use of *fanatic* has become rarer. This development can be perceived in historical corpora as having started already in earlier centuries (see Table 92). In the 1995 issues of *The Daily Telegraph, fanatic* was used as an adjective seven times (two instances being quotes from speech by non-native speakers of English), while the number of nominal uses of the word was 111. The same material contained 139 occurrences of the adjective *fanatical*.

Table 92. *Fanatic/fanatical* in the prose section of *Literature Online*.

	fanatic	*fanatical*	number of authors using both forms
1550–1599	-	-	-
1600–1649	4 (2)	-	-
1650–1699	6 (3)	5 (3)	1
1700–1749	-	-	-
1750–1799	2 (2)	4 (3)	-
1800–1849	7 (4)	22 (8)	2
1850–1903	4 (3)	30 (9)	-

The historical corpora also show competition between the adjective pairs *philosophic/philosophical* and *theoretic/theoretical*, which, like some of the earlier pairs discussed above, either relate to a scientific field or pertain to scientific methodology.[16] Although the corresponding nouns do not end in *-ic(s)*, the use of the adjective forms seems to have followed the same lines as, for example, *mathematic/mathematical*, i.e. the longer form has eventually become dominant. In the case of *philosophic/philosophical*, the longer form was considerably more common even in the sixteenth and seventeenth centuries, as can be observed from Tables 93 and 94, representing the uses of the adjectives in the fiction and non-fiction corpora studied.

Table 93. *Philosophic/philosophical* in the prose section of *Literature Online*.

	philosophic	*philosophical*	number of authors using both forms
1550–1599	-	12 (6)	-
1600–1649	-	7 (4)	-
1650–1699	1 (1)	23 (8)	-
1700–1749	6 (3)	22 (7)	2
1750–1799	61 (22)	43 (19)	13
1800–1849	57 (14)	124 (21)	10
1850–1903	75 (20)	114 (26)	13

---

16   The occurrences of *theoretic/theoretical* in the *Literature Online* prose fiction texts and the *OED* citations are presented in Appendix D, Tables 6 and 7. In the 1995 *DTL* material, *theoretical* occurred 162 times, while no instances of *theoretic* were found. Other nowadays prevalent adjectives in *-ical* relating to various fields of science or knowledge, or scientific methodology, include *anatomical, astronomical, botanical, chemical, methodical*, and *statistical*, let alone adjectives ending in *-logical*.

Table 94. *Philosophic/philosophical* in the non-fiction texts studied.

	philosophic	philosophical	number of authors using both forms
1550–1599	-	16 (4)	-
1600–1649	1 (1)	1 (1)	-
1650–1699	1 (1)	90 (13)	-
1700–1749	4 (3)	16 (12)	2
1750–1799	12 (6)	61 (17)	2
1800–1849	20 (3)	46 (13)	3
1850–1903	13 (5)	49 (11)	4
1900–1949	8 (3)	44 (4)	3

In the eighteenth century, the use of the shorter form seems to have increased, the -*ic* form actually being more frequent than *philosophical* in the *Literature Online* texts from the latter half of the century. In addition to being used in the classifying sense 'relating to philosophy or philosophers' (e.g. *philosophic(al) research/scholar*), the adjectives were also used in the descriptive sense 'calm', 'wise', or 'contemplative' (as in *philosophic(al) serenity/temper*). *Philosophic* was slightly more common than *philosophical* in the descriptive sense, but perhaps not to such an extent as to suggest a major semantic division between the two forms.

Attempting to discover patterns of differentiation between forms in -*ic* and -*ical*, Fowler (1926) s.v. *philosophic(al)* claimed that *philosophic* was the form preferred in "all the more specific senses", i.e. relating to (the study) of philosophy, while the longer form remained in use in the descriptive senses (see also Zandvoort 1948, §912). However, the historical corpora do not lend support to this observation. In fact, in the non-fiction texts studied, most of the occurrences of the adjectives related to the scientific aspects of philosophy, and *philosophical* was the preferred form at all times. In the fictional texts studied, after the latter half of the eighteenth century, the use of *philosophical* only appears to have increased compared to that of the form in -*ic*. One difference concerns the predicative uses: in the texts published between 1850 and 1903, six instances of *philosophic* were found in a predicative position, while *philosophical* was used predicatively on 23 occasions. As to the present-day situation, Fowler's outline of the use of the two forms – which he regarded as giving "a [further] basis for differentiation" – evidently did not come to fruition. The shorter form is considerably rarer than the longer one. In the 1995 issues of *The Daily Telegraph*, only ten occurrences of *philosophic* were found, as opposed to 266 occurrences of *philosophical* (in the *BNC*, the corresponding figures are 64 and 1288, respectively). The few instances of *philosophic* in the *DTL* material included both classifying and descriptive cases.[17] It therefore appears justifiable to place *philosophic/philosophical* in the column of those adjective pairs ending in *-ic/-ical* where usage is showing a tilt towards a preference for the longer form, without prominent semantic differentiation. This is also the view held by present-day lexicographers: in e.g. *LDEL* (1991) and *NODE* (1998), *philosophic* is given as an alternative adjective form under the entry for *philosophical*.

3.   General remarks

It is interesting to note that a greater number of relevant adjective pairs studied manifest a shift in favour of the shorter form. In the case of twenty adjective pairs, the competition between the two forms has resulted in either a complete attrition of the form in *-ical*, or at least a clear preference for the form in *-ic*. In contrast, only eight adjective pairs – i.e. *heretic/heretical, hysteric/hysterical, fanatic/fanatical, mechanic/mechanical, philosophic/philosophical, satiric/satirical, theoretic/theoretical*, and *tyrannic/tyrannical* – showed variation between the forms in *-ic* and *-ical* in earlier centuries with the result of the longer form being nowadays favoured. These figures as such could be interpreted as reflecting a greater overall tendency to prefer the forms in *-ic*. This would also parallel the overwhelming difference in the total numbers of adjectival coinages ending in *-ic* and *-ical*, observed in Chapter 4.

   As the collection of non-fiction texts studied was considerably smaller in size than the *Literature Online* prose material, the number of adjective pairs meeting the "analysability" level was naturally also smaller. It must be emphasized, however, that the smaller numbers of occurrences for the non-fiction corpus were usually in line with those for the fiction corpus. It is nevertheless possible that examination of a larger set of non-fictional texts – or large corpora of different types of non-fictional texts – would reveal historical shifts in the use of other *-ic/-ical* adjectives (e.g. relating to different fields of science), and the relation between those pairs showing a shift towards the *-ic* form and those showing a shift towards *-ical* could be different.

   As observed earlier in this chapter, it is possible to perceive semantically coherent groups of *-ic/-ical* pairs, such as terms relating to works of fiction (e.g.

---

17   The comments made by Burchfield (1996) s.v. *philosophic(al)* feature a distant echo of Fowler's original ideas, as he makes a specific point on *philosophical* being the preferred form in the sense of 'calm', as in "he took a philosophical view of [some setback]". Considering the uses of the adjectives in the *BNC* and the *DTL*, it would appear simpler to merely note that *philosophical* is the preferred form in all senses. After all, the use of *philosophic* in the descriptive sense, although rare compared to *philosophical*, is by no means awkward, as in "Whilst learning to take the rough and the smooth of rugby fortunes with a philosophic air, Townsend has already reacted to criticism with refinements to his play that have been a factor in his selection for Australia" (*BNC*, CKA 1156).

comic/comical, *dramatic/dramatical*, *epic/epical*, *farcic/farcical*, *poetic/poetical*, and *tragic/tragical*). However, the behaviour of these pairs is not always identical, and one often finds exceptions to the pattern that would appear to dominate. Where there are nominal uses of the shorter form, the pairs differ as to the preferred adjective form. For example, even though *academic*, *domestic*, *epidemic*, and *rustic* are prominently used as nouns, the adjectival uses of the forms in -*ic* have prevailed, while the opposite can be observed in the case of *hysteric*, *heretic*, *fanatic*, and *mechanic*.[18] As regards the meanings of the relevant nouns in -*ic*, with the exception of *epidemic*, all denote persons.

---

18   One is rather tempted, however, to point out that as many as four of the eight adjectives showing a shift towards the use of the -*ical* forms were ones where the -*ic* form has a nominal function.

Chapter 12

Some special cases

In addition to the six *-ic/-ical* pairs discussed in detail in Chapters 5–10, there are other pairs ending in *-ic/-ical* which today show semantic differentiation. The present chapter looks into the developments in the use of four such pairs, namely *diabolic/diabolical*, *fantastic/fantastical*, *optic/optical*, and *politic/political*.[1] Although sharp lines of differentiation can be observed in the uses of the two forms, these pairs are perhaps not as central to the average language user as *classic/classical*, *comic/comical*, *economic/economical*, *electric/electrical*, *historic/historical*, and *magic/magical*. The latter six pairs have a higher relative frequency of both forms in almost any corpus of present-day English. In fact, one feature peculiar to the four pairs to be discussed in the present chapter is that one of the forms has become considerably rarer than the other. In some cases, one might entertain the idea that the tendencies of semantic differentiation and deletion of one of the forms have here merged to some extent. Possibly because of the rareness of one of the forms, many usage manuals often do not include entries for the four *-ic/-ical* pairs.

As far as *-ic/-ical* adjective pairs are concerned in general, the role of *diabolic/diabolical*, *fantastic/fantastical*, *optic/optical*, and *politic/political* is by no means insignificant. In fact, the use of *politic/political* was singled out by Fowler (1926) s.v. *-ic, -ical*, who considered the pair to represent "[t]he final stage of differentiation", which is only emphasized by the fact that the word stresses in the two adjectives fall on different syllables (i.e. *'politic* and *po'litical*). The use of *politic/political* in present-day English shows that there is indeed little overlap between the two forms. With the exception of the fixed phrase *body politic* (which basically means the same as *political body*), the shorter form is used in the descriptive sense 'sensible', 'prudent', or 'skilful': "It is not always politic to disagree with England's craggy manager among whose many attributes is an acid tongue" (*The Daily Telegraph*, Feb. 18, 1995, "Rugby Union: Wales out to expose weaknesses in England armour").[2] *Political*, on the other hand,

---

1   There are, of course, even more *-ic/-ical* pairs where semantic differentiation is observed in present-day English, for example *graphic/graphical*. Although different corpora of present-day English do include numerous instances of such adjective pairs, many of them were relatively rare in the historical corpora examined. Therefore the discussion in the present study concentrates on those pairs which were represented in both the historical and the present-day corpora.

2   Some senses carried by *politic* have a negative shade, such as 'scheming' or 'devious'. These kind of instances were rare in the corpora examined; in the present-day materials, *politic* mostly had a positive loading. Furthermore, as in the *DTL* example quoted, many instances of *politic* today occur in a predicative position.

nowadays carries the classifying senses which can be paraphrased as 'relating to (the running of) the government or public affairs of a country' and 'relating to politics'. Of the two forms, *politic* entered the language first, and according to the *OED*, it used to carry both descriptive and classifying senses. The first recorded instances of the shorter form in the *OED* date from the fifteenth century, while the longer form is first attested in the sixteenth century. In the sixteenth century texts studied, altogether 62 instances of *politic* were found (in texts by 24 authors), most of them having the descriptive sense 'cunning' or 'sensible'. A good ten instances carried the classifying meaning 'civic' or 'relating to public affairs or politics' (including the phrase *body politic*). In contrast, the texts from this period included no instances of *political*. The longer form first appears in the seventeenth century material, and interestingly enough, most of the occurrences have to do with the classifying sense, with only a few instances having the descriptive meaning 'wise, prudent'. During this period, *politic* was still used in both the descriptive and classifying senses (more frequently in the former), and in the eighteenth century, the semantic division between the two forms along the lines of descriptive versus classifying became even sharper.

What is fascinating about the use of *politic/political* is that the shorter form is nowadays quite rare. In the 1995 issues of *The Daily Telegraph*, only 23 occurrences of *politic* were found, 16 of them in the fixed phrase *body politic*. The remaining seven instances carried the sense 'wise, prudent'. *Political*, on the other hand, is today one of the most frequently used words ending in *-ical* (with 10487 instances in the 1995 *DTL* CD-ROM). One could therefore argue that *politic/political* manifests both semantic differentiation and signs of one of the forms becoming rare, albeit perhaps not entirely obsolete. Other pairs showing the effects of both tendencies include *diabolic/diabolical* and *fantastic/fantastical*. However, these pairs differ from *politic/political* in that, judging from the historical corpora, one of the forms became weaker first, and then, at a relatively late stage, a new sense was assigned exclusively to the already more frequent form, while the less frequent form continued to be used in the older senses.

As regards *fantastic/fantastical*, the historical texts examined show no remarkable difference between the meanings carried by the two forms. Both forms are found in the senses 'imaginary', '(irrationally) fanciful', and 'characterised by fantasy or extravagance', as in the following examples:

(1)   a.   Her husband was a poor-spirited Fellow, which gave us the more leisure to make him a Cuckold. One day he observ'd his wife walking at her Country House in my Cloaths, which sometimes in a fantastic humor she would put on; he conjectur'd that I had let her know where I laid my Cloaths, and that I had given admission to the person that wore my Habit; and thence he began to conceive in his mind the Spoils that I had won by triumphing over his Honour: [...] (Charles Gildon, *The Post-boy rob'd of his Mail* (1692), 307)

b. Who, and what were his Parents and Relations, and the manner of his Education, his small Encouragements to Learning, and his great Inclination to read Books of Knight Errantry, of which he gives some particular account, and what fantastical humours they raised in him. (Francis Kirkman, *The Unlucky Citizen* (1673), 26)

c. The Maypole – by which term from henceforth is meant the house, and not its sign – the Maypole was an old building, with more gable ends than a lazy man would care to count on a sunny day; huge zig-zag chimneys, out of which it seems as though even smoke could not choose but come in more than naturally fantastic shapes, imparted to it in its natural progress; and vast stables, gloomy, ruinous and empty. (Charles Dickens, *Barnaby Rudge* (1840), 229–230)

d. The broad outer moat was dry and grassgrown, and the laden trees of the orchard hung over it with gnarled straggling branches that drew fantastical patterns upon the green slope. (M.E. Braddon, *Lady Audley's Secret* (1862), 6)

The definitions and citations for these adjectives in the *OED* give a very similar impression of their use in earlier centuries; in fact, many of the definitions listed for *fantastical* contain a mere cross-reference to those found under *fantastic*. As can be observed from Table 95, the occurrences of the adjectives in the *Literature Online* material show that *fantastic* became more frequent than the longer form, a development clearly visible in the texts from the late eighteenth century onwards.

Table 95. The numbers of occurrences of *fantastic/fantastical* in the prose section of *Literature Online*.

	fantastic	*fantastical*	number of authors using both forms
1550–1599	1 (1)	42 (16)	-
1600–1649	7 (5)	9 (7)	1
1650–1699	28 (13)	34 (10)	5
1700–1749	28 (4)	9 (5)	4
1750–1799	83 (17)	18 (9)	6
1800–1849	170 (23)	18 (8)	6
1850–1903	191 (41)	18 (8)	6

The table gives the numbers of occurrences of the adjectives in different fifty-year periods; the figures in parentheses denote the numbers of authors using the forms. Between 1550 and 1600, *fantastical* was used by a considerably greater number of authors, but in subsequent periods the use of *fantastic* appears to have increased. No sense seems to have been assigned exclusively to either form.

Instead, the change in preference from *fantastical* to *fantastic* affected all uses of the adjectives. A similar pattern in the occurrences of the adjectives was seen in the historical non-fiction texts examined.

Fantastic is also the more frequently used form in present-day English: the 1995 issues of *The Daily Telegraph* contain altogether 500 occurrences of *fantastic*, but only 38 occurrences of *fantastical*. One factor, however, which has a significant influence on the present-day figures is the use of *fantastic* for showing approval, as in *It was an absolutely fantastic performance*. This, nowadays perhaps the most prominent use of *fantastic*, came about during the twentieth century (the first recorded instance in the *OED* dating from 1938), and it appears to have been assigned only to the *-ic* form. *Fantastical* still survives in the older meanings 'incredible or fanciful' and 'characterised by lively imagination or fantasy', but *fantastic* is used in these meanings as well (roughly as often as *fantastical*), as in "They produced, at best, brilliantly and gaily coloured visions of monsters, fantastic animals, mothers, children, goblins and demons from Dutch and Scandinavian folk tales" (*The Daily Telegraph*, Dec. 9, 1995, "The Arts: When art took a new direction"). It therefore seems that the development of a new and eventually very popular use for the *-ic* form gave a new lease of life for *fantastical* in the older uses, for which it had, curiously enough, by then already become the less frequent form. On the other hand, because *fantastic* is still used in the same senses as *fantastical*, the destiny of the *-ical* form remains uncertain.

A pair resembling *fantastic/fantastical*, as far as the historical development of the forms is concerned, is *diabolic/diabolical*, except for the fact that with the latter pair, the *-ical* form is nowadays more common in everyday language. In the 1995 *DTL* material, only four instances of *diabolic* were found, as opposed to 65 of *diabolical*, and the corresponding figures in the *BNC* were 15 versus 110. The few occurrences of *diabolic* carry the senses 'pertaining to the devil' or 'devilish, evil', as in "It is an eye-catching portrait of twisted repression, but to my mind it fails to convey the essentially diabolic nature of Iago's negativity" (*BNC*, A1D 93). *Diabolical* is also used in this sense: "David Jones's production, ingeniously designed by Eileen Diss, never relaxes its grip and there is a splendidly unsettling soundtrack (Tom Lishman) featuring the whimpers and diabolical laughter of the inmates" (*The Daily Telegraph*, Aug. 24, 1995, "The Arts: Give the man an exploding cigar"). However, only *diabolical* is found in the sense 'disgraceful' or 'appalling', as in the following example:

(2)   'At the moment the whole system is a mess. The booking system is diabolical, only 40 per cent of people in the south-east know about the train service after all this time, their advertising is ill-conceived, the pricing structure does not allow discounts for corporate clients or frequent users. [...]' (*The Sunday Telegraph*, Oct. 29, 1995, "£200m rescue for struggling Channel train: Extra Treasury Cash to ease rail sale")

This use, labelled 'slang' in the *OED*, and in other dictionaries presented as informal and chiefly British English, developed in the twentieth century; the first citation in the *OED* dates from 1958. In the historical corpora, *diabolical* appears to have dominated over *diabolic* at all times, as seen from the figures for the *Literature Online* texts (Table 96). Both forms were used in the same meanings, with the *-ical* form nevertheless being more common in all senses.[3]

Table 96. The numbers of occurrences of *diabolic/diabolical* in the prose section of *Literature Online*.

	diabolic	*diabolical*	number of authors using both forms
1550–1599	-	-	-
1600–1649	-	18 (2)	-
1650–1699	1 (1)	13 (5)	-
1700–1749	2 (2)	22 (5)	-
1750–1799	2 (2)	68 (21)	2
1800–1849	1 (1)	81 (21)	1
1850–1903	16 (5)	81 (18)	4

In the same way as in connection with *fantastic/fantastical*, it is tempting to assume that the assignment of the most recent, popular use exclusively to the already more frequent form (*diabolical*) has resulted in the rarer form (*diabolic*) surviving, albeit only just, in the older senses.

As noted earlier, the relation between the semantic changes and frequency of use is in all likelihood remarkably different in the case of *politic/political* as opposed to *diabolic/diabolical* and *fantastic/fantastical*. The process of "dying out" of *politic* – if it is to be regarded as a genuinely ongoing process – began after the usage of the two forms had diverged. The decreasing use of the adjective is perhaps not primarily a result of the competition between *politic* and *political* at all, because *political* is not used in the sense assigned to *politic*. Instead, the decrease in the use of *politic* may simply be an independent process of a particular word gradually disappearing from common use, with alternative words or expressions (e.g. *wise, sound, effective*) being preferred in its place.

One rather peculiar pair, to a great extent conforming with the pattern in which the form ending in *-ic(s)* is reserved for the nominal, and *-ical* for the adjectival function, is *optic/optical*. As an adjective, *optic* seems to have been

---

3   When comparing the *OED*'s definitions for *diabolic* and *diabolical* to those for *fantastic* and *fantastical*, it is interesting to note that instead of cross-references to *diabolical* (the more common form), the glosses for *diabolic* are given in full, although they are practically identical to those given for the *-ical* form. In the case of *fantastic/fantastical*, the definitions of the rarer form (*fantastical*) involved mere cross-references to *fantastic*.

used earlier; the first citation of the shorter form in the *MED* dates from late fourteenth century, while *optical* has its first citation in the *OED* from 1570. However, although the nominal use of *optic(s)*, denoting the science of light and vision, has its beginnings in the late sixteenth century, in this period *optical* was not the dominant adjectival form, contrary to other -*ic*/-*ical* pairs where the form in -*ic* also had a nominal function denoting a branch of science. For example, as shown in Table 97, the seventeenth century non-fictional works studied include a greater number of authors using *optic* rather than *optical* as an adjective. In the *Literature Online* material, a similar tendency was observed, with eight authors in the seventeenth century using the adjective *optic*, but only one using *optical*. The shorter form was at first preferred in all senses of the pair, occurring in phrases such as *optic doctrine/glass/nerve/organ/perception/sense*. Quite interestingly, the nineteenth century texts witness a dramatic change in the use of the pair, with *optic* being used only when modifying the words *nerve* and *lens*, while *optical* was used with a variety of other head words, relating to both the scientific aspects of optics and the devices used therein, as well as to matters to do with vision in general (e.g. *optical illusion/instrument/ principles/science*).

Table 97.   The numbers of occurrences of *optic/optical* in the non-fiction texts studied.

	optic	*optical*	number of authors using both forms
1550–1599	2 (2)	-	-
1600–1649	1 (1)	-	-
1650–1699	55 (6)	1 (1)	-
1700–1749	12 (2)	1 (1)	-
1750–1799	2 (1)	1 (1)	-
1800–1849	11 (3)	40 (4)	2
1850–1903	2 (1)	12 (7)	1
1900–1949	-	2 (2)	-

The restriction of *optic* to only a few collocations can still be seen today. In the 1995 issues of *The Daily Telegraph*, the adjective *optic* occurred 18 times, eight of them in the fixed phrase *optic nerve*. A further eight cases had *optic* modifying the noun *fibre*. The latter collocation appears to manifest some variation in the use of the adjective form, as the phrase *optical fibre* was likewise found eight times (the adjective *optical* occurring 75 times in the material).[4] Interestingly, the shorter form is preferred in the corresponding compound adjective, i.e. *fibre-optic* (sometimes spelt without the hyphen). Definitions of *optic* in dictionaries suggest that it is the preferred form in relation to anatomy or medicine. In addition to the

---

4   In the *BNC* and the 1998 issues of *The Daily Telegraph*, however, *optical* appears to be notably more common than *optic* when modifying *fibre*.

phrase *optic nerve, NODE* (1998) gives separate entries to the phrases *optic chiasma/cup/disc/lobe/neuritis/tract*, while phrases containing *optical* defined separately in the dictionary mostly relate to physics or chemisty (e.g. *optical density/isomer/path/rotation*). The *BNC* also includes occurrences of anatomical or medical terms such as *optic atrophy/implant/lobe*, albeit only in a small number of texts. While the occurrences of *optic/optical* were not numerous enough to enable examination of the viability of *optic* in new phrases (most likely relating to anatomy or medicine), it would appear that the relation between the frequencies of *optic* and *optical* depends significantly on the subject matter.[5]

---

5   If it is the case that *optic* is no longer used in newly coined expressions – i.e. even in phrases relating to anatomy or medicine – the use of the adjective in a specific set of fixed (or "relic") phrases resembles the existing situation with *botanic/botanical*, where the shorter form mainly occurs in the phrase *botanic garden*.

Chapter 13

Concluding remarks

As was observed in Chapter 3, many of the general comments made by linguists on the use of adjective pairs in -ic/-ical appear somewhat unsatisfactory, mostly because of the numerous counterexamples to the tendencies proposed. In addition, the descriptions of the historical developments – both in general and as regards individual -ic/-ical pairs – have been notably inaccurate. Compared to earlier accounts on the subject, the major novelty in the present study is that the analyses are based on the examination of authentic instances of the words in large corpora of historical and present-day writings. The results from the corpora allow us to examine the validity of previously made statements and generalisations, and also to see whether other kinds of tendencies can be argued for. While it has already been noted in the analyses in the present study that there almost always tend to be some instances going against the observed tendency, the discussion that follows points out those generalisations which appear more justified than others.

Considering the overall tendencies in the entrance of new adjectives ending in -ic and -ical into the lexicon, the different sources and materials examined in the present study all provide similar results. As regards the present-day situation, the claims on the preference for -ic when forming new words seem perfectly justified: the first citations of adjectives in -ic and -ical indicate that the new adjectives in -ic in the twentieth century outnumber those in -ical by far. However, when it comes to the changes in the relative frequencies of new words ending in -ic and -ical through the centuries, a more detailed picture has been drawn here compared to earlier work. The citations for the adjectives in the *OED* show that the very first adjectives ending in -ic preceded those in -ical. Being basically anglicized versions of Latin or Greek adjectives ending in -icus and -ικος, the adjectives ending in -ic were in general more frequent than adjectives in -ical – the first instances of which were mainly adoptions of French adjectives in -ical – until the sixteenth century.

Interestingly, the sixteenth century was a period when new words ending in -ical became quite fashionable, and they were in general more frequent than those in -ic. According to the *OED*, many of these adjectives were formed by adding the suffix -al to the Latin and Greek adjectives in -icus and -ικος. In some cases, an adjective form in -ic was already in existence, but during this period, the corresponding new forms in -ical were generally more frequently used, as observed in the historical corpora. Also speaking of the sixteenth century as being the heyday for the forms in -ical are early English dictionaries from the late sixteenth century and early seventeenth century, which listed more adjectives ending in -ical than in -ic. Yet another factor supporting this diachronic outline, as noted in Chapter 4, was the number of rare items – the number of adjectives ending in -*ic* and -*ical* occurring only once – in the historical corpora. An examination of the numbers of the so-called *hapax legomena*, which have been considered to be indicative of the productivity of the morphological process that the words represent, showed that the sixteenth century materials included more hapax legomena in -*ical* than in -*ic*. It was observed, however, that instead of indicating changes in the productivity of the suffixes -*ic* and -*ical* as fully-fledged English suffixes, the analyses rather reflect the overall popularity of adjectival neologisms in -*ic* and -*ical*. This is simply because in many cases it is almost impossible to determine conclusively whether a word in -*ic* or -*ical* was an English formation or an adopted word (or, in the case of adjectives in -*ic*, even a shortening of the -*ical* form).

The relation between the numbers of neologisms ending in -*ic* and -*ical* began to change during the seventeenth century, with the adjectives in -*ic* gaining ground. This new development was also reflected in the use of the already existing lexemes. Based on the historical corpora, many of the once fashionable and dominant forms in -*ical* started to become less fashionable compared to their rivals in -*ic*, as in the case of *domestic/domestical, heroic/heroical, majestic/majestical*, and *rustic/rustical*. Similar changes occurred in the subsequent centuries in connection with a number of other -*ic*/-*ical* pairs, e.g. *angelic/angelical, democratic/democratical, ironic/ironical*, and *poetic/poetical*. One should emphasise, however, the gradual nature of the weakening of the forms in -*ical*, as regards both the word-formational level and the subsequent use of the words which had a competing form in -*ic*. In fact, new words ending in -*ical* still kept entering the lexicon whilst the competition between adjectives -*ic* and -*ical* was leading towards the ousting of several -*ical* forms. The change, in other words, was not drastic or sudden, nor did it affect all adjectives in -*ical*. In some cases the -*ical* forms remained vital, and the forms in -*ic* disappeared from use instead (e.g. *theoretic/theoretical, tyrannic/tyrannical*).

There are, as one would expect, some relatively low-frequency adjective pairs not examined here in greater detail where the competition still has not resulted in a clear preference for either of the forms. For example, the adjectives *pedagogic* and *pedagogical* both occur with roughly equal frequencies in the corpora of present-day English, with no apparent pattern governing the choice between the two. The very fact that the adjectives are not commonly used in everyday language probably also explains why variation still exists between the two forms. In other words, the more clearly one can observe variation between alternate forms, the more an natural impetus there will be to strive towards consistency in their use.

It nevertheless appears that the shift in preference for the forms in -*ic* as a process of language change has been on the whole stronger than than the tendency to favour the -*ical* forms. This becomes evident from the examination of those instances where competition between adjectives in -*ic* and -*ical* was most prominent in the historical corpora: a greater number of cases resulted in the obsolescence or considerable weakening of the form in -*ical*. It is true that some degree of variation has existed between several other -*ic*/-*ical* pairs in addition to the most frequently occurring ones investigated here, and the rivalry has in some cases resulted in a clear preference for the form in *-ic* (e.g. *gigantic*, *public*, *romantic*) or *-ical* (e.g. *mathematical*, *technical*, *typical*). Although the changes in the use of all the pairs in *-ic/-ical* have not been entirely uniform, linguists have nevertheless attempted to find at least some common features in the words manifesting a preference for either form. And there are indeed reasons to believe that in many instances the shift in preference for the form in *-ic* or *-ical* has affected particular groups of adjectives more or less consistently. Based on the *OED* entries and the historical corpora, the group showing the strongest uniformity in this respect are adjectives formed from names of people or places (e.g. *Aristotelic*, *Byronic*, *Icelandic*), typically denoting a relation to the person or place in question, or to the language spoken in the area referred to. This is also the group that has been most often singled out in grammar books and usage manuals discussing the *-ic* and *-ical* adjectives. Adjectives relating to sciences are an interesting group in that the older ones seem to show a preference for the form in *-ical* (e.g. *chemical*, *logical*, *mathematical*, and *physical*), while formations from the nineteenth century onwards favour the *-ic* form (e.g. *linguistic*, *phonetic*).

A number of adjectives also seem to conform with Elphinston's (1765; 1790) early theory, according to which words denoting something characteristically 'solemn', graceful, or powerful tend to favour the *-ic* form (e.g. *angelic*, *heroic*, *majestic*, *prophetic*, *seraphic*). However, as observed in Chapter 11, there are many other adjective pairs where a shift from *-ical* to *-ic* was noted during the same period, raising the question whether or not the shift genuinely affected the "solemn" adjectives or the adjectives derived from proper nouns as a distinct group. There are some additional cases where one would like to perceive groups of adjectives sharing certain semantic components and behaving in the same manner in their choice between the forms in *-ic* and *-ical*. However, one sooner or later encounters notable exceptions to the pattern. For example, all adjectives relating to forms of government or to literary genres "unfortunately" do not select the *-ic* or *-ical* ending in a similar fashion. The study of possible patterns, and the timing of the shifts of potential groups of adjectives, are questions which could be explored further through a detailed examination of both the *OED* and even larger historical corpora.

Six semantically differentiated *-ic/-ical* pairs were studied in greater detail. It was seen that in many cases the choice between the two forms involves rather fine semantic nuances, and there is thus a need for descriptions of the principles used in placing the individual occurrences of the words into different semantic categories. A particularly interesting finding concerns the different ways in which the two forms were distinguished. In most instances, the two forms themselves have clearly different senses. For example, while *historic* is most often used of events or things regarded as important or significant from the viewpoint of history, *historical* can have a neutral application, merely denoting the viewpoint of history, or, more specifically, emphasizing the authenticity of a referent's existence in the past. In other cases, however, the choice of the form depends to some extent on the collocating word. *Electric* and *electrical* can both be used of things that are powered by electricity, but *electric* is more often used in connection with terms of a greater specificity (e.g. *kettle*, *iron*, *toothbrush*), while *electrical* modifies superordinate terms such as *appliances* and *devices*. Some signs of collocational selection were also seen with *magic/magical*; the examination of further *-ic/-ical* pairs might shed more light on whether differentiation along these lines is a relatively recent feature.

As for the wider developments in the use of semantically differentiated pairs, some of the previous generalisations proved to be clearly unsatisfactory. As noted in Chapter 3, it has been argued by e.g. Schibsbye (1970) that semantically differentiated pairs show a degree of regularity as regards the adjectival functions of the forms, with the forms in *-ic* being more typically classifiers, the longer forms having a descriptive meaning. That argument did not find much support in the present study. The most notable "chiastic" examples in this respect are *economic/economical* and *historic/historical*: in the former pair, the shorter form carries the classifying sense, while in the latter, this function is assigned first and foremost to the longer form.[1]

There are grounds, however, for making a case for a general shift in favour of the shorter forms in connection with semantically differentiated pairs as well as with those pairs which have a clear preference for one of the forms. A comment to this effect was already made by Ross (1998: 42–43), who pointed out certain individual instances where the longer forms may be losing ground, i.e. cases where the shorter forms are increasingly found, and which go against the basic differentiation between the two forms said to exist today. The present corpus-based study into the changes in the use of the pairs, stretching as it does to the very early history of the words in question, gives rise to an observation of a notable increase in the use of the shorter forms. The tendency to favour the shorter form for conveying new senses also explains the eventual "chiasmus" in the assignment of the classifying and descriptive senses in the pairs

---

1   In his study of a number of *-ic/-ical* pairs, Marsden (1985) observed that the pairs behaved differently as regards the assignment of value judgement, the notion of resemblance, and the ability to occur in a predicative position. Since these features can be linked with the general distinction between classifying and descriptive senses, Marsden's findings basically confirms the observation that the forms in *-ic* and *-ical* may carry different kinds of senses from one pair to another. Considering the ability of an adjective to occur in a predicative position, this does not in general appear to have played a particularly important role in distinguishing between the uses of the two forms. In fact, the numbers of predicative instances in the material studied were rather low. As could be expected, the ability to occur in a predicative position is greater when the adjective describes rather than classifies. However, as observed in Chapter 11, some interesting differences in the predicative uses were seen when the forms in *-ic* and *-ical* were more or less synonymous: the nineteenth century texts examined contained a larger number of predicative instances of *ironical*, *poetical*, and *satirical*. Further study might provide more detailed information on whether one can perceive a more general tendency to prefer predicative forms in *-ical* in this period.

economic/economical and *historic/historical*. Considering *economic/economical*, the longer form used to be the dominant one until the introduction of a new sense, namely 'relating to the economy and management of wealth and other resources', which as a classifying sense contrasted with the descriptive meaning 'frugal, sparing'. Although the new sense was at first assigned to both forms, and the occurrences of *economical* even outnumbered those of *economic*, the shorter form eventually came to be the form carrying this meaning, with only a few exceptions. A similar change can be seen in connection with *historic/historical*: *historical* was initially the prevalent form, but the more recent meaning 'important in history' was, in the end, assigned to the shorter form. Yet another example is the assignment of the figurative use ultimately to *electric* instead of *electrical*. The analysis of the uses of *classic/classical* might be more difficult in this respect, because many of the senses are closely related to one another, but even in this case one could present the increasing use of *classic* in the sense of 'typical' as a relatively recent sense assigned to the shorter form. The changes in the uses of *comic/comical* and *magic/magical* do not provide notable instances in support of this idea, perhaps because the major classifying and descriptive senses were already in existence in the early stages of the adjectives' history.[2] The pair *diabolic/diabolical* actually seems to go against this observation, as the more recently developed sense 'disgraceful' or 'appalling' appears to have been assigned only to the longer form. This new sense, however, did not drastically differ from the previously existing senses as far as the distinction between classifying versus descriptive meanings is concerned, because the adjectives were already used in a classifying ('pertaining to the devil') and a descriptive sense ('devilish', 'wicked', 'malevolent'). It could be argued then that the new sense 'disgraceful' did not have so great a potential to semantically distinguish between *diabolic* and *diabolical* as the sense 'important in history' had in the case of *historic* and *historical*. One might suggest that in cases where a novel use of an adjective in -*ic*/-*ical* radically differed from the earlier uses, the sense in question was finally more often assigned to the shorter form. The examination into the historical developments of other semantically differentiated pairs, e.g. *graphic/graphical*, *mystic/mystical*, and *mythic/mythical*, would probably bring more light on the matter.

What predictions could we then make on the future developments in the use of adjective pairs ending in -*ic*/-*ical*? Based on some of the main observations made here, it could be argued that the major trend seems to favour the shorter forms. The most vulnerable cases are probably ones where the two competing

---

2   The idea does not quite seem to fit in with the developments of *politic/political*, either. However, the increase in the use of *political* was not linked to the introduction of the classifying sense it now carries, since the sense was already carried by the shorter form even before *political* entered the lexicon. One reason for *political* taking over the classifying sense ('relating to the government or public affairs of a country') may have been the use of the noun *politics* for "the art of government" in the sixteenth century, conforming to the pattern with scientific terms.

forms show no clear lines of differentiation. As for semantically differentiated pairs, the survival of the longer form depends to a large extent on the overall viability of the division of the senses between the two forms. The divergence of the senses obviously has to be sufficiently "perceivable" with little or no overlap, enabling the distribution of meaning between the two forms to gradually establish itself. Another essential factor is the existence of a reasonable need for the individual senses to be expressed by means of a separate lexeme. *Comical*, used particularly in contexts which suggest unintentionality of the humorous element, may be slowly disappearing from the lexicon because the more widely used adjective *comic* is also used in these kinds of contexts, and, as a result, conveys exactly the same meaning. When it comes to the semantically differentiated pairs examined in the present study, however, it does not seem that other forms in *-ical* besides *comical* are on the verge of becoming archaic.

Considering the materials used for purposes of the study, the examination of different sources – the second edition of the *OED*, the early English dictionaries in *EMEDD*, and the historical corpora – provide results which are remarkably similar to one another, and thus made possible the presentation of the overall developments in the occurrence and use of adjectives ending in *-ic* and *-ical*. The correspondence of the results is encouraging in the light of some of the doubts raised about the reliability and useability of the *OED*. While the concerns are undoubtedly justified, and call for a number of improvements (which are likely to be seen in the third edition of the dictionary), it is worth acknowledging the dictionary's value as a source of information (see also Bauer 2001: 156–157). One area where the dictionary was found lacking, however, was the definitions of the adjectives. When mirrored against the analysis of authentic examples of individual *-ic/-ical* adjectives in the corpora, an examination of the definitions of the adjectives – particularly the six main semantically differentiated *-ic/-ical* pairs – showed that a number of improvements could be made as regards the organisation and presentation of the different senses. The use of cross-references between the two forms could be made considerably more logical and consistent. Because of the occasionally rather confusing arrangement of all the information included, the entries are often not very helpful. This is especially true if one attempts to form a picture of the relation between the competing *-ic* and *-ical* forms, from either the diachronic or the synchronic point of view. The more recent dictionaries naturally fare rather well in their portrayal of the present-day situation; however, one might wish for more detailed information on the extent of interchangeability of the two forms, for which corpus analysis provides efficient means. Most of the usage manuals examined present a relatively accurate picture of the main differences that exist today between the most prominently differentiated pairs in *-ic/-ical*. The more recent works also aptly mention that some overlap may exist between the two forms. In general, given the main goals and the more or less normative nature of usage manuals, there is no need to criticize them very strongly for their occasional omissions or inaccuracies. However, Fowler (1926) is an interesting case with its explicitly stated call for clearer lines of semantic differentiation between the forms in *-ic* and *-ical* in many instances. Interestingly enough, not all the distinctions Fowler envisaged or promoted have materialized in real life.

While one still perhaps has to agree with Labov's (1994: 11) well-known assertion that historical linguistics is in reality very much "the art of making the best use of bad data", the large size of the historical corpora now available has opened up possibilities for research into linguistic processes which have previously been very difficult to examine. The study of lexical competition between adjective forms in -ic and -ical through times, particularly in conjunction with the study of the entrance of words carrying these endings in general into the lexicon, is definitely a field of research which benefits significantly from such corpora. The results are thus encouraging considering future work on the productivity of competing word-formational patterns examined together with the developments in the rivalry of the lexemes produced by these patterns. This is especially true for cases where the words can be clearly seen as English coinages, not loan words or items introduced by means other than derivation. Such studies would provide a significant addition to the study and understanding of the nature of competition in language in general. However, there is definitely room for further improvement as regards the corpora available to linguists today. As regards the study of adjectives ending in -ic/-ical, ever larger collections of texts would obviously enable a detailed examination of a greater number of adjective pairs, which would add to the overall picture to be drawn on the uses of the pairs. Some theories proposed in the present study, such as the role of prefixation in the use of -ic/-ical adjectives, would still require the examination of larger corpora to be validated. Another very important issue is the variety of different types of texts represented in a corpus. Larger collections of texts of different kinds would, in the future, enable more detailed investigations into possible genre-related differences in lexical usage.

Corpus linguistics, in recent years, has made great strides and provided lexicologists and lexicographers with research tools that earlier could only be dreamt of. The present study has, I believe, shown that by examining the historical and present-day corpora available, important new light can be shed on complex issues relating to English vocabulary and word-formation. Nevertheless, as pointed out above, even in the examination of the -ic and -ical forms, there is still room for more work which would benefit from further developments in corpus design, as well as the methods of examining corpora. As has been observed in the course of our investigation here, one is perhaps well advised to remember that no corpus (nor a dictionary or a usage manual) will ever be developed into such perfection that it would merit being examined alone as "the only trustworthy source". There will always be some limitations to the scope of corpus analysis as a tool to study language use, just as there are shortcomings with other sources and methods. The progress in the field has made the study of corpora increasingly more useful, and it appears that the future developments will make it an even more valuable piece in the linguists' toolbox.

References

Primary sources

A. The corpora and collections of texts examined

British National Corpus, World Edition. Oxford: Oxford University Computing Services. (*BNC*)

Century of Prose Corpus. (1990) Cleveland: Department of English, Cleveland State University.

Chadwyck-Healey Literature Online. (1996–2002). Cambridge: Chadwyck-Healey Limited. http://lion.chadwyck.co.uk. (*LION*)

Corpus of Early English Medical Writing, being compiled by I. Taavitsainen and P. Pahta (University of Helsinki).

A Corpus of Nineteenth Century English, being compiled by M. Kytö (Uppsala University) and J. Rudanko (University of Tampere).

The Daily Telegraph/The Sunday Telegraph on CD-ROM, 1 January 1993 – 31 December 1993. (1994) Database copyright The Telegraph Plc, software by Personal Library Software Inc. Cambridge: Chadwyck-Healey.

The Daily Telegraph/The Sunday Telegraph on CD-ROM, 1 January 1994 – 31 December 1994. (1995) Database copyright The Telegraph Plc, software by Personal Library Software Inc. Cambridge: Chadwyck-Healey.

The Daily Telegraph/The Sunday Telegraph on CD-ROM, 1 January 1995 – 31 December 1995. (1996) Database copyright The Telegraph Plc, software by Personal Library Software Inc. Cambridge: Chadwyck-Healey.

The Daily Telegraph/The Sunday Telegraph on CD-ROM, 1 January 1996 – 31 December 1996. (1997) Database copyright The Telegraph Plc, software by Personal Library Software Inc. Cambridge: Chadwyck-Healey.

The Daily Telegraph/The Sunday Telegraph on CD-ROM, 1 January 1997 – 31 December 1997. (1998) Database copyright The Telegraph Plc, software by Personal Library Software Inc. Cambridge: Chadwyck-Healey.

The Daily Telegraph/The Sunday Telegraph on CD-ROM, 1 January 1998 – 31 December 1998. (1999) Database copyright The Telegraph Plc, software by Personal Library Software Inc. Cambridge: Chadwyck-Healey.

The Daily Telegraph/The Sunday Telegraph on CD-ROM, 1 January 1999 – 30 June 1999. (1999) Database copyright The Telegraph Plc, software by Personal Library Software Inc. Cambridge: Chadwyck-Healey.

Helsinki Corpus = The Helsinki Corpus of English Texts: Diachronic Part. (1991) Helsinki: Department of English, University of Helsinki.

The Washington Post Ondisc. (1998) Articles of *The Washington Post* (January 1994 – December 1994) copyright 1996, software ProQuest Searchware, version 5.10, copyright 1998. UMI Company.

B. The non-fiction texts compiled from the Internet

(Note: Some of the texts gleaned from the Internet were presented in several parts, e.g. with each chapter of a book having its own URL address. Unless otherwise noted below, all parts of the original works were included in the study. Instead of listing all web addresses of a particular text, the list below includes the addresses either to the index page of an electronic edition of a text – with links to the different parts of the text – or to the first part of the electronic edition.)

Abbott, A.H. (1900) "Experimental psychology and the laboratory in Toronto", in *University of Toronto Monthly*, 1, pp. 85–98, 106–112. Electronic version located at http://psychclassics.yorku.ca/Abbott; retrieved Dec. 15, 2000.

Adriance, V. (1901) "Premature Infants", in *American Journal of the Medical Sciences*, 121, pp. 410–421. Electronic version located at http://www.neonatology.org/classics/adriance.html; retrieved Dec. 14, 2000.

Aikin, L. (1810) *Epistles on Women*. London: Printed for J. Johnson and Co. Electronic version located at http://www.lib.ucdavis.edu/English/BWRP/Works/AikiLEpist.sgm; retrieved Feb. 7, 2001.

Aletheia, M.D. (1897) *The Rationalist's Manual*. London: Watts & Co. Electronic version located at http://www.infidels.org/library/historical/m_d_aletheia/rationalists_manual. html; retrieved Dec. 15, 2000.

Allport, F.H. and Allport, G.W. (1921) "Personality traits: Their classification and measurement", in *Journal of Abnormal and Social Psychology*, 16, pp. 6–40. Electronic version located at http://psychclassics.yorku.ca/Allport/Traits; retrieved May 18, 2001.

Allport, G.W. (1927) "Concepts of trait and personality", in *Psychological Bulletin*, 24, pp. 284–293. Electronic version located at http://psychclassics.yorku.ca/Allport/concepts.htm; retrieved May 18, 2001.

Allport, G.W. (1937) "The functional autonomy of motives", in *American Journal of Psychology*, 50, pp. 141–156. Electronic version located at http://psychclassics.yorku.ca/Allport/autonomy.htm; retrieved May 18, 2001.

Allport, G.W. (1940) "The psychologist's frame of reference", in *Psychological Bulletin*, 37, pp. 1–28. Electronic version located at http://psychclassics.yorku.ca/Allport/frame.htm; retrieved May 18, 2001.

Angell, J.R. (1907) "The province of functional psychology", in *Psychological Review*, 14, pp. 61–91. Electronic version located at http://psychclassics.yorku.ca/Angell/functional.htm; retrieved Feb. 1, 2001.

Anger, J. (1589) *Jane Anger Her Protection for Women*. London: Printed by R. Jones, and T. Orwin. STC 644. Electronic version located at the *Renaissance Women Online* web site, retrieved Oct. 7, 2001.

Anonymous. (1606) *A True and Perfect Relation of the Proceedings at the Severall Arraignments of the Late Most Barbarous Traitors*. London:

Printed by R. Barker. Electronic version located at http://e3.uci.edu/ ~papyri/garnet; retrieved Feb. 21, 2001.

Anonymous. (1619) *The Wonderful Discoverie of the Witchcrafts of Margaret and Phillip Flower*. London: Printed by G. Eld for I. Barnes. STC 11107. Electronic version located at the *Renaissance Women Online* web site, retrieved Oct. 7, 2001.

Anonymous. (1623) *Certaine Sermons or Homilies appointed to be read in Chvrches*. London: Printed by I. Bill. STC 13675. Electronic version located at http://www.library.utoronto.ca/utel/ret/homilies/elizhom.html; retrieved Jan. 25, 2001.

Anonymous. (1641) *The Arminian Nunnery*. London: Printed for Thomas Underhill. Electronic version located at http://www.inform.umd.edu/ EdRes/Colleges/ARHU/Depts/English/englfac/WPeterson/GIDDING/ arminian-nunnery.pdf; retrieved May 14, 2001.

Anonymous. (1677) *England's Great Happiness*. London: Printed by J.M. for E. Croft. Electronic version located at http://panoramix.univ-paris1.fr/ CHPE/textes.html; retrieved Jan. 23, 2001.

Arbuthnot, J. (1710) "An argument for Divine Providence", in *Philosophical Transactions*, 27, pp. 186–190. Electronic version located at http://panoramix.univ-paris1.fr/CHPE/Textes/Arbuthnot/Arbuthnot.html; retrieved Feb. 7, 2001.

Arnold, M. (1865) "The Function of Criticism at the Present Time", in *Essays in Criticism*. London and Cambridge: Macmillan and Co. pp. 1–41. Electronic version located at http://www.library.utoronto.ca/utel/rp/ criticism/funct_il.html; retrieved Jan. 31, 2001.

Ascham, R. (1570) *The Scholemaster*. London: Printed by I. Daye. Electronic version located at the *Renascence Editions* web site, http:// darkwing.uoregon.edu/~rbear/ascham1.htm; retrieved Dec. 13, 2000.

Astell, M. (1700) *Some Reflections Upon Marriage*. London: J. Nutt. Electronic version located at http://www.pinn.net/~sunshine/book-sum/astl_ mrg.html; retrieved Feb. 7, 2001.

Aston, F.W. (1919) "The Constitution of the Elements", in *Nature*, 104, p. 393. Electronic version located at http://webserver.lemoyne.edu/faculty/giunta/ aston.html; retrieved Jan. 26, 2001.

Aston, F.W. (1920) "Isotopes and Atomic Weights", in *Nature*, 105, p. 617. Electronic version located at http://dbhs.wvusd.k12.ca.us/Chem-History/Aston-MassSpec.html; retrieved Jan. 26, 2001.

Ayres, L.P. (1919) *The War with Germany: a Statistical Summary*. 2nd edition. Washington: Government Printing Office. Electronic version located at http://cepa.newschool.edu/het/index.htm, retrieved Nov. 24, 2000.

Bacon, F. (1625) *The Essayes or Covnsels, civill and morall*. London: Printed by I. Haviland for H. Barret. Electronic version located at http:// www.library.utoronto.ca/utel/criticism/baconf_ess/ess_titlepage.html; retrieved Jan. 30, 2001.

Bagehot, W. (1848) "Principles of Political Economy, with some of their applications to Social Philosophy. By J.S. Mill", in *The Prospective Review*, vol. IV, 16, pp. 460–502. Electronic version located at http://socserv2.socsci.mcmaster.ca/~econ/ugcm/3ll3/mill/bagehot.html; retrieved Nov. 24, 2000.

Baines, M.A. (1862) *Excessive Infant-Mortality: How Can It Be Stayed?* London: J. Churchill and Sons. Brighton: Printed by J. Farncombe. Electronic version located at http://www.neonatology.org/classics/baines.html; retrieved Dec. 14, 2000.

Banks, J. (1768-1771) *The Endeavour Journal of Joseph Banks, 25 August 1768-12 July 1771*. Original manuscript held the by Mitchell Library. Electronic version located at http://www.slnsw.gov.au/Banks/series_03/03_ start.htm; retrieved Feb. 13, 2001.

Barbauld, A.L. (1793) *Sins of Government, Sins of the Nation*. London: Printed for J. Johnson. Electronic version located at gopher://dept.english.upenn. edu/00/Courses/Curran551/barbsins; retrieved Feb. 23, 2001.

Barbon, N. (1690) *A Discourse of Trade*. London: Printed by T. Milbourn for the Author. Electronic version located at http://socserv2.socsci.mcmaster.ca/ ~econ/ugcm/3ll3/barbon/trade.txt; retrieved Dec. 1, 2000.

Barker, T. (1659) *Barker's Delight: or, The Art of Angling*. 2nd edition. London: Printed for H. Moseley. Electronic version located at the *Renascence Editions* web site, http://darkwing.uoregon.edu/~rbear/barker1.html; retrieved Aug. 28, 2001.

Bateson, G. (1941) "The Frustration-Aggression Hypothesis and Culture", in *Psychological Review*, 48, pp. 350–355. Electronic version located at http://psychclassics.yorku.ca/FrustAgg/bateson.htm; retrieved Oct. 23, 2001.

Belisle, D.W. (1859) *History of Independence Hall*. Philadelphia: J. Challen & Son. Electronic version located at http://www.libertynet.org/ardenpop/ apphall.html; retrieved Jan. 2, 2001.

Bellasis, G.H. (1815) *Views of Saint Helena*. London: Printed by J. Tyler. Electronic version located at http://www.telepath.com/bweaver/ bellasis/bellasis.htm; retrieved Feb. 13, 2001.

Bennett, E. (ca 1620) *A treatise divided into three parts, touching the inconveniences, that the Importation of Tobacco out of Spain, hath brought into this land*. STC 1883. Electronic version located at the *Renascence Editions* web site, http://darkwing.uoregon.edu/~rbear/tobacco.html; retrieved Jan. 24, 2001.

Bentham, J. (1776) *A Fragment on Government*. London: Printed for T. Payne, P. Emily, and E. Brooks. Electronic version located at http:// socserv2.socsci.mcmaster.ca/~econ/ugcm/3ll3/bentham/government.html; retrieved Dec. 1, 2000.

Bewick, T. (1826) *A History of British Birds. Vol. I* (excerpts from the beginning of the book through the section on "The Scops Eared Owl"). Sixth edition. Newcastle: Printed by E. Walker. Electronic version located at http://faculty.plattsburgh.edu/peter.friesen/default.asp?go=273;   retrieved Feb. 1, 2001.

Biddle, H. (1660) *A Warning from the Lord God of Life and Power*. London: Printed for R. Wilson. Wing B2866. Electronic version located at the *Renaissance Women Online* web site, retrieved Oct. 7, 2001.

Biddle, H. (1662) *The Trumpet of the Lord Sounded Forth Unto These Three Nations*. London: [s.n.]. Wing B2865. Electronic version located at the *Renaissance Women Online* web site, retrieved Oct. 7, 2001.

Bigelow, H.J. (1846) "Insensibility during surgical operations produced by inhalation", in *Boston Medical and Surgical Journal*, 35, pp. 309–317. Electronic version located at http://www.anes.uab.edu/aneshist/bigelow1.htm; retrieved Feb. 1, 2001.

Boole, G. (1848) "The Calculus of Logic", in *Cambridge and Dublin Mathematical Journal,* Vol. III, pp. 183–198. Electronic version located at http://www.maths.tcd.ie/pub/HistMath/People/Boole/CalcLogic/CalcLogic.html retrieved Jan. 26, 2001.

Boring, E.G. (1929) "The psychology of controversy", in *Psychological Review*, 36, pp. 97–121. Electronic version located at http://psychclassics.yorku.ca/Boring; retrieved May 18, 2001.

Boyle, R. (1661) *The Sceptical Chymist* (excerpts). London: Printed by J. Cadwell for J. Crooke. Electronic version located at http://webserver.lemoyne.edu/faculty/giunta/boylesc.html; retrieved Jan. 25, 2001. Checked against page images of the original edition at http://www.library.upenn.edu/etext/collections/science/boyle/chymist/index.html; retrieved Jan. 25, 2001.

Bradbury, J. (1819) *Travels in the Interior of America*. 2nd edition. London: Sherwood, Neely, and Jones. Electronic version located at http://www.xmission.com/~drudy/mtman/html/bradbury.html;   retrieved Feb. 23, 2001.

Bray, T. (1700) *A Memorial Representing the Present State of Religion, on the Continent of North-America*. London: Printed by W. Downing. Electronic version located at http://www.mun.ca/rels/ang/texts/bray.html; retrieved Feb. 13, 2001.

Breland, K. and M. Breland. (1961) "The misbehavior of organisms", in *American Psychologist*, 16, pp. 681–684. Electronic version located at http://psychclassics.yorku.ca/Breland/misbehavior.htm; retrieved May 18, 2001.

Browne, E. (1677) *An Account of Several Travels Through a great part of Germany*. London: Printed for B. Tooke. Electronic version located at http://penelope.uchicago.edu/travels/index.html; retrieved June 12, 2001.

Browne, T. (1643) *A true and full coppy of that which was most imperfectly and surreptitiously printed before vnder the name of Religio medici*. [London]: Printed for A. Crooke. Electronic version located at http://penelope.uchicago.edu/relmed/relmed.html; retrieved Feb. 13, 2001.

Browne, T. (1658) *Hydriotaphia, Urne-buriall, or, A Discourse of the Sepulchrall Urnes lately found in Norfolk. Together with The Garden of Cyrus.* London: Printed for H. Brome. Electronic version located at http://penelope.uchicago.edu/hydrionoframes/hydrion.html; retrieved Feb. 13, 2001.

Browne, T. (1690) *To a Friend, Upon occasion of the Death of his Intimate Friend.* British Museum (643 L.24 (6)). Electronic version, based on a facsimile edition published in 1924 as No. 1 of "The Hazelwood Reprints", London, located at http://penelope.uchicago.edu/letter/letter.html; retrieved Feb. 15, 2001.

Browne, T. (1713) *Christian Morals.* Cambridge: Printed at the University-Press for C. Crownfield. Electronic version located at http://penelope.uchicago.edu/cmorals/cmorals.shtml; retrieved Feb. 13, 2001.

Brownson, O.A. (1866) *The American Republic: Constitution, Tendencies, and Destiny.* New York: P. O'Shea. Electronic version located at http://www.execpc.com/~berrestr/broame.html; retrieved Feb. 6, 2001.

Bruner, J.S. and C.C. Goodman. (1947) "Value and Need as Organizing Factors in Perception", in *Journal of Abnormal and Social Psychology*, 42, pp. 33–44. Electronic version located at http://psychclassics.yorku.ca/Bruner/Value; retrieved May 18, 2001.

Bruner, J.S. and L. Postman. (1949) "On the Perception of Incongruity: A Paradigm", in *Journal of Personality*, 18, pp. 206–223. Electronic version located at http://psychclassics.yorku.ca/Bruner/Cards; retrieved May 18, 2001.

Buchner, E.F. (1903) "A quarter century of psychology in America: 1878–1903", in *American Journal of Psychology*, 14, pp. 666–680. Electronic version located at http://psychclassics.yorku.ca/Buchner/quarter.htm; retrieved May 18, 2001.

Bulfinch, T. (1913) *The Age of Fable.* New York: Review of Reviews. Electronic version located at http://www.bartleby.com/bulfinch; retrieved Dec. 13, 2000.

Bunyan, J. (1679) *A Treatise of the Fear of God.* London: Printed for N. Ponder. Electronic version located at http://www.mountzion.org/text/bun-fear.txt; retrieved Feb27, 2001. Checked against the page images of the original edition on the *Early English Books Online* web site, http://wwwlib.umi.com/eebo.

Burrough, E. (1656) *The True Faith of the Gospel of Peace Contended for.* London: Printed for G. Calvert. Electronic version located at http://www.voicenet.com/~kuenning/qhp/bunyan/contend1.html; retrieved Dec. 4, 2000.

Burrough, E. (1657) *Truth (the Strongest of all) Witnessed forth in the Spirit of Truth.* London: Printed for G. Calvert. Electronic version located at http://www.voicenet.com/~kuenning/qhp/bunyan/witness1.html; retrieved Dec. 4, 2000.

Bury, C.R. (1921) "Langmuir's Theory of the Arrangement of Electrons in Atoms and Molecules", in *Journal of the American Chemical Society*, Vol. 43, pp. 1602–1609. Electronic version located at http://dbhs.wvusd.k12.ca.us/Chem-History/Bury-1921.html; retrieved Jan. 25, 2001.

Cadogan, W. (1749) *An Essay upon Nursing and the Management of Children, from their Birth to Three Years of Age.* London: Printed for J. Roberts. Electronic version located at http://www.neonatology.org/classics/cadogan.html; retrieved Dec. 14, 2000.

Calkins, M.W. (1892) "Experimental Psychology at Wellesley College", in *American Journal of Psychology*, 5, pp. 464–471. Electronic version located at http://psychclassics.yorku.ca/Calkins/lab.htm; retrieved May 18, 2001.

Calkins, M.W. (1896) "Association: An essay analytic and experimental", in *Psychological Review Monographs Supplement*, 1 (2). Electronic version located at http://psychclassics.yorku.ca/Calkins/Assoc; retrieved May 18, 2001.

Calkins, M.W. (1906) "A reconciliation between structural and functional psychology", in *Psychological Review*, 8, pp. 61–81. Electronic version located at http://psychclassics.yorku.ca/Calkins/reconciliation.htm; retrieved May 18, 2001.

Calkins, M.W.. (1908) "Psychology as science of self. I: Is the self body Or has it body?", in *Journal of Philosophy, Psychology and Scientific Methods*, 5, pp. 12–20. Electronic version located at http://psychclassics.yorku.ca/Calkins/SciSelf/index1.htm; retrieved May 18, 2001.

Calkins, M.W. (1908) "Psychology as science of self. II: The nature of the self", in *Journal of Philosophy, Psychology and Scientific Methods*, 5, pp. 64–68. Electronic version located at http://psychclassics.yorku.ca/Calkins/SciSelf/ index2.htm; retrieved May 18, 2001.

Calkins, M.W. (1908) "Psychology as science of self. III: The Description of Consciousness", in *Journal of Philosophy, Psychology and Scientific Methods*, 5, pp. 113–122. Electronic version located at http://psychclassics.yorku.ca/Calkins/SciSelf/index3.htm; retrieved May 18, 2001.

Calkins, M.W. (1915) "The self in scientific psychology", in *American Journal of Psychology*, 26, pp. 495–524. Electronic version located at http://psychclassics.yorku.ca/Calkins/self.htm; retrieved May 18, 2001.

Campion, T. (1602) *Observations in the Art of English Poesie.* London: Printed by R. Field for A. Wise. Electronic version located at the *Renascence Editions* web site, http://darkwing.uoregon.edu/~rbear/poesie.html; retrieved Dec. 13, 2000.

Carew, R. (1614) "The Excellencie of the English tongue", in *Camden's Remains.* British Library MS Cott. F. xi, f. 265. Electronic version located at http://www.library.utoronto.ca/utel/rp/criticism/engli_il.html; retrieved Jan. 31, 2001.

Carleton, M. (1663) *The Case of Madam Mary Carleton*. London: Printed for S. Speed. Wing C586A. Electronic version located at the *Renaissance Women Online* web site, retrieved Oct. 7, 2001.

Cartwright, J. (1649) *The Petition of the Jewes*. London: Printed for G. Roberts. Wing C695. Electronic version located at the *Renaissance Women Online* web site, retrieved Oct. 7, 2001.

Cary, E. (1680) *The History of the Life, Reign, and Death of Edward II*. London: Printed by J.C. for C. Harper. Wing F313. Electronic version located at the *Renaissance Women Online* web site, retrieved Oct. 7, 2001.

Cary, E. (1680) *The History of the Most Unfortunate Prince King Edward II*. London: Printed by A.G. and J.P. Wing F314. Electronic version located at the *Renaissance Women Online* web site, retrieved Oct. 7, 2001.

Cary, Mary. (1651) *The Little Horns Doom & Downfall*. London: Printed for the Author. Wing C737. Electronic version located at the *Renaissance Women Online* web site, retrieved Oct. 7, 2001.

Cattell, J.M. (1886) "The time taken up by cerebral operations, Parts 1 & 2", in *Mind*, 11, pp. 220–242. Electronic version located at http://psychclassics.yorku.ca/Cattell/Time/part1-2.htm; retrieved May 21, 2001.

Cattell, J.M. (1886b) "The time taken up by cerebral operations, Part 3", in *Mind*, 11, pp. 377–392. Electronic version located at http://psychclassics.yorku.ca/Cattell/Time/part3.htm; retrieved May 21, 2001.

Cattell, J.M. (1887) "The time taken up by cerebral operations, Part 4", in *Mind*, 11, pp. 524–538. Electronic version located at http://psychclassics.yorku.ca/Cattell/Time/part4.htm; retrieved May 21, 2001.

Cattell, J.M. (1888) "The psychological laboratory at Leipsic", *Mind*, 13, pp. 37–51. Electronic version located at http://psychclassics.yorku.ca/Cattell/leipsic.htm; retrieved May 21, 2001.

Cattell, J.M. (1890) "Mental tests and measurements", in *Mind*, 15, pp. 373–381. Electronic version located at http://psychclassics.yorku.ca/Cattell/mental.htm; retrieved May 21, 2001.

Cattell, J.M. (1898) "The psychological laboratory", in *Psychological Review*, 5, pp. 655–658. Electronic version located at http://psychclassics.yorku.ca/Cattell/lab.htm; retrieved May 21, 2001.

Cattell, J.M. (1928) "Early psychological laboratories", in *Science*, 67, pp. 543–548. Electronic version located at http://psychclassics.yorku.ca/Cattell/earlylabs.htm; retrieved May 21, 2001.

Cattell, J.M. (1943) "Proposed Changes in the American Psychological Association", in *Psychological Review*, 50, pp. 61–64. Electronic version located at http://psychclassics.yorku.ca/Cattell/founding.htm; retrieved May 21, 2001.

Cavendish, H. (1785) "Experiments on Air", in *Philosophical Transactions* 75, p. 372. Electronic version located at http://webserver.lemoyne.edu/faculty/giunta/cavendish.html; retrieved Jan. 25, 2001 .

Cavendish, M. (1655) *The Worlds Olio*. Wing N873. London: Printed for J. Martin and J. Allestrye. Electronic version located at the *Renaissance Women Online* web site, retrieved Oct. 7, 2001.

Cavendish, M. (1666) *Observations upon Experimental Philosophy*. London: Printed by A. Maxwell. Wing N857. Electronic version located at the *Renaissance Women Online* web site, retrieved Oct. 7, 2001.

Cavendish, M. (1667) *The Life of the Thrice Noble, High and Puissant Prince William Cavendishe*. London: Printed by A. Maxwell. Wing N853. Electronic version located at the *Renaissance Women Online* web site, retrieved Oct. 7, 2001.

Cawdrey, R. (1604) *A Table Alphabeticall*. London: Printed by I. R. for E. Weauer. STC 4884. Electronic version located at http:// www.library.utoronto.ca/utel/ret/cawdrey/cawdrey0.html; retrieved Jan. 25, 2001.

Chadwick, J. (1932) "Possible Existence of a Neutron", in *Nature*, Feb. 27, p. 312. Electronic version located at http://dbhs.wvusd.k12.ca.us/Chem-History/Chadwick-neutron-letter.html; retrieved Jan. 26, 2001.

Chidley, K. (1641) *The Justification of the Independent Churches of Christ*. London: Printed for W. Larnar. Source copy owned by British Library. Wing C3832. Electronic version located at the *Renaissance Women Online* web site, retrieved Oct. 7, 2001.

Chidley, K. (1645) *Good Counsell, to the Petitioners for Presbyterian Government*. [London: s.n.]. Wing C3831. Electronic version located at the *Renaissance Women Online* web site, retrieved Oct. 7, 2001.

Chidley, K. (1645) *A New-Yeares-Gift*. [S.l.: s.n.]. Wing C3833. Electronic version located at the *Renaissance Women Online* web site, retrieved Oct. 7, 2001.

Child, J. (1668) *Brief Observations Concerning Trade and Interest of Money*. London: Printed for E. Calvert. Electronic version located at http:// socserv2.socsci.mcmaster.ca/~econ/ugcm/3ll3/child/trade.txt; retrieved Dec. 2, 2001.

Clark, J.B. (1895) "The Origin of Interest", in *Quarterly Journal of Economics*, volume 10, pp. 257–278. Electronic version located at http:// socserv2.socsci.mcmaster.ca/~econ/ugcm/3ll3/clarkjb/clarkjb003.html; retrieved Nov. 24, 2000.

Clark, K.B. and M.K. Clark. (1939) "The development of consciousness of self and the emergence of racial identification in negro preschool children", in *Journal of Social Psychology, S.P.S.S.I. Bulletin*, 10, pp. 591–599. Electronic version located at http://psychclassics.yorku.ca/Clark/Self-cons; retrieved May 22, 2001.

Clark, K.B. and M.K Clark. (1940) "Skin color as a factor in racial identification of negro preschool children", in *Journal of Social Psychology, S.P.S.S.I. Bulletin*, 11, pp. 159–169. Electronic version located at http://psychclassics.yorku.ca/Clark/Skin-color; retrieved May 22, 2001.

Clinton, E. (1622) *The Countesse of Lincolnes Nurserie*. Oxford: Printed by John Lichfield and James Short. STC 5432. Electronic version located at the *Renaissance Women Online* web site, retrieved Oct. 7, 2001.

Clough, G.B. (1904) *A Short History of Education*. 2nd edition, 1st edition 1904. London: R. Holland & Co. Electronic version located at http://www.socsci.kun.nl/ped/whp/histeduc/clough/index.html; retrieved Jan. 23, 2001.

Cockaine, T. (1591) *A Short Treatise of Hunting*. London: Printed by T. Orwin for T. Woodcocke. Electronic version located at the *Renascence Editions* web site, http://darkwing.uoregon.edu/~rbear/hunting/cockaine.html; retrieved Dec. 13, 2000.

Coke, R. (1670) *A Discourse of Trade*. London: Printed for H. Brome and R. Horne. Electronic version located at http://socserv2.socsci.mcmaster.ca/~econ/ugcm/3ll3/ coke/coke.tx2; retrieved Dec. 1, 2000.

Colby, B. (1846) *A Guide to Health*. Milford, N.H.: J. Burns. Electronic version located at http://chili.rt66.com/hrbmoore/ManualsOther/Colby-1.txt; retrieved Feb. 1, 2001.

Coleridge. S.T. (1817) *Biographia Literaria; or Biographical Sketches of my Literary Life and Opinions. Vol. I.* London: Rest Fenner. Electronic version located at http://www.library.utoronto.ca/utel/rp/criticism/bio_1_0.html; retrieved Jan. 31, 2001.

Combe, A. (1837) *The Physiology of Digestion* (extracts). 4th edition. Boston: Marsch, Capen & Lyon. Electronic version located at http://www.gastrolab.net/ghe0.htm, retrieved Feb. 1, 2001.

Combe, G. (1834) *Elements of Phrenology*. 2nd edition. Boston: Marsh, Capen & Lyon. Electronic version located at http://faculty.plattsburgh.edu/peter.friesen/default.asp?go=218; retrieved Feb. 1, 2001.

Commons, J.R. (1931) "Institutional Economics", in *American Economic Review*, vol. 21, pp. 648–657. Electronic version located at http://socserv2.socsci.mcmaster.ca/~econ/ugcm/3ll3/commons/institutional.txt; retrieved Nov. 24, 2000.

Cooley, C.H. (1909) "Social and Individual Aspects of Mind", in *Social Organization* (Chapter 1). New York: Charles Scribner's Sons, pp. 3-12. Electronic version located at http://panoramix.univ-paris1.fr/CHPE/textes.html, retrieved Jan. 23, 2001.

Coolidge, S. (1880) *A Short History of the City of Philadelphia, From Its Foundation to the Present Time*. Boston: Roberts Brothers. Electronic version located at http://www.libertynet.org/ardenpop/appshort.html; retrieved Jan. 2, 2001.

Coote, E. (1596) *The English Schoole-maister*. London: Printed by the Widow Orwin, for R. Iackson and R. Dexter. Electronic version located at http://www.library.utoronto.ca/utel/ret/coote/coote.html; retrieved Jan. 25, 2001.

Cranmer, T. (1689) *The judgment of Archbishop Cranmer concerning the peoples right to, and discreet use of the H. Scriptures*. London: Printed for John

Taylor. Wing C6827. Electronic version located at http://www.hti.umich.edu/e/eebo/; retrieved May 18, 2001.

Creighton, J.E. (1902) "The purposes of a philosophical association", in *Philosophical Review*, 11, pp. 219–237. Electronic version located at http://psychclassics.yorku.ca/Creighton/purpose.htm; retrieved May 22, 2001.

Cronbach, L.J. (1957) "The two disciplines of scientific psychology", in *American Psychologist*, 12, pp. 671–684. Electronic version located at http://psychclassics.yorku.ca/Cronbach/Disciplines; retrieved May 22, 2001.

Cronbach, L.J. and P.E. Meehl. (1955) "Construct validity in psychological tests", in *Psychological Bulletin*, 52, pp. 281–302. Electronic version located at http://psychclassics.yorku.ca/Cronbach/construct.htm; retrieved May 22, 2001.

Crosby, E.H. (1903) *Tolstoy and His Message*. New York: Funk & Wagnalls. Electronic version located at http://www.boondocksnet.com/editions/tolstoy.html; retrieved Jan. 25, 2001.

Culpeper, N. (1652) *The English Physitian*. London: Printed by Peter Cole. Electronic version located at http://www.med.yale.edu/library/historical/culpeper/culpeper.htm; retrieved Dec. 14, 2000.

Dalton, J. (1805) "On the Absorption of Gases by Water and Other Liquids", in *Memoirs of the Literary and Philosophical Society of Manchester*, 1, pp. 271–287. Electronic version located at http://webserver.lemoyne.edu/faculty/giunta/dalton52.html; retrieved Jan. 25, 2001.

Dalton, J. (1805) "Experimental Enquiry into the Proportion of the Several Gases or Elastic Fluids, Constituting the Atmosphere", in *Memoirs of the Literary and Philosophical Society of Manchester* 1, pp. 244–258. Electronic version located at http://webserver.lemoyne.edu/faculty/giunta/dalton1.html; retrieved Jan. 25, 2001.

Dalton, J. (1808) *A New System of Chemical Philosophy* (excerpts). Manchester: Printed by S. Russell for R. Bickerstaff. Electronic version located at http://webserver.lemoyne.edu/faculty/giunta/dalton.html; retrieved Jan. 25, 2001.

Daniel, S. (1603) *A Defence of Ryme*. London: Printed by V.S. for E. Blount. Electronic version located at the *Renascence Editions* web site, http://darkwing.uoregon.edu/~rbear/ryme.html; retrieved Dec. 13, 2000.

Darwin, C. (1845) *The Voyage of the Beagle*. 2nd edition. London: J. Murray. Electronic version located at http://www.esp.org/books/darwin/beagle; retrieved Jan. 24, 2001.

Darwin, C. (1859) *On the Origin of Species by Means of Natural Selection, or the Preservation of Favoured Races in the Struggle for Life*. London: J. Murray. Electronic version located at ftp://ftp.mirror.ac.uk/sites/etalab.unc.edu/pub/docs/books/gutenberg/etext98/otoos10.txt; retrieved Jan. 24, 2001.

Darwin, C. (1877) "A biographical sketch of an infant", in *Mind*, 2, pp. 285–294. Electronic version located at http://psychclassics.yorku.ca/Darwin/infant.htm; retrieved Dec. 15, 2000.

Davenant, W. (1651) "Preface" to *Gondibert, An Heroick Poem*. London: Printed for J. Holden. Electronic version located at http://www.library.utoronto.ca/utel/rp/criticism/gondi_il.html; retrieved Jan. 31, 2001. Checked against the page images of the 1651 edition of the poem in the *Early English Books Online*.

Davies, E. (1644) *The Word of God*. [London: s.n.]. Wing D2018. Electronic version located at the *Renaissance Women Online* web site, retrieved Oct. 7, 2001.

Davies, E. (1652) *Tobits Book, A Lesson Appointed for Lent*. [S.l.: s.n.]. Wing D2016. Electronic version located at the *Renaissance Women Online* web site, retrieved Oct. 7, 2001.

Davis, J.B. (1817) *A Cursory Inquiry Into Some Of The Principle Causes Of Mortality Among Children*. London: Printed for the author. Electronic version located at http://www.neonatology.org/classics/davis.html; retrieved Dec. 14, 2000.

Davy, H. (1811) "On a Combination of Oxymuriatic Gas and Oxygene Gas", in *Philosophical Transactions of the Royal Society*, vol. 101, pp. 155–162. Electronic version located at http://dbhs.wvusd.k12.ca.us/Chem-History/Davy-Chlorine-1811.html; retrieved Jan. 25, 2001.

Dee, J. (1588) *Compendium Heptarchiæ Mysticæ*. British Library, Additional MS. 36674. Electronic version located at http://www.esotericarchives.com/dee/chm.htm; retrieved Aug. 13, 2001.

Dee, J. (159?) *De Heptarchia Mystica*. British Library, catalog number Sloane 3191. Electronic version located at http://www.esotericarchives.com/dee/hm.htm; retrieved Aug. 13, 2001.

Dee, J. (1599) *A Letter, Containing a most briefe Discourse Apologeticall*. London: Printed by P. Short. Electronic version located at http://www.esotericarchives.com/ dee/aletter.htm; retrieved Aug. 13, 2001.

Defoe, D. (1704) *Giving Alms no Charity*. London: [s.n.]. Electronic version located at http://instruct1.cit.cornell.edu/courses/ilrle140/defoe.htm; retrieved Dec. 12, 2001.

Dennis, J. (1704) *The Grounds of Criticism in Poetry*. London: George Straban. Electronic version located at http://www.library.utoronto.ca/utel/rp/criticism/groun_il.html; retrieved Jan. 31, 2001.

Dewey, J. (1894) "The ego as cause", in *Philosophical Review*, 3, pp. 337–341. Electronic version located at http://psychclassics.yorku.ca/Dewey/ego.htm; retrieved June 4, 2001.

Dewey, J. (1896) "The reflex arc concept in psychology", in *Psychological Review*, 3, pp. 357–370. Electronic version located at http://psychclassics.yorku.ca/Dewey/reflex.htm; retrieved June 4, 2001.

Down, J.L.H. (1866) "Observations on an Ethnic Classification of Idiots", in *London Hospital Reports*, 3, pp. 259–262. Electronic version located at http://www.neonatology.org/classics/down.html; retrieved Dec. 14, 2000.

Dudley, R. (1586) *Lawes and Ordinances militarie*. Leyden: Printed by Andries Derschout. Electronic version located at the *Renascence Editions* web site, http://darkwing.uoregon.edu/~rbear/dudley1.html; retrieved Sept. 5, 2001.

Dunbar, J. (1781) *Essays on the History of Mankind in Rude and Cultivated Ages*. Printed for W. Strahan, T. Cadell, and J. Balfour. Electronic version located at http://socserv2.socsci.mcmaster.ca/~econ/ugcm/3ll3/dunbar/dunbar01.txt; retrieved Dec. 1, 2000.

Dunlap, K. (1912) "The case against introspection", in *Psychological Review*, 19, pp. 404–413. Electronic version located at http://psychclassics.yorku.ca/Dunlap/introspection.htm; retrieved June 4, 2001.

Dryden, J. (1668) *Of Dramatick Poesie, An Essay*. London: Printed for H. Herringman. Electronic version located at http://www.library.utoronto.ca/utel/rp/criticism/of_dr_il.html; retrieved Jan. 31, 2001.

Eburne, R. (1624) *A Plaine Path-way to Plantations*. [S.l.]: Printed by G.P. for I. Marriott. Electronic version located at http://www.mun.ca/rels/hrollmann/relsoc/texts/eburne/etitle.html; retrieved Dec. 4, 2000.

Eccles, S. (1667) *The Musick-Lector*. London: [s.n.]. Electronic version located at http://www.voicenet.com/~kuenning/qhp/eccles.html; retrieved Dec. 4, 2000.

Elizabeth I. (1558) *The Passage of Our Most Drad Soveraigne Lady Quene Elyzabeth Through the Citie of London to Westminster the Daye before Her Coronacion*. STC 7590. Electronic version located at the *Renaissance Women Online* web site, retrieved Oct. 7, 2001.

Elizabeth I. (1586) *The true copie of a letter from the queenes majestie, to the Lord Maior of London, and his brethren*. London: Printed by C. Parker. STC 7577. Electronic version located at the *Renaissance Women Online* web site, retrieved Oct. 7, 2001.

Elizabeth I. (1601) *Her majesties most Princelie answere* (*The Golden Speech*). London: [s.n.]. STC 7578. Electronic version located at the *Renaissance Women Online* web site, retrieved Oct. 7, 2001.

Ellis, W. (1750) *The Country Housewife's Family Companion*. London: Printed for J. Hodges and B. Collins. Electronic version located at http://www.soilandhealth.org/03sovereigntylibrary/0302%20homestedlibrary/030205ellis/030205ellis.toc.html; retrieved Nov. 8, 2001.

Evans, K. (1662) *This is a short Relation Of some of the Cruel Sufferings (For the Truths sake) of Katharine Evans & Sarah Chever*. London: Printed for R. Wilson. Wing T935. Electronic version located at the *Renaissance Women Online* web site, retrieved Oct. 7, 2001.

Evelyn, J. (1661) *Fumifugium, or The Inconveniencie of the Aer and Smoak of London Dissipated*. London: Printed by W. Godbid for G. Bedel, and T. Collins. Electronic version located at http://users.synflux.com.au/~ant/Evelyn/ed_hold.html; retrieved Nov. 29, 2000.

Evelyn, J. (1661) *Tyrannus or, The Mode*. Facsimile of Evelyn's own copy of the only published edition, issued by the Luttrell Society, Oxford, 1951, and edited by J.L. Nevinson. Electronic version located at http://users.synflux.com.au/~ant/Evelyn/ed_hold.html; retrieved Nov. 29, 2000.

Faraday, M. (1834) "On Electrical Decomposition", in *Philosophical Transactions of the Royal Society*. Electronic version located at http://dbhs.wvusd.k12.ca.us/Chem-History/Faraday-electrochem.html; retrieved Jan. 25, 2001.

Fell, M. (1656) *A Loving Salutation to the Seed of Abraham*. London: Printed for T. Simmons. Wing F634. Electronic version located at the *Renaissance Women Online* web site, retrieved Oct. 7, 2001.

Fell, M. (1660) *A Declaration and an Information from us the People of God Called Quakers*. London: Printed for T. Simmons and R. Wilson. Wing F628. Electronic version located at the *Renaissance Women Online* web site, retrieved Oct. 7, 2001.

Fell, M. (1660) *An Evident Demonstration to Gods Elect*. London: Printed for T. Simmons. Wing F629. Electronic version located at the *Renaissance Women Online* web site, retrieved Oct. 7, 2001.

Fell, M. (1660) *This Was Given to Major Generall Harrison and the Rest*. London: Printed for T. Simmons. Wing F638. Electronic version located at the *Renaissance Women Online* web site, retrieved Oct. 7, 2001.

Fell, M. (1667) *Womens Speaking Justified, Proved and Allowed of by the Scriptures*. London: [s.n.]. Wing F643. Electronic version located at the *Renaissance Women Online* web site, retrieved Oct. 7, 2001.

Fell, M. (1677) *The Daughter of Sion Awakened*. [S.l.: s.n.]. Electronic version located at http://chaucer.library.emory.edu/cgi-bin/sgml2html/wwrp.pl; retrieved Feb. 13, 2001.

Fernberger, S.W. (1932) "The American Psychological Association: A historical summary, 1892–1930", in *Psychological Bulletin*, 29, pp. 1–89. Electronic version located at http://psychclassics.yorku.ca/Fernberger/1932/history.htm; retrieved June 12, 2001.

Fernberger, S.W. (1943) "The American Psychological Association 1892–1942", in *Psychological Review*, 50, pp. 33–60. Electronic version located at http://psychclassics.yorku.ca/Fernberger/1943; retrieved June 12, 2001.

Festinger, L. and J.M. Carlsmith. (1959) "Cognitive consequences of forced compliance", in *Journal of Abnormal and Social Psychology*, 58, pp. 203–210. Electronic version located at http://psychclassics.yorku.ca/Festinger/index.htm; retrieved June 12, 2001.

Finney, C.G. (1851) *Lectures on Systematic Theology*. London: W. Tegg and Co. Electronic version located at http://www.gospeltruth.net/1851Sys_Theo/index1851st.htm; retrieved Dec. 18, 2001.

Fisher, I. (1918) "Is 'Utility' the Most Suitable Term for the Concept It is Used to Denote?", in *American Economic Review*, volume 8 pp. 335–337. Electronic version located at http://socserv2.socsci.mcmaster.ca/~econ/ugcm/3ll3/fisher/utility.htm; retrieved Dec. 1, 2000.

Flower, B.O. (1914) *Progressive Men, Women, and Movements of the Past Twenty-Five Years*. Boston: The New Arena. Electronic version located at http://www.boondocksnet.com/editions/progressive; retrieved Oct. 27, 2001.

Fowler, L.N. (1840) "Phrenological Developments of Joseph Cinquez, Alias Ginqua", in *American Phrenological Journal and Miscellany*, 2, pp. 136-138. Electronic version located at http://amistad.mysticseaport.org/ library/images/people/phren.cinque.html; retrieved Feb.15, 2001.

Fowler, L.N. (1846) *Synopsis of Phrenology and Physiology*. Boston: Printed by S. Harris. Electronic version located at http://jefferson.village.virginia.edu/ whitman/classroom/student_projects/raglas/pamphlet.htm; retrieved Feb. 1, 2001.

Fox, G. (1661) *Some Principles of the Elect People of God Who in Scorn are called Quakers*. London: Printed for R. Wilson. Electronic version located at http://www.voicenet.com/~kuenning/qhp/gfprinc.html; retrieved Dec. 4, 2000.

Foxe, J. (1563) *Actes and Monuments* (the extract "The two examinations of the worthy servant of God, Maistris An Askew"). London: J. Day. Source copy owned by Henry E. Huntington Library. STC 11222. Electronic version located at the *Renaissance Women Online* web site, retrieved Oct. 7, 2001.

Franz, S.I. (1912) "New phrenology", in *Science*, N.S. 35 (No. 896), pp. 321-328. Electronic version located at http://psychclassics.yorku.ca/Franz/ phrenology.htm; retrieved June 12, 2001.

Fremantle, A.J.L. (1864) *Three Months in the Southern States: April, June, 1863.* Mobile: S.H. Goetzel. Electronic version located at http:// docsouth.unc.edu/imls/fremantle/fremantle.html; retrieved Dec. 14, 2000.

French, J. (1651) *The Art of Distillation*. London: Printed by R. Cotes. Electronic version located at http://www.levity.com/alchemy/jfren_ar.html; retrieved Jan. 29, 2001.

Fuller, T. (1710) *Pharmacopoeia Extemporanea*. London: Printed for B. Walford. Electronic version located at http://www.med.yale.edu/library/ historical/fuller/contents.htm; retrieved Dec. 15, 2000.

Fullerton, H.S. (1921) "Why Babe Ruth is Greatest Home-Run Hitter", in *Popular Science Monthly*, 99 (4), pp. 19–21, 110. Electronic version located at http://psychclassics.yorku.ca/Fullerton; retrieved June 12, 2001.

Galton, F. (1865) "Hereditary talent and character", in *Macmillan's Magazine*, 12, pp. 157–166, 318–327. Electronic version located at http:// psychclassics.yorku.ca/Galton/talent.htm; retrieved July 30, 2001.

Galton, F. (1880) "Statistics of mental imagery", in *Mind*, 5, pp. 301–318. Electronic version located at http://psychclassics.yorku.ca/Galton/ imagery.htm; retrieved July 30, 2001.

Gervaise, I. (1720) *The System or Theory of the Trade of the World*. London: Printed by H. Woodfall. Electronic version located at http:// socserv2.socsci.mcmaster.ca/~econ/ugcm/3ll3; retrieved Dec1, 2000.

Gordon, K. (1905) "Wherein should the education of a woman differ from that of a man", in *School Review*, 13, pp. 789–794. Electronic version located at http://psychclassics.yorku.ca/Gordon/education.htm; retrieved Aug. 6, 2001.

Guthrie, E.R. (1946) "Psychological facts and psychological theory", in *Psychological Bulletin*, 43, pp. 1–20. Electronic version located at http://psychclassics.yorku.ca/Guthrie; retrieved Aug. 6, 2001.

Graunt, J. (1662) *Natural and Political Observations Mentioned in a following Index, and made upon the Bills of Mortality*. London: Printed by T. Roycroft, for J. Martin, J. Allestry, and T. Dicas. Electronic version located at http://panoramix.univ-paris1.fr/CHPE/textes.html; retrieved Jan. 23, 2001.

Green, D. (1864) *Facts and Suggestions Relative to Finance & Currency*. Augusta, Ga.: J.T. Paterson & Co. Electronic version located at http://docsouth.unc.edu/greend/green.html; retrieved Dec. 14, 2000.

Griffith, C.R. (1921) "Some neglected aspects of a history of psychology", in *Psychological Monographs*, 30, pp. 17–29. Electronic version located at http://psychclassics.yorku.ca/Griffith/neglected.htm; retrieved Aug. 6, 2001.

Griffith, C.R. (1922) "Contributions to the history of psychology – 1916-1921", in *Psychological Bulletin*, 19, pp. 411–428. Electronic version located at http://psychclassics.yorku.ca/Griffith/contributions.htm; retrieved Aug. 6, 2001.

Grymeston, E. (1604) *Miscelanea, Meditations, Memoratives*. London: Printed by Melch. Bradwood for F. Norton. STC 12407. Electronic version located at the *Renaissance Women Online* web site, retrieved Oct. 7, 2001.

Hale, M. (1683) *A Discourse Touching Provision for the Poor*. London: Printed for W. Shrowsbery. Electronic version located at http://socserv2.socsci.mcmaster.ca/~econ/ugcm/3ll3/hale/poor; retrieved Dec. 1, 2000.

Hall, W.A. (1864) *The Historic Significance of the Southern Revolution*. Petersburg: Printed by A.F. Crutchfield. Electronic version located at http://docsouth.unc.edu/imls/hall/hall.html; retrieved Dec. 14, 2000.

Hamilton, W. (1830) "On the Error of a received Principle of Analysis, respecting Functions which vanish with their Variables", in *Transactions of the Royal Irish Academy*, vol. 16, part 1. Dublin: Royal Irish Academy. pp. 63–64. Electronic version located at http://www.maths.tcd.ie/pub/HistMath/People/Hamilton/Received; retrieved Jan. 26, 2001.

Hamilton, W. (1833) "On a general Method of expressing the Paths of Light, and of the Planets, by the Coefficients of a Characteristic Function", in *Dublin University Review and Quarterly Magazine*, Vol. I, 1833. pp. 795-826. Electronic version located at http://www.maths.tcd.ie/pub/HistMath/People/Hamilton/LightPlanets/LightPlanets.html; retrieved Jan. 26, 2001.

Hamilton, W. (1834) "On Some Results of the View of a Characteristic Function in Optics", in *Report of the Third Meeting of the British Association for the Advancement of Science held at Cambridge in 1833*. London: J. Murray.

pp. 360–370. Electronic version located at http://www.maths.tcd.ie/
pub/HistMath/People/Hamilton/BARep33/BARep33.html;   retrieved Jan.
26, 2001.

Hamilton, W. (1835) ""On a View of Mathematical Optics", in *Report of the
First and Second Meetings of the British Association for the Advancement
of Science; at York in 1831, and at Oxford in 1832*. London: J. Murray. pp.
545–547. Electronic version located at http://www.maths.tcd.ie/pub/Hist
Math/People/Hamilton/BARep32/BARep32.html; retrieved Jan. 26, 2001.

Hamilton, W. (1843) "On a new Species of Imaginary Quantities connected with
a theory of Quaternions", in *Proceedings of the Royal Irish Academy, Nov.
13, 1843*, vol. 2. Dublin: Royal Irish Academy. pp. 424–434. Electronic
version located at http://www.maths.tcd.ie/pub/HistMath/People/Hamilton/
Quatern1/Quatern1.html; retrieved Jan26, 2001.

Hamilton, W. (1847) "On Quaternions", in *Proceedings of the Royal Irish
Academy, Nov. 11, 1844*, vol. 3. Dublin: Royal Irish Academy. pp.1-16.
Electronic version located at http://www.maths.tcd.ie/pub/HistMath/
People/Hamilton/Quatern2/Quatern2.html; retrieved Jan26, 2001.

Hariot, T. (1588) *A briefe and true report of the new found land of Virginia*.
London: [s.n.]. Electronic version located at http://www.people.virginia.
edu/~msk5d/hariot/main.html; retrieved March 5, 2001.

Harlow, H.F. (1958) "The nature of love", in *American Psychologist*, 13, pp. 573-
685. Electronic version located at http://psychclassics.yorku.ca/Harlow/
love.htm; retrieved Aug. 14, 2001.

Hart, R. (1859) "Reminiscences of James Watt", in *Transactions of the Glasgow
Archæological Society*, 1st Series, Vol. 1, No. 1, pp. 1–7. Electronic
version located at http://www.history.rochester.edu/steam/hart; retrieved
Feb. 1, 2001.

Hartmann, G.W. (1941) "Frustration Phenomena in the Social and Political
Sphere", in *Psychological Review*, 48, pp. 362–363. Electronic version
located at http://psychclassics.yorku.ca/FrustAgg/hartmann.htm; retrieved
Oct. 23, 2001.

Hayter, T. (1780) *Remarks on Mr. Hume's Dialogues concerning Natural
Religion*. Cambridge: Printed by J. Archdeacon for T. Cadel. Electronic
version located at   http://www.utm.edu/research/hume/com/hayter.htm;
retrieved Feb. 13, 2001.

Hebb, D.O. (1955) "Drives and the C.N.S. (conceptual nervous system)", in
Psychological Review, 62, pp. 243–254. Electronic version located at
http://psychclassics.yorku.ca/Hebb; retrieved Aug. 14, 2001.

Hobbes, T. (1651) *Philosophicall Rudiments Concerning Government and
Society*. London: Printed by J.C. for R. Royston. Electronic version located
at   http://socserv2.socsci.mcmaster.ca/~econ/ugcm/3ll3/hobbes/hobbes1;
retrieved Dec. 1, 2000.

Hollander, J.H. (1904) "The Development of Ricardo's Theory of Value", in
Quarterly Journal of Economics, volume 18, pp. 455–491. Electronic

version located at http://socserv2.socsci.mcmaster.ca/~econ/ugcm/ 3ll3/hollander/value.html; retrieved Dec. 1, 2000.

Hollander, J.H. (1910–11) "The Development of the Theory of Money from Adam Smith to David Ricardo", in *Quarterly Journal of Economics*, volume 25, pp. 429–470. Electronic version located at http:// socserv2.socsci.mcmaster.ca/~econ/ugcm/3ll3/hollander/money.html; retrieved Dec. 1, 2000.

Hollingworth, L.S. (1914) "Variability as related to sex differences in achievement: A critique", in *American Journal of Sociology*, 19, pp. 510-530. Electronic version located at http://psychclassics.yorku.ca/ Hollingworth/sexdiffs.htm; retrieved Oct. 19, 2001.

Hollingworth, L.S. (1916) "Social devices for impelling women to bear and rear children", in *American Journal of Sociology*, 22, pp. 19–29. Electronic version located at http://psychclassics.yorku.ca/Hollingworth/children.htm; retrieved Oct. 19, 2001.

Hollingworth, L.S. (1922) "Differential action upon the sexes of forces which tend to segregate the feebleminded", in *Journal of Abnormal Psychology and Social Psychology*, 17, pp. 35–57. Electronic version located at http://psychclassics.yorku.ca/Hollingworth/Differential; retrieved Oct. 19, 2001.

Hooke, R. (1665) *Micrographia: or some Physiological Descriptions of Minute Bodies made by Magnifying Glasses with Observations and Inquiries thereupon* (excepts). London: Printed by J. Martyn, and J. Allestry. Electronic version located at http://www.roberthooke.org.uk/micro1.htm; retrieved Feb. 6, 2001.

Hortop, J. (1591) *The Travailes of an English man*. London: W. Wright. Electronic version at http://penelope.uchicago.edu/hortop/hortop.html; retrieved Aug. 14, 2001

Howes, Ethel Puffer. (1922) "Accepting the Universe", in *Atlantic Monthly*, 129, pp. 444-453. Electronic version located at http://psychclassics.yorku.ca/Howes/ accepting.htm; retrieved Oct. 19, 2001.

Hull, C.L. (1934) "The concept of the habit-family hierarchy and maze learning: Part I", in *Psychological Review*, 41, pp. 33–54. Electronic version located at http://psychclassics.yorku.ca/Hull/Hierarchy/part1.htm; retrieved Oct. 19, 2001.

Hull, C.L. (1934) "The concept of the habit-family hierarchy and maze learning: Part II", in *Psychological Review*, 41, pp. 134-152. Electronic version located at http://psychclassics.yorku.ca/Hull/Hierarchy/part2.htm; retrieved Oct. 19, 2001.

Hull, C.L. (1935) "The conflicting psychologies of learning – A way out", in *Psychological Review*, 42, pp. 491–516. Electronic version located at http://psychclassics.yorku.ca/Hull/Conflict; retrieved Oct. 19, 2001.

Hume, D. (1783) *Essays on Suicide and the Immortality of the Soul*. London: Printed for M. Smith. Electronic version located at http://www.infidels.org/library/historical/david_hume/suicide.html; retrieved Dec. 15, 2000.

Hume, J.G. (1892) "Physiological psychology", in *Minutes of the Twenty-First Annual Convention of the Ontario Teachers' Association*, pp. 86-106. Electronic version located at http://psychclassics.yorku.ca/Hume/physpsych.htm; retrieved Oct. 19, 2001.

Hume, J.G. (1897) *The practical value of psychology to the teacher*. Toronto: G.N. Morang. Electronic version located at http://psychclassics.yorku.ca/Hume/teacher.htm; retrieved Oct. 19, 2001.

Hume, J.G. (1898) "Contributions of psychology to morality and religion", in *Psychological Review*, 5, pp. 162–163. Electronic version located at http://psychclassics.yorku.ca/Hume/morality.htm; retrieved Oct. 19, 2001.

Hume, J.G. (1909) "The Import of Pragmatism for the History of Philosophy", in *Philosophical Review*, 18, pp. 176–177. Electronic version located at http://psychclassics.yorku.ca/Hume/pragmatism.htm; retrieved Oct. 19, 2001.

Hume, J.G. (1909) "The Proper Affiliation of Psychology: With Philosophy or the Natural Sciences", in *Psychological Bulletin*, 6, pp. 65–67. Electronic version located at http://psychclassics.yorku.ca/Hume/affiliation.htm; retrieved Oct. 19, 2001.

Hume, J.G. (1910) "The Significance of Suicide", in *Philosophical Review*, 19, pp. 179–180. Electronic version located at http://psychclassics.yorku.ca/Hume/suicide.htm; retrieved Oct. 19, 2001.

Hume, J.G. (1916) "Scientific Truth and the Scientific Spirit", in *University of Toronto Monthly*, 16, pp. 443–445. Electronic version located at http://psychclassics.yorku.ca/Hume/scientifictruth.htm; retrieved Oct. 19, 2001.

Hume, J.G. (1922) "Evolution and Personality", in *Philosophical Essays Presented to John Watson*. Kingston, ON: Queen's University. pp. 298–330. Electronic version located at http://psychclassics.yorku.ca/Hume/evolution.htm; retrieved Oct. 19, 2001.

Hutton, J. (1798) "Theory of the Earth", in *Transactions of the Royal Society of Edinburgh, Volume I*. Edinburgh: The Royal Society of Edinburgh. Electronic version located at http://www.mala.bc.ca/~johnstoi/essays/Hutton.htm; retrieved Feb. 13, 2001.

Inglis, C. (1780) *The Duty of Honouring the King*. New York: Printed by H. Gaine. Electronic version located at http://justus.anglican.org/resources/pc/charles/inglis.html; retrieved Nov. 15, 2001.

Ireland, W.H. (1796) *An Authentic Account of the Shaksperian Manuscripts*. London: [s.n.]. Electronic version located at http://andromeda.rutgers.edu/~jlynch/Texts/ireland.html; retrieved May 18, 2001.

James, E. (1687) *Mrs. James's Vindication of the Church of England*. London: Printed for E. James. Electronic version located at http://chaucer.library.emory.edu/cgi-bin/sgml2html/wwrp.pl; retrieved Feb. 13, 2001.

James, W. (1884) "What is an emotion?", in *Mind*, 9, pp. 188–205. Electronic version located at http://psychclassics.yorku.ca/James/emotion.htm; retrieved Oct. 19, 2001.

James, W. (1892) *Psychology* (chapter XI). Cleveland & New York: World. Electronic version located at http://psychclassics.yorku.ca/James/jimmy11.htm; retrieved Oct. 23, 2001.

James, W. (1904) "Does consciousness exist?", in *Journal of Philosophy, Psychology, and Scientific Methods*, 1, pp. 477-491. Electronic version located at http://psychclassics.yorku.ca/James/consciousness.htm; retrieved Oct. 23, 2001.

James, W. (1904b) "A world of pure experience", in *Journal of Philosophy, Psychology, and Scientific Methods*, 1, pp. 533–543, 561–570. Electronic version located at http://psychclassics.yorku.ca/James/experience.htm; retrieved Oct. 23, 2001.

James, W. (1907) "The energies of men", in *Science*, N.S. 25 (No. 635), pp. 321–332. Electronic version located at http://psychclassics.yorku.ca/James/energies.htm; retrieved Oct. 23, 2001.

Jastrow, J. (1891) "A study in mental statistics", in *New Review*, 5, pp. 559–568. Electronic version located at http://psychclassics.yorku.ca/Jastrow/Mental; retrieved Oct. 23, 2001.

Jastrow, J. (1893) "The section of psychology", in M. P. Hardy (Ed.), *Official Catalogue – World's Columbian Exposition* (Part. vii, pp. 50–60). Chicago: W.B. Conkey Company. Electronic version located at http://psychclassics.yorku.ca/Jastrow/section.htm; retrieved Oct. 23, 2001.

Jastrow, J. (1896) "Community of ideas of men and women", in *Psychological Review*, 3, pp. 68–71. Electronic version located at http://psychclassics.yorku.ca/Jastrow/community.htm; retrieved Oct, 23, 2001.

Jevons, W.S. (1866) "Brief Account of a General Mathematical Theory of Political Economy", in *Journal of the Royal Statistical Society*, XXIX, pp. 282–287. Electronic version located at http://socserv2.socsci.mcmaster.ca/~econ/ugcm/3ll3/jevons/mathem.txt; retrieved Dec. 1, 2000.

Jevons, W.S. (1881) "A Review of Edgeworth's Mathematical Psychics", in *Mind*, Vol. 6, pp. 581–583. Electronic version located at http://cepa.newschool.edu/het/texts/jevons/jevonsedgew81.htm; retrieved Feb. 14, 2001.

Jobson, R. (1623) *The Golden Trade* (extracts). London: Printed by N. Okes. Electronic version located at http://penelope.uchicago.edu/jobson/jobson1.html; retrieved Feb. 13, 2001.

Jocelyn, J. (1718). *An Essay on Money and Bullion*. London: Printed for B. Lintot. Electronic version located at from http://socserv2.socsci.mcmaster.ca/~econ/ugcm/3ll3/jocelyn/Money.pdf; retrieved Dec. 1, 2000.

Johnson, S. (1755) "Preface" to *A Dictionary of the English Language*. 2 vols. London: J.F. & C. Rivington. Electronic version located at http://andromeda.rutgers.edu/~jlynch/Texts/preface.html; retrieved Feb. 14, 2001.

Johnson, S. (1765) "Preface" to *Shakespear's Plays*, edited by S. Johnson. London: J. and R. Tonson. Electronic version located at http://www. library.utoronto.ca/utel/rp/criticism/johns_il.html; retrieved Jan. 31, 2001.

Jones, M.C. (1924) "A laboratory study of fear: The case of Peter", in *Pedagogical Seminary*, 31, pp. 308–315. Electronic version located at http://psychclassics.yorku.ca/Jones; retrieved Oct. 23, 2001.

Jones, R. (1831) *An Essay on the Distribution of Wealth and on the Sources of Taxation*. London: J. Murray. Electronic version located at http://socserv2.socsci.mcmaster.ca/~econ/ugcm/3ll3/jones/Wealth000.html; retrieved Feb. 27, 2001.

Jones, S. (1644) *To Sions Lovers, Being a Golden Egge, to avoide Infection*. [S.l.: s.n.]. Wing J990. Electronic version located at the *Renaissance Women Online* web site, retrieved Oct. 7, 2001.

Jonson, B. (1641) *Timber*. London: [s.n.]. Electronic version located at http://www.library.utoronto.ca/utel/rp/criticism/timbe_il.html;   retrieved Jan. 31, 2001.

Joplin, T. (1718) *An Essay on Money & Bullion*. London: Printed for B. Lintot. Electronic version located at http://socserv2.socsci.mcmaster.ca/~econ/ ugcm/3ll3/joplin/money.txt; retrieved Dec. 1, 2000.

Kelvin, Lord (W. Thomson). (1902) "Aepinus Atomized", in *The Philosophical Magazine*, Vol 3, No. 15 (Sixth Series), March, p. 257ff. Electronic version located at http://dbhs.wvusd.k12.ca.us/Chem-History/Aepinus-Atomized.html; retrieved Jan. 25, 2001.

Knight, F.H. (1921) *Risk, Uncertainty, and Profit*. Boston and New York: Houghton Mifflin Co. Electronic version located at http:// www.econlib.org/library/Downloads/knRUPdownload.html;   retrieved Nov. 27, 2000.

Knight, F.H. (1922) "Ethics and the Economic Interpretation", in *Quarterly Journal of Economics*, 36, pp. 454–481. Electronic version located at http://www.augustana.ab.ca/~emmer/Texts/harvard_lecture1_1922.html; retrieved Dec. 1, 2000.

Knight, F.H. (1923) "The Ethics of Competition", in *Quarterly Journal of Economics*, 37, pp. 579–624. Electronic version located at http:// www.augustana.ab.ca/~emmer/Texts/harvard_lecture2_1923.html; retrieved Dec. 1, 2000.

Knox, J. (1558) *The first blast of the trumpet against the monstrvovs regiment of women*. Geneva: Printed by J. Poullain and A. Rebul. STC 15070. Electronic version located at http://www.hti.umich.edu/e/eebo/; retrieved May 18, 2001.

Krohn, W.O. (1894) "Facilities in experimental psychology in the colleges of the United States", in *Report of the Commissioner of Education for the year 1890-'91*. Vol. 2. pp. 1139–1151. Electronic version located at http://psychclassics.yorku.ca/Krohn/report.htm; retrieved Oct. 23, 2001.

Langmuir, I. (1919) "The Arrangement of Electrons in Atoms and Molecules", in Journal of the *American Chemical Society*, Vol. 41, No, 6, p. 868.

Electronic version located at http://dbhs.wvusd.k12.ca.us/Chem-History/ Langmuir-1919b.html; retrieved Jan. 25, 2001.

Langmuir, I. (1919) "The Structure of Atoms and the Octet Theory of Valence", in *Proceedings of the National Academy of Science*, Vol. V, p. 252. Electronic version located at http://dbhs.wvusd.k12.ca.us/Chem-History/ Langmuir-1919.html; retrieved Jan. 25, 2001.

Lapsley, G.T. (1902-3) "The Origin of Property in Land", in *American Historical Review*, volume 8, pp. 426–448. Electronic version located at http:// socserv2.socsci.mcmaster.ca/~econ/ugcm/3ll3/misc/lapsley.html; retrieved Dec. 1, 2000.

Lashley, K.S. (1923) "The behavioristic interpretation of consciousness", in *Psychological Bulletin*, 30, pp. 237–272, 329–353. Electronic version located at http://psychclassics.yorku.ca/Lashley/consciousness.htm; retrieved Oct. 23, 2001.

Lashley, K.S. (1930) "Basic neural mechanisms in behavior", in *Psychological Review*, 37, pp. 1–24. Electronic version located at http://psychclassics. yorku.ca/Lashley/neural.htm; retrieved Oct. 23, 2001.

Law, J. (1705) *Money and Trade Considered with a Proposal for Supplying the Nation with Money*. Edinburgh: Printed by the Heirs and Successors of A. Anderson. Electronic version located at http://socserv2.socsci. mcmaster.ca/~econ/ugcm/3ll3/law/mon.txt; retrieved Dec. 1, 2000.

Law, W. (1740) *An Appeal to All that Doubt, or Disbelieve, the Truths of the Gospel*. London: Printed for W. Innys and J. Richardson. Electronic version located at http://www.ccel.org/l/law/appeal/appeal.txt; retrieved Feb. 14, 2001.

Lead, J. (1681) *The Heavenly Cloud Now Breaking*. London: Printed for J. Lead. Electronic version located at http://www.passtheword.org/Jane-Lead/ heav-cld.htm; retrieved Feb. 14, 2001.

Lead, J. (1683) *The Revelation of Revelations*. [S.l.]: J. L. Electronic version located at http://www.passtheword.org/Jane-Lead/revelatn.htm; retrieved Feb. 14, 2001.

Lead, J. (1694) *The Enochian Walks with God*. [S.l.: s.n]. Electronic version located at http://www.passtheword.org/Jane-Lead/enocwalk.htm; retrieved Feb. 14, 2001.

Lead, J. (1695) *The Laws of Paradise*. London: Printed by T. Sowle. Electronic version located at http://www.passtheword.org/Jane-Lead/paradise.htm; retrieved Feb. 14, 2001.

Lead, J. (1695) *The Wonders of God's Creation Manifested in the Variety of Eight Worlds*. London: [s.n.]. Electronic version located at http:// www.passtheword.org/Jane-Lead/8-worlds.htm; retrieved Feb. 14, 2001.

Lead, J. (1696) *A Message to the Philadelphian Society*. London: Printed by J. Bradford. Electronic version located at http://www.passtheword.org/Jane-Lead/philadel.htm; retrieved Feb. 14, 2001.

Lead, J. (1696) *The Tree of Faith*. London: Printed by J. Bradford. Electronic version located at http://www.passtheword.org/Jane-Lead/trefaith.htm; retrieved Feb. 15, 2001.

Lead, J. (1697) *A Revelation of the Everlasting Gospel-Message*. London: [s.n.] Electronic version located at http://www.passtheword.org/Jane-Lead/gospel.htm; retrieved Feb. 15, 2001.

Lead, J. (1698) *The Messenger of An Universal Peace*. London: [s.n.]. Electronic version located at http://www.passtheword.org/Jane-Lead/msgpeace.htm; retrieved Feb. 15, 2001.

Lead, J. (1699) *The Ascent to the Mount of Vision*. London: [s.n.]. Electronic version located at http://www.passtheword.org/Jane-Lead/ascent.htm; retrieved Feb. 15, 2001.

Lead, J. (1699) *The Signs of the Times*. [S.l.: s.n]. Electronic version located at http://www.passtheword.org/Jane-Lead/signs.htm; retrieved Feb. 15, 2001.

Lead, J. (1700) *The Wars of David*. London: Printed by J. Bradford. Electronic version located at http://www.passtheword.org/Jane-Lead/warsofdavid.htm; retrieved Feb. 14, 2001.

Lead, J. (1702) *A Living Funeral Testimony*. Printed by J. Bradford. Electronic version located at http://www.passtheword.org/Jane-Lead/funeral.htm; retrieved Feb. 14, 2001.

LeConte, J. (1862) *Instructions for the Manufacture of Saltpetre*. Columbia, S.C.: C.P. Pelham. Electronic version located at http://docsouth.unc.edu/lecontesalt/leconte.html; retrieved Dec. 14, 2000.

Leigh, D. (1616) *The Mother's Blessing*. London: John Budge. STC 15402. Electronic version located at the *Renaissance Women Online* web site, retrieved Oct. 7, 2001.

Leslie, T.E.C. (1870) "The Political Economy of Adam Smith", in *Fortnightly Review*, 14, November 1, pp. 549–563. Electronic version located at http://socserv2.socsci.mcmaster.ca/~econ/ugcm/3ll3/leslie/leslie01.html; retrieved Dec. 30, 2000.

Leslie, T.E.C. (1876) "On the Philosophical Method of Political Economy", in *Hermathena*, vol. 2, No. iv, pp. 1–32. Electronic version located at http://socserv2.socsci.mcmaster.ca/~econ/ugcm/3ll3/leslie/leslie02.html; retrieved Dec. 30, 2000.

Leslie, T.E.C. (1879) "Political Economy and Sociology", in *Fortnightly Review*, January 1. Electronic version located at http://socserv2.socsci.mcmaster.ca/~econ/ugcm/3ll3/leslie/leslie06.html; retrieved Dec. 30, 2000.

Leslie, T.E.C. (1880) "Political Economy in the United States", in *Fortnightly Review*, October 1st, pp. 488–509. Electronic version located at http://socserv.socsci.mcmaster.ca/econ/ugcm/3ll3/leslie/leslie05.html; retrieved Dec. 30, 2000.

Levy, D.M. (1941) "The Hostile Act", in *Psychological Review*, 48, pp. 356-361. Electronic version located at http://psychclassics.yorku.ca/FrustAgg/levy.htm; retrieved Oct. 23, 2001.

Lewis, G.N. (1916) "The Atom and the Molecule", in *Journal of the American Chemical Society*, Volume 38, pp. 762–786. Electronic version located at http://dbhs.wvusd.k12.ca.us/Chem-History/Lewis-1916/Lewis-1916.html; retrieved Jan. 25, 2001.

Lilburne, E. (1646) *To the Chosen and Betrusted Knights*. [London: s.n.]. Wing L2077. Electronic version located at the *Renaissance Women Online* web site, retrieved Oct. 7, 2001.

Linnett, J.W. (1947) "Structure of Ethylene Oxide and Cyclopropane", in *Nature*, 160, pp. 162–163. Electronic version located at http://www.bluffton.edu/~bergerd/chem/walsh/160-163.html; retrieved Jan. 26, 2001.

Little, W.J. (1861) "On The Influence of Abnormal Parturition, Difficult Labours, Premature Birth, and Asphyxia Neonatorum, on the Mental and Physical Condition of the Child, Especially in Relation to Deformities", in *Transactions of the Obstetrical Society of London*, 3. pp. 243–344. Electronic version located at http://www.neonatology.org/classics/little.html; retrieved Dec. 14, 2000.

Locke, J. (1691) *Some Considerations of the Consequences of the Lowering of Interest and the Raising the Value of Money*. London: Printed for Awnsham and J. Churchill. Electronic version located at http://socserv2.socsci.mcmaster.ca/~econ/ugcm/3ll3/locke/consid.txt; retrieved Dec. 1, 2000.

The London Gazette, Numb. 937. (1674). London: Printed by T. Newcomb. Electronic version located at http://www.history.rochester.edu/London_Gazette/0937/lgazette.htm; retrieved Feb. 6, 2001.

The London Gazette, Numb. 1040. (1675). London: Printed by T. Newcomb. Electronic version located at http://www.history.rochester.edu/London_Gazette/1040/plain.htm; retrieved Feb. 6, 2001.

The London Gazette, Numb. 1089. (1676). London: Printed by T. Newcomb. Electronic version located at http://www.history.rochester.edu/London_Gazette/1089/lgazette.htm; retrieved Feb. 6, 2001.

The London Gazette, Numb. 1319. (1678). London: Printed by The: Newcomb. Electronic version located at http://www.history.rochester.edu/London_Gazette/ 1319/plain.htm; retrieved Feb. 6, 2001.

The London Gazette, Numb. 2838. (1692). London: Printed by E. Jones. Electronic version located at http://www.history.rochester.edu/London_Gazette/2838/plain.htm; retrieved Feb. 6, 2001.

Long, T. (1684) *Moses and the Royal Martyr Parallel'd*. London: Printed by J.C. and F. Collins. Electronic version located at http://justus.anglican.org/resources/pc/charles/long.html; retrieved Nov. 15, 2001.

Love, M. (1663) *Love's Name Lives*. London: [s.n.]. Wing L3142. Electronic version located at the *Renaissance Women Online* web site, retrieved Oct. 7, 2001.

Lurting, T. (1711) *The Fighting Sailor*. London: Printed by J. Sowle. Electronic version located at http://www.voicenet.com/~kuenning/qhp/lurting.html; retrieved Dec. 4, 2000.

MacCorquodale, K. and P.E. Meehl. (1948) "On a distinction between hypothetical constructs and intervening variables", in *Psychological Review*, 55, pp. 95–107. Electronic version located at http://psychclassics.yorku.ca/MacMeehl/hypcon-intvar.htm; retrieved Oct. 23, 2001.

Mackay, C. (1852) *Memoirs of Extraordinary Popular Delusions and the Madness of Crowds*. 2nd edition, 1st edition 1841. London: Office of the National Illustrated Library. Electronic version located at http://www.econlib.org/library/Mackay/macEx.html; retrieved Feb. 15, 2001.

MacMahon, T.W. (1862) *Cause and Contrast: an Essay on the American Crisis*. Richmond, Va.: West & Johnston. Electronic version located at http://docsouth.unc.edu/cause/cause.html; retrieved Dec. 14, 2000.

Maine, H.S. (1875) *Lectures on the Early History of Institutions*. London: J. Murray. Electronic version located at http://socserv2.socsci.mcmaster.ca/~econ/ugcm/3ll3/maine/lect01; retrieved Dec. 1, 2000.

Maine, H.S. (1915) *International Law: a Series of Lectures Delivered before the University of Cambridge, 1887*. 2nd edition, 1st edition 1887. London: J. Murray. Electronic version located at http://socserv2.socsci.mcmaster.ca/~econ/ugcm/3ll3/maine/intlaw.htm; retrieved Dec. 1, 2000.

Maitland, F. (1900) "The Corporation Sole", in *Law Quarterly Review*, 16, pp. 335–354. Electronic version located at http://socserv2.socsci.mcmaster.ca/~econ/ugcm/3ll3/maitland/maitland; retrieved Dec. 1, 2000.

Maitland, F. (1901) "The Crown as Corporation", in *Law Quarterly Review*, 17, pp. 131–46. Electronic version located at http://socserv2.socsci.mcmaster.ca/~econ/ugcm/3ll3/maitland/crowncor.mai; retrieved Dec. 1, 2000.

Malthus, T. (1798) *An Essay on the Principle of Population*. London: Printed for J. Johnson. Electronic version located at http://socserv2.socsci.mcmaster.ca/~econ/ugcm/3ll3/malthus/popu.txt; retrieved Dec. 1, 2000.

Malthus, T. (1800) *An Investigation of the Cause of the Present High Price of Provisions By the Author of the Essay on the Principle of Population*. London: Printed for J. Johnson, by Davis, Taylor, and Wilks. Electronic version located at http://socserv2.socsci.mcmaster.ca/~econ/ugcm/3ll3/malthus/highpric.txt; retrieved Dec. 1, 2000.

Malthus, T. (1814) *Observations on the Effects of the Corn Laws*. London: Printed for J. Johnson and Co. Electronic version located at http://socserv2.socsci.mcmaster.ca/~econ/ugcm/3ll3/malthus/cornlaws; retrieved Dec. 1, 2000.

Malthus, T. (1815) *An Inquiry into the Nature and Progress of Rent, and the Principles by which it is regulated*. London, Printed for J. Murray. Electronic version located at http://socserv2.socsci.mcmaster.ca/~econ/ugcm/3ll3/malthus/rent; retrieved Dec. 1, 2000.

Malthus, T. (1815) *The Grounds of an Opinion on the Policy of Restricting the Importation of Foreign Corn*. London: Printed for J. Murray and J. Johnson and Co. Electronic version located at http://socserv2.socsci. mcmaster.ca/~econ/ugcm/3ll3/malthus/grounds.txt; retrieved Dec. 1, 2000.

Makin, B. (1673) *An Essay to Revive the Antient Education of Gentlewomen*. London: Printed by J.D. Electronic version located at http://www.pinn.net/ ~sunshine/book-sum/makin1.html; retrieved Apr. 20, 2001.

Malynes, G. (1622) *The Maintenance of Free Trade*. London: Printed by I.L. for W. Shefford. Electronic version located at http://socserv2.socsci.mcmaster. ca/~econ/ugcm/3ll3/malynes/malynes.txt; retrieved Dec. 1, 2000.

Maslow, A.H. (1941) "Deprivation, Threat and Frustration", in *Psychological Review*, 48, pp. 364–366. Electronic version located at http:// psychclassics.yorku.ca/FrustAgg/maslow.htm; retrieved Oct. 23, 2001.

Maslow, A.H. (1943) "A theory of human motivation", in *Psychological Review*, 50, pp. 370–396. Electronic version located at http:// psychclassics.yorku.ca/Maslow/motivation.htm; retrieved Oct. 23, 2001.

Mason, J. (1620) *A Briefe Discourse of the New-found-land*. Edinburgh: Printed by Andro Hart. Electronic version located at http://www.mun.ca/rels/ hrollmann/relsoc/texts/mason.html; retrieved Dec. 4, 2000.

Masters, E.L. (1904) *The New Star Chamber and Other Essays*. Chicago: Hammersmark Publishing Co. Electronic version located at http://www. boondocksnet.com/masters/elm_newstar.html; retrieved Jan. 25, 2001.

Maxwell, J.C. (1872) "Limitation of the Second Law of Thermodynamics", in *Theory of Heat*, New York: D. Appleton & Co., pp. 308-9. Electronic version located at http://webserver.lemoyne.edu/faculty/giunta/ demon.html; retrieved Jan. 26, 2001.

Maxwell, J.C. (1873) "Molecules", in *Nature*, 8, pp. 437-441. Electronic version based on a reproduction in D.M. Knight, ed., *Classical scientific papers: chemistry*, New York: American Elsevier (1968), and located at http://webserver.lemoyne.edu/faculty/giunta/maxwell.html; retrieved Jan. 25, 2001.

Maxwell, J.C. (1875) "On the Dynamical Evidence of the Molecular Constitution of Bodies", in *Journal of the Chemical Society*, 28, pp. 493–508. Electronic version based on a facsimile published in M.J. Nye, *The Question of the Atom*, Los Angeles: Tomash (1984), and located at http:// webserver.lemoyne.edu/faculty/giunta/maxwell1.html; retrieved Jan. 25, 2001.

McDonald, W. (1865) *The Two Rebellions; or, Treason Unmasked*. Richmond: Smith, Bailey & Co. Electronic version located at http://docsouth.unc.edu/ imls/mcdonald/mcdonald.html; retrieved Dec. 14, 2000.

McDowell, C.A. (1947) "Structures of Ethylene Oxide and Cyclopropane", in *Nature*, 159, p. 508. Electronic version located at http://www.bluffton.edu/ ~bergerd/chem/walsh/159-508.html; retrieved Jan. 26, 2001.

Mead, G.H. (1913) "The social self", in *Journal of Philosophy, Psychology, and Scientific Methods*, 10, pp. 374–380. Electronic version located at http://psychclassics.yorku.ca/Mead/socialself.htm; retrieved Oct. 23, 2001.

Mill, J.S. (1850) "The Negro Question", in *The Living Age*, March 9, 1850, vol. 24, issue 303 pp. 465–69. Electronic version located at http://cepa. newschool.edu/het/texts/carlyle/millnegro.htm; retrieved Dec. 1, 2000.

Mill, J.S. (1869) *On liberty*. 4th edition, 1st edition 1859. London: Longman, Roberts & Green. Electronic version located at http://www.bartleby.com/ 130; retrieved Feb. 15, 2001.

Millar, J. (1806) *The Origin of the Distinction of Ranks*. 4th edition, 1st edition 1771. Edinburgh: Printed for W. Blackwood, and Longman, Huest, Rees, & Orme. Electronic version located at http://socserv2.socsci.mcmaster.ca/ ~econ/ugcm/3ll3/millar/rank; retrieved Dec. 1, 2000.

Miller, G.A. (1956) "The magical number seven, plus or minus two: Some limits on our capacity for processing information", in *Psychological Review*, 63, pp. 81–97. Electronic version located at http://psychclassics.yorku.ca/ Miller; retrieved Oct. 23, 2001.

Miller, N.E. (1941) "The Frustration-Aggression Hypothesis", in *Psychological Review*, 48, pp. 337–342. Electronic version located at http://psychclassics. yorku.ca/FrustAgg/miller.htm; retrieved Oct. 23, 2001.

Milton, J. (1641) *The Reason of Church-governement Urg'd against Prelaty*. In 2 volumes. London: Printed by E. G. for I. Rothwell. Electronic version located at http://www.dartmouth.edu/~milton/reading_room/reason/ titlepage/index.html; retrieved Feb. 14, 2001.

Milton, J. (1644) *The Doctrine and Discipline of Divorce*. In 2 volumes. London: [s.n.]. 2nd edition, 1st edition 1643. Electronic version located at http:// www.shu.ac.uk/schools/cs/emls/iemls/work/etexts/mdoctrin.txt; retrieved Jan. 10, 2002.

Milton, J, trans. (1644) *The Judgment of Martin Bucer, Concerning Divorce*. London: [s.n.] Electronic version located at http://www.shu.ac.uk/schools/ cs/emls/iemls/work/etexts/mmartb.txt; retrieved Jan. 10, 2002. Checked against the page images of the original edition on the *Early English Books Online* web site, http://wwwlib.umi.com/eebo.

Milton, J. (1644) *Areopagitica*. London: [s.n.]. Electronic version located at http://www.dartmouth.edu/~milton/reading_room/areopagitica/part_1/ index.html; retrieved Feb. 14, 2001; checked against page images of the original on the *Octavo* web site at http://www.octavo.com/collection/ mltare.html, retrieved Feb. 14, 2001.

Milton, J. (1645) *Tetrachordon*. London: [s.n]. Electronic version located at http://www.shu.ac.uk/schools/cs/emls/iemls/work/etexts/mtetrac.txt; retrieved Jan. 10, 2002. Checked against the page images of the original edition on the *Early English Books Online* web site, http://wwwlib.umi.com/eebo.

Milton, J. (1645) *Colasterion: a Reply to a Nameles Ansvver against the Doctrine and Discipline of Divorce*. [London: s.n.] Electronic version located at http://www.shu.ac.uk/schools/cs/emls/iemls/work/etexts/mcolast.txt; retrieved Jan. 10, 2002. Checked against the page images of the original edition on the *Early English Books Online* web site, http://wwwlib.umi.com/eebo.

Misselden, E. (1622) *Free Trade or, The Meanes To Make Trade Florish*. London: Printed by J. Legatt, for S. Waterson. Electronic version located at http://socserv2.socsci.mcmaster.ca/~econ/ugcm/3ll3/misselden/freetrad.txt; retrieved Dec. 1, 2000.

More, P.E. (1912) *Nietzsche*. Boston and New York: Houghton Mifflin Company. Electronic version located at http://www.execpc.com/~berrestr/mornie.html; retrieved Feb. 6, 2001.

Moseley, H.G.J. (1913) "The High Frequency Spectra of the Elements", in *The Philosophical Magazine*, p. 1024. Electronic version located at http://dbhs.wvusd.k12.ca.us/Chem-History/Moseley-article.html; retrieved Jan. 26, 2001.

Mulcaster, R. (1582) *The First Part of the Elementarie which entreateth of right writing of our English tung*. [s.l.]: Printed by T. Vautroullier. STC 18250. Electronic version located at the *Humanities Text Initiative* web site, http://www.hti.umich.edu; retrieved Sept. 5, 2001.

Mun, T. (1664) *Englands Treasure by Forraign Trade*. London: Printed by J.G. for T. Clark. Electronic version located at http://socserv2.socsci.mcmaster.ca/~econ/ugcm/3ll3/mun/treasure.txt; retrieved Dec. 1, 2000.

Munda, C. (1617) *The Worming of a mad Dogge*. London: Printed for L. Hayes. STC 18257. Electronic version located at the *Renaissance Women Online* web site, retrieved Oct. 7, 2001.

Nevers, C.C. and M.W. Calkins. (1895) "Dr. Jastrow on community of ideas of men and women", in *Psychological Review*, 2, pp. 363-367. Electronic version located at http://psychclassics.yorku.ca/Special/Women/nevers.htm; retrieved Oct. 30, 2001.

Newlands, J. (1863) "On Relations among the Equivalents", in *Chemical News*, Vol. 7, pp. 70–72. Electronic version located at from http://webserver.lemoyne.edu/faculty/giunta/newlands.html; retrieved Jan. 26, 2001.

Newlands, J. (1864) "Relations between Equivalents", in *Chemical News*, Vol. 10, pp. 59–60. Electronic version located at from http://webserver.lemoyne.edu/faculty/giunta/newlands.html; retrieved Jan. 26, 2001.

Newlands, J. (1864) "On Relations Among the Equivalents", in *Chemical News*, Vol. 10, pp. 94–95. Electronic version located at from http://webserver.lemoyne.edu/faculty/giunta/newlands.html; retrieved Jan. 26, 2001.

Newlands, J. (1865) "On the Law of Octaves", *Chemical News* Vol. 12, p. 83. Electronic version located at from http://webserver.lemoyne.edu/faculty/giunta/newlands.html; retrieved Jan. 26, 2001.

North, D. (1691) *Discourses Upon Trade*. London: Printed for Tho. Basset. Electronic version located at http://socserv2.socsci.mcmaster.ca/~econ/ugcm/3ll3/north/trade.txt; retrieved Dec. 1, 2000.

Overbury, T. (1611) *Sir Thomas Ouerburie his wife with new elegies vpon his (now knowne) vntimely death*. London: Printed by E. Griffin for L. L'isle. Electronic version located at http://www.hti.umich.edu/e/eebo; retrieved May 18, 2001.

Owen, J. (1634) *An Antidote Against Purgatory*. Source copy owned by Bodleian Library. STC 18984. Electronic version located at the *Renaissance Women Online* web site, retrieved Oct. 7, 2001.

Paley, W. (1809) *Natural Theology; or, Evidences of the Existence and Attributes of the Deity*. 12th edition, 1st edition 1802. London: Printed for J. Faulder. Electronic version located at http://www.hti.umich.edu/cgi/p/pd-modeng/pd-modeng-idx?type=HTML&rgn=TEI.2&byte=53049319; retrieved Feb. 12, 2001.

Parr, S. (1659) *Susanna's Apologie against the Elders*. [S.l.: s.n.]. Wing P551. Electronic version located at the *Renaissance Women Online* web site, retrieved Oct. 7, 2001.

Pater, W. (1865) "Coleridge", in *Appreciations* (1890). London: Macmillan and Co. pp. 64–106. Electronic version located at http://www.library.utoronto.ca/utel/rp/criticism/coler_il.html; retrieved Jan. 31, 2001.

Pater, W. (1874) "Wordsworth", in *Appreciations* (1890). London: Macmillan and Co. pp. 37–63. Electronic version located at http://www.library.utoronto.ca/utel/rp/criticism/words_il.html; retrieved Jan. 31, 2001.

Pater, W. (1888) "Style", in *Appreciations* (1890). London: Macmillan and Co. pp. 1–36. Electronic version located at http://www.library.utoronto.ca/utel/rp/criticism/style_il.html; retrieved Jan. 31, 2001.

Pemell, R. (1653) *De Morbis Puerorum, or, a Treatise of The Diseases of Children*. London: Printed by J. Legass. Electronic version located at http://www.neonatology.org/classics/pemell.html; retrieved Dec. 14, 2000.

Petty, W. (1662) *A Treatise of Taxes & Contributions*. London: Printed for N. Brooke. Electronic version located at http://socserv2.socsci.mcmaster.ca/~econ/ugcm/3ll3/petty/taxes.txt; retrieved Dec. 1, 2000.

Petty, W. (1690) *Political Arithmetick*. London: Printed for R. Clavel and H. Mortlock. Electronic version located at http://socserv2.socsci.mcmaster.ca/~econ/ugcm/3ll3/petty/poliarith.html; retrieved Dec. 1, 2000.

Poole, Eh. (1648) *A Vision: Wherein is manifested the disease and cure of the Kingdome*. London: [s.n.]. Wing P2810. Electronic version located at the *Renaissance Women Online* web site, retrieved Oct. 7, 2001.

Pope, A. (1715) "Preface" to *The Iliad of Homer. Vol. I*. London: W. Bowyer for B. Lintott. Electronic version located at http://www.library.utoronto.ca/utel/rp/criticism/prefa_il.html; retrieved Jan. 31, 2001.

Potter, S.O.L. (1902) *A Compend of Materia Medica, Therapeutics, and Prescription Writing With Especial Reference to the Physiological Actions of Drugs*. 6th edition, 1st edition 1894. Philadelphia: P. Blakiston's Son & Co. Electronic version located at http://www.ibiblio.org/herbmed/eclectic/potter-comp/main.html; retrieved Feb. 1, 2001.

Priestley, J. (1772) *Impregnating Water with Fixed Air*. London: Printed for J. Johnson. Electronic version created from page images at http://dbhs. wvusd.k12.ca.us/Chem-History/Priestley-1772; retrieved Jan. 26, 2001.

Priestley, J. (1775) *Experiments and Observations on Different Kinds of Air. Vol. II* (Section III). 2nd edition. London: Printed for J. Johnson. Electronic version located at http://webserver.lemoyne.edu/faculty/giunta/ priestley.html; retrieved Jan. 25, 2001.

Priestley, J. (1789) "Objections to the Experiments and Observations relating to the Principle of Acidity, the Composition of Water, and Phlogiston", in *Philosophical Transactions*, 79, p.7–11. Electronic version located at http://webserver.lemoyne.edu/faculty/giunta/priesteau.html; retrieved Jan. 25, 2001.

Priestley, J. (1796) *Considerations on the Doctrine of Phlogiston and The Decomposition of Water*. Philadelphia: Printed by T. Dobson. Electronic version located at http://webserver.lemoyne.edu/faculty/giunta/ phlogiston.html; retrieved Jan. 25, 2001.

Prout, W. (1815) "On the Relation between the Specific Gravities of Bodies in their Gaseous State and the Weights of their Atoms", published anonymously in *Annals of Philosophy* 6, pp. 321–330. Electronic version based on a reproduction in D.M. Knight, ed., *Classical Scientific Papers: Chemistry*. Second Series (New York: American Elsevier, 1970), located at http://webserver.lemoyne.edu/faculty/giunta/prout.html; retrieved Jan. 25, 2001.

Puttenham, G. (1589) *The Arte of English Poesie*. London: R. Field. British Library G.11548. STC 20519. Electronic version located at http:// www.library.utoronto.ca/utel/rp/criticism/artofp_all.html; retrieved Jan. 31, 2001.

Quiller-Couch, A. (1916) *On the art of writing: Lectures delivered in the University of Cambridge, 1913-1914*. Cambridge: University Press. Electronic version located at http://www.bartleby.com/190; retrieved Apr. 17, 2001.

Quiller-Couch, A. (1921) *On the art of reading: Lectures delivered in the University of Cambridge, 1916-1917*. Cambridge: University Press. Electronic version located at http://www.bartleby.com/191; retrieved Apr. 17, 2001.

R., M. (1630) *The Mothers Counsell*. London: for Iohn Wright. STC 20583. Electronic version located at the *Renaissance Women Online* web site, retrieved Oct. 7, 2001.

Rae, J. (1834) *Statement of Some New Principles on the Subject of Political Economy*. Boston: Hilliard, Gray & Co. Electronic version located at http://socserv2.socsci.mcmaster.ca/~econ/ugcm/3ll3/rae/newprin.html; retrieved Dec. 1, 2000.

Raleigh, W. (1595) *The discouerie of the large, rich, and bevvtiful empire of Guiana*. London: Printed by R. Robinson. STC 20634. Electronic version located at http://www.hti.umich.edu/e/eebo; retrieved May 18, 2001.

Ramsay, W. (1897) "An Undiscovered Gas" in *Nature* 56, p. 378. Electronic version based on a facsimile in D. Knight, ed., *Classic Papers in Chemistry*, second series, New York: American Elsevier (1970), and located at http://webserver.lemoyne.edu/faculty/giunta/ramsay.html; retrieved Jan 26, 2001.

Ravenstone, P. (1824) *Thoughts on the Funding System, and its Effects*. London: J. Andrews and J.M. Richardson. Electronic version located at http://panoramix.univ-paris1.fr/CHPE/textes.html; retrieved Feb. 27, 2001.

Ray, J. (1717) *The Wisdom of God Manifested in the Works of the Creation*. 7th edition, 1st edition 1691. London: Printed by R. Harbin, for W. Innys. Electronic version located at http://www.jri.org.uk/wisdom/wisd_fr.htm; retrieved Feb. 6, 2001.

Rayleigh, Lord. (1892) "Density of Nitrogen", in *Nature*, 46, p. 512. Electronic version located at http://webserver.lemoyne.edu/faculty/giunta/ rayleigh0.html; retrieved Jan. 25, 2001.

Rayleigh, Lord (1895) "Argon", in *Royal Institution Proceedings*, 14, p. 524. Electronic version located at http://webserver.lemoyne.edu/faculty/giunta/ rayleigh.html; retrieved Jan. 25, 2001.

Reed, J. (1922) *Ten days that shook the world*. New York: Boni & Liveright. Electronic version located at http://www.bartleby.com/79; retrieved Dec. 13, 2000.

Renaissance Women Online. (1999) Providence, RI: Brown University. Web site located at http://www.wwp.brown.edu/texts/rwoentry.html.

Renascence Editions. (1992-2003) Eugene, OR: R. Bear and The University of Oregon. Web site located at http://www.uoregon.edu/~rbear/ren.htm.

Ricardo, D. (1810) *The High Price of Bullion*. London: Printed for J. Murray. Electronic version located at http://socserv.mcmaster.ca/econ/ugcm/3ll3/ ricardo/bullion; retrieved Feb. 17, 2001.

Ricardo, D. (1815) *An Essay on the Influence of a low Price of Corn on the Profits of Stock*. London: Printed for J. Murray. Electronic version located at http://socserv2.socsci.mcmaster.ca/~econ/ugcm/3ll3/ricardo/profits.txt; retrieved Feb. 17, 2001.

Ricardo, D. (1821) *On The Principles of Political Economy and Taxation*. 3rd edition, 1st edition 1817. London: J. Murray. Electronic version located at http://socserv.mcmaster.ca/econ/ugcm/3ll3/ricardo/Principles.pdf; retrieved Feb. 18, 2001.

Ripley, G. (1683) *The Bosome-Book of Sir George Ripley, Canon of Bridlington*. London: Printed for W. Cooper. Electronic version located at http:// www.levity.com/alchemy/bosom.html; retrieved Feb. 1, 2001.

Robinson, R. (1947) "Structures of Ethylene Oxide and Cyclopropane", in *Nature*, 159, pp. 400–401. Electronic version located at http:// www.bluffton.edu/~bergerd/chem/walsh/159-400.html; retrieved Jan. 26, 2001.

Robinson, R. (1947) "Formulæ for Ethylene Oxide and Cyclopropane", in *Nature*, 160, p. 162. Electronic version located at http://www.bluffton.edu/~bergerd/chem/walsh/160-162.html; retrieved Jan. 26, 2001.

Rogers, C.R.. (1946) "Significant aspects of client-centered therapy", in *American Psychologist*, 1, pp. 415–422. Electronic version located at http://psychclassics. yorku.ca/Rogers/therapy.htm; retrieved Oct. 30, 2001.

Rogers, C.R.. (1947) "Some observations on the organization of personality", in *American Psychologist*, 2, pp. 358–368. Electronic version located at http://psychclassics.yorku.ca/Rogers/personality.htm; retrieved Oct. 30, 2001.

Rosenzweig, S. (1941) "Need-persistive and Ego-defensive Reactions to Frustration as Demonstrated by an Experiment on Repression", in *Psychological Review*, 48, pp. 347–349. http://psychclassics.yorku.ca/FrustAgg/rosenzweig.htm; retrieved Oct. 23, 2001.

Ross, A. (1652) *Arcana Microcosmi. Book II*. London: Printed by T. Newcombe. Electronic version located at http://penelope.uchicago.edu/ross/index.html; retrieved Feb. 13, 2001.

Royce, J. (1902) "Recent logical inquiries and their psychological bearings", in *Psychological Review*, 9, pp. 105–133. Electronic version located at http://psychclassics.yorku.ca/Royce; retrieved Oct. 30, 2001.

Rozeboom, W.W. (1960) "The fallacy of the null-hypothesis significance test", in *Psychological Bulletin*, 57, pp. 416–428. Electronic version located at http://psychclassics.yorku.ca/Rozeboom; retrieved Oct. 30, 2001.

Rutherford, E. (1899) "Uranium Radiation and the Electrical Conduction Produced by It", in *The Philosophical Magazine*, January 1899, ser. 5, xlvii, pp. 109–163. Electronic version located at http://dbhs.wvusd.k12.ca.us/Chem-History/Rutherford-Alpha&Beta.html; retrieved Jan. 26, 2001.

Sanford, E.C. (1891–1892). "A laboratory course in physiological psychology", in *American Journal of Psychology*, 4, pp. 141–155, 303–322, 474–490; 5, pp. 390–415, 593–616. Electronic version located at http://psychclassics.yorku.ca/Sanford; retrieved Oct. 30, 2001.

Savery, T. (1702) *The Miners Friend*. London: Printed for S. Crouch. Electronic version located at http://www.history.rochester.edu/steam/savery; retrieved Oct. 10, 2001.

Schreiner, O. (1896) *The Political Situation*. London: T. Fisher Unwin. Electronic version located at http://www.indiana.edu/~letrs/vwwp/schreiner/politsit.html; retrieved Jan. 2, 2001.

Scott, T. (1624) *Certaine reasons and argvments of policie*. [London: s.n.] Electronic version located at the *Renascence Editions* web site, http://darkwing.uoregon.edu/~rbear/spain.html; retrieved Dec. 13, 2000.

Scudder, J.M. (1870) *Specific Medication and Specific Medicines*. Cincinnati: Wilstach, Baldwin & Co., Printers. Electronic version located at http://www.ibiblio.org/herbmed/eclectic/spec-med/main.html; retrieved Feb. 1, 2001.

Sears, R.R. (1941) "Non-aggressive Reactions to Frustration", in *Psychological Review*, 48, pp. 343–346. Electronic version located at http://psychclassics. yorku.ca/FrustAgg/sears.htm; retrieved Oct. 23, 2001.

Selden, J. (1640) *A Briefe Discovrse Concerning the Povver of the Peeres*. [London]: Printed [by T. Paine]. STC 22165. Electronic version located at http://socserv.socsci.mcmaster.ca/econ/ugcm/3ll3/selden/peeres.htm; retrieved Jan. 30, 2001.

Seligman, E. (1902) "The Economic Interpretation of History", in *Political Science Quarterly*, volume 16, pp. 612–640; volume 17, pp. 71–98, 284–312. Electronic version located at http://panoramix.univ-paris1.fr/CHPE/ textes.html; retrieved Feb. 27, 2001.

Senior, N. (1830) *Three Lectures on the Rate of Wages*. 2nd edition, 1st edition 1830. London: J. Murray. Electronic version located at http://socserv2. socsci.mcmaster.ca/~econ/ugcm/3ll3/senior/wages.html; retrieved Feb. 17, 2001.

Senior, N. (1854) *Political Economy*. 3rd edition, 1st edition 1848. London and Glasgow: R. Griffin and Company. Electronic version located at http:// www.econlib.org/library/Senior/snPtoc.html; retrieved Feb. 21, 2001.

Shelley, P. (1821) *Defence of Poetry. Part First*. Bodleian Library Ms. Shelley e.6. Electronic version based on a facsimile in *The Bodleian Shelley Manuscripts: A Facsimile Edition* (1994), edited by M. O'Neill, New York and London: Garland. Located at http://www.library.utoronto.ca/utel/rp/ criticism/shell_il.html; retrieved Jan. 31, 2001.

Sibly, E. (1795) *A New and Complete Illustration of the Occult Sciences* (Book IV). London: Printed for the Author. Electronic version located at http:// www.esotericarchives.com/solomon/sibly4.htm; retrieved Aug. 13, 2001.

Sidgwick, H. (1877) "Bentham and Benthamism in Politics and Ethics", in *The Fortnightly Review*, 21, January-June 1877, pp. 627–652. Electronic version located at http://panoramix.univ-paris1.fr/CHPE/Textes/Sidgwick/ Bentham0. html; retrieved Dec. 1, 2000.

Sidgwick, H. (1879) "The Wages Fund Theory", in *The Fortnightly Review*, volume 25, July–December, pp. 401–413. Electronic version located at http://panoramix.univ-paris1.fr/CHPE/Textes/Sidgwick/Wf.html; retrieved Dec. 1, 2000.

Sidgwick, H. (1879) "What is Money?" in *The Fortnightly Review*, 25, January-June, pp. 563–575. Electronic version located at http://panoramix.univ-paris1.fr/CHPE/Textes/ Sidgwick/Money0.html; retrieved Dec. 1, 2000.

Sidgwick, H. (1886) "Economic Socialism", in *The Contemporary Review*, volume 50, pp. 620–631. Electronic version located at http://phare.univ-paris1.fr/textes/Sidgwick/_Social.html; retrieved Dec. 1, 2000.

Sidney, P. (1595) *The Defence of Poesie*. London: William Ponsonby. British Library C.57.b.38. Electronic version located at http://www.library. utoronto.ca/utel/rp/criticism/defen_il.html; retrieved Jan. 31, 2001.

Skinner, B.F. (1935) "Two types of conditioned reflex and a pseudo type", in *Journal of General Psychology*, 12, pp. 66–77. Electronic version located at http://psychclassics.yorku.ca/Skinner/Twotypes/twotypes.htm; retrieved Oct. 30, 2001.

Skinner, B.F. (1937) "Two types of conditioned reflex: A reply to Konorski and Miller", in *Journal of General Psychology*, 16, pp. 272–279. Electronic version located at http://psychclassics.yorku.ca/Skinner/ReplytoK/reply.htm; retrieved Oct. 30, 2001.

Skinner, B.F. (1948) "'Superstition' in the pigeon", in *Journal of Experimental Psychology*, 38, pp. 168–172. Electronic version located at http://psychclassics.yorku.ca/Skinner/Pigeon; retrieved Oct. 30, 2001.

Skinner, B.F. (1950) "Are theories of learning necessary?", in *Psychological Review*, 57, pp. 193–216. Electronic version located at http://psychclassics.yorku.ca/Skinner/Theories; retrieved Oct. 30, 2001.

Slater, E.A. (1878) *Treatise on the Relation of Christians to Earthly Governments, or the Kingdom of Christ among the Nations*. Lexington, KY: Transylvania Printing and Publishing Co. Electronic version located at http://www.ag.uiuc.edu/~mcmillan/Restlit/Etexts/slater.html; retrieved Dec. 14, 2000.

Sledd, R.N. (1861) *A Sermon Delivered in the Market Street*. Petersburg: A.F. Crutchfield & Co. Electronic version located at http://docsouth.unc.edu/sledd/sledd.html; retrieved Dec. 14, 2000.

Smellie, W. (1762) *A Treatise on the Theory and Practice of Midwifery, Vol. 1* (Book 4, Chapter II). London: [s.n.]. Electronic version located at http://www.neonatology.org/classics/smellie.html; retrieved Dec. 14, 2000.

Smith, A. (1759) *The Theory of Moral Sentiments*. London: Printed for A. Millar, A. Kincaid and J. Bell. Electronic version located at http://socserv2.socsci.mcmaster.ca/~econ/ugcm/3ll3/smith/moral.1; retrieved Dec. 1, 2000.

Smith, S. (1864) "Amputations", in *Military Medical and Surgical Essays Prepared for the United States Sanitary Commission*, edited by W.A. Hammond. Philadelphia: J.B. Lippincott & Co. Electronic version located at http://www.netwalk.com/~jpr/amputate.htm; retrieved Feb. 1, 2001.

Smith, W.R. (1861) *The History and Debates of the Convention of the People of Alabama, Begun and held in the City of Montgomery, on the Seventh Day of January, 1861*. Montgomery; Tuscaloosa; Atlanta: White Pfister & Co.; D. Woodruff; Wood, Hanleiter, Rice & Co. Electronic version located at http://docsouth.unc.edu/imls/smithwr/smith.html; retrieved Dec. 14, 2000.

Snow, J. (1855) *On the Mode of Communication of Cholera*. London: J. Churchill. Electronic version located at http://www.ph.ucla.edu/epi/snow/snowbook.html; retrieved Feb. 1, 2001.

Sowernam, E. (1617) *Ester Hath Hang'd Haman*. London: Printed for N. Bourne. STC 22974. Electronic version located at the *Renaissance Women Online* web site, retrieved Oct. 7, 2001.

Spearman, C. (1904) "'General intelligence,' objectively determined and measured", in *American Journal of Psychology*, 15, pp. 201–293. Electronic version located at http://psychclassics.yorku.ca/Spearman/chap1-4.htm; retrieved Oct. 31, 2001.

Speght, R. (1617) *A mouzell for Melastomus, the cynical bayter of, and foule barker against Evahs sex*. London: Printed by N. Okes for T. Archer. STC 23058. Electronic version located at the *Renaissance Women Online* web site, retrieved Oct. 7, 2001.

Sprat, T. (1667) *The History of the Royal-Society of London* (extracts). London: Printed by T. R. and J. Allestry. Electronic version located at http://andromeda.rutgers.edu/~jlynch/Texts/sprat.html; retrieved Feb. 14, 2001.

Stagg, A., et al. (1641) *A True Copie of the Petition of the Gentlewomen, and Tradesmens-wives, in and about the City of London*. London: Printed by R. O. & G. D. for J. Bull. Wing T2656. Electronic version located at the *Renaissance Women Online* web site, retrieved Oct. 7, 2001.

Starr, L. (1889) *Hygiene of the Nursery*. 2nd edition. Philadelphia: P. Blakiston, Son. & Co. Electronic version located at http://www.neonatology.org/classics/starr/starr.html; retrieved Dec. 14, 2000.

Stephen, L. (1900) *The English Utilitarians. Volume Two: James Mill*. New York: G. P. Putnam's Sons. Electronic version located at http://socserv2.socsci.mcmaster.ca/~econ/ugcm/3ll3/mill/utila2.htm; retrieved Jan. 20, 2001.

Stephen, J.F. (1873) *Liberty, Equality, Fraternity*. London: Smith, Elder, & Co. Electronic version located at http://www.execpc.com/~berrestr/stelib.html; retrieved Feb. 6, 2001.

Stewart, J. (1767) *An Inquiry into the Principles of Political Economy*. 2 vols. London: Printed for A. Millar and T. Cadell. Electronic version located at http://socserv2.socsci.mcmaster.ca/~econ/ugcm/3ll3/steuart/princi1; retrieved Dec. 1, 2000.

Stoney, G. (1894) "Of the 'Electron,' or Atom of Electricity", in *The Philosophical Magazine*, Series 5, Volume 38, pp. 418–420. Electronic version located at http://dbhs.wvusd.k12.ca.us/Chem-History/Stoney-1894.html; retrieved May 18, 2001.

Stroop, J.R. (1935) "Studies of interference in serial verbal reactions", in *Journal of Experimental Psychology*, 28, pp. 643–662. Electronic version located at http://psychclassics.yorku.ca/Stroop; retrieved Oct. 31, 2001.

Strunk, W. (1918) *Elements of Style*. Ithaca, N.Y.: Privately printed. Electronic version located at http://www.bartleby.com/141; retrieved Dec. 13, 2000.

Sutcliffe, A. (1634) *Meditations of Man's Mortalitie*. London: Printed by B.A. and T.F. for H. Seyle. 2nd edition. STC 23447. Electronic version located at the *Renaissance Women Online* web site, retrieved Oct. 7, 2001.

Swetnam, J. (1617) *The Schoole of the Noble and Worthy Science of Defence* (excerpts). London: Printed by N. Okes. Electronic version located at http://jan.ucc.nau.edu/~wew/fencing/swetnam-man.html; retrieved Feb. 8, 2001. Checked against page images of the original edition at http://www.schooleofdefence.fsnet.co.uk/page9.html; retrieved Feb. 8, 2001.

Swift, J. (1732) *A Proposal For an Act of Parliament, To Pay off the Debt of the Nation, Without Taxing the Subject*. Dublin: [s.n.]. Electronic version located at http://socserv2.socsci.mcmaster.ca/~econ/ugcm/3ll3/swift/debt; retrieved Dec. 1, 2000.

Swift, J. (1736) *Reasons Why We Should not Lower the coins now current in this Kingdom*. Dublin: Printed by E. Waters. Electronic version located at http://socserv2.socsci.mcmaster.ca/~econ/ugcm/3ll3/swift/coins; retrieved Dec. 1, 2000.

Tattle-well, M. (1640) *The Womens Sharp Revenge*. London: I.O. Source copy owned by Bodleian Library. STC 23706. Electronic version located at the *Renaissance Women Online* web site, retrieved Oct. 7, 2001.

Terman, L.M. (1916) "The uses of intelligence tests", in *The Measurement of Intelligence* (chapter 1). Boston: Houghton Mifflin. Electronic version located at http://psychclassics.yorku.ca/Terman/terman1.htm; retrieved Oct. 31, 2001.

Thomson, J.J. (1897) "Cathode Rays", in *The Philosophical Magazine*, 44, p. 293. Electronic version based on a facsimile in S. Wright, ed. *Classical Scientific Papers, Physics*. London: Mills and Boon (1964), located at http://webserver.lemoyne.edu/faculty/giunta/thomson1897.html; retrieved Jan. 25, 2001.

Thomson, J.J. (1899) "On the Masses of the Ions in Gases at Low Pressures", in *The Philosophical Magazine*, Series 5, Vol. 48, No. 295. pp. 547–567. Electronic version located at http://dbhs.wvusd.k12.ca.us/Chem-History/Thomson-1899.html; retrieved Jan. 25, 2001.

Thomson, J.J. (1904) "On the Structure of the Atom: an Investigation of the Stability and Periods of Oscillation of a number of Corpuscles arranged at equal intervals around the Circumference of a Circle; with Application of the Results to the Theory of Atomic Structure", in *The Philosophical Magazine*, Series 6, Volume 7, Number 39, pp. 237–265. Electronic version located at http://dbhs.wvusd.k12.ca.us/Chem-History/Thomson-Structure-Atom.html; retrieved Jan. 25, 2001.

Thomson, J.J. (1906) "On the Number of Corpuscles in an Atom", in *The Philosophical Magazine*, vol. 11, June 1906, pp. 769–781. Electronic version located at http://dbhs.wvusd.k12.ca.us/Chem-History/Thomson-1906/Thomson-1906.html; retrieved Jan. 25, 2001.

Thomson, T. (1813) "On the Daltonian Theory of Definite Proportions in Chemical Combinations", in *Annals of Philosophy* 2, p. 32. Electronic version based on a reproduction in D.M. Knight, ed., *Classical Scientific Papers: Chemistry* (New York: American Elsevier, 1968), located at http://webserver.lemoyne.edu/faculty/giunta/tthomson.html; retrieved Jan. 25, 2001.

Thorndike, E.L. and R.S. Woodworth. (1901) "The influence of improvement in one mental function upon the efficiency of other functions (I)", in *Psychological Review*, 8, pp. 247–261. Electronic version located at http://psychclassics.yorku.ca/Thorndike/Transfer/transfer1.htm; retrieved Oct. 31, 2001.

Thorndike, E.L. and R.S. Woodworth. (1901) "The influence of improvement in one mental function upon the efficiency of other functions: II. The estimation of magnitudes", in *Psychological Review*, 8, pp. 384-395. Electronic version located at http://psychclassics.yorku.ca/Thorndike/ Transfer/transfer2.htm; retrieved Oct. 31, 2001.

Thorndike, E.L. and R.S. Woodworth. (1901) "The influence of improvement in one mental function upon the efficiency of other functions: III. Functions involving attention, observation, and discrimination", in *Psychological Review*, 8, pp. 553–564. Electronic version located at http://psychclassics. yorku.ca/Thorndike/Transfer/transfer3.htm; retrieved Oct. 31, 2001.

Thorndike, EL. (1910) "The contribution of psychology to education", in *Journal of Educational Psychology*, 1, pp. 5–12. Electronic version located at http://psychclassics.yorku.ca/Thorndike/education.htm; retrieved Oct. 31, 2001.

Thornton, W.T. (1869) "On Labour, its Wrongful Claims and Rightful Dues, its Actual Present and Possible Future", in *Fortnightly Review*, May 1869, pp. 505–518 (part I), and June, 1869 (part II), pp. 680–700. Electronic version located   at   http://socserv2.socsci.mcmaster.ca/~econ/ugcm/3ll3/mill/ thorn.html; retrieved Dec. 1, 2000.

Thurstone, L.L. (1934) "The vectors of mind", in *Psychological Review*, 41, pp. 1–32. Electronic version located at http://psychclassics.yorku.ca/ Thurstone; retrieved Oct. 31, 2001.

Titchener, E.B. (1898) "The postulates of a structural psychology" , in *Philosophical Review*, 7, pp. 449–465. Electronic version located at http:// psychclassics.yorku.ca/Titchener/structuralism.htm; retrieved Oct. 31, 2001.

Titchener, E.B. (1898) "A psychological laboratory", in *Mind*, 7, pp. 311–331. Electronic version located at http://psychclassics.yorku.ca/Titchener/ lab.htm; retrieved Oct. 31, 2001.

Titchener, E.B. (1912) "The schema of introspection", in *American Journal of Psychology*, 23, pp. 485–508. Electronic version located at http:// psychclassics.yorku.ca/Titchener/introspection.htm; retrieved Oct. 31, 2001.

Titchener, E.B. (1914) "On 'Psychology as the behaviorist views it'", in *Proceedings of the American Philosophical Society*, 53, pp. 1–17. Electronic version located at http://psychclassics.yorku.ca/Titchener/ watson.htm; retrieved Oct. 31, 2001.

Titchener, E.B. (1921) "Brentano and Wundt: Empirical and experimental psychology", in *American Journal of Psychology*, 32, pp. 108–120. Electronic version located at http://psychclassics.yorku.ca/Titchener/ brentano-wundt.htm; retrieved Oct. 31, 2001.

Tolman, Edward C. (1922) "A new formula for behaviorism", in *Psychological Review*, 29, pp. 44–53. Electronic version located at http://psychclassics.yorku. ca/Tolman/formula.htm; retrieved Oct. 31, 2001.

Tolman, E.C. (1948) "Cognitive maps in rats and men", in *Psychological Review*, 55(4), pp. 189–208. Electronic version located at http://psychclassics. yorku.ca/Tolman/Maps/maps.htm; retrieved Oct. 31, 2001.

Tooke, T. (1844) *An Inquiry into the Currency Principle.* London: Printed for Longman, Brown, Green, and Longmans. Electronic version located at http://socserv2.socsci.mcmaster.ca/~econ/ugcm/3ll3/tooke/currency.html; retrieved Dec. 1, 2000.

Torrens, R. (1834) *On Wages and Combination.* London: Longman, Rees, Orme, Brown, Green & Longman. Electronic version located at http://socserv2. socsci.mcmaster.ca/~econ/ugcm/3ll3/torrens/wages.html; retrieved Dec. 1, 2000.

Trapnel, A. (1654) *The Cry of a Stone or a Relation of Something spoken in Whitehall.* London: [s.n.]. Wing T2031. Electronic version located at the *Renaissance Women Online* web site, retrieved Oct. 7, 2001.

Trapnel, A. (1654) *Strange and Wonderful Newes 3 from White-hall.* London: Printed for Robert Sele. Wing T2034. Electronic version located at the *Renaissance Women Online* web site, retrieved Oct. 7, 2001.

Triplett, N. (1898) "The dynamogenic factors in pacemaking and competition", in *American Journal of Psychology*, 9, pp. 507-533. Electronic version located at http://psychclassics.yorku.ca/Triplett; retrieved Oct. 31, 2001.

Vanderlint, J. (1734) *Money Answers All Things.* London: Printed for T. Cox. Electronic version located at from http://socserv2.socsci.mcmaster.ca/ ~econ/ugcm/3ll3/vanderlint/money; retrieved Dec. 1, 2000.

Vaughan, R. (1675) *A Discourse of Coin and Coinage.* London: Printed by Thomas Dawks. Electronic version located at http://socserv2.socsci. mcmaster.ca/~econ/ugcm/3ll3/vaughan/coin; retrieved Dec. 1, 2000.

Vaughan, W. (1626) *The Golden Fleece.* London: Printed for F. Williams. Electronic version located at http://www.mun.ca/rels/hrollmann/relsoc/ texts/vaughan/fleece1.html; retrieved Dec. 4, 2000.

Walpole, H. (1768) *Historic Doubts on the Life and Reign of King Richard the Third.* London: Printed for J. Dodsley. Electronic version located at http://www.r3.org/bookcase/walpole/index.html; retrieved Feb. 28, 2001.

Walsh, A.D. (1947) "Structures of Ethylene Oxide and Cyclopropane", in *Nature*, 159, p. 165. Electronic version located at http://www.bluffton.edu/ ~bergerd/chem/walsh/159-165.html; retrieved Jan. 26, 2001.

Walsh, A.D. (1947) "Structures of Ethylene Oxide and Cyclopropane", in *Nature*, 159, pp. 712–713. Electronic version located at http://www.bluffton.edu/ ~bergerd/chem/walsh/159-712.html; retrieved Jan. 26, 2001.

Warburton, W. (1757) *Remarks on Mr. David Hume's Essay on The Natural History of Religion.* London: Printed for M. Cooper. Electronic version located at http://www.utm.edu/research/hume/com/warbnhr.htm; retrieved Feb. 14, 2001.

Warren, E. (1863) *An Epitome of Practical Surgery, for Field and Hospital.* Richmond, VA: West & Johnston. Electronic version located at http:// docsouth.unc.edu/imls/warrene/warrene.html; retrieved Dec. 14, 2000.

Washburn, M.F. (1922) "Introspection as an objective method", in *Psychological Review*, 29, pp. 89–112. Electronic version located at http://psychclassics. yorku.ca/Washburn; retrieved Oct. 31, 2001.

Watson, J.B. (1913) "Psychology as the behaviorist views it", in *Psychological Review*, 20, pp. 158–177. Electronic version located at http://psychclassics. yorku.ca/Watson/views.htm; retrieved Oct. 31, 2001.

Watson, J.B. (1916) "Behavior and the concept of mental disease", in *Journal of Philosophy, Psychology, and Scientific Methods*, 13, pp. 589–597. Electronic version located at http://psychclassics.yorku.ca/Watson/ mental.htm; retrieved Oct. 31, 2001.

Watson, J.B. (1920) "Is thinking merely the action of language mechanisms?", in *British Journal of Psychology*, 11, pp. 87–104. Electronic version located at http://psychclassics.yorku.ca/Watson/thinking.htm; retrieved Oct. 31, 2001.

Watson, J.B. and R. Rayner. (1920) "Conditioned emotional reactions", in *Journal of Experimental Psychology*, 3, pp. 1–14. Electronic version located at http://psychclassics.yorku.ca/Watson/emotion.htm; retrieved Oct. 31, 2001.

Watson, R. (1789) "Of Fire, Sulphur, and Phlogiston", in *Chemical Essays*. 5th edition. London: T. Evans. Electronic version located at http://webserver. lemoyne.edu/faculty/giunta/Watsonphlogiston.html; retrieved Jan. 21, 2002.

Watt, J. (1784) "Thoughts on the Constituent Parts of Water and of Dephlogisticated Air" (excerpt), in *Philosophical Transactions*, 74, p. 329. Electronic version located at http://webserver.lemoyne.edu/faculty/giunta/ watt.html; retrieved Jan. 25, 2001.

West, E. (1815) *Essay on the Application of Capital to Land.* London: Printed for T. Underwood. Electronic version located at http://socserv2.socsci. mcmaster.ca/~econ/ugcm/3ll3/west/west.txt; retrieved Dec. 1, 2000.

Whewell, W. (1862) *Six Lectures on Political Economy.* Cambridge: Printed at the University Press. Electronic version located at http://phare.univ-paris1.fr/textes/Whewell/lecture0.htm; retrieved Feb. 15, 2001.

Whitbourne, R. (1620) *A Discovrse and Discoverie of Nevv-found-land.* London: Printed by F. Kingston, for W. Barret. Electronic version located at http://www.mun.ca/rels/hrollmann/relsoc/texts/whitbourne/whit.html; retrieved Dec. 4, 2000.

Wicksteed, P.H. (1914) "The Scope and Method of Political Economy", in *Economic Journal*, volume 24, pp. 1–23. Electronic version located at http://socserv2.socsci.mcmaster.ca/~econ/ugcm/3ll3/wicksteed/scope.html; retrieved Jan. 20, 2001.

Wigington, L. (1684) *The Confession and Execution of Letitia Wigington of Ratclif.* London: Printed for L. Curtiss. Electronic version located at http://chaucer.library.emory.edu/cgi-bin/sgml2html/wwrp.pl; retrieved Feb. 13, 2001.

Williams, R.P. (1896) *An Introduction to Chemical Science.* Boston: Ginn and Company. Electronic version located at ftp://ftp.mirror.ac.uk/sites/metalab. unc.edu/pub/docs/books/gutenberg/etext03/aitcs10.txt; retrieved Aug. 6, 2001.

Wilson, T. (1585) *The Arte of Rhetorique.* London: Printed by G. Robinson. Electronic version located at the *Renascence Editions* web site, http://darkwing.uoregon.edu/~rbear/arte/arte.htm; retrieved Jan. 24, 2001.

Withers, T.J. (1862) *"Cato" on Constitutional "Money" and Legal Tender.* Charleston: Steam-Power Presses of Evans & Cogswell. Electronic version located at http://docsouth.unc.edu/witherst/witherst.html; retrieved Dec. 14, 2000.

Witmer, L. (1907) "Clinical psychology", in *Psychological Clinic*, 1, pp. 1-9. Electronic version located at http://psychclassics.yorku.ca/Witmer/clinical.htm; retrieved Oct. 31, 2001.

Woolley, H. (1664) *The Cooks Guide: or, Rare Receipts for Cookery.* London: Printed for P. Dring. Wing W3276. Electronic version located at the *Renaissance Women Online* web site, retrieved Oct. 7, 2001.

Woolley, H. (1675) *The Gentlewoman's Companion: or, A Guide to the Female Sex.* [S.l.]: Printed for E. Thomas Bookseller. Electronic version located at http://chaucer.library.emory.edu/cgi-bin/sgml2html/wwrp.pl; retrieved Feb. 13, 2001.

Woolley, H.T. (1910) "A Review of the recent literature on the psychology of sex", in *Psychological Bulletin*, 7, pp. 335–342. Electronic version located at http://psychclassics.yorku.ca/Thompson/psychsex.htm; retrieved Oct. 31, 2001.

Wordsworth, W. (1798) "Preface" *Lyrical Ballads, with a Few Other Poems.* London: Printed for J. and A. Arch. Electronic version located at http://www.library.utoronto.ca/utel/rp/criticism/lyrb1_il.html; retrieved Jan. 31, 2001.

Yerkes, R.M. and J.D. Dodson. (1908) "The relation of strength of stimulus to rapidity of habit-formation", in *Journal of Comparative Neurology and Psychology*, 18, pp. 459–482. Electronic version located at http://psychclassics.yorku.ca/Yerkes/Law; retrieved Oct. 31, 2001.

Yerkes, R.M. and S. Morgulis. (1909) "The method of Pawlow in animal psychology", in *Psychological Bulletin*, 6, pp. 257–273. Electronic version located at http://psychclassics.yorku.ca/Yerkes/pavlov.htm; retrieved Oct. 31, 2001.

Young, A.A. (1911) "Some Limitations of the Value Concept", in *Quarterly Journal of Economics*, volume 25, pp. 409–428. Electronic version located at http://socserv2.socsci.mcmaster.ca/~econ/ugcm/3ll3/young/value; retrieved Dec. 1. 2000.

Young, A.A. (1928) "Increasing Returns and Economic Progress", in *The Economic Journal*, volume 38, pp. 527–42. Electronic version located at http://socserv2.socsci.mcmaster.ca/~econ/ugcm/3ll3/young/increas.html; retrieved Oct. 28, 2001.

Young, E. (1759) *Conjectures on Original Composition*. London: Printed for A. Millar. Electronic version located at http://www.library.utoronto.ca/utel/rp/ criticism/conje_il.html; retrieved Jan. 31, 2001.

C. General dictionaries

Allen, R.E., ed. (1990) *The Concise Oxford Dictionary of Current English*. 8th edition, 1st edition 1911. Oxford: Clarendon Press.

Allen, R., ed. (2000) *The New Penguin English Dictionary*. London: Penguin Books.

Bailey, N. (1721) *An Universal Etymological English Dictionary*. London: E. Bell, J. Darby, A. Bettesworth, F. Fayram, J. Pemberton, J. Hooke, C. Rivington, F. Clay, J. Batley, and E. Symon.

Bailey, R.W., ed. (1978) *Early Modern English: Additions and Antedatings to the Record of English Vocabulary 1475-1700*. Hildesheim: Georg Olms Verlag.

Barclay, J. (1819) *A Complete and Universal English Dictionary*. London: T. Kelly.

Blount, T. (1656) *Glossographia*. London: Printed by T. Newcomb. Wing B3334. Included in the *Early Modern English Dictionaries Database* (*EMEDD*), edited by I. Lancashire.

Blount, T. (1661) *Glossographia*. 2nd edition, 1st edition 1656. London: Printed by T. Newcomb. Wing B3335.

Bullokar, J. (1616) *An English Expositor: teaching the interpretation of the hardest words in our language*. London: Printed by J. Legatt. STC 4083. Included in *EMEDD*, edited by I. Lancashire.

Bullokar, J. (1680) *An English Expositor: teaching the interpretation of the hardest words in our language*. 6th edition, 1st edition published 1616. Cambridge: J. Hayes.

Cawdrey, R. (1604) *A Table Alphabeticall*. London: Printed by I.R. for E. Weauer. STC 4884. Electronic version located at http://www.library. utoronto.ca/utel/ret/cawdrey/cawdrey0.html; retrieved Jan. 25, 2001. Included in *EMEDD*, edited by I. Lancashire.

Cockeram, H. (1623) *The English Dictionarie*. London: Printed by Eliot's Court Press for N. Butter. STC 5461. Included in *EMEDD*, edited by I. Lancashire.

Cockeram, H. (1626) *The English Dictionarie*. 2nd edition, 1st edition 1623. London: Printed by I. Haggard for E. Weaver. STC 5462.

Coles, E. (1676) *An English Dictionary*. London: Printed for S. Crouch at the Corner Shop of Popes-head. Wing C5070.

Coote, E. (1596) *The English Schoole-maister*. London: Printed by the Widow Orwin, for R. Iackson and R. Dexter. Electronic version located at http:// www.library.utoronto.ca/utel/ret/coote/coote.html; retrieved Jan. 25, 2001. Included in *EMEDD*, edited by I. Lancashire.

Cotgrave, R. (1611) *A dictionarie of the French and English tongues*. London: Printed by A. Islip. STC 5830. Included in *EMEDD*, edited by I. Lancashire.

Craig, J. (1848) *A New Universal Technological, Etymological and Pronouncing Dictionary of the English Language. Vol. 2*. London: H.G. Collins.

Craig, J. (1852) *A New Universal Technological, Etymological and Pronouncing Dictionary of the English Language. Vol. 1*. London: G. Routledge & Co.

Davidson, T., ed. (1914) *Chambers's English Dictionary*. London: W. & R. Chambers.

Engineer, S. and H. Gay, eds. (1991) *Longman Dictionary of the English Language*. Burnt Mill: Longman. (*LDEL*)

Florio, J. (1598) *A worlde of wordes, or most copious, dictionarie in Italian and English*. London: Printed by A. Hatfield for E. Blount. STC 11098. Included in *EMEDD*, edited by I. Lancashire.

Glare, P.G.W., ed. (1982) *Oxford Latin Dictionary*. Oxford: Clarendon Press.

Gove, P.B., ed. (1993) *Webster's Third New International Dictionary of the English Language*. (1961 edition with six subsequent Addenda.) Springfield, Ma.: Merriam-Webster.

Higgleton, E. et al, eds. (1993) *The Chambers Dictionary*. Edinburgh: Chambers Harrap Publishers Ltd.

Hornby, A.S. (1995) *Oxford Advanced Learner's Dictionary of Current English*. 5th edition, edited by J. Crowther. Oxford: Oxford University Press. (*OALD*)

Hornby, A.S., E.V. Gatenby, and H. Wakefield. (1963) *The Advanced Learner's Dictionary of Current English*. 2nd edition. London: Oxford University Press.

Johnson, S. (1755) *A Dictionary of the English Language: in which the Words are deduced from their Originals, and illustrated in their Different Significations by Examples from the Best Writers*. 2 volumes. London: J.F. & C. Rivington.

Kersey, J. (1702) *A New English Dictionary*. London: Printed for H. Bonwicke.

Kurath, H., S.M. Kuhn et al, eds. (1956-2001) *Middle English Dictionary*. Ann Arbor: The University of Michigan Press.

Lancashire, I., ed. (1999) *Early Modern English Dictionaries Database*. Internet site at http://www.chass.utoronto.ca/english/emed/emedd.html. (*EMEDD*)

Latham, R.E. (1965) *Revised Medieval Latin Word-List from British and Irish Sources*. London: The British Academy by the Oxford University Press.

Lewis, C.T. and C. Short. (1879) *A Latin Dictionary*. Oxford: Clarendon Press.

Liddell, H.G. and R. Scott. (1940) A Greek-English Lexicon. 9th edition, revised by H.S. Jones. 1st edition published 1843. Oxford: Clarendon Press.

McIntosh, E., ed. (1951) *The Concise Oxford Dictionary of Current English*. 4th edition, 1st edition 1911. Oxford: Clarendon Press.

Minsheu, J. (1617) *The Guide into the Tongues*. London: J. Browne. STC 17944.

Mulcaster, R. (1582) *The First Part of the Elementarie which entreateth of right writing of our English tung*. Printed by T. Vautroullier. STC 18250.

Electronic version located at http://www.hti.umich.edu; retrieved Sept. 5, 2001. Included in *EMEDD*, edited by I. Lancashire.

Murray, J.A.H., H. Bradley, W.A. Craigie, and C.T. Onions, eds. (1992) *The Oxford English Dictionary*, 2nd edition on compact disc, prepared by I.A. Simpson and E.S.C. Weiner. 1st ed. published 1933. Oxford: Oxford University Press and Software. (*OED*)

Ogilvie, J. (1882) *The Imperial Dictionary of the English Language*, edited by C. Annandale. London: Blackie & Son.

Onions, C.T., ed. (1966) *The Oxford Dictionary of English Etymology*. Oxford: Clarendon Press.

Palsgrave, J. (1530) *Lesclarcissement de la langue francoyse*. Printed by R. Pynson and J. Haukyns. STC 19166. Included in *EMEDD*, edited by I. Lancashire.

Pearsall, J, ed. (1998) *The New Oxford Dictionary of English*. Oxford: Clarendon Press. (*NODE*)

Phillips, E. (1658) *The New World of English Words; or, a General Dictionary*. London: E. Tyler for N. Brooke at the Sign of the Angel in Cornhill.

Pickett, J.P. et al, eds. (2000) *The American Heritage Dictionary of the English Language*. 4th edition. Boston: Houghton Mifflin Co.

Procter, P. et al, eds. (1995) *Cambridge International Dictionary of English*. Cambridge: Cambridge University Press. (*CIDE*)

Robert, P. (2001) *Le Grand Robert de la Langue Française*. 2nd edition. Paris: Dictionnaires le Robert.

Richardson, C. (1836) *A New Dictionary of the English Language*. London: W. Pickering.

Rooney, K. et al, eds. (1999) *Encarta World English Dictionary*. London: Bloomsbury.

Rundell, M. et al, eds. (2002) *Macmillan English Dictionary for Advanced Learners*. Oxford: Macmillan.

Sheridan, T. (1780) *A General Dictionary of the English Language*. London: Printed for J. Dodsley, Pall-Mall; C. Dilly, in the Poultry; and J. Wilkie, St. Paul's Churchyard.

Sinclair, J., ed. (1995) *Collins COBUILD English Dictionary*. 2nd edition, 1st edition 1987. London: HarperCollins.

Sinclair, J., ed. (2001) *Collins COBUILD English Dictionary for Advanced Learners*. 3rd edition, 1st edition 1987. Glasgow: HarperCollins. (*COBUILD*)

Soukhanov, A.H. et al, eds. (1999) *Encarta World English Dictionary*. New York: St. Martin's Press.

Steinmetz, S.l et al., eds. (1996) *Random House Compact Unabridged Dictionary*. Special 2nd edition, 1st edition 1966. New York: Random House.

Thomas, T. (1587) *Dictionarium Linguae Latinae et Anglicanae*. London: R. Boyle. STC 24008. Included in the *Early Modern English Dictionaries Database* (*EMEDD*), edited by I. Lancashire.

Todd, H.J., ed. (1827) *A Dictionary of the English Language*. 2nd edition. London: Longman, Rees, Orme, Brown, and Green.

Treffry, D. et al, eds. (1998) *Collins English Dictionary*. 4th edition, 1st edition published 1979. Glasgow: HarperCollins.

Walker, J. (1791) *A Critical Pronouncing Dictionary and Expositor of the English Language*. London: G.G.J. and J. Robinson, Paternoster Row; and T. Cadell, in the Strand.

Webster, N. (1828) *American Dictionary of the English Language*. 2 vols. New York: S. Converse. Facsimile edition from the original 1828 copy, published by the Foundation for American Christian Education in 1967.

Webster's New Encyclopedic Dictionary. (1993) Cologne: Könemann. (editor not mentioned)

Wright, J., ed. (1896–1905) *The English Dialect Dictionary*. 6 vols. London: Oxford University Press.

Wright, T., ed. (1862–1867) *The Royal Dictionary-Cyclopædia*. London: London Printing and Publishing Company.

Secondary sources

Adams, V. (1973) *An Introduction to Modern English Word-formation*. London: Longman.

Adams, V. (2001) *Complex Words in English*. Harlow: Longman.

Alexander, L.G. (1994) *Right Word Wrong Word*. Burnt Mill: Longman.

Allaby, A. and M. Allaby. (1990) *The Concise Oxford Dictionary of Earth Sciences*. Oxford: Oxford University Press.

Anshen, F. and M. Aronoff. (1989) "Morphological productivity, word frequency and the *Oxford English Dictionary*", in *Language Change and Variation*, edited by R.W. Fasold and D. Schiffrin. Amsterdam: John Benjamins. pp. 197–202.

Apel, W. (1944) *Harvard Dictionary of Music*. London: Routledge and Kegan Paul.

Arnold, D., ed. (1983) *The New Oxford Companion to Music*. Oxford: Oxford University Press.

Aronoff, M. and F. Anshen. (1998) "Morphology and the lexicon: Lexicalization and productivity", in *The Handbook of Morphology*, edited by A. Spences and A.M. Zwicky. Oxford: Blackwell. pp. 237–248.

Aston, G. and L. Burnard. (1998) *The BNC Handbook: Exploring the British National Corpus with SARA*. Edinburgh Textbooks in Empirical Linguistics. Edinburgh: Edinburgh University Press.

Baayen, H. (1993) "On frequency, transparency and productivity", in *Yearbook of Morphology 1992*, edited by G. Booij and J. van Marle. Dordrecht: Kluwer. pp. 181–208.

Baayen, H. and R. Lieber. (1991) "Productivity and English derivation: a corpus-based study", in *Linguistics*, 29, pp. 801–843.

Baayen, R.H. and A. Renouf. (1996) "Chronicling the times: productive lexical innovations in an English newspaper", in *Language*, 72, pp. 69–96.

Bache, C. and N. Davidsen-Nielsen. (1997) *Mastering English: An Advanced Grammar for Non-native and Native Speakers*. Berlin: Mouton de Gruyter.

Bailie, J. and M. Kitchin. (1988) *The Essential Guide to English Usage*. London: Chancellor Press.

Bain, A. (1879) *A Higher English Grammar*. London: Longmans and Co.

Barbeau, J. and J. Barbeau. (2000) "Random acts of American and European adjectives", http://praxis.md/post/healingwords/092000; retrieved March 19, 2001.

Barber, C. (1964) *Linguistic Change in Present-Day English*. Edinburgh: Oliver & Boyd.

Barber, C. (1976) *Early Modern English*. London: A. Deutsch.

Barber, C. (1993) *The English Language: A Historical Introduction*. Cambridge: Cambridge University Press.

Barnet, S., M. Berman, and W. Burto. (1964) *A Dictionary of Literary Terms*. London: Constable.

Baugh, A.C. (1959) *A History of the English Language*. 2nd edition, 1st edition 1951. London: Routledge & Kegan Paul Ltd.

Bauer, L. (1983) *English Word-formation*. Cambridge Textbooks on Linguistics. Cambridge: Cambridge University Press.

Bauer, L. (1994) *Watching English Change*. London: Longman.

Bauer, L. (1998) "Is there a class of neoclassical compounds, and if so is it productive?", in *Linguistics* 36-3. pp. 403–422.

Bauer, L. (2001) *Morphological Productivity*. Cambridge: Cambridge University Press.

Beckson, K. and A. Ganz. (1990) *Literary Terms: A Dictionary*. 3rd edition. London: Andre Deutsch.

Bernstein, T.M. (1965) *The Careful Writer: A Modern Guide to English Usage*. New York: Atheneum.

Biber, D. (1993) "Co-occurrence Patterns among Collocations: A Tool for Corpus-Based Lexical Knowledge Acquisition", in *Computational Linguistics* 19. pp. 531-538.

Boland, D.G. (1997) "Economics and Aristotle's *Division of the Sciences*". Retrieved April 22, 2002, from the World Wide Web: http://www.cts.org.au/1997/aristotl.htm.

Bolozky, S. (1999) *Measuring Productivity in Word Formation: The Case of Israeli Hebrew*. Leiden: Brill.

Brengelman, F.H. (1980) "Orthoepists, Printers, and the Rationalization of English Spelling", in *Journal of English and Germanic Philology* 3. pp. 332–354.

Bremner, J.B. (1980) *Words on Words: a dictionary for writers and others who care about words*. New York: Columbia University Press.

Brook, G.L. (1958) *A History of the English Language*. London: Andre Deutsch.

Bryson, B. (1984) *The Penguin Dictionary of Troublesome Words.* Harmondsworth: Penguin.

Burchfield, R., ed. (1996) *The New Fowler's Modern English Usage.* 3rd edition, 1st ed. 1926. Oxford: Clarendon Press.

Cannon, G.. (1987) *Historical Change and English Word-Formation.* New York: Lang.

Chapman, R.W. (1939) "Adjectives from Proper Names", in *S.P.E. Tract No. LII.* Oxford: Clarendon Press.

Chilvers, I. and H. Osborne. (1988) *The Oxford Dictionary of Art.* Oxford: Oxford University Press.

Chomsky, N. and M. Halle. (1968) *The Sound Pattern of English.* New York: Harper & Row.

Church, K.W., W. Gale, P. Hanks, and D. Hindle. (1991) "Using Statistics in Lexical Analysis", in *Lexical Acquisition: Exploiting On-line Resources to Build a Lexicon*, edited by U. Zernik. Hillsdale, NJ: Lawrence Erlbaum. pp. 115–164.

Clark, J.O.E. (1987) *Word Perfect – A Dictionary of Current English Usage.* London: Harrap Ltd.

Clark, J.O.E. (1990) *Harrap's Dictionary of English Usage.* London: Harrap.

Collins WordbanksOnline. (2002) Birmingham: HarperCollins Publishers and the University of Birmingham.

Copperud, R.H. (1964) *A Dictionary of Usage and Style.* New York: Hawthorn Books.

Cowie, C. and C. Dalton-Puffer. (2002) "Diachronic word-formation and studying changes in productivity over time: theoretical and methodological considerations", in *A Changing World of Words: Studies in English Historical Lexicography, Lexicology and Semantics*, edited by J.E. Díaz Vera. Amsterdam: Rodopi. pp. 410–437.

Crystal, D. (1991) *Making Sense of English Usage.* Edinburgh: Chambers.

Dalton-Puffer, C. (1996) *The French Influence on Middle English Morphology: a Corpus-Based Study on Derivation.* Berlin: Mouton de Gruyter.

Danielsson, B. (1948) *Studies on the Accentuation of Polysyllabic Latin, Greek, and Romance Loan-Words in English with Special Reference to Those Ending in -able, -ate, -ator, -ible, -ic, -ical, and -ize.* Stockholm Studies in English III. Stockholm: Almqvist and Wiksell.

Downing, A. and P. Locke. (1992) *A University Course in English Grammar.* New York: Prentice Hall.

Earle, J. (1871) *The Philology of the English Tongue.* Oxford: Clarendon Press.

Earle, J. (1892) *The Philology of the English Tongue.* 5th edition, 1st edition 1871. Oxford: Clarendon Press.

Early English Books Online. (1999-2003) Web site at http://wwwlib.umi.com/ eebo. University of Michigan, Oxford University, and ProQuest Information and Learning Company.

Ebbitt, W.R. and D.R. Ebbitt. (1990) *Index to English.* 8th edition. New York and Oxford: Oxford University Press.

Elphinston, J. (1765) *The Principles of the English Language Digested*. London: J. Bettenham.

Elphinston, J. (1790) *Inglish Orthoggraphy Epittomized: and Propriety's Pocket-Diccionary*. London: Sold by W. Ritchardson, Royal-Exchainge; J. Deighton, (N.274) Holboarn, and W. Clark (N. 38) New Bond-street: by R. Cheyn, and J. Hill, Eddinburrough.

Evans, B. and C. Evans. (1957) *A Dictionary of Contemporary American Usage*. New York: Random House.

Follett, W. (1966) *Modern American Usage. A Guide*. Edited and completed by J. Barzun in collaboration with C. Baker et al. London: Longmans.

Fowler, H.W. (1926) *A Dictionary of Modern English Usage*. Oxford: Clarendon Press.

Fowler, H.W. (1965) *Modern English Usage*. 2nd edition, edited by E. Gowers, 1st edition 1926. Oxford: Clarendon Press.

Fudge, E. (1984) *English Word-Stress*. London: George Allen & Unwin.

Gowers, E. (1973) *The Complete Plain Words*. Revised edition by B. Fraser. Harmondsworth: Penguin Books Ltd.

Graf, R.F. (1977) *Modern Dictionary of Electronics*. 5th edition. Indianapolis: H.W. Sams and Co.

Green, J. (1991) *Neologisms – new words since 1960*. London: Bloomsbury.

Greenbaum, S. (1996) *English Grammar*. Oxford: Oxford University Press.

Greenbaum, S. and J. Whitcut. (1988) *Longman Guide to English Usage*. Harlow: Longman.

Gries, S.T. (2001) "A Corpus-linguistic Analysis of English *-ic* vs *-ical* Adjectives", in *ICAME Journal*, No. 25, pp. 65–107.

Gries, S.T. (2003) "Testing the sub-test: a collocational-overlap analysis of English *-ic* and *-ical* adjectives", in *International Journal of Corpus Linguistics*, 8.1. pp. 31–61.

Görlach, M. (1991) *Introduction to Early Modern English*. Cambridge: Cambridge University Press.

Görlach, M. (1999) *English in Nineteenth-Century England: An Introduction*. Cambridge: Cambridge University Press.

Haggar, R.G. (1984) *A Dictionary of Art Terms*. Dorset: New Orchard Editions Ltd.

Halliday, M.A.K. (1985) *An Introduction to Functional Grammar*. London: Edward Arnold.

Handel, S. (1971) *A Dictionary of Electronics*. 3rd edition. Harmondsworth: Penguin Books.

Hann, M. (1992) *The Key to Technical Translation. Volume One: Concept Specification*. Amsterdam: John Benjamins.

Hansen, E. and H.F. Nielsen. (1986) *Irregularities in Modern English*. Odense: Odense University Press.

Hardie, R.G. (1991) *Collins Gem Dictionary of English Usage*. Glasgow: HarperCollins.

Hawkes, H. (1976) "'-ic' and '-ical': the terrible twins", in *Lenguaje y Ciencias*, 16:2. pp. 91–99.

Heller, L., A. Humez, and M. Dror. (1983) *The Private Lives of English Words*. London: Routledge & Kegan Paul.

Herbst, R. and S.T. Herbst. (1995) *Wine Lover's Companion*. Hauppauge, NY: Barron's.

Hill, A.A. (1974) "Word Stress and the Suffix *-ic*", in *Journal of English Linguistics*, 8. pp. 6–20.

Howard, G. (1993) *The Good English Guide. English Usage in the 1990s*. London: Macmillan.

Hudson, K. (1977) *The Dictionary of Diseased English*. London: Macmillan.

Ilson, R. and J. Whitcut. (1994) *Mastering English Usage*. New York: Prentice Hall.

Jespersen, O. (1935) *Growth and Structure of the English Language*. 8th edition. Leipzig: B. G. Teubner.

Jespersen, O. (1942) *A Modern English Grammar on Historical Principles. Part VI: Morphology*. Copenhagen: E. Munksgaard.

Kaunisto, M. (1999) "*Electric/electrical* and *classic/classical*: variation between the suffixes *-ic* and *-ical*", in *English Studies,* 80:4. pp. 343-370.

Kaunisto, M. (2001) "Nobility in the History of Adjectives Ending in *-ic* and *-ical*", in *LACUS Forum XXVII*. Edited by R.M. Brend, A.K. Melby, and A.L. Lommel. Fullerton: Linguistic Association of Canada and the United States. pp. 35–45.

Kaunisto, M. (2002) "The parallel adjectival suffix pairs: the English *-ic/-ical* and the Finnish *-inen/-llinen*", in *Studies in Contrastive Linguistics: Proceedings of the 2nd International Contrastive Linguistics Conference, Santiago de Compostela, October, 2001*, edited by L. Iglesias Rábade and S.M. Doval Suárez. Santiago de Compostela: Universidade de Santiago de Compostela. pp. 543–549.

Kennedy, A.G. (1935) *Current English*. Boston: Ginn and Company.

Kjellmer, G. (2001) "Why *weaken* but not **strongen*? On deadjectival verbs", in *English Studies*, 82:2. pp. 154–171.

Krapp, G.P. (1927) *A Comprehensive Guide to Good English*. Chicago: Rand McNally & Company.

Kwon, H.-S. (1997) "Negative prefixation from 1300 to 1800: A case study in *in-/un-* variation", in *ICAME Journal*, 21. pp. 21–42.

Labov, W. (1994) *Principles of Linguistic Change: Internal Factors*. Oxford: Blackwell.

Langlotz, E. (1960) "Classic art", in *Encyclopedia of World Art. Vol. 3*. (1960) New York: McGraw-Hill.

Maetzner, E. (1874) *An English Grammar: Methodical, Analytical, and Historical*. Translated from German by C.J. Grece. London: J. Murray.

Manser, M.H., ed. (1988) *Bloomsbury Good Word Guide*. London: Bloomsbury.

Marchand, H. (1969) *The Categories and Types of Present-Day English Word-Formation*. 2nd edition, 1st edition 1960. München: C.H. Beck.

Marsden, P. (1985) "Adjective Pairs in *-ic* and *-ical*", in *Lebende Sprachen*, 1. pp. 26–33.

Marshall, D., ed. (1996) *Changing Times CD-ROM*. A selection of 10,000 articles from the *Times* of London, 1785–1985. Cambridge: Chadwyck-Healey Ltd.

McArthur, T., ed. (1992) *The Oxford Companion to the English Language*. Oxford: Oxford University Press.

McDermott, A. (2002) "Early dictionaries of English and historical corpora: In search of hard words", in *A Changing World of Words: Studies in English Historical Lexicography, Lexicology and Semantics*, edited by J.E. Díaz Vera. Amsterdam: Rodopi. pp. 197–226.

McGlynn, H., ed. (1995) *The Hutchinson Concise English Usage*. Oxford: Helicon.

McKaskill, S.G. (1977) *A Dictionary of Good English*. Edited by J. van Emden. Melbourne: Inkata Press.

Meiklejohn, J.M.P. (1890) *The English Language: its Grammar, History, and Literature*. 5th edition. London: A.M. Holden.

Metcalfe, J.E. and C. Astle. (1995) *Correct English*. Tadworth: Clarion.

Morris, R. (1872) *Historical Outlines of English Accidence, comprising chapters on the history and developments of the language, and on word-formation*. London: Macmillan and Co.

Morris, W. and M. Morris. (1985) *Harper Dictionary of Contemporary Usage*. 2nd edition, 1st edition 1975. New York: Harper & Row

Morrish, J. (1995) "Keeping tabs on changing language: classic", *Telegraph Magazine (The Daily Telegraph)*, 29 July, 1995, p. 8.

Nevalainen, T. (1999) "Early Modern English Lexis and Semantics", in *The Cambridge History of the English Language, Volume III: 1476–1776*, edited by R. Lass. Cambridge: Cambridge University Press. pp. 332–458.

The New Encyclopedia Britannica. Micropedia and Macropedia. (1974) 15th edition. Chicago: Encyclopedia Britannica Inc.

Opdycke, J.B. (1935) *Get It Right! A Cyclopedia of Correct English Usage*. New York: Funk & Wagnalls Company.

Osselton, N.E. (1984) "Informal Spelling Systems in Early Modern English: 1500–1800", in *English Historical Linguistics: Studies in Development*, edited by N.F. Blake and C. Jones. CECTAL Conference Papers Series, No. 3. Sheffield: University of Sheffield. pp. 123–137.

Palmer, F.R. (1976) *Semantics: A New Outline*. Cambridge: Cambridge University Press.

Partridge, E. (1957) *Usage and Abusage*. Harmonsworth: Penguin Books.

Phythian, B.A. (1979) *A Concise Dictionary of Current English*. Totowa: Rowman & Littlefield.

Plag, I. (1999) *Morphological Productivity: structural constraints on English derivation*. Berlin: Mouton de Gruyter.

Plag, I. (2000) "On the mechanisms of morphological rivalry: A new look at competing verb-deriving affixes in English", in *Anglistentag 1999 Mainz*, edited by B. Reitz and S. Rieuwerts. Trier: Wissenschaftlicher Verlag Trier. pp. 63–76.

Quirk, R., S. Greenbaum, G. Leech, and J. Svartvik. (1985) *A Comprehensive Grammar of the English Language*. London: Longman.

Ramsey, S. (1892) *The English Language and English Grammar*. New York: G.P. Putnam's Sons.

Reuter, O. (1936) *Verb Doublets of Latin Origin in English*. Helsinki: Societas Scientiarium Fennica.

Richardson, J.L. (1885) *"English" Practice in Analysis, Parsing, Word-formation, Composition, and Paraphrasing*. London: George Philip & Son, 32 Fleet Street, E.C.

Rissanen, M. (1989) "Three problems connected with the use of diachronic corpora", in *ICAME Journal*, No. 13. pp. 16–19.

Roberts, P. (1967) *Modern Grammar*. New York: Harcourt, Brace & World, Inc.

Room, A. (1985) *Dictionary of Confusing Words and Meanings*. London: Routledge & Kegan Paul.

Room, A. (1988) *A Dictionary of Contrasting Pairs*. London: Routledge.

Ross, N.J. (1998) "The *-ic* and *-ical* Pickle", in *English Today*, 54:2. pp. 40–44.

Roth, P. (1998) *American Pastoral*. London: Vintage.

Rowling, J.K. (1997) *Harry Potter and the Philosopher's Stone*. London: Bloomsbury.

Salmon, V. (1999) "Orthography and Punctuation", in in *The Cambridge History of the English Language, Volume III: 1476–1776*, edited by R. Lass. Cambridge: Cambridge University Press. pp. 13–54.

Schibsbye, K. (1970) *A Modern English Grammar*. 2nd edition. London: Oxford University Press.

Scholes, P.A. (1970) *The Oxford Companion to Music*. 10th edition, revised by J.O. Ward. London: Oxford University Press.

Shaw, H. (1975) *Dictionary of Problem Words and Expressions*. New York: McGraw-Hill.

Sinclair, John, ed. (1991) *Collins COBUILD English Guides 2: Word Formation*. London: HarperCollins Publishers.

Slevin, P. and D. Balz. (2000) "Fla. High Court Considers Recounts", on *The Washington Post* Internet site, http://washingtonpost.com/wp-dyn/articles/A46540-2000Nov20.html, retrieved Nov. 21, 2000.

Smith, L.P. (1943) *Words and Idioms*. 5th edition. London: Constable & Company Ltd.

Speake, G., ed. (1994) *A Dictionary of Ancient History*. Oxford: Blackwell.

Sundby, B. (1995) *English Word-formation as Described by English Grammarians 1600–1800*. Oslo: Novus Forlag.

Swan, M. (1980) *Practical English Usage*. Oxford: Oxford University Press.

Swan, M. (1995) *Practical English Usage*. 2nd edition, 1st edition 1980. Oxford University Press.

Sweet, H. (1891) *A New English Grammar. Part I: Introduction, Phonology, and Accidence*. Oxford: Clarendon Press.

Tennant, J. (1964) *A Handbook of English Usage*. London: Longmans, Green and Co.

Todd, L. (1997) *The Cassell Dictionary of English Usage*. London: Cassell.

Todd, L. and I. Hancock. (1986) *International English Usage*. London: Croom Helm.

Turton, N.D. and J.B. Heaton. (1996) *Longman Dictionary of Common Errors*. 2nd edition. Edinburgh: Longman.

Urdang, L. (1982) *Suffixes and Other Word-Final Elements of English*. Detroit: Gale Research Company.

Urdang, L. (1988) *Dictionary of Differences*. London: Bloomsbury.

Urdang, L. (1994) "Classic Problem", in *Verbatim*, XXI:1. p. 21.

Vallins, G.H. (1965) *Spelling*. Revised edition by D.G. Scragg, 1st edition 1954. London: A. Deutsch.

Walker, P., ed. (1988) *Chambers Science and Technology Dictionary*. Cambridge: Chambers.

Warren, B. (1984) *Classifying Adjectives*. Gothenburg: Acta Universitatis Gothoburgensis.

Weiner, E.S.C., ed. (1996) *Oxford Dictionary and English Usage Guide*. Oxford: Oxford University Press.

Westrup, J. and F.L. Harrison. (1976) *Collins Encyclopedia of Music*. Revised by C. Wilson. London: Collins.

Wilson, G.B.L. (1974) *A Dictionary of Ballet*. 3rd edition. London: A. & C. Black.

Wood, F.T. (1962) *Current English Usage*. London: Macmillan.

Wrenn, C.L. (1949) *The English Language*. London: Methuen & Co.

Wyld, H.C. (1921) *A Short History of English*. 2nd edition, 1st edition 1914. London: J. Murray.

Zandvoort, R.W. (1948) *A Handbook of English Grammar*. 3rd edition. Groningen: J.B. Wolters.

Appendices

1. Appendix A: *classic/classical*

Table 1. *Classic/classical* in the non-fiction texts studied, 1900–1949 (British authors).[1]

	classic	classical
1. positive value judgement: 'of the first rank', 'of high quality', 'belonging to a canon', 'authoritative'	-	2
2. being representative of a type: 'typical', 'regular', 'archetypal', 'traditional', 'quintessential'	-	1
3. pertaining to a historical period in a particular culture: a. ancient Greece or Rome		
1. arts, literature	-	4
2. others	1 (1)	7
a'. pertaining to the study and knowledge of ancient Greek/ Latin cultures	1	7
a''. pertaining to people learned in ancient Greek/Latin cultures	-	3
4. 'pertaining to classicism', 'characterised by simplicity, harmony, symmetry, etc.'	-	6
5. pertaining to traditional and (formerly) accepted methods, systems, or ideas	-	7 (1)
total	**2 (1)**	**37 (1)**
# of authors using the forms: # of authors using both forms: 1	1	6

---

1   The figures in Tables 1 and 2 in Appendix A include a large number of uses by some individual authors, e.g. 18 occurrences of *classical* by Arthur Quiller-Couch (British), and 98 occurrences of *classical* by C.E. Ayres (American). However, the major distinctions between the adjective forms that can be deduced from the tables are not drastically affected by idiosyncratic uses; i.e. the conclusions would be similar even if the instances by Quiller-Couch or Ayres were excluded from the figures.

Table 2. *Classic/classical* in the non-fiction texts studied, 1900–1961 (American authors).

	classic	*classical*
1. positive value judgement: 'of the first rank', 'of high quality', 'belonging to a canon', 'authoritative'	6 (1)	1
2. being representative of a type: 'typical', 'regular', 'archetypal', 'traditional', 'quintessential'	6	1
3. pertaining to a historical period in a particular culture: a. ancient Greece or Rome		
1. arts, literature	1	2
2. others	3	6
a'. pertaining to the study and knowledge of ancient Greek/ Latin cultures	-	3
4. 'pertaining to classicism', 'characterised by simplicity, harmony, symmetry, etc.'	-	1
5. pertaining to traditional and (formerly) accepted methods, systems, or ideas	4 (1)	148
6. pertaining to old, "pure" literary forms of languages	-	1
total	**20 (2)**	**163**
# of authors using the forms:	13	17
# of authors using both forms: 4		

2. Appendix B: *electric/electrical*

Table 1. *Electric/electrical* in the non-fiction texts examined, 1850–1899 (American authors).

	electric	electrical
1. 'having to do with electricity as a physical phenomenon'		
a. research: ~ *analysis/work*/etc.	-	3
b. ~ *machine*	-	1
c. ~ *battery*	2	1
d. general terms: ~ *conditions*	-	1
e. others: ~ *current/power*/etc.	13	2
2. 'having to do with the transmission of electricity'		
a. 'carrying electricity': ~ *wire/* etc.	7	1
b. 'having to do with the supply of electricity': ~ *supply*	-	2
3. 'charged with electricity'	1	-
4. 'caused by electricity': ~ *shock/ spark*	3	-
5. 'powered by electricity':		
a. appliances, specific ~ *bell/light*/etc.	10	-
b. actions, processes, illumination, etc.	4	8
6. others: ~ *taste*	-	1
7. figurative: 'full of tension', 'exciting'	1	-
total	**41**	**20**
# of authors using the forms:	8	8
# of authors using both forms: 7		

Table 2. *Electric/electrical* in the non-fiction texts examined, 1900–1961 (American authors).

	electric	electrical
1. 'having to do with electricity as a physical phenomenon'		
a. ~ *machine*	-	1
b. ~ *battery*	1	-
c. general terms: ~ *condition/ properties*	-	2
d. others: ~ *current/power*/etc.	17	11
2. 'carrying electricity'	4	3
3. 'caused by electricity': ~ *shock/spark*/etc.	10	1
4. 'powered by electricity':		
a. appliances, specific ~ *bell/light*/etc.	42	-
b. vehicles: ~ *car/coach*	2	-
c. actions, processes, illumination, etc.	6	10
5. figurative: 'full of tension', 'exciting'	3 (2)	-
total	**85 (2)**	**28**
# of authors using the forms:	18	12
# of authors using both forms: 8		

Table 3. *Electric/electrical* in the 1995 issues of *The Daily Telegraph* (semantic groups 2.a and 2.b).

	electric	electrical
2.a 'carrying electricity'		
~ *cable*	9	8
~ *cabling*	-	2
~ *circuit*	1	5
~ *conductor*	1	1
~ *connection*	-	1
~ *contact*	1	1
~ *cord*	-	2
~ *flex*	2	1
~ *line*	-	1
~ *power line*	1	-
~ *pylon*	1	-
~ *route*	1	-
~ *umbilicals*	-	1

~ *wire*	5	-
~ *wiring*	1	3
2.b 'having to do with the supply of electricity'		
~ *clamp*	1	-
~ *connector*	-	1
~ *feeder*	-	1
~ *fuse*	1	-
~ *link*	-	1
~ *outlet*	-	1
~ *plug*	1	1
~ *point*	2	-
~ *power point*	1	-
~ *power supply*	-	1
~ *power system*	-	1
~ *socket*	3	1
~ *supply*	-	2
~ *switch*	3	2
~ *switch(ing) gear*	-	2
~ *workings*	1	-

Table 4. *Electric/electrical* in the *British National Corpus* (semantic groups 2.a and 2.b).

	electric	*electrical*
2.a 'carrying electricity'		
~ *cable*	29 (23)	5 (5)
~ *cabling*	2 (2)	1 (1)
~ *circuit*	8 (5)	31 (27)
~ *flex*	6 (4)	4 (4)
~ *wire*	4 (4)	9 (9)
~ *wiring*	9 (7)	18 (18)
2.b 'having to do with the supply of electricity'		
~ *plug*	3 (3)	-
~ *point*	2 (2)	2 (2)
~ *socket*	11 (10)	6 (6)
~ *supply*	-	13 (12)
~ *switch*	4 (3)	2 (2)

3.   **Appendix C:** *historic/historical*

Table 1. *Historic/historical* in the non-fiction texts studied, 1850–1899 (American authors).[2]

	historic	*historical*
1. a. 'having to do with history'	23	36 (1)
b. 'recording history'	-	3
2. 'belonging to history', 'existed in the past'	4	6
3. 'important or famous in history'	5 (1)	1
4. 'genuinely existed or occurred in the past', 'authentic'	2	3 (1)
5. 'having a long history'	5	1
total	**39 (1)**	**50 (2)**
# of authors using the forms:	4	11
# of authors using both forms: 3		

Table 2. *Historic/historical* in the non-fiction texts studied, 1900–1949 (British authors).

	historic	*historical*
1. a. 'having to do with history'	1	27 (2)
b. 'having to do with the research of history'	-	4
2. 'based on history'		
a. writing	-	2
b. painting	-	2
3. 'belonging to history', 'existed in the past'	-	6
4. 'having a long history'	-	1
total	**1**	**42 (2)**
# of authors using the forms:	1	5
# of authors using both forms: 1		

---

2   It is possible that the figures in Table 1 do not properly represent the use of *historic/historical* in American non-fictional writings in this period. The number of authors using the two adjectives in this period is rather small, and 31 of the 39 instances of *historic* were found in a text by William Hall, which possibly distorts the overall picture of the uses of the adjective.

Table 3. *Historic/historical* in the non-fiction texts studied, 1900–1961 (American authors).

	historic	historical
1. a. 'having to do with history'	21	112 (4)
a'. ~ *importance*	-	1
~ *significance*	-	1
~ *value*	-	3
b. 'recording history'	-	6
c. 'having to do with the research of history'	-	33
2. 'based on history' (writing)	2	-
3. 'belonging to history', 'existed in the past'	12	20 (2)
4. 'important or famous in history'	9	-
5. 'having a long history'	10	2
total	**54**	**178 (6)**
# of authors using the forms:	9	24
# of authors using both forms: 8		

Table 4. *Historic/historical* in different domains of written language in the *British National Corpus* (the numbers in parentheses indicating the texts in which the adjectives occurred).

A = # of occurrences
B = # of occurrences per 1 million words

	historic		historical	
	A	B	A	B
1. Imaginative	81 (66)	4.9	145 (90)	8.8
2. Natural and pure sciences	15 (11)	4.0	134 (47)	35.4
3. Applied sciences	113 (53)	15.9	295 (85)	41.5
4. Social sciences	181 (71)	13.0	1731 (213)	124.5
5. World affairs	560 (191)	32.7	1112 (237)	64.9
6. Commerce and finance	189 (75)	26.0	331 (105)	45.6
7. Arts	290 (66)	44.5	890 (132)	136.5
8. Belief and thought	46 (26)	15.3	386 (53)	128.4
9. Leisure	508 (126)	41.7	275 (110)	22.6
total	**1983 (685)**	**22.7**	**5299 (1072)**	**60.7**

4.   Appendix D: Obsolescence of one of the forms

Table 1. The numbers of occurrences of *heroic/heroical* in the *OED* citations, 1500–1799.[3]

	heroic	heroical
1500–1549	1	3
1550–1599	15	25
1600–1649	22	12
1650–1699	59	14
1700–1749	27	4
1750–1799	23	3

Table 2. The numbers of occurrences of *majestic/majestical* in the *OED* citations, 1550–1749.[4]

	majestic	majestical
1550–1599	1	10
1600–1649	8	13
1650–1699	20	8
1700–1749	31	2

Table 3. The numbers of occurrences of *rustic/rustical* in the prose section of *Literature Online*.

	rustic	rustical	number of authors using both forms
1550–1599	10 (7)	15 (6)	-
1600–1649	14 (8)	1 (1)	-
1650–1699	11 (8)	5 (4)	-
1700–1749	10 (5)	1 (1)	1
1750–1799	80 (17)	1 (1)	1
1800–1849	123 (23)	-	-
1850–1903	163 (30)	5 (2)	2

---

3   The last citation in the second edition of the *OED* containing *heroical* dates from 1880.

4   The last citation in the second edition of the *OED* containing *majestical* dates from 1879.

Table 4. The numbers of occurrences of *poetic/poetical* in the *OED* citations, 1550–1989.

	poetic	poetical
1550–1599	1	29
1600–1649	4	29
1650–1699	17	28
1700–1749	21	30
1750–1799	34	46
1800–1849	53	67
1850–1899	97	76
1900–1949	47	17
1950–1989	70	3

Table 5. The numbers of occurrences of *heretic/heretical* in the prose section of *Literature Online*.

	heretic	heretical	number of authors using both forms
1550–1599	-	3 (3)	-
1600–1649	-	-	-
1650–1699	2 (2)	3 (3)	1
1700–1749	1 (1)	3 (2)	-
1750–1799	4 (3)	11 (8)	2
1800–1849	13 (4)	19 (7)	3
1850–1903	7 (5)	22 (16)	3

Table 6. The numbers of occurrences of *theoretic/theoretical* in the prose section of *Literature Online*.

	theoretic	theoretical	number of authors using both forms
1550–1599	-	-	-
1600–1649	-	-	-
1650–1699	-	-	-
1700–1749	-	-	-
1750–1799	-	3 (3)	-
1800–1849	3 (2)	15 (10)	1
1850–1903	21 (5)	17 (11)	4

Table 7. The numbers of occurrences of *theoretic/theoretical* in the *OED* citations, 1600–1989.

	theoretic	*theoretical*
1600–1649	1	2
1650–1699	4	5
1700–1749	2	2
1750–1799	9	4
1800–1849	8	20
1850–1899	12	50
1900–1949	5	83
1950–1989	5	156